CALL ME CAPTAIN

A Memoir of a Woman at Sea

SUSAN SCOTT

A Latitude 20 Book

University of Hawai'i Press

HONOLULU

19 18 17 16 15 14   5 4 3 2 1

Some names and details in this book have been changed to protect
individuals' privacy.

Library of Congress Cataloging-in-Publication Data
Scott, Susan, author.
   Call me captain : a memoir of a woman at sea / Susan Scott.
        pages cm
   "A latitude 20 book."
   ISBN 978-0-8248-3981-9 (alk. paper)
  1. Scott, Susan   2. Women marine biologists—Biography.   3. Women
sailors—Oceania—Biography.   4. Natural resources—Line Islands—
Palmyra Atoll.   I. Title.
   QH91.3.S36 2014
   570.92—dc23
   [B]   2014005522

Designed by George T. Whipple

Printed by Sheridan Books, Inc.

CALL ME CAPTAIN

Susan Scott.

For Craig

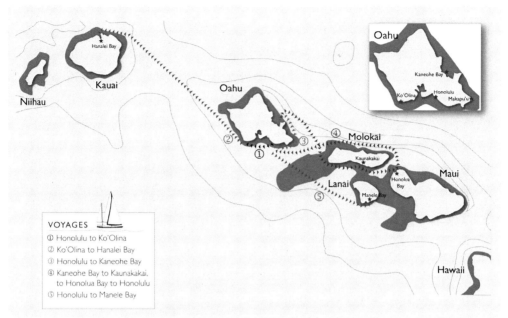

VOYAGES

① Honolulu to Ko'Olina
② Ko'Olina to Hanalei Bay
③ Honolulu to Kaneohe Bay
④ Kaneohe Bay to Kaunakakai,
   to Honolua Bay to Honolulu
⑤ Honolulu to Manele Bay

Map of practice voyages through main Hawaiian Islands. Map by Bruno Davis.

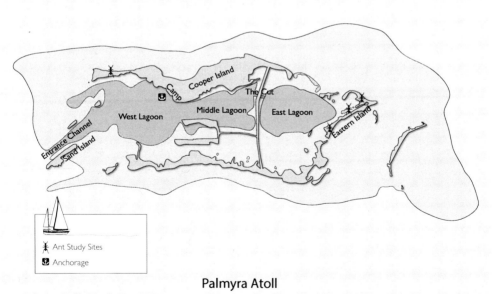

✳ Ant Study Sites
⚓ Anchorage

Palmyra Atoll

Palmyra Atoll. Map by Bruno Davis.

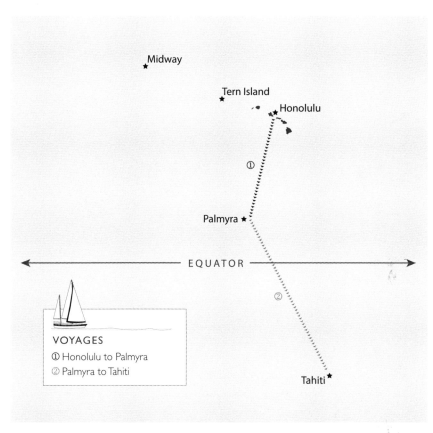

Midway ★

Tern Island ★

● ★ Honolulu

①

Palmyra ★

← EQUATOR →

②

VOYAGES
① Honolulu to Palmyra
② Palmyra to Tahiti

Tahiti ★

Large-scale map showing relative distances between Tern Island, Honolulu, Palmyra, and Tahiti. Map by Bruno Davis.

1

*L*OOKING down the companionway, I watched Alex remove my husband's foul weather gear in the red night-light of the navigation station below. This was no small task. The storm waves were rolling my thirty-seven-foot sailboat *Honu* so violently that he had to hang onto an overhead rail and shake his shoulder to remove first one sleeve and then the other. Unclipping the fasteners on the yellow overalls caused them to fall to his knees, and he used his feet to push them from his ankles. Free of the outer clothes, he stretched out on the sea bunk, filling it from end to end.

Alex was tall and slim, sweet and sensitive. He was also twenty-nine years old. Watching him from above like that made me, at fifty-six, feel like a perverted old lady. Was I? Who knew? I didn't know myself any better than I knew the mechanics of the diesel engine beneath my feet. A year earlier an acquaintance posed the question: "If you had to describe yourself in one word, what would it be?" An uncomfortable silence followed, and as it lengthened, my face flushed hot. I shrugged, embarrassed. I couldn't come up with a single word.

This was our first night offshore, and it was so dark we couldn't see the ocean over the rail. But, oh, we could hear it. Avalanches of water thundered toward the boat like freight trains, their roars getting louder and louder as they raced toward us. Hearing an explosive wave approaching, I would wedge my icy bare feet against the cockpit bench opposite me, grip the steel compass mount as hard as my arthritic hands could hold it, and brace for the hit, only to have the monster smoothly lift the boat and roll beneath. Other times, the gentle whoosh of a small wave would trick me into relaxing, and with a foaming hiss of power, *wham*. It slammed the hull and sent me flying.

I tightened the Velcro closures of my yellow jacket until I could barely turn my head, but the sea wormed its way in anyway. Occasionally a wave ambushed from an odd angle and struck with such force it felt as if someone had heaved a bucket of water in my face. Salt water dribbled down my cheeks, onto my neck, and into my clothes. Just sitting there was exhausting.

"This is the funhouse ride from hell," I said to Alex earlier, when he was still sitting next to me in the cockpit.

"I'm getting queasy again," he said.

I looked at my watch. "I'll get us another pill." Over our foul weather gear we wore safety harnesses, with leashes clipped to the boat. I freed myself, climbed down the ladder, and worked my way hand over hand across the heaving floor to the medicine cabinet, where I found the anti-nausea medication and swallowed a tablet dry. It tasted salty. Everything tasted salty. By the time I got back to the cockpit to give Alex his scopolamine, I had to clench my teeth to keep from retching.

We sat across from one another in that stiff silence that ensues when people are concentrating on not throwing up and listened to the boat creak and groan in the twelve-foot seas. In preparation for this voyage I had installed a windmill high on the mizzenmast, the secondary mast to the rear of the main mast. The windmill did a fine job of making electricity, but that night in the thirty-mile-per-hour wind it sounded like a maniac was up there with a chainsaw.

Alex flinched, and something hit the deck behind him with a thud. "Wow," he said. "A seabird flew right past my ear. It came so close I heard it go by."

Kneeling on the bench, we leaned over the cockpit edge as far as our leashes would allow and looked at the deck. There lay a flying fish at least a foot long, its winglike fins flailing, its silver body thumping. Alex snatched the fish and dropped it overboard.

"Hey, I wanted to look at that," I said. "I've never seen a flying fish that big." I had been the "Ocean Watch" columnist for the *Honolulu Star-Advertiser* for twenty-three years and would have liked to examine and write about the fish.

"It was suffering," he said.

What could I say? Alex, a University of Hawai'i doctoral candidate studying tropical island ecosystems, was the guy I once watched catch a three-inch-long flying cockroach, known as a B-52 in Hawai'i, in his bare hands, carry it outside, and set it gently on the ground. It occurred to me as we sat there that the fish could easily have hit him in the eye. I worried about a thousand things regarding this voyage, but never once did I think that Alex might get brained by a fish.

"How are you?" I said.

"Were we crazy to do this?" he asked. "Or just adventurous?"

"I don't know that they're two different things."

"I didn't think I'd be scared, but I am," he said. "Are you?"

Scared? The ocean was tossing my ten-ton sailboat around like a blade of seaweed. Sometimes when a particularly ambitious wave struck the boat, I imagined *Honu* rolling over or splitting open, and panic would strike, my body insisting I do something, anything, right now. With nowhere to run and nothing to fight, the rush went to my stomach as if to say, "Okay, then, vomit." The happy pills, as Alex named our anti-nausea medication, took care of seasickness but didn't do a thing for fear sickness.

"Yes, I'm scared," I said. "The only thing between us and drowning is a half-inch-thick sheet of fiberglass. Every new bang or squeak makes me feel that the boat is breaking up." I had been on this boat with my husband, Craig, in seas worse than this, so I knew it was built to take it. But I hadn't been the captain, and that made all the difference. If something broke, it would now be my responsibility to diagnose it, fix it, and keep us afloat and alive. I reviewed the abandon-ship procedures in my mind for the zillionth time: don the emergency backpack, turn on the emergency satellite beacon, heave the life raft over the rail, and chant the sailors' creed: *Only get into a life raft when you have to step up.* This means don't step off the deck until it's actually underwater, because a panicked mind can make an intact boat seem to be sinking. Countless sailboats have been found afloat minus their life rafts and people.

"The boat is doing fine," I said, as much to convince myself as Alex. *Honu* was racing along at six to seven miles per hour, fast for a thirty-seven-footer. Its four-story mast, the pillar of sailing activity, and its web of support wires shuddered with the hardest hits, but that was normal. The so-called tuning of the rig had been done just before the boat left harbor, with each wire adjusted taut enough to make the mast stand secure yet loose enough to let the system absorb the shocks. As I watched the mast and wires flex and recover, I could see the boat taking the wind and waves in stride. It was her passengers who weren't doing so hot.

Seawater soaked my T-shirt in front, sweat made my back feel clammy, and the salt on my face crackled like a mud pack. It had been eighty degrees Fahrenheit during the day, but that night the tropical air felt impossibly cold. My wet hands were freezing, but I knew if I took them off the handhold and tucked them in my armpits or under my legs, I would fall off the bench.

A rowdy wave rolled the boat onto its side farther than usual, and my dinner of Cheez-Its and canned frosting leaped toward my throat. I focused on the wheel, trying to dredge up a meditation mantra I once learned but could never remember. The word *relax* came to mind instead, so I repeated it silently over and over and concentrated on watching the ghostly autopilot we had nicknamed "Alphie" turn the wheel, left, right, left, right. . . .

Honu's GPS map cast a small circle of dim light in the cockpit, but beyond that I could see nothing except the boat's running lights, intended to indicate our presence to another vessel, should one happen to be nearby. Given that the Pacific Ocean is sixty-four million square miles, this is so unlikely that some captains and their crews just go to bed at night and hope for the best. I was far too nervous for that and insisted on night watches. On this seven-day trip with just two of us, we were in for some long nights.

I hated the thought of being alone in the cockpit in all that blackness with waves bashing and wind howling and fish trying to skewer us, but I couldn't make Alex stay there all night just to keep me company. "I'll take the first watch," I said. "Try to get some sleep."

"I won't be able to sleep."

"We can at least take turns getting in out of the weather."

"It sounds even worse down there," he said. He was right. The rolling boat caused the teak wood of the interior to squeak and groan like cracking ribs.

"I know. But try."

He went below, and that's when I became a peeping Tommette. *Nothing wrong with admiring a handsome man*, I thought, as he peeled off his wet T-shirt, revealing broad shoulders and muscled abs. But the red light gave the cabin a hint of the pornographic, and I felt creepy looking at him. I was old enough to be the guy's mother, for God's sake. What was wrong with me?

If Alex knew I was watching him, he didn't care. We had met a year earlier while working as biologists at Tern Island, the main biological research station of the tongue-twisting Papahānaumokuākea Marine National Monument. Native Hawaiians gave this long name to the Hawaiian Islands National Wildlife Refuge when President George W. Bush declared the area a monument (an upgrade from refuge) in 2007. Most people, including many Hawai'i residents, have a hard time pronouncing the name, but the beauty of the Hawaiian language is that it has only thirteen letters, and long words can be broken down to manageable bits. With a word like this, I reminded myself to start small: *papa*—easy enough—*ha-now* (halfway there), *mow-koo*, and finally, *ah-kay-ah*.

Papa-hanau-moku-akea. After about a hundred repetitions, the name just rolled off my tongue.

On Tern, a fifty-four-acre islet about five hundred miles northwest of Honolulu, Alex and I lived in an old Coast Guard barracks with several other biologists. We banded seabirds together, tagged sea turtles together, ate together, and snorkeled together. At the time, Alex and I, both grieving over lost love, became close friends, sharing secrets, dreams, and sorrows. When I told Alex that he felt like a trusted girlfriend, he took it the way I meant it—as my highest compliment. After three months, he and I knew more about each other than most people know about their spouses. I had a feeling that if I told Alex what had occurred to me—that he was an attractive man and I felt like a geriatric deviant for thinking so—he would laugh and we'd end up discussing ageism, sexism, his girlfriends, my husband, and eventually the subject we usually ended up pondering: the meaning of life, our own in particular.

It was Alex who convinced me to sail to Palmyra Atoll, a remote wildlife refuge a thousand miles south of Hawai'i and one of the most spectacular marine wilderness areas on Earth. Alex, working in Palmyra on his doctoral thesis, lured me with stories of fearless manta rays and photos of crabs as big as toaster ovens, giant clams in psychedelic colors, melon-headed whales, sharks and fish of every variety. He could not sail there with me, he had said, because his research on the interaction among rats, crabs, and seedlings was at a crucial point, but he wanted to share the joy of the place. From Palmyra he had sent an e-mail: "Palmyra is more influential than beautiful, more exciting than paradise, and more real than Eden. It's still all sinking in with every plunge off the rope swing." I didn't know what that meant exactly, but his description kindled my passion for seeking out new marine animals and ocean experiences. I wanted to immerse myself in the atoll's wildlife with the same fervor that my dog rolled around in dead fish. Palmyra, I decided, would be my kind of heaven.

It was also as hard to get to as heaven. The rare flights to Palmyra were private charters in eighteen-passenger planes, and commercial boats were not allowed in the refuge. Even if I somehow managed to get myself there, the refuge managers had no place for me to stay.

"Well, you have a sailboat, don't you?" Alex had said.

Sort of. I had a boat the way some women have a Harley. My husband, Craig, and I owned it jointly, and I rode on it with him, but *Honu* was far more his boat than mine. And Craig would not sail to Palmyra. He didn't like off-shore passages because they offered no physical exercise, a facet of his life essential to his sense of well-being. When I proposed that he and I sail to Palmyra, Craig was training for an Ironman competition, a race composed of a 2.4-mile swim, 112-mile bicycle ride, and 26-mile run. Between that and his job as an emergency doctor in Hawai'i, he had neither the time nor the interest in refitting our neglected boat and taking me where I wanted to go. The fact that we were barely speaking to each other at the time probably didn't add to the appeal either.

Craig knew I had little appreciation for the difficulties of skippering a sailboat offshore in the Pacific and thought sailing from Honolulu to Palmyra would be a dangerous undertaking for me. He was a firm believer, however, in learning by doing, and although he hadn't encouraged me to do it, he hadn't discouraged me either. ("If it's something you feel you need to do, you should go.") And so, with Alex urging me on, I had decided to sail to Palmyra without Craig.

Now here I was in the middle of the Pacific Ocean scared to death, on a boat I could barely manage, with a young man who knew little about sailboats. Suddenly every cell in my body missed my husband, my soul mate, the person with whom I had spent most of my adult life. Being separated from Craig felt like someone had ripped my Siamese twin from my side.

Alex turned off the red light, and I sat hunched on the teak cockpit bench in the dark, feeling old, cold, wet, abandoned, and more alone than I had ever been in my life.

CRAIG and I really had been like twins. We called each other "Twinoid" and our bond the "Twinship," words we made up the first year we lived together. Craig even called me Twinoid in public, as in, "Twinoid, what's the name of that novel we liked?" This was a little embarrassing because people asked what the term meant, and it was a bed thing. When tangled limb over limb in the heated waterbed of our cold basement flat, we imagined this was what twins must feel like inside a uterus. Since being twins seemed a little incestuous, we decided we were twinlike or, as Craig put it, twinoid.

Some nights, cuddled up with him in that cozy bed, I could barely believe he was real. Here, warm and breathing, was the man I dreamed up for myself when I was fourteen years old reading *Gone with the Wind*. I saw Craig as a blend of the kind, gentle Ashley Wilkes striving to do the right thing (not always successful, but trying hard) and the strong, free-spirited Rhett Butler, an alpha male charging through life with the confidence of a grizzly bear.

Craig was like a girlfriend without being girly, masculine without being macho. A twofer: yin and yang in one fine package.

And the package was nicely wrapped. Craig stood six-one, with olive-tinged skin and a riot of never-combed curly dark hair. Soon after I met him, I overheard two women friends talking as they stared at an eight by ten picture of him on my wall. A professional photographer in Aspen had captured Craig skiing down a steep run in perfect form, the powder snow flying like wings in his wake.

"This is the new boyfriend?" said one woman, leaning in for a closer look. "If you think he looks good there," the other said, "wait until you see him in person."

Craig didn't see himself as good-looking, though, and almost never looked in a mirror. Appearances held little importance to him. (He once cut his hair with a rigging knife.) The one thing that mattered most to him in life, above all else, was being a good person and a good doctor. In those goals, he succeeded. Craig was the most generous and caring man I had ever known. Others thought so, too.

"You're lucky," one of his fellow interns told me at a party soon after we met. "Craig is really a great guy."

I was a young nurse at the time and adored this smart, gorgeous man. And a miracle occurred: he adored me back.

The Twinship blossomed over the years, and Craig and I became the king and queen of our own fairytale. We lived on a sailboat in Hawai'i. I earned a bachelor's degree in biology and got a dream job writing about marine science for the *Honolulu Star-Bulletin* (later changed to the *Star-Advertiser*). Craig's career as an emergency doctor took off, and he became president of his physician group. It wasn't long before I was known on Oahu for "Ocean Watch," my weekly newspaper column, Craig for his AED (automatic external defibrillator) work with the Honolulu police and fire departments, and the two of us for coauthoring local medical books. (Our favorite is *All Stings Considered*, which answers such popular questions as, "Does urinating on Portuguese man-of-war stings do any good?" Answer: no.) We appeared on local TV shows, talked on the radio, and were invited as guest speakers. A Hollywood director once hired us as medical consultants on a Bruce Willis film shot in Hawai'i. At one lecture, a friend introduced us as a renaissance couple.

As best friends, even after twenty years together, we rarely spent a night apart. In this, Craig was adamant. I would call him at work from our condo in

Waialua to say I had to sleep on the boat in the Waikiki marina thirty-five miles away because of an early meeting. His drive to Waikiki from the hospital was an hour long, and his shift went late. He was fifteen minutes from home.

"Just go home," I would say, and mean it. "You'll be tired."

"No, no, I'll come to the boat with you."

We had countless conversations like this, Craig always doing whatever it took for us to sleep together. Really sleep. It was as much about breathing in unison, hearing the sounds of our hearts beating, and sharing body heat as it was about sex. It was about the Twinship.

Life in Hawai'i was wonderful, and our trips together superb. We volunteered as a doctor-nurse team in the Philippines, China, and Vanuatu. We helped start a clinic and school in Bangladesh that today serve thousands of adults and children. Together we hiked up Mount Kilimanjaro, worked on a cruise ship in Antarctica, and trekked to Mount Everest base camp. On my fiftieth birthday we crossed Pakistan's Baltoro Glacier and camped at the foot of K2. Our health was excellent, we had enough money, and we liked each other more than any other couple we knew. The sex was great. Life was good. I believed our soulmateness would never end.

Then "something alarming" happened. My Japanese friend uses this expression when speaking of a mishap large or small, from committing suicide to falling in a mud puddle. Recounting events in this passive way saves face, his American wife explained, because it's disrespectful in Japan to place blame or name names. I'm not trying to be respectful in using the phrase. I just don't know who or what to blame. All I know was that when I reached my midfifties, life as I had known it for two decades was over.

I tried sticking various labels on it—menopause, midlife crisis, job stress, Christine. Sometimes I thought my misery came from all of the above, a cosmic convergence of negative forces; other times I thought they were all the same thing with different names. But no matter what I called it, or how much I pondered, I could not figure it out.

2

 $\mathscr{I}_T$ was easy to blame Christine for my troubles, and I did on and off, but when I was truthful with myself, I knew her arrival in our lives was only the spark that lit the fire. Besides that, she considered me her friend. When I talked about her and my situation, people judged her to be either conniving or crazy, and since I knew that to be untrue, I hated myself for even bringing her up.

For a year Craig and I knew this athletic thirty-year-old woman, a molecular biologist whom Craig had met during one of his lectures at the local medical school. She had come to meet him because she was interested in two jellyfish sting studies Craig and I had published. Christine had a sweet farm-girl kind of innocence, so young looking and freckle-faced that students, mistaking her for a teaching assistant, frequently asked her if they could talk to the professor. "I am the professor," she said, to which at least one student replied, "I want to see a real professor."

Craig met Christine over coffee to discuss our studies and her research. I asked him how it went.

"I liked her," he said. "Her theories are interesting. But the meeting was weird. She brought a guy named Steve with her who talked nonstop."

"One of her grad students?"

"No, someone in the pharmaceutical business. Her boyfriend, I believe."

Later, Christine invited Craig and me to join her and Steve for dinner at their Kaneohe house. I had the same impression as Craig: Christine was a shy, smart researcher who lived with a pushy drug representative. It was not a good "couples" match, and I shrugged them off. Craig and Christine, however, communicated about her toxicology studies by e-mail, phone, and occasionally in person since they both liked to jog.

One day while running, Christine told Craig she was having serious money problems. Craig, always the helper, asked if there was anything he could do to help. Soon she was at our kitchen table, twisting strands of her long brown hair around her finger as she talked.

"I had no idea what Steve was doing," she said. "I trusted him."

After inheriting from her grandfather a rundown house on Kaneohe Bay, Christine had put Steve, recently laid off, in charge of remodeling, giving all of her savings and paychecks directly to him. It wasn't enough money for the elaborate renovations, but rather than tell her, Steve started borrowing, saying yes to the many credit card offers banks sent Christine in the mail and maxing them out. For two years Christine thought her fiancé was building their dream house. He did, in fact, get the place finished, but the house on the hill cost more than she earned, and Steve could no longer make the minimum payments. Collection agencies began hunting Christine down. When she learned her house was a sand castle crumbling under waves of debt, she stopped the cash flow and put the house up for sale.

"He's furious with me," she said. "He won't move out."

"Are you afraid of him?" Craig said.

"No, but he's so angry. . . . I feel like I don't know him anymore."

"Where are you staying?" I said.

"There. I don't have any other place to go."

Craig and I simultaneously invited her to stay with us. The next day Christine moved into our guest room. I thought she would be there for a week or two, a month max, while she sorted out her financial difficulties. She stayed nearly a year.

People gasp, but it was fun for a while. This quiet, amiable woman slipped comfortably into our *ohana* (a Hawaiian concept meaning one's circle of family and close friends), and since my sister, Michele, and her family lived in the townhouse adjoining ours, and also liked Christine, we enjoyed a kind of dormitory life. Each of us had his and her own space, but we could easily share meals, holidays, parties, and evenings out.

Besides liking one another's company, we all had a soft spot in our hearts for Christine, who gave new depth to the expression "painfully shy." She told me she had a problem with shyness, but I didn't get it until the day she, Craig, and I went scuba diving on Maui. On the dive boat, a single, good-looking man asked Christine, "Where are you from?" When she didn't answer, I nudged her with my knee. She looked at me in panic, her eyes wide and her face blotchy red. "We're from Oahu," I said, and Christine nodded. The conversation went on in this absurd manner. The man would ask Christine something, she would look at me, and I would answer for her. "Join us for dinner?" I said to the guy as we left the boat. He agreed to meet us at the restaurant.

"Christine, what on earth . . . ?" I said after he left. "Why didn't you talk to him? He's interested in you and seemed nice."

"I told you I was shy."

"I know, but you can't even say 'I'm a molecular biologist' when someone asks you what you do?"

"Sometimes I panic and can't talk. My whole body shuts down. Feel this." She raised her hand to my cheek. The weather was hot and humid yet her fingers were icy cold.

"How do you work?" I said.

"It doesn't happen with students or colleagues. It's a social thing."

Why such an attractive, smart, talented person would have paralytic panic attacks over a question like "What's your name?" was a mystery to me, but there it was. I gave her a hug and encouraged her for the upcoming dinner. She did a little better with conversation that evening, but not much.

Christine had gone to college on a track scholarship, and as her separation from Steve became more and more rancorous, she relieved her stress by running marathons. Off she would go at four or five in the morning, come back blistered and limping, and still go with us to dinner and a movie.

Soon marathons weren't enough. She began training for triathlons with the goal of qualifying for, and competing in, Ironman competitions. While pushing herself so hard, she said, she was unable to think about anything else, a state of mind she craved during this difficult time in her life. Craig, a former Olympic-class athlete and bicycle enthusiast, began training with her. He liked exercising hard again, and Christine liked the challenge of keeping up with him.

Their workouts increased, and soon they were running, swimming, and bicycling, together and separately, during most of their free time. Craig shed twenty-five unwanted pounds and began to look different, his bulging muscles, tan skin, and graying temples making him more handsome than ever, distinguished with a rakish, outdoorsy air. Christine looked different to me too, but only because I got to know her better. It was a slow process. I lived with Christine for two months before I found out that besides being a molecular biologist and triathlete, she was also a concert violinist and fluent in German, Russian, and Lithuanian, her grandparents' native language. Some days I felt as if my roommates were the X-Men mutants Wolverine and Storm.

That was my sentiment, though, not theirs, because even with all their achievements, neither Craig nor Christine viewed themselves or each other as anything special, certainly not superheroes. They both thought they were average people with hobbies. (I found out about Christine's musical talent when she asked me if I minded her playing her violin in the house because she had a concert that weekend and needed to practice.) This genuine humility was a large part of Christine's charm, and Craig's as well.

Often the two of them invited me to join them on their exercise outings, and occasionally I did, but it wasn't much fun. When we went snorkeling, they wore goggles instead of masks and fins, and swam the crawl stroke at a workout pace. If we hiked, they either gave me a head start and I walked alone, or they passed me and I walked alone. And forget bicycling with them. I never even tried.

Eventually they stopped asking me to come along, but I barely noticed. Mostly I was glad they were gone because I was working on the Great American Novel, a story featuring Hawai'i's marine animals.

One of my intentions in writing fiction was similar to what I hoped I was doing in my newspaper column, and that was to change the way many people thought about the oceans and marine life. A steady stream of bad news about oil spills, the "Pacific Garbage Patch" (a mass of plastic bits in the North Pacific Gyre), and global warming, as well as marine animal horror stories—turtles with tumors, seabirds choking on trash, and fish stocks gone—made it easy to imagine that Earth's vast blue oceans were nothing but cesspools of dying creatures tangled in six-pack rings.

This was not true. Week after week in "Ocean Watch" I shared my positive, often glorious, experiences in the ocean to show readers that countless invertebrates, seabirds, fish, and mammals survive, and sometimes thrive, in spite of us.

Response to the column over the years made it clear that the more people learn about the marine world, the more they appreciate it and want to take care of it. Sometimes this comes as a life-changing revelation. When the cynical and funny author David Sedaris went snorkeling off Maui, a large sea turtle swam close and looked him in the eye: "That, to me," he wrote in the *New Yorker*, "was worth the entire trip, worth my entire life, practically. For to witness majesty, to find yourself literally touched by it—isn't that what we've all been waiting for?"

As a Hawai'i columnist, I had a platform from which I could communicate how and where to find such majesty. But as a novelist, whoa. I could broadcast from the Space Needle, the Empire State Building, Big Ben (I dreamed big). Through my future international best seller, readers would discover that sharks are not mindless killers, nor are dolphins supernatural psychics. These and all animals deserve respect and awe just for being themselves. My novel would reverse *Jaws*. Fix *Flipper*. I could *really* free Willy.

Because I had been writing every day for years, churning out popular science books, magazine articles, journal papers, and newspaper columns, I knew how to write and how to get my work published. *How hard*, I thought, *could a novel be?*

Harder than I dreamed possible. The book consumed me, keeping me awake nights and demanding all my concentration. For months I didn't answer phone calls or e-mails, got snappish when interrupted, and ignored Craig and Christine. When I complained to Craig that Christine's presence in the house on her days off made it hard for me to write, he arranged a month for me in a friend's Maui condominium. I loved him for understanding.

The week I returned from Maui, my sister said, "Susan, people are talking." "About what?"

"Well, wives don't usually leave their husbands alone for a month with a beautiful thirty-year-old woman living in their house."

"Oh. I never thought about it," I said. And I never did. Craig and I weren't so naïve as to think neither of us would ever be attracted to someone else, or even that our great love affair would never end. We did, however, swear we'd tell each other if a flirtation ever got serious, or if it seemed time to move on. Worse than an affair or a change of heart, we agreed, was the humiliation of being the last to know.

Years earlier, a devastated acquaintance told me she discovered her husband had been having affairs throughout their twenty years together. "You had no idea?" I said, unable to imagine such cruelty on his part, such gullibility on hers. "None at all?"

"Oh, don't sit there all smug like it could never happen to you," she snapped. "You think you know Craig? Believe me, you don't."

But I did know Craig, at least the part of him that would sleep with someone else. If he decided to do it, he would tell me, not because I demanded it but because he thought it was the right thing to do. Much as he loved sex, he would not trade his integrity for it. He had become the good man and good doctor he set out to be.

Nor was Christine romantically interested in him. "No," she once said when my sister asked if she found Craig attractive. "He's *old*." While she lived with us, Christine had been invited to join a running group and through it found a boyfriend in Oregon. The man, about her age, was a talky type who spoke for both of them, and the two were carrying on a long-distance love affair.

Besides a romance between Craig and Christine being of no concern, I was obsessed with my brilliant new novel. I gave the half-finished manuscript to Craig and a trusted friend and waited for the rave reviews.

Neither told me the novel wasn't any good, but I could tell immediately through their polite suggestions that I had missed the mark. The fun I had describing wildlife in my column each week got lost in human plot points and obligatory sex scenes. I felt like a bird flying into a window. I couldn't work on my book anymore, and in losing it, I lost a dream.

I also lost my hormones. Years earlier, at forty-eight, when my periods got irregular, I cried when stuck in a traffic jam, flew into a rage over missing the mail carrier, and couldn't sleep through the night. "I feel like I'm going crazy," I told my longtime family doctor. "I know menopause can throw you, but *this*. Missing a UPS delivery depressed me for two days."

"I could recommend a counselor," he said, "and if that doesn't help, I'll write you a prescription for estrogen. Or I could just write the prescription now. My patients your age with these symptoms usually thank me for the prescription but not for the counselor."

Of course, I knew the controversy over hormone replacement therapy—some studies suggested it increased the risk of breast cancer, while others did not. But breast cancer was less scary to me than being nuts. The memory of my mother's last years haunted me. She started crying at fifty and didn't stop until sixty-eight and only then because she died. During those awful years she spoke of suicide, not as a threat but as an explanation of how bad she felt.

My mother didn't commit suicide, but an acquaintance from Scotland told me her aunt and two cousins did. "They got depressed during their change," Jess said. "My aunt was saved, sort of. She took pills, but her husband found her in time."

"What do you mean, sort of?" I said. "Did the drugs do permanent damage?"

"No, but a year later, they found her in the closet. You know. Hanging."

I skipped the counseling and went for the drugs.

A lot of my women friends were horrified over my taking these medications, as if I was shooting up heroin for a hangnail. They argued that drug companies represent menopause as a disease to sell more drugs, that the media report menopause as mental illness to sensationalize the news, that male doctors think this natural biological process needs medical intervention. It surprised me to learn that taking medication to ease menopause symptoms could be a political issue. Some women believed ageism, sexism, and medicalization had elbowed their way into our middle-aged consciousness to convince us we were old, sick, and sexless.

Not me. I felt old, sick, and sexless all on my own, and light years better on the drugs. What scared me more than the drugs' possible adverse effects was what would happen to me if I didn't take them. I worried I would collapse like a beached jellyfish.

And then a study called the Women's Health Initiative made headline news. It concluded that the drugs millions of women were taking to ease menopause symptoms not only increased our risk of breast cancer but also upped our odds of having a stroke. I went cold turkey and felt fine, even when Christine announced that we were out of laundry detergent, clearly expecting me to buy some more. I laughed and she apologized.

Six weeks later, though, when I discovered Costco had discontinued my favorite mouthwash, I became enraged and broke down crying. (Shopper alert: if a middle-aged woman is cursing and weeping in your aisle, change aisles fast.) Two months later I was freaking out over life's little practical jokes, such as a flat tire on my VW Beetle, as well as the big ones, such as a spreading spare tire around my middle. (My mother gained nearly a hundred pounds in her fifties.) The worst of it was not being able to tell the difference between an annoyance and a catastrophe. It was a fine line, I discovered, between laughing off Christine's long-term occupation of our spare bedroom and scheming to change the locks when her presence struck a hormone-frayed nerve. My life felt like one big bad acid trip.

I was not alone. Because of the Women's Health Initiative study results, hormone replacement therapy for treating hot flashes was getting a lot of press, but no one was talking much about the other symptoms of menopause that women suffered. I went on an Internet search and found dozens of forums in which middle-aged women wrote about anxiety, paranoia, and altered perception of reality.

"Is anyone else but me having these symptoms?" asked a fifty-year-old woman on a women's health site. "It's so hard to describe what I'm going through, but it's awful. My concentration and cognitive skills feel like I have

Alzheimer's. My mind is racing all over the map with things popping into my head. It doesn't seem like it's me creating this. It's just happening."

A woman replied, "At fifty-one, I am a year now on the same scary roller coaster you describe."

On another site: "Anxiety attacks, dizzy spells, memory loss, cognitive issues. At one point I was unable to . . . run my business, shop a grocery list, drive, hold a decent conversation, sleep. I thought I must have a tumor or something, it came on so fast. Neurology tests were negative. Rapid menopause runs in the family—my sister went crazy before I did [my behavior, by the way, was striking terror in my much younger sister]—and testing confirmed it. HRT stabilized it so I can function, but I still have that lovely Alzheimer's thing going on."

"At fifty-one," wrote another, "I thought I had early-onset Alzheimer's and spent the next five to six years in a nightmare. Insomnia alone was bad enough, but almost as bad was having to withdraw socially because I couldn't trust myself not to say something totally 'wrong' and embarrass myself. I couldn't remember what I was saying halfway through a sentence. I would wake up and not know what day it was. I was scared for years."

A Harvard Health Publication called these symptoms "mood swings" and reported that no direct link between mood and diminished estrogen had been proved.

What, then, was happening to me and countless other aging women? Why are these awful symptoms nonexistent for some and devastating for others? And my burning question remained: will this menopause madness ever end, or was I nuts for life? I had no idea.

"Thanks for the coffee," I said to Craig and Christine one morning while holding up the empty pot. During our years together Craig had always made the morning coffee, often delivering it to me in bed. Sometimes if I had to get up early—not my time of day—he would dip his finger in the creamy-sweet brew and dab it lovingly on my lips to gently wake me. He still made the coffee, except now he and Christine drank it all before I got up.

"I'll make some more," Craig said, rising from his chair.

"Forget it," I said. "Just leave me alone."

And he did.

3

I worked in my home office feeling anxious and unsure, not knowing if Craig would be home for dinner, or even home before I went to bed. My protests over his lengthy workouts triggered arguments, and for the first time in our life together, we fought. He wanted me to encourage him in his athletic endeavors. I wanted him to spend his free time with me.

I behaved like an empty nester—except my nest was not empty. I didn't even have a nest. I lived free-range, exploring my home islands of Hawai'i and visiting the wildlife of the world, while writing nature books and my newspaper column. Even my job title was loose: free-lance writer. (I contributed "Ocean Watch" every week not as an employee of the newspaper but as an independent contractor.) When people asked about my line of work, though, I usually called myself a marine biologist because I had a degree in biology with a certificate in marine journalism from the University of Hawai'i's Marine Option Program, and because saying that made me feel like I was the guest of honor at a party of fish.

I had enrolled in the university's course on ichthyology (study of fish) after moving temporarily, I thought, to Honolulu with new boyfriend, Craig. During that semester, I learned how gills extract oxygen from water, the way you can tell a fish's age (by its ear stones), why some fish should be the poster animals for the transgender community (changing sex halfway through adult life), and a hundred other amazing facts. I was not one of those students obsessed with memorizing the scientific names of each species—although I did it when required—but instead loved discovering how fish breathed, reproduced, communicated, swam. Once I understood the rarity of shark attacks and discovered how humans mindlessly persecuted these fantastic fish, I overcame my fear of sharks and loved them, too.

The next semester I learned that tides, waves, and currents make beaches wide, narrow, or steep, and oceanography became my favorite class. Invertebrate zoology sealed the deal: looking at a sea urchin in a lab, I amused my Hawaiʻi-born classmates, so ho-hum over such creatures, by exclaiming, "Look. Its little tube feet are filled with water!"

"You should be a writer," a rather cranky UH professor told me one day, handing back several papers I had written for her classes. I had taken two classes from her that semester, one in women's studies, another in Latin American history.

"I want to be a marine biologist," I said.

"You have a talent for writing," she said.

"I'm having a full science year," I told her. "I took your classes because they required writing papers, and after physics and analytical chemistry, that's easy. Fun, even."

"Not everyone thinks writing is easy and fun," she said. "It means you're a natural."

"But I love marine biology."

"Then write about that," she snapped.

She had a point. I enjoyed writing, and the more I thought about it, the more appealing it became to share with others my marine animal thrills.

Craig often read sailing magazines, and it surprised me to discover that they contained nothing about marine life. I thought mariners would appreciate some facts I was learning, such as the size of barnacle penises. Barnacles have the longest penises of any animal, up to eight times their body length. In a six-foot-tall man, that would be a forty-eight-footer. Now there was something for sailors to think about as they labored to clean their hulls.

While still a student, I wrote articles about barnacles on your (boat) bottom, sea turtles humping rowboats, and why dolphins ride bow waves (to play). When several national sailing magazines bought the stories, that clinched it. I decided that, when I graduated, I would write about Hawaiʻi's ocean animals in a local newspaper and, in that, do my part to save them. I took to heart the popular 1968 quote by Senegalese environmentalist Baba Dioum: "In the end, we will conserve only what we love, we will love only what we understand, and we will understand only what we are taught."

Writing professionally was easier said than done. When I suggested I write a weekly newspaper column about marine life, one editor told me, "No, we tried that once. It didn't work." Another said, "You mean something about diving? Call the sports editor." After a year of free-lance writing in which I put together a portfolio of my work, in 1987 I proposed writing a column called "Sea Watch" to a new-to-Hawaiʻi editor of the other Honolulu daily. (The city had two, which later merged.) "Let's try it for a few weeks and see how it goes," he said. "And since we live in the middle of the Pacific Ocean, let's call it 'Ocean Watch.'"

Readers liked my nontraditional approach to marine biology, such as avoiding use of scientific names. Greek and Latin words don't paint a picture and often aren't accurate. The species name, for instance, of the largest animal on Earth, the hundred-foot-long blue whale, is *musculus*, meaning "small mouse." And as for scientists insisting on calling jellyfish "sea jellies" because the animals aren't fish, and sea gulls simply "gulls," because some live far from the sea, well, that seems to me to be one more way to alienate people from wildlife. Call them whatever you want. My goal as a marine science writer was to make my stories as much fun as the animals were to me.

Soon, "Ocean Watch" topics were generating letters to the editor, letters to me, and verbal comments. Most were supportive, but not all, including my own managing editor.

"People are starting to recognize me," I said, excited about the positive response to the column.

"It's easy to be a big fish in a small pond," he said. "Don't let it go to your head."

It was the beginning of some lesson learning for me. One was that, as a free-lance writer, I would always be an outsider among the newspaper staff.

Nor was I welcomed in university circles. "You do not have my permission to write about my research," a UH biologist told me at a party as we discussed my fledgling column.

"You don't want people to know what you're doing?" I said.

"Not in a *newspaper*." He said this as if I wrote on toilet paper and hung it on an outhouse wall.

Another negative was that in academic circles I had no authority. "Who are you to write a book about fish?" a museum ichthyologist once said to me. "That's *my* field."

I adopted historian Barbara Tuchman's attitude about academics: screw them. I doubt she ever said that in so many words, but it's what she meant. Tuchman (1912–1989) wrote popular world history and won two Pulitzer Prizes for her books, but some academics disparaged her work. When an interviewer asked Tuchman why she had not gone to graduate school, she said, "It's what saved me, I think. If I had taken a doctoral degree, it would have stifled any writing capacity."

Tuchman did not regret her decision to pass on a PhD, and for most of my life neither did I. But as I marched toward my sixties, a sense of finality bored into my consciousness like a shipworm. Old-person notions popped into my head, such as *this might be my last car, the pain in my side is probably cancer,* and *now I'm too old for grad school.* Living with Craig and Christine, two people who had a stack of university degrees, language skills, athletic feats, and musical accomplishments, made it worse, as did the hormone storms that kept me awake at two in the morning with my mind leaping like a hooked marlin.

During those tormented times, I was beset by soul-shaking doubts about my abilities, my body, my worthiness as a partner. Occasionally I thought I might as well kill myself and get it over with. I knew this was hormonal lunacy speaking, that I had it all and should be grateful. When you're depressed, though, counting blessings doesn't help.

I forced myself off the couch, using my free time to exercise like mad (though about a quarter as much as Craig and Christine), running, hiking, and swimming until I dropped. I learned transcendental meditation, bought new clothes, colored my hair, joined a professional writing group and a book club, and went to meetings just to get out of my office. Nothing worked. (Well, going blonde helped a little.)

Craig, in the meantime, lost nearly all his body fat. His muscles grew ropey, and his slightly high blood pressure dropped to normal. He started to look like he did when I met him: a trim, tanned, muscled athlete, except now the silver streaks in his hair made him a dignified trim, tanned, muscled athlete. Oh, and another difference—he moved to Mars.

I never read the 1992 bestseller *Men Are from Mars, Women Are from Venus,* but for as much as Craig and I were communicating, we might as well have been two species from different planets. I was lonely and depressed. He was angry that I was lonely and depressed. I was angry that he was angry.

Day after day I wondered: *Where is that darling man who used to call me several times a day just to say hi? That thoughtful guy who rubbed my back without asking? The cheery one who sang in the shower? Who had always chosen to make love over all athletic activities?* It seemed as if the two of us had become entirely different people. Some days I would see Craig's strained, stoic expression and wonder,

Who is this guy? I would like to say he wondered the same about me, but I had no idea what he wondered. We lived in parallel universes.

I found a marriage counselor, and Craig agreed to go with me, but couples therapy got us nowhere. The counselor, a man about our age, took Craig's side. Craig's desire for a new athletic challenge—he was now training for an Ironman competition—was reasonable, he thought, and it was also reasonable that Craig had a workout friend in Christine.

I balked. This workout friend happened to be a beautiful, brilliant woman half my age whom everyone I knew reminded me almost daily to be worried about.

"What if Christine were a man?" the counselor asked me one day when I was there without Craig.

"It doesn't matter," I nearly shouted. "The point is all the time he spends with him. Her. Whoever. There's none left for me." The counselor urged me to concentrate on my own life. But in the ways I had come to depend on him as best friend/lover/Twinoid/travel partner and movie/book/newspaper buddy, Craig *was* my life.

Craig's secession from our nation-of-two turned into a civil war. We both despised and regretted the angry, hurtful words that came spurting from our mouths.

"Tell her to move out," I said when I learned in an e-mail that he and Christine were going to Yellowstone for a marathon. "I can't do this anymore."

"Where do you expect her to go? She's got no money."

"No money? She flew to Australia for a race. She's flying with you to Wyoming."

"She's meeting her boyfriend there."

I didn't know if this meant the boyfriend was paying for the trip, or if this was supposed to be some kind of reassurance for me, but Craig wouldn't or couldn't elaborate, and I wouldn't or couldn't keep asking. It became easier—but no less painful—to just stop speaking. I wanted to throw pies at every hand-holding couple I saw on the street. Often I drove to our sailboat in the city marina and slept there so I could mope in private.

"What do you want?" I asked him time and again, and always got the same two answers. I understood the first: he wanted to exercise with friends of his own choosing. I got that. It was his second point that threw me: he wanted me to be happy. "You mean I should get a life? Go somewhere? Leave you alone? I don't know what you mean. Why won't you talk to me?"

"I am talking to you," he would say. "You aren't listening."

Craig believed he was explaining himself, but understanding his cryptic messages was like reading smoke signals from the next hill over.

"I'm fine," he said to the counselor, setting his jaw the way he does when he's done talking. "She's the one who's upset."

Craig shut down during our last session together, and afterward I screamed at him in the car. "Talk to me."

"Okay," he said. "I haven't been happy for a long time."

I nearly fainted. (Not good. I was driving.)

"A long time?" I said. "How long?"

"I don't know," he said. "It's been gradual."

"Why didn't you tell me?" I said.

"I did."

"What? When?"

"A while ago."

"Well, remind me what we said when we talked about this, because I don't remember the conversation." For a panicky moment, I wanted to stick my fingers in my ears and yell LA LA LA LA . . . but apparently he thought I had already been doing that.

I listened hard, but he could explain only in halting and imprecise terms. "When you're going to work," he would start, "you don't want someone saying something that just hangs there all day."

"What, for example?" I said.

He could not give examples. Craig got so uncomfortable articulating his feelings that I felt sorry for him and began asking questions that he could answer with a yes or no. After a while of this, I thought I got it. He felt I didn't appreciate the difficulties of his job, realize how hard he worked at it, or understand its stresses.

This was true. It's a common problem among physicians and their families and friends. None of the E.R. doctors I knew, including Craig, liked to talk about their work, because no one, not even other physician specialists, could appreciate what life was like in the trenches of emergency medicine. I rarely knew when he was suffering or, if he was, about what. Once I eavesdropped when he and a colleague were talking in low voices and to my shock learned that Craig had treated the little boy whose aunt was pulling her car out of the garage and accidentally backed over him, a tragedy that had been all over the news. The toddler died in the E.R., and Craig had to make this announcement to the family members who were already wild with grief. How awful for him to come home after such anguish and have to listen to my story about the dog peeing on the carpet. But how was I to know he had a horrible day if he didn't tell me?

Craig also felt I ignored his desire and need to exercise. Well, okay. But the amount of aerobic activity he needed to feel good was so far off my ability chart, I couldn't even imagine it. At the beginning of our troubles, I signed us up for a trek in Morocco's Atlas Mountains. After hiking all day, the porters set up camp, we trekkers collapsed in our tents, and Craig went jogging.

Our lives had become too domestic, too traditional, he added. Hard to argue with that when, at the time, we were sitting in the remodeled living room of our large townhouse, in a gated community, on the golf course of an affluent Honolulu suburb. It had shocked our friends, and us too, that we alternative-lifestyle people of the 1960s had moved to such a place, but there we were. We wanted a home that we could leave for a month or two and not worry about roof leaks or break-ins. That ruled out a house, and condominiums near Craig's main hospital had been in short supply.

Craig said he wanted a partnership where each of us supported the other's endeavors, whatever those happened to be. Plus putting the blame for our problems on Christine, who was having a terrible time of her own, was short-sighted and mean on my part, he said.

That he saw me as the roadblock to his ideal life seemed short-sighted and mean. Where was his support to me during this hard and confusing time in my life? His idea of support was what? Riding his bicycle around the island so I could fight my demons alone?

One morning after he left for work, I sat on the couch and burst into tears with my face in the dog's neck. When I opened my swollen, fur-laden eyes, I looked at our lives from Craig's point of view. In this twenty-three-year show we'd been performing together, he saw me as producer, director, star, set artist, costume designer, stage hand, and caterer. Oh, and travel agent. I planned all our trips. Was his burst of athleticism his attempt to break out? Break away?

Why had he not said anything? Oh, that's right. He thought he had. But if I didn't respond, surely he knew I didn't get the message. And all this time I was thinking we were so close, such special friends. Looking around the room, I wondered: *Had I been so busy remodeling our condominium, searching for workers in our Bangladesh clinic, and planning trekking trips that I lost him?*

The realization of how unhappy he was, and how oblivious I had been to it, paralyzed me. I could barely get out of bed, and when I did, I walked around like a zombie. How could I have been so blind? Had my view of our relationship ever been correct?

"Don't rewrite your history together," the counselor counseled. (I was seeing him alone.) "If you felt happy all those years, you were."

"But was he? Maybe our wonderful love affair never existed at all. Did I want it so badly that I made it up?"

He handed me a tissue. "It's like this: You had a good life together. Now things have changed, and you have to figure out how you're going to deal with it."

Changed? Good Lord. When my mother's generation called menopause "the change of life," they weren't kidding. My body, my thinking, my spouse, my writing, even my sleep patterns had changed, and none for the better.

Often I felt like a sniveling mess, wondering, *Who am I without Craig? Without hormones? Without my goal of being a novelist?* Other times I was so furious with him for not talking, for blaming me, for allowing Christine to live with us for a year that I decided to leave him. He can live with his workout friend, I thought. But I don't have to.

"Be absolutely sure you want to leave him," the counselor said. "Living alone is awfully hard."

"I don't *want* to leave him," I said. "I just can't think of what else to do."

My brain was trying to kill me.

I decided to exchange my urban nightmare for a wilderness dream by volunteering to work at Tern Island, the main biological field station in Hawai'i's northwest chain. This wildlife refuge, designated the Papahānaumokuākea (*papa*-hah-*now-mow*-koo-ah-*kay-ah*) Marine National Monument, consists of dozens of isolated islands, islets, and atolls stretching over a thousand miles from Oahu and is the breeding ground of nearly all Hawai'i's sea turtles, monk seals, and seabirds. For me, a naturalist, photographer, nature writer, and lover of marine wildlife, Tern Island was paradise.

Two U.S. Fish and Wildlife Service workers ran the station with a handful of volunteers, most of them young adults with new degrees in biology or wildlife management. This was to be my fifth time at Tern, an unusual number of visits granted one person there, but Honolulu directors respected my column and its educational effect on the public, and knew me as a good wildlife worker besides.

I knew Tern Island well and felt, like most workers there, privileged to be allowed another stretch. Tern was one of the few places left in Hawai'i where workers lived so close to wildlife that we became wildlife ourselves. It seemed perfectly normal on Tern Island to walk around with a red-footed booby chick on your head.

In Hawai'i, the red-footed booby is the seabird most likely to land on your boat or, if you're working in a seabird colony like Tern, on your head. This is no fluttery little landing. The birds are twenty-eight inches long, head to tail, and have a wingspan of forty inches. It's like having a mallard duck settle in your hair.

Only juvenile red-footed boobies use people's heads and boats for landing practice, and only at a specific time in their development, which is after they've learned to fly but before their fishing skills are good enough to feed themselves. The young birds are adult size but not yet adult colored: their feet are gray, and their feathers a mottled brown. Red-footed boobies earn their tomato-red feet and snow-white body feathers by surviving for four years, the age of sexual maturity.

For a few weeks, the adolescent birds are in training, gliding on the wind and practice landing on stationary objects. In the late afternoon, the rehearsing-for-life youngsters go home for supper, delivered by parents who spent the day at sea plunge diving for fish and squid.

While working on Tern Island, I learned to play games with red-footed booby chicks. On a windy day, if you hold a branch bearing a horizontal stick in the air, feathered teenagers will try to land on it. If they miss the branch, or your arm wobbles under their two- to three-pound weight, they might settle on your head instead, bending the toenails of their flat webbed feet into your hair. Booby bird toenails are short and don't hurt the scalp, even through fine, straight hair like mine. But my straight hair offered little for the birds to grip, and they soon slipped down the side of my head and flew off. Alex's thick curly hair gave the birds a good foothold, and they liked riding on him. I once saw Alex walk the length of Tern Island with a red-footed booby perched on his head like a hood ornament.

It's great fun wearing a bird for a hat, but there's a downside. Just before they take flight, seabirds defecate to lighten their load, and since caps are hard to keep on in the strong wind there, the squirts often land in our hair. Receiving this splash of guano, however, was just a matter of attitude. One day when a glob landed on top of my hatless head, I reached up and touched the wet deposit.

"Yuck," I said, looking at my hand.

"Think of it as Tern Island creme rinse," Alex said.

This was one reason I had come to love Alex: his sense of humor lifted problems right off my shoulders—and occasionally off my head.

The wildlife jobs on Tern Island were nearly endless, but my favorite was fastening aluminum ID bands on the legs of seabirds, because this was one of the few times you could legally hold—and hug—federally protected animals. Cradling a Laysan albatross in my arms was a joy like no other. The feathers of the goose-sized birds with seven-foot wingspans were so soft that my work-calloused hands could barely feel them. But my lips could. To band an albatross, one person picked it up and held it while another applied a numbered ring to its right leg. When it was my turn to hold, I would lower my face to the bird's head, inhale its fresh smell of the open ocean, and press my lips to its velvety feathers. With this kiss I delivered to the bird my message: *You are magnificent and I adore you.*

Because albatrosses and Hawai'i's other native seabirds, turtles, and seals evolved with no land predators, they were easy to approach, fun to work with, and lovable as puppies. A bird would sometimes look at me with such confusion, such innocence, I would get teary. "You're going to be okay," I sometimes whispered to the white terns I held. "We do this because we love you." Banding is the only way researchers can learn a seabird's age, know where it flies, or study its nesting patterns.

Fortunately, the albatrosses (and most other seabirds) were quick to forgive and forget, being single-minded in their drive to find a lifetime mate, lay an egg, and raise a chick. Usually the birds didn't care much about the two-legged creatures that insisted on giving them bracelets or reading the numbers on their bands. Even when we inched our hands beneath their egg-sitting bodies and extracted a leg to read a band number, the brooding birds mostly ignored us.

It felt wonderful knowing that my hours of labor and buckets of sweat would ultimately help the creatures I so admired. Also wonderful was the fact that I could expand the help through my "Ocean Watch" column. Some days I could barely rush to the barracks fast enough to write down an extraordinary experience, such as cradling in my T-shirt a dozen baby sea turtles that had lost their way to the beach, and e-mail the column to my editors. At Tern Island my entire body felt glowing with good news, and my urge to share it with people who couldn't see it for themselves grew stronger with each fluffy chick, each sleek shark, each bustling crab. Sure, the oceans had problems, but there was so much more going on than the gloom and doom of the daily news. Where other writers saw loss and death, I saw life.

The work at Tern Island also involved dozens of maintenance chores, such as keeping the bicycles in working shape, servicing the boats' outboard motors, and washing guano off solar panels. At day's end, when I was soaked in sweat, splattered with bird shit, dusted with dirt, and smeared with grease and oil, I felt like a breaded pork chop. Showers at Tern felt like gifts from the gods.

Tern Island is located inside French Frigate Shoals, an atoll five hundred miles north of Honolulu. This fifth time in the refuge would be my longest stint there, because the volunteer coordinator insisted I commit to the three-month minimum requirement for volunteers. (I was there for four months due to the plane schedule.) Craig didn't like the idea but didn't say why. Maybe he thought I was running away from my troubles. True, but still, if he wouldn't talk, I didn't care if he liked it or not. Things could hardly get worse between us, and I thought three months apart would give us some needed distance from each other. Maybe at Tern I would start another novel in which female monk seals transformed into mermaid militias that sabotaged long-liners' fishing gear. Maybe Christine would move out and Craig would miss me. Maybe he would be happy I was gone, in which case I would move on. Whatever happened, I would not keep living as I had been.

Before I left, however, some disturbing symptoms developed that I attributed to menopause. One was the inability to make decisions. This struck me at odd times, like at a video store, where I once dithered and dithered until, finally, miserable and frustrated, I left empty-handed. And I had really wanted to see some of those movies. It scared me to think that at Tern Island I would miss the shorebird count or a turtle-tagging event because I couldn't decide which T-shirt to wear.

I also developed the Lord Voldemort of menopause, the-symptom-that-must-not-be-named: vaginal burning. (Harry Potter's nemesis, Lord Voldemort, is so evil you can't say his name out loud.) This depressing state of affairs threatened to sever one of the bonds Craig and I still had. As angry and aggravated as we were, our attraction to each other still held. Even though our lovemaking felt like we were communicating over a tin can telephone—*Hello? Are you there? Can you hear me?*—the spark we'd had from the start remained, and that had given me hope. Now this.

The pain I experienced wasn't as bad as a bladder infection, but getting there. I had heard of vaginal atrophy, but I wasn't sure what that meant. No one mentioned that it hurt just walking around. Wondering about this, I quietly mentioned this odd ache to a friend in my book group, which consisted of eight women in their fifties and sixties. To my surprise, all of them leaped into the conversation, each with her own story about symptoms, remedies, and relationships.

"Of course marriage changes when you get old," one friend said. "It's not how good the sex is anymore. It's how good you are as *companions*."

We forgot our book, *Suite Française*. Sex, that evening, trumped literature.

"That kind of discomfort is common," an E.R. doctor friend told me later when we talked about my nagging bladder-infection feeling. "I have patients in their eighties who ask for prescriptions for estrogen cream."

"No. Women come to the emergency room for that? *At eighty?*"

He assured me they did.

My family doctor prescribed the cream, and it relieved the burning, but it did nothing for my dry, flaky skin or the itching sensation on my arms and legs. Sometimes the itching was so intense that during the night I unconsciously scratched myself to bleeding.

Those were my excuses for taking the hormones again. But I resumed estrogen therapy for another secret reason: fear. I feared that this crumbling of my excellent life with Craig, this wreckage of our wonderful Twinship, was all in my head, that I made it up. I feared that hormone withdrawal had turned me into a lunatic, that a bunch of kid biologists working at Tern Island would think I was a loopy old lady. More important, I feared that my disturbed state of mind might keep me from enjoying this rare opportunity to work, live, and be one with the animals I loved. There's no place in the world like Tern Island, and only a select few get to go there. At Tern, hope for the world shines bright. I would risk breast cancer for it.

I read the professional criticisms of the Women's Health Initiative estrogen study and went back to my doctor. "I felt better on the hormones," I said.

He smiled as he took out his prescription pad. "Most of the women who quit say the same."

Back on estrogen, I flew to Tern Island in a six-passenger plane without bathroom, heat, or other passengers. Besides the two pilots, my companions consisted of broccoli heads, asparagus stalks, and crates of apples and oranges, fresh food for the island's workers. Three hours later, French Frigate Shoals, the coral reef surrounding Tern Island, appeared.

This was no subtle sight. The deep blue of the open ocean contrasted dramatically with the turquoise waters inside the reef ("shoals" means shallows, an older term for reef), and the undersides of the fluffy white clouds bore the lagoon's soft pastels. As we approached the island, the pilots slipped on life jackets and donned helmets. Thousands of seabirds breed on Tern Island, some species right on the coral rock runway, and the approaching plane startled them into flight. The concern is that a bird will crash through the windshield and knock out the pilot and we end up on the bottom of the ocean.

I tightened my seatbelt and held my breath. In a heart-leaping maneuver, the experienced pilot dropped the plane nearly vertically through the black ball of screeching birds. Even over the roar of the plane's engines, the hits were audible—*thud, thud, thud*—as birds struck the fuselage, wings, and propellers. Seconds later, we touched down and rolled to a halt.

The airplane hit seven sooty terns, a small number given the tens of thousands of panicked seabirds that had been circling the runway. But still, several stricken birds lived, flopping pitifully with amputated wings. Before the airplane rolled to a full stop, island workers ran to the unfortunate terns and put them out of their misery with a primitive but effective form of euthanasia: a rock to the head. This was an awful chore, but we all did it without delay. To hesitate was to see the birds suffer.

Except for emergencies, airplane landings at Tern Island have since been discontinued. People now come and go only by boat.

The pilot opened the door, and I took a deep breath, inhaling the strong odor of guano, so rich in phosphorus and nitrogen that people have destroyed seabird colonies the world over by collecting and selling the stuff as fertilizer. When I first arrived in guano-reeking seabird colonies, the smell was so overpowering I felt short of breath, as if the odor somehow interfered with my oxygen intake. But noses fatigue, and in a day or so, I said, along with the other workers, "Smell? What smell?"

The U.S. Navy made Tern Island what it is today, fifty-four acres of pancake-flat, blinding-white sand and coral relieved by only a few imported coconut palms and hundreds of low-lying, half-dead bushes. They are half dead because seabirds perch, nest, and poop on them nearly constantly, as well as on nearly every other square yard of island, including the six or so old Coast Guard buildings and their surrounding water tanks and courtyards. The sound of hundreds of thousands of seabirds calling merged into a screeching wail that caused workers there to sometimes wear earplugs.

Plane Day occurred only once every six weeks or so and was therefore a big event. With little contact to the outside world, workers on the island greeted me warmly.

While the four workers staying on the island hugged good-bye to the four workers leaving, I dragged my duffel bag into the former Coast Guard barracks and chose an empty room. Sun and salt had weathered the wooden furniture gray, rust stains made the linoleum floor orange, and a windowpane was missing. To most people who work and live there, these dilapidated accommodations are better than five-star lodgings. They're the best rooms in the world. Nowhere else can a person have a fairy tern chick living on her windowsill as I did, its gray, downy body balancing on the narrow ledge while waiting for its fish dinner. Monk seals snorted outside, just feet from my bed. I watched baby sea turtles hatch in our backyard beach and each night fell asleep to wedge-tailed shearwaters moaning for mates.

For me, working in Hawai'i's wildlife refuges was like intense exercise had become for Christine and Craig: it consumed me, and while doing it I couldn't think about anything else. I don't know how much the estrogen contributed to my delight in working at Tern Island, but I kissed, cuddled, and banded albatrosses, booby birds, wedge-tailed shearwaters, and fairy terns in a state of bliss. I pulled alien weeds to clear nesting sites until my hands were so sore I could barely open a door. I swam with turtles, sharks, and eagle rays. I rescued (and nuzzled) baby turtles that hatched from their sand nests at night and couldn't find the ocean.

For fun, often I played toss-the-stick with juvenile frigatebirds, seabirds that catch objects naturally as they train for their future part-time jobs as pirates. (Sailors of old named the birds after the small, fast ships called frigates that were preferred by buccaneers.) As adults, frigatebirds often harass flying booby birds until they regurgitate their fresh-caught fish. At that, the frigatebird swoops down and, with amazing dexterity, catches its loot in midair.

Frigatebirds have bad reputations as a result of this behavior, but in fact, they catch most of their food on their own, plucking fish from the water's surface. This is tricky work for birds that can't land on a flat surface. If frigatebirds accidentally get grounded, either on land or on water, they usually can't lift off since those big wings need to flap to get going.

Most of my days contained activities I could hardly call work, such as rescuing seabirds that got stuck in the island's crumbling, World War II–era breakwater, a metal wall around the edges of the man-made island. Over the years, the ocean had reclaimed a considerable amount of sand, soil, and coral rubble from inside the breakwater, leaving a narrow gap between wall and island that trapped birds, turtles, and seals. Frigatebirds got grounded there most often, but they seemed to know I was trying to help them and never pecked my hand when I reached down to give their astonishingly light bodies a lift. (Frigatebirds have the largest wingspan-to-body-weight ratio of any bird: seven feet of wingspan on two- to three-pound bodies.) Other times, I spent back-breaking hours in the broiling sun raking the airplane runway, pulling weeds, and banding birds.

Even with all the physical work, I rose early each morning to write my columns and work on a five-part newspaper series about the atoll. Getting up at four in the morning would have been tough normally, especially after all that labor, but I didn't even need an alarm to wake up. From the feedback I received, I knew that my readers loved these stories, looked forward to them, and wanted more. At Tern Island, I had an opportunity to share the extraordinary experience of working with wildlife that had no fear of human beings. Hawai'i residents lived right next door to this little Galapagos-style wonderland, but few even knew it existed.

I made friends with Tasha, a twenty-five-year-old seabird biologist who arrived on the island with her researcher boyfriend in the middle of my Tern tenure.

The first evening there, she knocked on my door. "Do you mind if I move into the room next to you?" she said. "You see, Jim and I aren't really together," she said.

"Oh. The Honolulu office told us you were a couple." As a result of this report, we women had fixed up a room for them with twin beds pushed together to make a double.

"We were, but. . . ." She glanced over her shoulder. "I don't want him to hear us talking about it. He's pretty upset."

"Come in," I said, and closed the door behind us.

Tasha, a West Coast sailor from childhood, was also having a relationship problem, but even with our age difference (Tasha's mother was only a few years older than me) our conversations were never the mother-daughter kind, where I offered sage advice and she nodded gratefully. No, in the evenings we discussed our man problems as mature women, while polishing our toenails and sharing clothes like girls in junior high.

We were typical girlfriends, but with one huge exception: we lived on Tern Island, a place where the universe clobbered us with perspective. During the day, I sometimes helped Tasha and Jim fasten tiny satellite tracking tags on the legs of Laysan albatrosses. As we worked among tens of thousands of wild animals—monk seals, green sea turtles, and eighteen species of seabirds—each one in its own life-and-death struggle to avoid predators, find food, attract mates, and raise offspring, Tasha's and my problems dried up and blew away on the northeast trade winds. There was nothing more effective to remind me that my problems were tiny and irrelevant than watching an albatross head into the vast blue Pacific Ocean. When I stepped outside the barracks at Tern Island, I became a speck of dust in an infinite galaxy chugging along in its own unfathomable way. A happy speck. At Tern Island, I felt good when I woke up in the morning, grateful to live another day.

The physical work did my body good, too. Most of the chores at Tern required strength—volunteers had to be able to lift fifty pounds of food bins, propane tanks, boat gear, trash, and dozens of other items essential to life in a biological field station. To increase my strength and stamina, most days I jogged four island lengths (two miles total) and afterward lifted weights in the workout room, a routine I enjoyed because it had such noticeable results, one being that as the weeks rolled on, the same weights got easier to lift. For the first time in my life, my muscles grew defined, and I worked my way up to four chin-ups. I had to stand on a chair under the bar, but even so. I had never done a chin-up in my life. Sometimes I surprised myself with this newly acquired strength, hoisting an old mattress or large gas can with ease. One young biologist told me I was the strongest woman she had ever known.

Getting strong, trim, and aerobically fit gave me some insight into the differences between Craig and me regarding exercise. My fitness occurred almost as an accident, the result of the passion I had for living and working on Tern Island. For Craig, however, the exercise itself was the passion. For him, the goal was not to go anywhere in particular, or to look good, or even to win a race, but rather to push his body as hard as it would go. I didn't know what kind of feeling that gave him, exactly, because to me it sounded like torture. But for Craig it was a potent drug. He wanted it every day, the more the better, and withdrawal caused him to suffer.

I enjoyed an occasional exercise endorphin rush, and my little muscle bulges amused me, but I felt just as content lying on a beach watching ghost crabs dig holes and frigatebirds dip and glide overhead. No wonder the two of us had disagreements over exercise.

ALEX wasn't on the island when I arrived. He had gone to his parents' home to lick his wounds, I was told, after a love affair at Tern Island went bad. Gossip is practically theater in biological field stations, where sex is one of the workers' few diversions, and the six workers there talked often about the affair between Alex, who had fallen in love, and Tiffany, a monk seal worker returned to Canada, who apparently had not. Alex hadn't known that for Tiffany the affair was a temporary fling, and he had committed himself to the relationship in a far more emotionally responsible way than most men his age would have done. When he discovered that the love of his life had been, um, entertaining another man on the opposite side of the barracks, it broke his heart.

When speaking of Alex, people often used terms such as "sensitive" and "vulnerable," and I pictured a shy, milquetoasty type, eager to be liked. Not so. When Alex returned to Tern Island, about two weeks after my arrival, his self-assured bearing and long-legged stride from the plane exuded confidence, and his greeting—a hug rather than a handshake—warmed me to him instantly.

Alex possessed the surety of youth. His proclamations reminded me of a comment made by Craig's older friend a few years earlier: "You sure have gone downhill, Craig," Ed said, smiling. "When I met you, you were eighteen and knew everything."

Alex's approach to life contained few gray areas—a thing was either good or bad, right or wrong. His ideas were cast not in stone, however, but in sponge, making him charmingly open-minded. Alex shaped his ideologies by reading scientifically thoughtful books (Michael Pollan's *Botany of Desire* was one of his favorites), but if challenged with realities, or corrected with facts, he cheerfully reconsidered his position and, if warranted, would change his mind.

I learned those things about him over a bunch of bugs.

It was true that Alex cared deeply about others, and not just humans. His empathy extended to all living creatures.

"What are you doing?" he said when he found me placing cockroach traps around the teeming kitchen at Tern. His tone sounded as if he caught me drowning a sack of kittens.

"Cleaning," I said. "The roaches are practically carrying off the silverware."

"Cockroaches have a right to exist," he said.

"Sure they do. But they aren't native here, and they can carry pathogens."

He worked his jaw, clearly torn. "I wish you wouldn't kill them."

"I wrote a book about Hawai'i's animal pests," I said, "and believe me, we don't want roaches in our food and on our dishes."

"What about in the bedrooms?"

"You can keep pet roaches in your room if you want," I said, smiling. "Just tell them to stay home."

Another day, to mop the floor, I turned some dining room chairs upside down and found in their corners several black widow spiders, their white egg cases suspended in silky dense webs. As I was carrying the chairs outside to the airplane runway to spray them with pressurized seawater from a hose, Alex appeared.

"Look what I found under our chairs," I said.

We stared at the lovely mother spiders. "They're beautiful," he said.

"Yes. They look like they're wearing evening attire," I said, "little black dress, red bow."

"Killing a few won't get rid of them," Alex said. "They're all over the island."

"But we could accidentally grab them when we pull in our chairs, and they'll bite us to protect themselves," I said. "They have to go."

"I know," he said. "But it makes me feel bad. I don't want to watch."

Alex's aversion to killing these creatures came out of his respect for all living things, and in that, he did not discriminate between cuddly cuties and creepy crawlies. I appreciated his idealism. I killed the spiders alone.

Alex, I soon learned, never thought lack of knowledge or experience stood in the way of doing anything, large or small. I discovered this when the refuge manager gave me an unusual assignment. Each of us performed a daily chore to help keep the station functional, and one morning when I checked the grease board for my task, it said: "Fix front doorknob—Susan."

Fix front doorknob? I had never fixed a doorknob in my life. I didn't know what doorknobs looked like inside or even how they worked. I walked down the hallway to the front door and turned the knob. The metal bar that goes into the slot did not move. During storms, this door had to be closed securely or the wind would whip and whirl through the barracks, ripping papers off bulletin boards, pulling down wall maps, and even tipping over oil lamps. But how was I to fix it? In the midst of my hemming and hawing, Alex, not a morning person, walked past, his dark hair tousled, his eyes puffy with sleep. "Alex, wait," I said. "Do you know what's wrong with this doorknob?"

He turned back and tried the door. "It's seized," he said.

"I know. I got assigned to fix it, but I don't know how."

He stared at the doorknob, at me, and back at the knob. "Do it anyway," he said, and off he strode, leaving me blinking in the bright morning sun.

Thanks for nothing, I thought in a flash of anger. But Alex used the same standard for himself. He would never say "I don't know how" without trying first, and he would not accept it from anyone else. If I tried and failed and couldn't think of another approach, he would take a crack at it, but not before.

I reexamined the device and went to the tool room for a screwdriver and pair of pliers. With the screws out, it was easy to remove the knobs from each side of the door, and that exposed the frozen latch. *So that's how doorknobs work*, I thought, examining the simple mechanism. I chipped the salt and corrosion off the fastener, sanded it smooth, oiled it with WD-40, and screwed it back in the door—and the bolt slid home. This was a tiny achievement as mechanical things go, and it took me most of the morning to do it, but it made a big impression. I don't imagine doorknobs have changed many people's lives, but that one changed mine. *Do it anyway* became my silent vow.

I saw little of Alex for the next week. Still hurting from Tiffany's betrayal, he chose solitary work and spent his free time alone.

One day he knocked on my door with my camera in hand. "I thought you might be looking for this," he said.

"I was. Thanks. Want to come in?" I said.

If a man could look sadder, I hadn't seen it. "I spent a lot of time in here," he said. "My ex-girlfriend had this room."

"I didn't know. I picked it because it's across from the bathroom. And the fact that the walls are orange." The hue caught the shades of Tern Island's spectacular sunrises, which I paused during my writing each morning to admire.

"I would rather not come in," he said, straining his neck to peer in without stepping across the threshold. Alex braced himself for signs of Tiffany but instead saw on the orange wall hangings of cowfish exoskeletons mixed with bits of rubbish I found on the beach.

"Your art is cool," he said.

I don't know if my interest in found art came from living at Tern Island, or if my changing hormones caused some kind of left-brain/right-brain shift, but while I was there, a creative streak came out in me.

The Hawaiian island chain lies near the center of several oceanic currents known as the North Pacific Gyre, and certain of Hawai'i's beaches, Tern Island's south side being one, are landfalls of drifting trash. One day after doing a beach cleanup, I dumped the broken red, yellow, green, and blue plastic pieces I collected into a heap on the concrete floor to count and catalogue (we kept track of the junk that washed in) and found the colors and shapes intriguing.

It was quite an assortment: toothbrushes, cigarette lighters, and doll heads, mixed with plastic bottles, rubber flip flops, and nylon nets, to name a few. I picked out my favorite pieces and that evening strung fishnet floats to pearly shells and glued toy soldiers on leggy driftwood as room decorations. The result—a colorful statement of humanity's effect on the nature of the ocean—was pleasing and disturbing at the same time. The process of making the mobiles, my first attempt at art, was so much fun and so surprisingly satisfying that I vowed to make more when I got home.

"Want to help me organize the seal tagging gear?" he said.

We moved to the messy storage room, currently strewn with sandy kneepads, salty dry bags, and ice chests filled with warm water. As we cleaned up, Alex talked about his grief. I, in turn, poured my heart out about Craig and Christine. Alex was such a good listener, and so sympathetic, that I even told him about the confusion and shock I felt about aging. Sharing our pain gave us comfort, and because neither of us had any interest in watching DVDs, the preferred evening pastime of the other workers, Alex and I spent after-dinner hours editing and sharing our wildlife photos and walking the starlit airplane runway that takes up three-quarters of the island. On windy, moonlit nights, the runway felt like a walk through a haunted house, because the dark shadows of the night-gliding frigatebirds against the crushed white coral made us wince and duck. As the two of us walked, we talked and talked and talked. Our nighttime chats became a pleasant habit that continued throughout our three months of barracks life.

Alex had spent nearly two years on Tern Island as an employee of the U.S. Fish and Wildlife Service, but this was to be his last assignment. When he left, about the same time as me, he would fly to Palmyra Atoll, another National Wildlife Refuge a thousand miles south of Hawai'i, to finish research for his doctoral dissertation. He had been there several times and spoke glowingly of Palmyra, an atoll I had heard about but not visited. By Alex's accounts, the place was another wildlife paradise: while Tern was a desert island where we had to make freshwater from seawater, Palmyra Atoll, being near the equator, was deluged with rain, averaging 175 inches per year. (In Honolulu, the average rainfall is about twenty inches per year. In New York, it's forty-five inches; Chicago, thirty-nine; San Francisco, twenty-two.)

The difference between an atoll and a tropical island can be hard to sort out, because when it came to names, the military, sailors of old, and scientists each had their own version of what they were seeing. The U.S. Navy, for instance, erected a huge sign over their hangar at Midway saying "NAF [Naval Air Force] MIDWAY ISLAND." There is no Midway Island. The hangar is on Sand Island inside Midway Atoll.

In another example, a French explorer, Captain Jean-Francois de Galaup La Perouse, named the coral reef surrounding Tern Island and several other islands "French Frigate Shoals" because he nearly ran his two frigates aground there. La Perouse used the term "shoal" to mean shallow water. Technically, though, a shoal is an underwater sandbank visible at low tide. Later, scientists recognized La Perouse's "shoals" as coral reefs and renamed the area French Frigate Shoals Atoll.

Once you're past the creative naming, though, an atoll is easy to picture. A basic atoll looks like a loosely strung flower lei floating in a pot of boiling blue water. Coral reefs line the outside edge of the lei. The individual flowers are the atoll's islands, some lying so close together they are nearly connected, and some separated by spaces. A rare few of these spaces are naturally deep enough to allow boats to enter the lagoon at the center. Because the coral reefs and islands absorb the brunt of the force of open-ocean waves, atoll lagoons can be calm havens for boats—if the skippers can safely enter.

"Palmyra is as wonderful as Tern," Alex told me, "but different. It's rain forest. Jungly. Wet."

Tern Island is five hundred miles north of Honolulu, and Palmyra is a thousand miles south, which explains the climate difference.

"And the animals?"

"Awesome. You should think about volunteering."

Now there's an idea, I thought. Craig and I could sail our boat *Honu* there. It would be like our old days of togetherness, sailing, singing, sharing an adventure. I told Craig my idea on the single-sideband radio from Tern Island one evening after he called from the boat's radio. "Susan, I can't sail to *Palmyra*." He said this as if I had suggested we visit the International Space Station for a weekend escape.

"You couldn't take a month off?"

"No."

I had trouble for a moment drawing a breath. This blunt refusal was so un-like Craig. He had taken a month off for many of our trips in the past. I went to my room and sat on my bed watching a white tern parent stuff a silvery blue fish into its chick's upraised mouth. The fish looked ridiculously large for the baby bird, the rear half poking far out of the chick's beak. The youngster, how-ever, recently hatched on my windowsill, gulped and gulped, putting its entire body into the effort of swallowing until, finally, it got the meal down. The chick looked so smug over this accomplishment that I had to smile, and that made the world a bit brighter. Still, I went to Alex for sympathy.

"Craig won't sail to Palmyra with me," I said glumly as we unpacked crates of canned goods that had arrived by ship.

"Well, then," he said, without missing a beat, "I guess you'll have to sail there without him."

4

$\mathscr{A}$FTER nearly four months at Tern Island, I came home to Oahu proud of my bulging new muscles, my "Ocean Watch" columns, and my articles and photos of Tern Island. I felt upbeat on the flight home, sure that life would get good again.

Life got worse. While working at Tern, the joints in my hands began to hurt. Sometimes my fingers ached so much I had trouble holding a fork or pulling open a heavy door. We were banding albatrosses at the time, though, and no way was I going to give up my opportunity to handle those remarkable birds just because my fingers were sore. They'll get back to normal when the work is over, I told myself.

Back home, I was taking Tylenol for the still-painful joints when Craig saw my knuckles. He took my hands in his and turned them doctor-like back and forth. We stared at my fingers for a long moment. "Susan, how long have your hands been like this?"

"I don't know. They don't hurt as much as they did at Tern, but now they're getting lumpy."

"This looks inflammatory," he said. "I'm worried it might be rheumatoid, but it's not something I know much about. You need to see a rheumatologist."

It never occurred to me I might have an injury that wouldn't mend or had developed a debilitating disease. When something hurt in the past, it always healed. "Are you saying rheumatoid *arthritis?*"

"I'm not saying you have it. I just think it's something you should see a specialist about."

I sank into the sofa. "Rheumatoid is the kind Iris had." Iris was a former editor whose hands had turned so claw-like she could barely hold a pencil.

"Rheumatoid arthritis isn't as bad as it used to be," he said. "There are drugs for it now that help a lot."

"What kind of drugs?"

"One treats some kinds of cancers. Apparently, it works well in small doses for rheumatoid arthritis." He paused. "I'll get the name of a rheumatologist for you to see."

Chemotherapy? I stared at my hands for a long time that evening, remembering people who lived in denial about their illnesses. Several of my family members had "weak" livers. (They were alcoholics.) The lesion on a friend's leg that wouldn't heal was a little infection. (It was a melanoma.) A girlfriend's obesity was caused by a sluggish metabolism. (She ate too much.) I had thought it bizarre of these people to avoid such simple and obvious truths. Now here I was pretending my swollen, painful joints would get better because arthritis was an old person's malady, and therefore I couldn't have it.

I saw the specialist. I had arthritis. Thankfully it was not rheumatoid. It was wear-and-tear arthritis brought on by the repetitive motion of banding birds and clearing weeds from nest sites. *Well,* I thought, as I looked at my misshapen fingers, *I wish it hadn't happened, but some people injure themselves sitting at a desk. At least I hurt myself working with the wildlife I love.* I was clearly prone to arthritis and would have gotten it anyway, the doctor said, but the recurring strain had likely accelerated it. My joints were now permanently damaged, making four of my fingers lie crooked, sometimes dislodging in my sleep. While awake, the doctor explained, my subconscious brain kept the fingers in line with muscles. When I slept, however, the muscles relaxed, the damaged surfaces slipped sideways, and I'd wake up in torment. To get relief, I had to pull on the fingertip—quick, don't think—straightening the wayward digit with an agonizing pop.

Try not to injure them further, I was told, and take Tylenol for pain. A hand surgeon said he could fuse the joints straight, but they would be frozen in that position forever. He did not recommend it. Another hand surgeon wrote a prescription to have me fitted for finger braces.

"Will the braces make them grow straight again?" I said as we looked at my fingers. With their bends and knobs, they resembled twigs, reminding me of a witch's clutch.

"No, braces just straighten the joints while you're wearing them," he said.

"Joints heal, don't they?"

"Susan, the cartilage is gone. Cartilage doesn't regenerate."

"I've worked harder and longer in the past. Why this time? What caused this?"

He smiled and said, kindly, "Birthdays."

ASIDE from Craig's genuine concern about my arthritis, we picked up where we left off.

"Just because you take off and have a good time for four months doesn't mean life stopped here," he snapped the day I returned home.

"What does that mean?" I said.

He sighed. If I didn't get it, the sigh implied, he wasn't going to try to explain.

This pissed me off so much, I said, "You wanted me to go live my life and I did. Now you're mad at me for leaving? What's the matter with you?"

And we were off and running, saying things we wished we hadn't. I did not know what he wanted, or what I should do.

Christine finally got her own apartment, two blocks away, but her moving out made little difference in our lives. Occasionally she went to see her Portland boyfriend. When she was gone, Craig rode, ran, and swam alone. When she returned, they rode, ran, and swam together. I guess. Since she and Craig launched most of their expeditions from her place, I rarely saw either of them.

I hated them both, and I hated myself for hating them. Of course, I *didn't* hate Craig. I loved him and wanted him back in my life. And in my better moments, I felt sorry for Christine, who besides being shy had lost a man she trusted and a house she loved. When I told her Craig and I were having serious problems, she said, "I asked my sister what she would do if Mike [the sister's husband] worked out with a woman the way Craig works out with me. She said she'd kill him."

I thought that was charitable of the sister. I wanted to kill them both.

"I'll stop working out with him if you want me to," she told me.

A tempting offer, but the counselor warned me: Craig will go to the mat on this. Not for Christine specifically, but for the right to choose his own friends.

"That won't work, Christine. It can't come from me."

"But I don't even like riding with him anymore. He's too competitive."

"Do what you need to for yourself," I told her. "This thing between Craig and me isn't about you."

"What is it about?"

I shrugged. "I don't know."

My sister, Michele, didn't know either. "I can't talk to Craig anymore," she told me one day. The two had always been close, and he had been discussing our troubles with Michele far more than with me. I didn't mind. She was a friend to us both.

"Why?" I asked, thinking she would say she didn't want to be in the middle anymore. I nearly fell off my chair when she said, "It's too frustrating. He cries all the time."

"He cries all the time?" Since the beginning of this disaster, I'd been bawling my eyes out but never saw Craig shed one tear. "Why?"

"That's what's so frustrating," she said. "You know how he is. He won't say."

To Craig, being a good person meant not pushing his opinions on others or saying things that might cause hurt feelings or disappointment. In his professional life as a doctor and business manager, this was a gift. Rather than bark orders or announce a policy change, Craig made subtle suggestions, letting people believe an idea was their own. He would not embarrass an older doctor whose medical knowledge wasn't up-to-date, for example. Instead, he'd hint that the doctor had worked so hard all his life that he deserved an early retirement. To a nurse who was persistently slow in giving medications, Craig might say, "We should think about ways to make this work more efficiently." These suggestions came with such subtlety, and people were so glad to make their own decisions, that few realized Craig had been planting seeds of change for months. When this worked, it was a beautiful thing to watch. Sometimes, though, his comments were so cryptic that people didn't get it.

"Was that a yes or a no from Craig?" a doctor asked me after an Aloha Medical Mission meeting. (Craig and I were active members of this volunteer organization.)

"A no," I would say, usually with confidence. I knew Craig well enough to pick up key words and interpret his body language.

But I wasn't always right. My sister once planned a surprise birthday party for me, and because she lived in the townhouse next to us, Craig's job was to keep me away from home until six that evening. I needed new trail shoes at the time, and while we were out, I asked him to stop at a sporting goods store. He suggested we "go home to beat the rush-hour traffic," which I misinterpreted as his long-standing hatred of shopping.

"Come on, Craig," I said. "We're right there, and it will only take a few minutes."

At six o'clock, my sister called him to see where we were. "Jesus, Craig," she said when he told her. "I have thirteen people here waiting to jump out and yell 'Surprise' and you let her go *shopping?*"

Craig hadn't convinced me to leave, and since he was incapable of uttering even a tiny lie, he was stuck. "She needs new hiking boots," he said. "We'll be there pretty soon."

My sister could lie for this party, no problem. She made up an urgent story—an angry outburst from her teenage son had scared her—so I would have a good reason to hurry home.

When she told everyone at the party what Craig had done, no one was surprised. "That's our Craig," they laughed. And it was. When it came to life or death, Craig was top dog—the guy you wanted in your life raft (and your E.R.). He might prefer leading by innuendo, but if someone's health or life was in jeopardy, and people weren't following his cues, or were panic-stricken, he'd step up, coolly and with confidence, make eye contact, and say, "Trust me." And people did.

In all the years I knew him, I rarely saw Craig get angry, and I never saw him threaten violence, yet people instinctively knew not to cross him. During our years together, quite a few of his acquaintances and colleagues asked me, "What's Craig really like?" I didn't have a good answer until years ago, while writing a column about bottlenose dolphins.

In the late 1990s, researchers estimated that about 60 percent of harbor porpoises found on a Scottish beach had been pummeled to death by male bottlenose dolphins competing for food and space. As Charles Darwin noted: "Each organic being . . . has to struggle for life and suffer great destruction. The vigorous, the healthy, the happy survive and multiply."

Craig seemed to me the personification of a bottlenose dolphin, born with a smile on his face, joy in his heart, and a tireless drive to compete. Winning dolphins got to pass along their genes; Craig got diplomas, trophies, and a rewarding career. But it was not prizes that motivated Craig, nor was it even winning. He simply liked being at the front of the pack, "in the hunt," as he would say—alert, capable, and ready to rise to whatever challenge presented itself. Emergency medicine suited him well.

Socially, however, Craig could be oblivious, misjudging time, missing awkward silences, dressing dweebishly, dodging conflict. This was often intentional—to the doctor in him, if life or health didn't depend on it, he didn't care and wouldn't try—but sometimes he was clueless, an absent-minded professor in bike shorts.

"Craig, I would have thought you earned enough money to upgrade your rash guard now and then," said a grinning friend as he pointed to a flap of torn fabric in the middle of Craig's surf shirt. Both sleeves of the unevenly faded garment trailed pink threads down Craig's tanned arms, and sunscreen stained the rim of the stretched-out neck.

Craig looked down at the shirt, and said, "I'm not an upgrade kind of guy."

Given this don't-sweat-the-small-stuff life that Craig adhered to, I took his tears with Michele as code for something huge that he couldn't bring himself to say. Needing to know how huge, I asked him if he felt our time together had run its course, and I promised that if his answer was yes I would not freak out. For the first time in months, he looked me in the eye and I saw the old Craig, the one I knew: the honest guy who, when asked a straight question, gave a straight answer. His answer was no. My heart hopped back in my chest. He did not want a separation or a divorce, he said. He wanted to pursue his athletic activities with my blessing, wherever they took him, for however long they lasted, and with friends of his choosing. As for me, he wanted me to do what-ever I wanted.

What I wanted was to have him back at my side as my best friend, and to be considered his best friend in return, but I didn't say that. Craig was telling me he loved me and wanted to remain a couple, *and* he wanted us to follow our separate paths. How did that work?

I grew so weary of the angst, I stopped talking to Craig about anything other than food (did you eat yet?), and the weather (how about that Kona storm?). This seemed fine with him. He didn't know what medications I was taking (on hormones and antidepressants), what I was writing (columns but no books), or how I felt (insane), and he didn't ask. He just continued to train for, and com-pete in, races with Christine and, when the events were taking place on the mainland, with Christine and her boyfriend.

Confused and miserable, I decided to again go live with animals, only this time I wouldn't set a return date. I would immerse myself in the wildlife work I loved, write about it in my columns, and come home when it felt right. If that was never, so be it. Taking Alex's advice, I volunteered to work at Palmyra Atoll, the wildlife refuge a thousand miles south, co-owned by the Nature Con-servancy and U.S. Fish and Wildlife Service. Alex was, at the time, immersed in his research, an investigation into the effects of alien black rats and native crabs on the atoll's plant species, both native and introduced.

Researchers thought that rats originally arrived in Palmyra as stowaways on ships between 1940 and 1945 during the Navy's construction of buildings, runways, roads, and wharves. Without predators, and given abundant crabs, insects, and seeds to eat, the black rat population had grown to an estimated 30,000 on Palmyra's twenty-five islets, a land area less than one square mile. If the rat population continued unchecked, Palmyra Atoll could never be the haven for native species it was intended to be. Alex's research was part of a seven-year analysis regarding a rat eradication plan.

I admired Alex to no end for taking on that study, because eliminating harmful alien species from wildlife refuges is a distasteful part of biology work. In addition, this was the guy who thought so highly of all living creatures that he couldn't bear to kill a cockroach. But the scientist in Alex understood the necessity of ecological balance, and rising above his personal feelings, he took on as his PhD thesis the task of quantifying the damage caused by Palmyra rats.

If I could make it to Palmyra, Alex said, he and I would work together on some projects, separately on others. Palmyra Atoll, a thousand miles south of Oahu, almost to the equator, was famous in Hawai'i for its jungles, sharks, and especially its ten-pound coconut crabs, also called robber crabs for their thieving ways. The Honolulu managers knew me, needed a worker, and agreed. But they had no way to get me there and no place for me to live. A boat solved both problems.

Alex had been right on Tern Island when he said I would have to sail to Palmyra without Craig, because that's exactly what I intended to do.

Our sailboat *Honu* needed an enormous amount of work to make the week-long, open-ocean voyage, and I was not good at such things. Crewing I understood: you do what the captain says, such as pull in a line, drop the mainsail, or haul up the anchor. But when it came to *being* the captain, which included responsibility for all the boat systems (mechanical, electrical, navigational, domestic), I was a preschooler. I didn't even know the names of tools or understand most of their functions.

Nor did I know how to sail very well. The basic premise was simple enough. The wind blew against the sails and pushed the boat forward. But, oh, so many details in that airy push. Because pushing made sailboats want to roll over, they possessed a giant blade below, called a keel, filled with something super-heavy, usually lead.

Experienced sailors don't worry about keeled sailboats capsizing, but I had been worried sick about it the first time Craig took me sailing on his father's twenty-five-foot Erickson. The boat rolled sideways in a gust of wind, and I nearly fell overboard leaning to the high side, believing that only my weight kept us from tipping over and drowning in the freezing green waters of Puget Sound.

It hadn't occurred to Craig, sailing since he could crawl, that I might not understand the physics of sailboats, but when he noticed the terror on my face, he explained: "The boat can't capsize. I promise. There's a big fin, called the keel, that runs under it along its centerline, and it's filled with lead. When the boat leans over on its side, the weight in the keel pulls the boat back to its upright position."

"Can't the wind get strong enough to beat the lead?" I said, when the little Erickson rolled so far that, while clinging to the mast, I got a glimpse of that keel. (For those who know sailing, a gusty wind shift had caused the boat to broach under spinnaker.)

I took comfort forever after in Craig's answer: "No. Because when the wind pushes the boat over on its side, the sails lay down too, and the wind spills out. And there goes your power."

"We can't capsize," he promised.

"Okay. What else do I need to know?" I said.

"Nothing," he said.

He meant it. Craig had been driving, fixing, and building sailboats and powerboats most of his life. In 1981, during our first trip together to his parents' house in the Pacific Northwest, Craig appeared on the dock looking like a young Hemingway with sandaled feet, shaggy beard, faded T-shirt, and a duffle bag slung over his shoulder. Rugged, handsome, and nautical, he strode to his father's waiting boat with the confidence of a man who had met boats on distant shores a hundred times before—and he had.

The instant he stepped onto that sailboat, Craig was in charge. The traditional gender politics of sailing—men were captains, women their crew—was fine with me. Boats, I thought, were for someone else to take me where I wanted to go, which for the past twenty-five years had been to see marine animals.

Alex had great faith in my nautical abilities and was unwavering in his conviction that I could sail to Palmyra. He had little idea, however, what was involved in sailing offshore, or how frightening and miserable sailboats could be in the open ocean. I knew this because in 1986 Craig and I sailed *Honu* from

Connecticut, where we bought it, to Hawai'i, where we lived. We took nine months to make the journey, motoring down the Atlantic coastline, sailing through the Caribbean Sea, transiting the Panama Canal, and proceeding half-way across the Pacific Ocean.

When something broke, Craig repaired it, and when he couldn't repair it, he improvised. When he couldn't improvise, he sailed to a marina and got help, all quietly and often without discussion. When he told the Connecticut-to-Hawai'i story, he always surprised me by going into detail about the things that failed and what he did about them. As chief sandwich maker, I barely realized what was happening.

People marveled over our courage in purchasing two one-way plane tickets to Connecticut, knowing that to get home to Honolulu we would have to sail there. But our plan didn't seem particularly daring to me. Sailing was Craig's area of expertise, and on boats he exuded self-confidence. With him in charge, I told myself since our first voyage together, what could be scary?

Oh, we had our moments. When we sailed from the Bahamas to Puerto Rico, a some seven-hundred-mile stretch of contrary winds, waves, and currents that sailors call—here's a clue—the Thorny Passage, it was one of the most frightening experiences of my life. As we ventured into the open ocean, a gale with winds over thirty miles per hour descended upon us. The boat lurched back and forth in the angry waves, and I threw up. *Honu* forged through the descending dusk as her bow smacked against towering waves in explosions that sent sheets of water into the cockpit and rolled the boat farther to its side than I had thought possible. I threw up some more, so seasick I couldn't even get to the head (bathroom), let alone help Craig, who terrified me by crawling out of the cockpit to shorten the mainsail while clinging to the mast. In that screaming black night, with the boat pitching and pounding, he could have been flicked off the deck like a bug from a leaf. He wasn't sure, he told me, looking grim and exhausted, where we were in relation to Silver Reef, a circle of exposed coral heads that would sink us if we hit. For the first time, I realized the gravity of what we'd taken on. Even with Craig doing everything brilliantly, we could die.

We didn't die, of course (we missed the reef by miles), but that nine-month voyage taught me how indifferent the ocean is to little blobs of life floating on its surface, and how balky and fragile sailboats can be if every adjustment isn't just so.

That trip had been Craig's scheme, and he did all the planning, sailing, improvising, and repairing. He called me his first mate, but that was a gift. For as much as I knew, and for the amount of boat work and sailing I did, I was more like a half-mate.

I explained all this to my friend Alex, but as usual, he thought I should do it anyway. I remembered my doorknob vow. Easy to say, though, with just a latch at stake. If I took half a day to fix a broken seacock, the boat would be sitting on the ocean floor.

Back home, I lay awake at night desperately wanting to go to Palmyra. The wildlife potential there thrilled me. I'd never seen a live coconut crab. In photos, it looked like a cross between a tarantula and a Maine lobster, something you might see in an old Japanese horror flick. And all I knew about the bright red, tangerine-sized hermit crabs were the four words Alex wrote about them in an e-mail. He had sent a picture of dozens of the red crabs in white snail shells crawling over his hiking boots. The caption read: "They love things stinky." I wondered if they destroyed the boots, licked off the sweat, or just inhaled the fumes. And tupas? Looking them up, I found hand-sized crabs with rainbow-colored bodies and white pincers. I could not wait to live among, and write about, the towering tropical trees, colossal crabs, and extensive reefs that had caused Palmyra to be declared a National Wildlife Refuge. Lots of people knew Palmyra was special, but few, including me, knew exactly why. I had to see for myself.

Yet there was no way to get there except by boat, and Craig wouldn't go. I could not picture myself as the captain of *Honu*, but those six words—*you have a boat, don't you?*—haunted me. Why didn't I think the boat was mine, too? In doubt over every aspect of my life, I went to dinner with a friend who brought several people I didn't know. I was busy forcing food down my dry throat (I'd lost so much weight, people had begun asking if I was sick) when one of the men, in midstory, caught my attention.

"So this crewman, a Solomon Islander, says to me, 'Do you know how to skipper a cargo ship?' And I'm thinking, well, I always *wanted* to skipper a cargo ship, and at least I'm sober. So I say, 'Sure,' and he motions for me to step up to the wheel. I don't even know where the throttle is, but the captain is passed-out-drunk . . . so off we went." He paused. "It was pretty crazy at first, but I told the crew that this boat was different from what I was used to. Which was true, because I was used to *no boat at all*." He chuckled. "And that was the start of my career in the merchant marines."

As the others laughed and chatted, I sat staring at the guy, flabbergasted. This is how men learn to manage boats? While we women sit in classes, read how-to books, take notes, and ask experts, men are stepping up to wheels thinking, *Let's see, now, how do you make this thing go?*

That did it. I would sail *Honu* to Palmyra. It would be dangerous for a novice like me, but so what if I drowned? I was going down anyway. And on the plus side, if I pulled it off, I would get what I wanted: a hands-on adventure with new wildlife and, at the same time, some distance from the gridlock that had become my life.

Even the name "Palmyra," with its warrior woman history, spurred me on. Palmyra is now a Syrian city in ruins about 150 miles from Damascus, but it was once a desert oasis captured by the bold and beautiful Queen Zenobia, who rose to power in 266 AD after her husband's assassination. Zenobia seized Palmyra—along with Syria, Egypt, and Arabia—from Rome. This angered the emperor Aurelian so much that he torched the city and killed its people. But not Zenobia. After a grand chase, Aurelian caught the defiant queen and took her back to Rome in golden chains, so the story goes. She managed to come to a good end, but maybe she didn't think so. She married a Roman governor and moved to a villa in Tivoli.

It's easy to be brave when you think you have nothing to lose. I announced to Craig that I would sail our boat to Palmyra. He stared at me for a long moment and said quietly, "It's not as easy as I make it look." This was not arrogance speaking. Craig had been an Olympic-class sailor. One of his former sailing partners, who went on to win a gold medal, told me that Craig was one of the best sailors in the world. He had quit racing to go to medical school. Besides that, he worked his way through college building boats, and was exceptionally good at figuring out how machines function, especially those nautical, and improvising ways to make them work.

"I won't tell you not to do it," Craig said, "but offshore sailing is hard. There's a lot more to it than the sailing." He rubbed his beard. "You know what I remember most about our trip here? What shadows all other memories? Fixing things. Almost every day that year, something broke and I had to fix it."

I fixed that doorknob, didn't I? "I'll learn," I said.

"The boat needs a complete refit."

"I'll make it so," I said. A captain already!

"I don't have time to help you."

"I don't want you to help me. I can do it myself."

"You're not thinking of sailing there alone, are you?" he said.

Dear God, I was already half dead from loneliness. "Tasha wants to go," I said. This was the twenty-five-year-old seabird biologist I had met at Tern Island, and although she hadn't actually committed to the Palmyra trip, her enthusiasm for going was good enough. Alex, my first choice, said he couldn't leave his research at Palmyra. He would be there when I arrived.

Craig sighed deeply like a frustrated parent, an infuriating habit he'd picked up to express disapproval. How I despised these father-daughter characters we were playing lately. I felt like a little girl pestering her dad to use the car. But this voyage was no joyride. Sailing offshore is a life-or-death undertaking, and few people knew that as well as Craig.

Craig was an adventurer to the core, however, and would never, ever discourage me, or anyone, from trying something new or hard. "If you think sailing will make you happy," he said, "you should do it."

Happy? Hardly. I just needed a ride to Palmyra.

5

To some sailors, changing a boat's name is bad luck, but that superstition came from men who thought taking a bath made you sick and women on ships caused storms. Craig and I had changed our boat's name to *Honu*, the Hawaiian word for green sea turtle, because above water she reminded us of those serene seaweed grazers with shell homes wide and heavy yet efficient and seaworthy. Green sea turtles can weigh up to four hundred pounds with shells about four feet long, yet like *Honu*'s hull, they cut through the water as effortlessly as the dolphins that surfed her bow.

When frolicking off the front of the boat, dolphins sometimes turn on their sides, revealing to a watcher on the bow an intelligent-seeming eye. With natural upturns at the corners of the mouth, it looks as if the dolphin is looking up and smiling. During those times, I felt we were all smiling: the dolphins up front, the turtles below, and the people on deck—all with *Honu* cheering us on.

As *Honu*'s original blue paint, cushions, and sail covers wore out, we replaced them in forest green to match her name, even though green sea turtle shells are not green but shades of gold and brown. The green in the name comes from the turtles' green fat, once prized in soup. People have eaten sea turtles and their eggs to such excess that today all seven species of the world's marine turtles are listed as threatened or endangered. In Hawai'i, however, since protection began in 1978, the population has rebounded. Today, only in Hawai'i can you watch sea turtles sleep on beaches and have them swim up to you, unafraid, to gaze placidly into your eyes.

When we found *Honu*, we had been shopping for two years for a boat to live aboard in Hawai'i. Craig wanted one in the forty-foot-or-less size range. His boat had to sail well and be built for offshore sailing. I didn't know what that meant, but building and racing sailboats had once been his career, and I trusted his opinions. All I wanted in a boat was comfort, since it was to be our only home.

The combination proved hard to find. The boats Craig liked were fast and sturdy but bleak below deck, some even lacking a head or galley. "I like it but you won't," he would say as I headed below deck. "It'll be a cave inside." And he was right. The boats that appealed to me had microwave ovens, shower stalls, and lots of windows. Craig vetoed my choices. Those boats were coastal cruisers, not made for the violence of the open ocean.

Finally, it happened. Stepping aboard *Honu*, Craig began examining the exterior and I went below. By the time we met in the companionway, we were both smiling, trying not to act excited in front of the broker.

For those who know boats, *Honu* was designed by English naval architects Holman and Pye for French builder Henri Wauquiez. The boat was designed to go to sea. The solid fiberglass construction (called the lay-up) was built to withstand the force of pounding waves, and the heavy, robust shrouds (wires), including a beefy forestay (the wire supporting the mast from the bow), could easily support the mast and sails in strong, sustained winds. Craig approved of the boat's canoe-shaped hull and fin keel, both shaped for stability, and he liked the sharp bow, broad beam, and full stern. Those features meant that the boat would sail fast for a cruiser, yet have more stability than a race boat. He liked the high center cockpit, which would keep occupants relatively dry, and the boat's length suited him. A thirty-seven-footer could be sailed single-handed, important to him since, with me for crew, he practically sailed alone. He wasn't crazy about having two masts, a main one and the smaller rear mizzenmast. Some sailors think a sailboat is better balanced when you have one sail at the front (the jib), one in the middle (the main), and one at the back (the mizzen). Craig felt that the tiny mizzen sail wasn't worth the trouble of hoisting it, but over the years we grew fond of the little mast. It was great for mounting radar, hauling dinghies to the deck, and hanging laundry. Later we learned that seabirds loved to hitch rides on its flat top.

For me, *Honu*'s cabins were as good as they get. She had a warm teak interior with charming French touches, such as arched doorways and cabinets with invisible latches. To open them you stuck your finger in a teak-rimmed hole and popped the latch from the inside. The master cabin had a double bed, a sofa, and a dressing table complete with a mirror and little compartments for combs, jewelry, and coins.

Since the cockpit was in the middle of the boat instead of the rear, the cabins were divided into three separate rooms, with doors for privacy. The ceilings (called overheads in boats) seemed impossibly high for a boat that length. Craig at six foot one could walk upright comfortably throughout the boat, and in some places the head room rose to eight feet.

Charming as *Honu* was, however, by the time of the refit, nearly twenty years after our purchase, she had issues. For years we had been using the boat as an apartment, a place we stayed in Honolulu when we didn't want to drive to our home on the North Shore of Oahu, up to two hours away in commuter traffic. Having electricity from a shore-side outlet in Waikiki's Ala Wai Small Boat Harbor, we installed central air conditioning, cable TV, a microwave oven—all the conveniences of a condominium in miniature. My chief role in boat maintenance had been interior decorator. I chose rich upholstery for the cushions, made sliding curtains for her rectangular windows, bought nautical-theme quilts and towels, and glued a four-foot-long glass figure of a green- and yellow-striped moray eel to a wall. To the main mast base, which was a stainless steel pole standing from ceiling to floor, I bungeed a koa wood vase and kept it filled with fresh anthuriums, torch ginger, or birds of paradise. The boat's living space looked neat and cheery, a dollhouse for grown-ups.

But playing house was over. *Honu* hadn't been sailed offshore for nearly fifteen years, and that meant an entire refit.

I wasn't sure what the word "refit" meant and looked it up in a book of nautical terminology. It means an overhaul, as in, "I'm taking the boat to the yard for a refit." It also means to carry out the overhaul, as in, "I'm out of my mind to think I can refit this boat." During the refit it would be my job to examine each piece of equipment and declare it sound, repair it, replace it, or decide it unnecessary and throw it out. After that, as the captain, I would own those systems in all ways. They were mine to operate, fix, and maintain.

My first approach to this way-over-my-head project was to go shopping. I drove to Honolulu's West Marine store (West Marine is a U.S. chain of nautical stores known by sailors worldwide) and bought a T-shirt in my size that said "Captain," a nautical chart of Palmyra Atoll, and since there was the possibility that I might never come home, charts of Tahiti and a cruising guide to Australia.

But wherever I ended up, my first stop would be Palmyra. It's a classic atoll: a circle of reef around a ring of about twenty-five islets that surround a peaceful lagoon. (Before the U.S. military dredged and filled parts of the atoll during World War II, Palmyra had about fifty islets.) Still, the place is just a dot in the ocean, its total land area not quite one square mile. Cooper Island, at 242 acres, or about one-third of a square mile, is the largest of Palmyra's islands and the only one inhabited by humans. The atoll lies 956 nautical miles (1,100 land miles) south of Honolulu and 352 nautical miles (405 land miles) north of the equator. (A nautical mile is 1.15 times longer than a land mile.) If all went well, it would take *Honu* about a week to sail there. I tried to adopt Alex's upbeat attitude. Of course I could sail downwind for seven days and seven nights in tropical seas to an atoll paradise. If other people did it, so could I.

Getting down to business (still shopping), I bought repair manuals: *The Boat Owner's Mechanical and Electrical Manual* and *Troubleshooting Marine Diesels*. To those I added books about storm sailing, how machines work in general, and how boats work in particular. Paging through the books felt like paging through my physics textbook the first day of class, thinking I may have made a terrible mistake.

"She needs new sails," Craig said when I announced that today was the official start of the refit. Once he knew I was serious about this trip, he seemed less patronizing and freely offered advice. Sometimes I took this as a plus, sometimes a minus, depending on my frame of mind. On my good days, I thought he was glad to be getting the boat fixed without having to do it himself and that he was proud of me for embarking on such a big, scary venture. On my middle days, I believed the voyage gave us an excuse to avoid talking about anything personal because now we talked almost exclusively about the boat. And on my darkest days, the ones when I could barely drag myself out of bed because there was nothing to live for, I thought he was encouraging me to sail to Palmyra to get rid of me.

This was a middle day. "All new sails?" I said.

"The main and the working jib at least," Craig said. "The mizzen if you want, but that doesn't matter much. And new rigging. She's overdue. Replace the lifelines and jack lines, too."

These are the plastic-covered wires that run around the edge of the deck to keep a person, in theory, from falling off the boat.

"Who does that?"

"Either the yard or the rigger [one who specializes in sailboat rigging] can do it." He paused. "The windlass needs rebuilding—its motor is seized. And you should lay the anchor chain out on the dock. Check for rusted links."

I knew the names and functions of these sailboat parts, but didn't know how they worked, exactly, and certainly didn't know how to fix or replace them. "Hold on," I said, and rose from the kitchen table to get pencil and paper. *Replace jack lines, rebuild windlass, check anchor chain. . . .*

"Pull the masts, of course." He meant take down both masts, the aluminum pillars that hold up the sails. Good grief. That's like taking down two telephone poles, wire supports included. Masts, and the wires that keep them standing, are the hearts of sailboats, like flippers on a sea turtle or wings on an albatross. Without masts to hang sails on, you stay afloat, but you don't go anywhere. Old-fashioned masts are made of wood, but most modern boats, including *Honu*, have aluminum masts. These are lighter and stronger than wood, and tall as street lights. *Honu*'s biggest mast, called the main mast, rises about forty-two feet off the deck (about four stories), and the smaller one, the mizzen, is about thirty feet. A web of wires runs from fasteners on the tops and sides of the masts to the deck, mostly around its perimeter. On *Honu*, one wire with the charming name of baby stay, because it is half the length of the others, attaches from the middle of the mast to the middle of the deck.

The end of each wire connects to the deck with a string of stainless steel hardware, and each part of that string has its own name. Upper shrouds, lower shrouds, forestay, split backstay, spreaders, turnbuckles, toggles, clevis pins, cotter pins, deck plates. You could play an entire game of Scrabble using only words having to do with rigging.

"Check out everything on the rigging," he said.

I had seen *Honu*'s masts taken down in the distant past but had no idea how Craig had arranged this massive job or what his role in it had been. Nor had I ever climbed the masts from the deck, something he did often. "What's up there besides lights?"

"VHF antenna, radar, anemometer, Windex. . . ." These I knew. Windex was the brand name of the sailboat version of a wind vane, and an anemometer was the whirly thing that measures wind speed. I scribbled as Craig talked. "Look at all the through-hulls while you're out of the water. Make sure the seacocks are sound and working."

Seacocks, I wrote on my yellow pad.

"And . . . um . . ." Craig said, hitting the scroll keys on his laptop.

I stared at the word "cock," wondering how the same term had come to mean a rooster, a penis, and a valve on a boat. "What else?" I said.

Craig was eating Raisin Bran, reading the *New York Times* online, listening to NPR's *Morning Edition* on the radio, rubbing the dog's belly with his foot, and instructing me in boat repairs all at the same time. If his cell phone rang, he would answer it and might walk upstairs and pee while talking. I once saw him take a shower while on the phone. This multitasking, as he called it (a new word at the time), could be annoying because it was often hard to get his full attention. But it was also an asset. Besides making him a good E.R. doctor, it meant Craig was usually up for just about anything. Whether he'd worked all night and hadn't slept, or had five other things to do that day, he'd respond to the suggestion of a hike, dinner out, or a movie with, "Sure. What time?"

It takes most people a lifetime to accomplish the things Craig could pack into a year. Those of us who know and love him enjoy his cheery, seize-the-day kind of energy, but some people resent it. Years earlier, a boat neighbor had the same birthday as Craig, and when we discovered this, he said to me, "I'm fifty-one. How old is Craig?"

"Thirty-four."

He stopped smiling. "You're telling me this guy raced sailboats all over the world, lived in New Zealand for a year, became a doctor, and sailed from Connecticut to Hawai'i all before he was thirty-four? I've been working in a fuck-ing *office* all my life." He stomped back to his boat and remained cool to Craig ever after.

"What should I check besides seacocks?" I said.

Type, type, type. Apparently he'd switched from news to e-mail. "One second . . ." he said. More typing. Finally he said, "Um . . . the stuffing box needs repacking." Dozens of times I had stared at Craig's sweat-soaked back as he bent over some dark and dirty place in the boat, such as this so-called stuffing box. I passed tools, found rags, and held flashlights but rarely knew what he was doing. That stuffing box and I were to become intimately ac-quainted, but right now I jotted the words in my column called "Things to Google."

Craig said, "That stuffing box nearly sunk us, remember?"

No.

"Have someone who knows diesel engines go over the motor," he went on.

"What should he be looking at specifically?" I said.

He typed. His phone rang. "One second." He answered, holding the tiny phone to his ear with a cocked shoulder while he continued tapping the keys. A few minutes later he hung up, hit Send on the computer, and said, "Where were we?"

"The engine. Its service. Who should . . . ?" I wrote frantically as Craig spewed out a dozen more boat items to get checked, have fixed, or be replaced. Some I couldn't even spell.

I looked at my list. "This is going to cost a fortune."

"It doesn't matter. It had to be done eventually, and the boat has to be safe as well as functional." He paused and looked up from the computer. "Safety is key, Susan." We looked into each other's eyes, and for a moment there was my old Craig, my Twinoid. "I want you to be safe," he said.

I nodded. The moment passed. "Where should I start?"

He glanced at his watch. "Shit, I'm late," he said, springing from his chair.

"How does a person go about buying new sails?" I said.

He shut down his computer and stood. "I've got to go to work."

My first task was to make an appointment at the boatyard for the haul-out. *Honu*'s home was in Waikiki's Ala Wai Boat Harbor, which hosted a private boatyard called Ala Wai Marine. The business had fallen on hard times (along with the harbor) and reminded me of a wreckage scene from the movie *Waterworld*. Piles of metal, discarded wood, and plastic junk littered every corner of the work area, and the shelves in the store contained more empty spaces than supplies. Outside on the concrete slab, sailboats and powerboats crowded together, their makeshift stands surrounded by do-it-yourself scaffolds. A bedraggled mango tree grew on the grounds, adding the sweet-sour smell of rotting fruit to the odors of toxic paint and drying epoxy.

I had no idea who managed the boatyard business now, but traditionally the men in this line of work considered women bubbleheads, and since I felt like one around boats anyway, it made Ala Wai Marine more intimidating than ever. I took a deep breath, pushed open the door, and walked to the doorway of the manager's glassed-in office where a man sat with his back to me, studying a computer screen full of numbers.

"Excuse me?" I said. "I'd like to haul my sailboat?" Hearing women turn statements into questions always made me wince, yet there I was practically begging for permission to exist.

Swiveling around and rising to shake my hand was the nicest guy I've ever met in a boatyard. He happened to be movie-star good-looking, too, and at five feet four inches or so, as short as many movie stars. "Hi there," he said, smiling warmly. "My name is Henry. Have a seat. Let's have a look at the schedule and see what we can do for you." I relaxed in the presence of this pleasant man, in his early forties. He had an easy manner and gleaming white teeth. "How long?" Henry said, smiling.

"Well, it needs a lot of work, so it will probably take at least two or three weeks."

"Your boat," he said. "How long is your boat?"

"Oh. Thirty-seven feet."

"And it needs what?" he said.

"The masts taken down, bottom paint and . . . um . . . most everything in between."

"Ah, a complete refit," he said. Henry got out a form, searched his cluttered desk for a pen, and began to write. "Number of stays?" he said. He meant how many wires hold up the masts. A stay is the nautical term for such a wire.

"It's a ketch."

Henry looked up. "And how many stays does your ketch have?"

"It's not a standard number?"

"Nope. Each boat is different."

Nuts, I thought. This was like memorizing a few phrases of a foreign language. You start out okay, but quickly the native speaker leaves you in the weeds. "I'll get back to you on that," I said.

"What kind of keel?"

Boat people talk a lot about these fin-like structures that hang from the bottom, along the centerline of their sailboat hulls. I knew what keels were, but I had never paid much attention to *kinds* of keels.

"What are my choices?" I asked Henry.

"Fin, full, or custom."

"Fin. I think."

"You need to be sure. If we don't get the straps in the right place we'll snap your shaft."

Snap my shaft? Oh, dear. The shaft is a pipe connecting the transmission inside the boat to the propeller outside.

My pink T-shirt felt damp all over, and my scalp prickled with moisture. But this was no hot flash. It was the shock, and embarrassment, of realizing how little I knew about our boat.

"I'll find out," I said.

"Bring a schematic [diagram showing the layout] if you have one." Henry leaned back in his chair and folded his arms, all the while smiling. "Do you know how tall your main mast is?"

Dang. "I'll have to get back to you on that, too."

We studied the yard calendar and chose the first date available, nearly a month away. Spring was a busy time in the yard, Henry explained. For me, though, the delay was a four-week reprieve. "How do I go about getting new rigging?"

"I can take care of that for you."

Wow, that was easy. "Thank you, Henry." He shook my hand warmly, and I went back to the boat. An hour later I stood in the doorway of Henry's office. "*Honu* has eighteen stays, a fin keel, and her main mast is forty-two feet tall." I had counted the stays and found the boat's papers in our files for keel type and mast height. It felt good obtaining these facts without asking Craig. He could rattle off *Honu*'s design details in his sleep, but I forgot them over and over. Never again.

"Good," Henry said, writing the numbers on *Honu*'s soon-to-be-enormous bill. "See you in a month."

I left feeling great about the refit. Why, I had a friend in the boatyard.

I did not, however, have a friend in the bathroom mirror. More and more during this time, I would pass a mirror and freeze, stunned. I wasn't myself anymore.

"What does it feel like to be ninety-two?" I once asked Craig's healthy, energetic grandmother.

"I feel the same as I always did," she said. "But when I look in a mirror now, I think, *Who in the world is that old lady?*"

Grandma Mary said she took care of those unnerving moments by getting rid of the mirrors in her house, but I wasn't quite there yet. *The light in here is terrible*, I thought, as I leaned over the bathroom sink to examine my face. But lighting had nothing to do with it. I had to fetch reading glasses to see my face clearly, and after donning the glasses I wished I hadn't. Several coarse white hairs stuck out from my eyebrows, and brown blotches marked my newly sagging cheeks. Also clear was a stubble of whiskers on my chin, which I had started shaving because I was too busy for plucking or waxing. (Electrolysis had seemed like the perfect solution a year earlier, but it hurt too much to continue.) My face had permanently changed in only a few years. When I looked in the mirror now, I thought the same as Grandma Mary: *Who in the world is that old lady?*

Maybe I should start wearing cosmetics again, I thought, but quickly decided not to. Years earlier I'd discarded not only makeup but also the notion that it made me look better. "Why do you do that?" Craig asked me soon after we met. He was standing in the doorway of my bathroom watching me apply mascara. "You look beautiful without it."

He told me this often during our first year together, and I grew to like my natural look. I tossed the makeup, let my legs and underarms go furry, and had my hair cut very short. It was heavenly having a man think I looked my best hairy and plain and sweaty. Happily, I became his cavewoman.

Over the years, I customized this Amazon image. When I spotted a forty-ish hairy-legged woman in a Hilo grocery store, my first thought was *hippie aging poorly*, and I went home and shaved my legs. It wasn't so much the hair I wanted to shed but rather the impression of being a woman who couldn't move on. Later I let the extremely short hair (for a few years, I went only to barbers) grow out and another time tried coloring it red, figuring hair might as well be fun. (It turned out to be more work than fun.) Makeup, however, I never resumed. Pale cheeks and blond lashes became my permanent fashion statement.

I didn't worry about wrinkles or gray hair, either, believing Craig loved me however I looked. He would stick with me through thick and thin, age and infirmity.

In my heart, however, I never believed that I'd actually get old. Moving into my fifties, I was dumbfounded to see signs of aging advancing upon me like an army of ants. Some days I was so surprised by the symptoms it felt like bombs falling. Incoming! Arthritis assault in the wings. Wrinkles taking the rear. Vagina down. Husband MIA. At those moments my heart pounded and panic swept over me. Or maybe it was a hot flash.

A few friends fought this onslaught of age with breast tucks, face-lifts, and take-him-for-everything-he's-worth divorces. Some of their stories could have been screenplays for Lifetime TV. One woman told me she knew something was wrong when her heart-surgeon husband started wearing aloha shirts and sandals to work. In Minnesota. In winter. He later ran off with his scrub nurse. Another friend discovered pornography and proposals to prostitutes on her husband's computer. Male prostitutes.

These women had my sympathy, but no matter how many people told me I was being naïve about Christine, I refused to believe that Craig led a secret life.

While I was away at Tern Island, Honolulu's Ala Wai Boat Harbor, a state facility, had fallen even further into its shameful state of disrepair, with piers broken and dock box doors dangling. When Hawai'i's Department of Land and Natural Resources condemned *Honu*'s longtime slip, we were assigned a temporary mooring on a somewhat isolated row intended for transient boats, a place with a reputation for drug dealing, trespassing, and violence. Because the transient row lacked piers alongside the boats, we had to tie *Honu*'s bow to a floating white ball chained to a concrete block on the harbor floor, and the stern to the dock. The space we were given was too small for *Honu*. Often she tugged her mooring ball underwater, and sometimes only a fender (an air-filled bumper shaped like a sausage) separated the neighbors' hulls from hers. Driving one's vessel in and out of this kind of mooring was challenging for all boaters, and the tight fit made it even more so.

Craig, alone, had backed *Honu* into this mooring, tied her bow to the ball, and her stern to the pier. Before leaving, he had shortened the bow's mooring lines to lengths that kept her rear from bumping and strangers from boarding. As a result, it took all my strength to tug the boat close enough to the dock to leap aboard the aft deck. When I pointed out to Craig that I could barely get aboard my own boat in this mooring, he suggested I make a gangplank, as others in the row had done. It had to be removable, to deter thieves when I wasn't there, yet practical enough for me to use with ease.

After examining other gangplanks in the harbor, off I went to the lumberyard and bought a piece of wood. I screwed little wheels on the dock end of my board so it would move with surges and tides, and experimented with pulley systems to draw the plank up when I left. It took an entire week and several design corrections to make my gangplank workable, and even then it ended up too narrow. I had to learn to "walk the plank" with my arms full of gear, but I was proud of my invention. It might have been a small achievement, and not particularly nautical, but it was my first baby step toward the refit.

This triumph was short-lived. I learned that, to have new sails made, I had to remove the old ones (kept under UV-resistant canvas covers in their places at the bow, center, and back of the boat) to use as patterns. But when I took the sail cover off *Honu*'s mainsail, I saw only a crumpled mass of yellowish fabric. How on earth was I going to manage a total refit when I didn't even know one of a sailboat's most basic procedures, how to remove its sails? I examined the sail and saw that the triangular sail attached to the mast by dozens of plastic sliders threading vertically up a track on one side. A similar slot stretched horizontally across the boom, a perpendicular pole attached about five feet up the mast, which as the boat turned could swing across the cockpit like a giant baseball bat and knock you in the water. I decided that to get the sail off, I would have to haul it up, loosen the nut that stopped the sliders from falling out, and pull the sail from the slots as I eased it down.

Hoisting a sail in a slip on a calm day is no big deal. The sail hangs there like a limp bed sheet. But when it's windy, as it was that day, the breeze can fill the sail and propel the boat. When the boat is tied up, this is a problem. It either crashes into the pier or, in *Honu*'s position, into one of the neighbor boats at her sides.

I wasn't entirely sure I had to haul the sail up the mast to pull its sliders off (I did not, I later learned), but it didn't matter because I couldn't loosen the nut that held them in place. Stumped by this tiniest of tasks, my spirits fell. *I can't even turn a wingnut*, I thought. Below deck, I opened the tool locker for a pair of pliers but instead found a dozen screwdrivers, several rolls of duct tape, spare knobs for the hatches, two kinds of hammers, and a huge, heavy tool with adjustable jaws (Channellock pliers, I later learned) that reminded me of a *Tyrannosaurus rex*. Everything but simple pliers. I pulled out my To Do list and jotted: "Organize tools." Before starting the refit in earnest, I would have to learn the names of tools, create a system for finding them, and make labels for their lockers.

Finally I located a pair of pliers, loosened the nut locking the mainsail to the mast track, and hauled up the sail. Right on schedule, a gust of wind filled the sail and pushed *Honu* into the neighbor's boat three feet away, making an ugly scraping noise. I had forgotten to release the rope that controlled the sail.

Real sailors, by the way, never call ropes "ropes." They call them "lines." Except when the lines pull sails in and out. Then they're "sheets." When they haul up sails, though, they're "halyards." Craig didn't care about nautical jargon—he thought a lot of it was pretentious and needlessly confusing—but having grown up with it as part of his everyday vocabulary, he knew the terms so well that he often used them unconsciously. Still, there was nothing sacred to him about boat lingo, and we had made jokes about ropes having formal names, calling them things like Sir Halyard and Lady Mainsheet. I usually called them the first thing that popped into my mind, such as "that blue rope tangled up over there." Eventually I, too, would learn and use the terms, because they made it easier to be clear.

With the boat slamming into its neighbor, I ran to the cockpit and yanked on the blue rope (okay, the main sheet) attached to the boom. Once the boom swung free, the wind spilled out of the sail, and it lost its power to push. *Honu*'s hull had already struck the neighbor's boat in the only spot not protected by fenders. I leaned over the rail to check the damage. A rusty exposed screw from the neighbor's decrepit rail had carved a deep scratch across the middle of *Honu*'s center Plexiglas window. Nice. My first ten minutes of working on the boat alone ended up disfiguring her.

The owner of the boat, apparently in his usual alcoholic stupor below deck, did not emerge. I didn't know the man's name, since he was rarely sober enough to climb the ladder to his cockpit, and when he did, he couldn't focus past the rail. I felt lucky to have such a neighbor. Most boat owners would be apoplectic if someone rammed their boat that hard. Not this guy. Most days I could have untied his mooring lines and set him adrift and he wouldn't have noticed.

Back at the mast, I eased the main halyard and . . . success. The sail began falling to the deck in a heap.

Removing the other sail, called the jib, at the bow presented a new problem because it attached to a furler that rolled and unrolled the sail around the forestay like a window shade. On *Honu*, and most modern sailboats, the forestay is a big fat wire at the front of the boat with one end fastened to the bow and the other end to the top of the mast. Covering the forestay almost entirely is an aluminum tube—the furler—and rolled around the furler is the jib. For those who have never seen a sailboat up close, imagine a toilet paper holder: the metal rod holding the toilet paper roll is the forestay, the cardboard tube that rotates around the metal rod is the furler, and the toilet paper wrapped around the tube is the jib. Since jibs are big, heavy sails, and it's hard to roll and unroll them around the furler by hand (like you do toilet paper), you instead roll and unroll the jib from the cockpit using ropes and a pulley.

When I unrolled the jib from around the furler, I remembered to release its lines, but the wind still filled it, this time yanking *Honu* away from the dock and turning the jib sheets into whips that lashed my arms, legs, and face as painfully as leather belts.

"I will help you?" a male voice with a heavy German accent called from the dock. I looked up from my flogging to see a pleasant-looking blond man in his midthirties holding up the end of my precious gangplank. "It fell down," he said of the board, "and caught in . . . in this place." He nodded to the edge of the concrete dock. "There it would cause damage to your boat." The man wore nothing but baggy, low-hung shorts. His bare torso was smooth and tan with a slight roundness in the middle, a beer belly in the making, and he'd bound his shoulder-length blond hair into a ponytail doubled back on itself.

At that instant, by chance, the jib halyard came loose and the sail dropped to the deck with a *whomp*. With the sail depowered, the whipping stopped and the rope snakes lay dead on the deck. *Honu* drifted back to her resting position.

The man set the gangplank on the concrete, "You must secure your boat more tightly in the future," he said. I busied myself gathering the sail. "Your lines must be more tight," he said, louder. "I am Fritz. My boat is this one." He pointed to the catamaran a foot from *Honu*'s other side. "I am from Germany."

No kidding, I thought. The guy looked and sounded like a Teutonic knight. I introduced myself and continued folding my sails.

"You are repairing your sails? I have a sewing machine. I will do it for you." When I explained I was replacing, not repairing, Fritz invited me onto his boat, an easy step away, while he fetched the phone number of a sailmaker he knew. Well, why not? My next chore would be getting estimates for new sails. I stepped aboard his boat. His living space was clean and uncluttered, everything neatly stowed. "You are not married?" he said, eyebrows raised. He was staring at my ringless left hand.

Now why did he have to go and ask me that? The subject carried more baggage than the Queen Mary.

6

THE first year Craig and I knew each other, there had been some urgency to our affair, partly because of the three-hour drive that separated our towns and partly because we were both divorced and half believed that true love did not exist. But suddenly, there it was. We found each other, love was easy, life was beautiful, and Craig wanted to get married. It was his idea, and he said it several times that first year. Marry me. Be my wife. I thought this a little premature and somewhat clingy, but he was the most wonderful man I ever met, and we were sick in love. Okay, I said, let's get married.

We moved in together. I enrolled at the University of Colorado and, with Craig's encouragement, registered for a set of rigorous premed courses. I nearly wept when I got a B in general chemistry (respectable in retrospect, but premeds need As) and expected Craig to help me. He was, after all, the one who convinced me I could go to medical school, something I formerly thought impossible because I wasn't smart enough. Now I had proved I wasn't smart enough.

Craig did not agree. Efficient studying was a learned skill, he said, but he couldn't explain how one goes about acquiring it. Nor did he have time to help me. As a medical resident, he worked day and night and was half dead from sleep deprivation.

Before meeting Craig, I dated a ranger at Rocky Mountain National Park and loved his stories about marmots, elk, and other animals living in that spectacular range. I had a notion since that time to study wildlife management and work for the National Park Service. The idea of working with animals appealed to me a lot more than the reality of nursing sick people. I could not picture myself as a doctor, but there I was, competing with thousands of others for a coveted seat in an American medical school.

Stressed like never before, I became the clingy one. I drank too much, smoked pot, and grew fond of cocaine. Sometime during that year, Craig decided he didn't want to get married after all but could not bring himself to tell me. Of course, I knew things weren't going well, but I went on foolishly planning an elopement the groom had no intention of attending. One afternoon I came home with a pile of brochures from a travel agency.

He continued reading the newspaper.

"Don't you want to look at these?" I said.

When he lowered the newspaper, he looked tired and sad. A long silence passed between us. "You don't want to get married, do you?" I said.

"I don't think it's a good idea." He said it so softly I could barely hear him. He rose to get ready for work.

After he left for the hospital, I went running to my hippie girlfriend. "He doesn't want to marry me," I said.

"Good," she said, not looking up from her painting. "Marriage sucks."

"I don't think he loves me anymore."

"Because he doesn't want to get married? Give me a fucking break. We spent half the sixties and most of the seventies trying out new lifestyles because our parents were miserable, and we hated their whole hypocritical-marriage-farce thing, and now you're upset because this guy won't marry you? Please."

"Can I bum a cigarette?" I said.

"I thought you quit."

"I did, but he nagged me to it."

"Believe me," she said, as we lit up. "You're lucky you didn't go through with it."

I decided to believe that and went on a feminist antimarriage rant, to Craig's great relief, while continuing to poison myself with drugs, alcohol, and tobacco, to Craig's great dismay. During the second year of this he issued the inevitable ultimatum: I must stop abusing myself or he was leaving. He said this with so much love and such heart-rending tears, I vowed to end my self-destructive behavior that moment. It was time to snap out of the seventies and pay attention to a person I loved deeply. I quit smoking, threw out the drugs, gave up drinking. I joined Jazzercise and got new friends. I ate healthier food, bought running shoes, and rode my bicycle everywhere I could. Craig supported these changes wholeheartedly, sharing his time and money (precious gifts since both were extremely limited at the time), and encouraging me to enter whatever field I felt was right for me.

When he finished his residency that year, we flew to Hawai'i for an extended windsurfing vacation (Craig wanted to surf and sleep for as long as our student loan lasted) and immediately fell in love with island culture, the subtropical Pacific Ocean, and Hawai'i's jungled mountains. I enrolled at the University of Hawai'i in Manoa, where I discovered the enchanted world of marine biology, for me a thrilling new field. Each day I came home excited about puffer fish, ghost crabs, moray eels, albatrosses, and a hundred other native species. Together, Craig and I got scuba certified and explored the islands above water and below. That I felt relief to be off the medical school track, and delight in learning marine science, told me the latter was right for me.

After living on *Honu* for several years, we bought a condominium on Oahu's North Shore, and several lawyers, including Craig's feminist lawyer mother, advised us to get married, citing insurance issues, joint ownership matters, lawsuits, and taxes. It seemed stupid not to do it. Craig agreed, but reluctantly, disliking being forced by bureaucracy to conform. We decided to do it quietly, just the two of us, making it not exactly a secret, but not a celebration either. And so, after eleven years of living together, Craig and I got married in a private, five-minute ceremony at the Wahiawa courthouse.

It was a colossal mistake.

After that, when people asked me when we were going to get married, I had no good answer. If I said never, they assumed we were having relationship problems and patted my arm in sympathy ("Susan, if you ever need to talk . . ."). If I said I didn't know, they thought Craig was a jerk ("After all these years, he still won't marry you?"). If I said we didn't believe in marriage, people sniffed ("Why, how *enlightened* of you"). And if I whispered we already got married in secret, inevitably came, "Congratulations!" I would leap to explain—legal issues, insurance, the IRS—sounding like I was apologizing for being married and feeling like a fool.

Hawai'i is a small place, and word got around quickly. It astonished me to learn how much Craig disliked being called a husband, and how much he disliked anyone, including me, to refer to me as his wife. I came to dislike the label, too, when I discovered, in this culture of physician-as-shaman, that I had lost my identity. "This is Dr. So-and-So," people would say, "and his wife." The reality of marriage turned out to be worse than I thought. I felt like the family dog.

Before we were married, Craig introduced me as his friend. After we got married, he said, "This is Susan," leaving strangers wondering who this Susan person was to him. When Christine moved in ten years later, and Craig and I started fighting, he stopped introducing me at all, leaving the person I was meeting ill at ease and me furious. "Do I embarrass you?" I said as we argued over what to call each other. "People think we met last week, for God's sake."

"Since when do you care what people think?" he said. "Marriage is a trap. People [apparently meaning him and me] think they aren't going to fall into the husband-wife stereotype and they do it anyway."

One evening, shortly after Christine moved in, Craig and I attended a business dinner with several hospital administrators and their spouses. "How long have you and Craig been dating?" the wife of one of Craig's colleagues asked me. "Twenty-three years," I snapped. She gave a nervous little laugh and turned back to her salad.

We never resolved the husband-wife issue because once the marriage certificate was issued, there was no going back. Getting divorced would have been ludicrous, making us an ex-wife and ex-husband happily living together. Over the years, however, the subject grew toxic, the M-word deadly. The fact that we had gotten married became one of those steer-clear subjects that long-term couples collect over the years. We occasionally celebrated the anniversary of our meeting, but never, ever the anniversary of our marriage.

As Fritz stood waiting for me to tell him whether I was married or not, I realized that "Are you married?" should not be a trick question. *I must get away from this husband I am not married to*, I thought, *and from this marriage in which I am nobody's wife.*

"No," I said. "I'm not married."

Fritz nodded. "I understand," he said, softly. "My girlfriend has left me, too."

I could have killed him, gleefully.

"Where's that phone number for the sailmaker?" I said.

He took too long to find it in that super tidy boat. "Tell me your needs," he said, brushing my hand as he passed me the business card. "I can provide you with anything."

Living in Hawai'i with its large number of immigrants and tourists made me accustomed to hearing skewed phrases from people who spoke English as a second language. But the gleam in those piercing blue eyes and the suggestive smile he shot me as I stepped off his boat and onto mine told me this was not the case. Fritz meant exactly what he said.

AFTER helping sail *Honu* over ten thousand miles and living on her for five years, I was constantly astonished by how little I knew. When we bought *Honu*, Craig tried to teach me how to sail and maintain her, but he was raised living and breathing sailboats in Seattle, while I grew up in rural Wisconsin where sailboats were as alien as Batmobiles. I was so far behind him in terminology, experience, and skill that I didn't understand most of what he told me.

"You're pinching," he would murmur when I was at the wheel. "Fall off a bit." He meant I was steering too close to the direction of the wind. I would turn the boat away. "Head up some, you're reaching now," meaning I had turned too far. Often he would offer such advice while soldering loose wires in the autopilot, or oiling a seized turning block, and not even look up. Craig could determine wind direction and strength by the boat's performance, but by the time I felt it we were stalled or off course.

Craig's favorite subject in college was physics. He enjoyed figuring out how gears and switches and springs and levers worked or didn't work. Not me. I had studied physics, too, but combustion engines and electric circuits didn't zing me. (Well, electricity occasionally did. I once shocked myself and tripped a breaker trying to wire a homemade lamp, and gave up using voltage in my art projects.) During Craig's explanations about fuel injectors, water pumps, or sail dynamics, I'd start out listening attentively, but his accounts were long-winded and too detailed for what I wanted to know. As he talked, a bird might fly into view and my mind would fly with it. *I wonder if that's a red-footed booby or masked booby*, I would think, and Craig's details were lost.

Sailboats were so strange to me, and so second nature to Craig, it was easier to just let him do it. That left me as crew, a worthy enough job but secondary to the decision-making duties of the captain. When we sailed *Honu* from Connecticut to Hawai'i, and later when we sailed in Hawaiian waters, some of the roughest in the world, Craig skippered and I crewed. A good crew member does what the captain says, and since I trusted Craig's judgment, this worked for us.

Unlike couples who were both learning to sail, Craig and I never argued. My main jobs were to drop and retrieve the anchor, haul up the mainsail, and unless I got seasick—usually remedied with drugs we kept aboard—make the meals. It was Craig who trimmed sails, checked rigging, replaced hoses, caulked leaks, fiberglassed holes, tightened fittings, scraped barnacles, set the course, listened, tinkered, coaxed, maintained, and a hundred other things a captain must do on offshore voyages. Still, I enjoyed the teamwork I felt crewing for Craig, and even though the reasons behind his decisions weren't always clear to me, I didn't care. Besides, back then I believed I would never do anything, especially *sail*, without him.

Craig kindly led me to believe that he needed me to sail *Honu*, that I was, if not entirely a cocaptain, at least a capable crew member. Now, standing befuddled on the deck, I understood for the first time how generous—and competent—he had been. I felt like a novice boat owner in desperate need of a captain.

I needed help. Tasha, who had arrived in Honolulu after finishing her albatross work at Tern Island, fit the bill. She had two weeks to spare and offered to pitch in with the refit.

"Where do we start?" she said, looking over the long list of tasks.

"How about at the bow?" I said. "Let's get the windlass off the deck and take it for a diagnosis." Because one of my jobs as crew had been to manage the anchor, I knew the electric windlass better than other systems. I also knew that its motor was not working.

Tasha agreed to tackle the heavy anchor-hauling machine with me, and soon we were shouting to one another through the deck as we pulled bolts and severed electrical wires, she on the deck, me below. We lugged the fifty-pound machine to the dock, and as we were congratulating our sweating and panting selves for getting the thing disconnected and off the boat (down that made-by-me plank, no less), gray grease began oozing onto the concrete. I hurried to the boat for some rags, and when I returned, there was Fritz, crouched over the windlass, shoulder to shoulder with Tasha. "It must have a new gasket," he said to her, pointing out the obvious leak.

"Hello," he said, talking to me while gazing dreamily at Tasha. "I hear this pretty lady is going to sail with you to Palmyra."

"Her name is Tasha," I said, wiping the sweat off my forehead with the sleeve of my T-shirt. Tasha shot me a look of thanks.

"Yes, I know," he said, staring at her breasts. "We've been talking." With a good-looking, twenty-five-year-old woman aboard my boat, Fritz paid no attention to me. A long silence followed. Unsure, Tasha stared at Fritz, uncomfortable with his fawning but not knowing what to say. Finally, he dragged his eyes from her chest and announced, "I will help you with your boat work. I am an expert."

"I already have an agreement with the boatyard," I said.

Disregarding me, Fritz murmured tender instructions about the windlass—my windlass—into Tasha's ear. I had heard older women complain about feeling invisible, but I never got what they meant. That day I got it like a bug gets a windshield.

"Fritz," I said, "I already have someone to fix this."

"The casing is damaged here," he said to Tasha who had to pull back slightly to avoid skin contact. "You see?"

Apparently my voice had become inaudible as well. Whether it was because Fritz was drooling over Tasha and ignoring me, or because he so blatantly disregarded my authority over my own boat, or because I was just a tad low on estrogen, or all three, I snapped. "Leave us," I said. "I mean it. *Go away.*"

He stood slowly, leaning his face to mine, far past my comfort zone. "You have insulted me," he said in a scary whisper, his eyes narrowing.

"Oh, please," I said, stepping back.

His face turned red and his biceps bulged as he clenched and unclenched his fists. My God, he was going to hit me. Tasha's eyes grew wide, and I wondered if I should try dialing 911 on the phone in my shorts or toss it to her so she could call while I got slugged. As my hand slid into the pocket, Fritz apparently thought better of striking a woman in broad daylight on a public pier. He gave me a murderous look, turned, and stomped off down the dock.

This was my first experience with having a young person think I was too old to be worth speaking or listening to, and it shocked me at how much it hurt and how angry I felt. Tasha shrugged, murmured a thank-you, and helped me avoid Fritz for the rest of the day.

She and I became a party of two, calling ourselves Team Estrogen. (She had her own natural supply; mine came in pills.) What we lacked in efficiency and know-how we made up for in fun and enthusiasm. At the end of our week together, Tasha had to leave Hawai'i abruptly to visit her sick mother (close to my age) on the East Coast, and when I heard from her again she choked out bad news. Her mother's ovarian cancer had spread, and she had only six months, a year at most, to live. There was no way Tasha could sail with me to Palmyra.

I e-mailed Alex in Palmyra. He replied that although he would love to crew for me, he couldn't at that point leave his crab/plant/rat research, an investigation, in part, into how nature balanced Palmyra's native land crabs, scavengers that ate everything they came across, with Palmyra's native trees, plants that dropped their seed-laden fruit on the ground. Crabs, he was learning, routinely ate the fleshy parts of fallen fruits, but mostly left the inner, hard-shelled seeds intact to sprout. Palmyra's nonnative rats, however, ate the seeds as well as the fruit, and in doing so, prevented several native tree species from producing seedlings.

Okay, so I'd have to find another crew member. I did not lack volunteers. Even though I never mentioned a need for crew when I wrote in my newspaper column that I planned to sail to Palmyra, an acquaintance I barely knew phoned begging me to take her husband along, because sailing the South Pacific was his lifelong dream. A woman pharmacist I knew in Michigan showed the online column to a male friend who told her to tell me that he would do anything to go—quit his job to cook, scrub decks, anything. Quite an offer, I thought, for a practicing physician. A Toronto college student also read my column about my upcoming plans for the voyage and sweetly pleaded his case, via e-mail, to be a crew member, even sending me his stellar grades in oceanography.

I had no idea so many men dreamed so passionately about sailing the South Pacific. The women I knew did not, nor did I. Long-distance cruising had never been my dream. Oh, it had its moments, but I had sailed enough with Craig to know that offshore sailing was an odd mix of greasy work and boredom punctuated by panic. For me this voyage wasn't a test of myself against the elements, a journey of self-discovery, or thumbing my nose at old age. The driving force was my interest in marine animals and atoll ecology. Palmyra became an obsession. I had not lived, I decided, until I was One with a coconut crab.

I accepted none of the crew offers. Hey, I'd seen the film *Becalmed*. Nicole Kidman's character may have been the dumbest sailor on the planet, but who could forget that homicidal rapist chasing her around the boat? It was a silly movie, and some of my applicants would probably have made excellent crew members, but some could be psychopaths, too. Years earlier, a European sailor told me about a young woman who offered to help him and his wife with night watches on the way to England. Almost immediately the new crew member got horribly seasick, claimed she was dying, and demanded he stop the boat and let her get off. Gladly, he said, but it would be a couple of days before they could reach land. The woman began banging the back of her head against a wall, harder and harder until blood smeared the wood and soaked her hair. The captain told me, "I had to tie her up."

"You tied her up?" I said. "Weren't you afraid she'd have you arrested when you got to England?"

"Yes," he said, "but I thought that was better than arriving with a dead body."

No, I would sail with someone I knew.

Whoever crewed for me, though, also had to apply for, and get accepted as, a Palmyra volunteer by the U.S. Fish and Wildlife Service or the Nature Conservancy. This was something I had barely managed to do, and I knew people. Plus, the four-month time commitment meant either quitting a job or getting a long leave of absence. When I thought about it, I had to admit that finding someone with all those qualities was extremely unlikely. But I didn't worry about it. With so much to do on the refit, and so many changes happening in my life, I just put my head down and kept on working. *Something*, I thought, *will happen.*

I worked on the boat alone, rewiring the bilge pump wrong (it would not work despite repeated tries), ordering new sails, and just learning how things worked. Since I was starting at the basics, the going was slow, and I spent hours on the Internet looking up GPS systems, satellite phones, and flexible fuel tanks.

Fritz got more and more creepy. Occasionally I would catch him peering out of his porthole at me as I worked. Seeing him coming down the long, narrow pier got to be spooky, and after he once bumped my shoulder hard in passing, I began checking the pier from a distance to make sure he was not there. Sometimes I sat in my car waiting for Fritz to leave the dock, fuming over the injustice of being afraid to go to my own boat.

It was bad enough that I had to worry about this transient sailor hurting me, but he was also spoiling my enjoyment of the harbor, and for that I could not forgive him. One of the reasons I liked staying on the boat was that I regarded the marina as my personal saltwater aquarium with constantly changing exhibits. A few regulars there were longtime friends, such as the pair of scribbled filefish that hung out near my pier. The three-foot-long fish have tails nearly as wide and long as their bodies, making them look like fish trailing whisk brooms. Bright blue iridescent scribbles with black spots between them cover the pale blue bodies of these striking fish, and seeing the couple in the morning as I walked the dock made my day. I also loved the busy, boxy trunkfish, a spotted blue-and-white suitcase-with-eyes that nibbled the seaweed at *Honu*'s waterline.

My favorite underwater neighbor was a resident snowflake moray eel that poked its snout in the cracks and crevices of the rocky reef. The attractive black-and-yellow eel, covered in a flurry of white spots, is one of the few morays to start life as female and later change to male. In one way, these fish, as well as some members of the wrasse and parrotfish families, go through the ultimate change of life. Called broadcast spawners because both sexes eject their gametes into the water, the females of some species not only lose their estrogen and egg-production ability but also start manufacturing testosterone. Eventually, the she fish becomes a he fish, growing testes that spew out sperm. Talk about hormone storms. I wondered if fish had hot flashes.

It was also hard to appreciate my favorite fish when I was half sick with dread over having to drive the boat from its buoy at one end of the harbor to the work dock at the other, where a crane would lift the masts off the deck. Later the same day, I would have to maneuver into the haul-out slot called the slipway. An outgoing stream created a current in that part of the harbor, plus the dock jackals would be out—men with pursed lips and folded arms who never seemed to have anything better to do than watch someone screw up. Drivers of both sexes drew critical stares, but women learning to drive *really* got their attention. I knew I should ignore them, but having an audience set off my alarms. If I didn't humiliate myself by crashing into the dock, I worried that I would stop too far from it and not be able to throw my lines ashore. And then what? I didn't know how to handle the boat well enough to have contingency plans.

I told Craig of my fears. "I'll help you," he said.

"Thank you."

"You're welcome," he said, formally.

After he left for work, I wondered if I'd thanked him for things he did for me in the past few years. I couldn't remember, which probably meant I had not, and that made my stomach hurt. I forced myself to stop thinking about this terrible possibility and drove to the boat, where I prepared to loosen my stays. *Such a Scarlet O'Hara phrase*, I thought, smiling. But having no one there to laugh with, my little joke drifted out with the tide, silent and sad.

Kneeling on the deck in the bright Waikiki sun, I set to work removing a bunch of stiff little wires called cotter pins. These look like beefy bobby pins, and since their job is to keep wire end fittings called turnbuckles from turning, they're hard to remove. There's a trick to getting cotter pins out—you straighten their little legs and twist their heads with a pair of pliers—but I didn't know it. My arthritic fingers, already weak and wobbly, pushed and pulled for thirty minutes to remove two pins from one turnbuckle, and it took another ten minutes to figure out how a turnbuckle turns. Ten more minutes passed before the first wire was done. I looked at my watch: nearly an hour to loosen one shroud. With joints already aching, I had seventeen more to go.

By that evening my back ached, my pockets tinkled with mangled cotter pins, and I had eighteen slack stays and shrouds.

Craig was asleep when I fell exhausted into bed, and when I woke the next morning, he had already left for work. I telephoned, an uncommon event these days, to remind him of my scheduled time at the crane dock. He rarely drove or rode in cars anymore, preferring to get around by bicycle. He said he would ride from the hospital to the boat, about twenty miles, in time to make my five o'clock appointment.

I worked on my tool organizing systems. As the day wore on, my nerves wore out, and I began pacing. Craig was late. Nothing new there. Craig lived in a state of eternal optimism about leaving work on time (rare), traffic jams (widespread), flat tires on his bike (routine), or phone calls from the hospital (common). Usually I forgave him his tardiness, because, well, people were sick and needed the doctor. But this time, given the state of our relationship in general, and my exasperation with work on the boat specifically, plus the knowledge that I would be watched and judged, it drove me crazy. Did he forget me? Blow it off? Get in an accident? Please, not today. I needed his help to drive the boat to the crane. I'd had a month to mentally prepare for my appointment with the long-armed machine that would lift *Honu*'s masts from her deck, but I wasn't ready. I would never be ready.

I stepped into the cockpit to start the motor. My hand trembled when I flipped the engine's start switch, the first time by myself. Back on the deck, when I bent down to check the mooring lines on the cleats, I got woozy. I hadn't eaten much that day, and when I stood up, the marina began to spin. *Great start*, I thought as I squatted on the deck to help blood make its way back to my throbbing head. *Susan couldn't bring the boat to the crane dock because she fainted.*

When I lifted my eyes, there was Craig, standing on the dock looking trim and handsome in his body-hugging bike clothes.

"Ready to go?" he said.

"You're here."

"I said I'd come," he said.

"Yes, well." Deep breath. This was not the time to start a fight over how late he was (one hour) or his chronic tardiness. "I loosened all the shrouds," I said, wiggling one with a finger. "I didn't know how loose to make them. I worried the mast would fall down if I went too far."

He looked up. "As long as all the wires are still attached and the boat isn't sailing, the mast will be fine."

"It took me the whole day and half the evening to loosen them all," I said.

"You're learning by doing. It's the best way."

"Maybe, but I'm afraid of learning *to drive* by doing."

"You'll be fine," he said.

Easy for him to say, I thought. *The guy's been driving boats since he was six.*

I wiped the sweat from my eyes. "Okay," I said. "Let's go."

7

$\mathcal{O}$NE of my biggest fears about driving the boat was that I would hit the dock. I hit the dock.

At the moment Craig cast off mooring lines and I shifted into gear, an avalanche of wind came roaring down the mountains.

"Goose it," he said. "In this wind, you need power." I revved the engine, and the boat began to move. Backward. Into the pier. "Stop, stop," Craig shouted. On our boat, pulling the shift lever back put the transmission in forward gear; pushing it forward put it in reverse. This was the opposite of other boats, and the opposite of logic. Craig had been forced to move the shift cable in the engine room years earlier to make room for a generator, figuring that once you knew it went the wrong way, you knew it.

The sound of wood creaking—okay, breaking—came from the back of the boat as it banged into the dock railing.

"You're in REVERSE," Craig shouted so loudly I was sure every person in the harbor heard him. I pulled the shift lever back and gunned it again. This time, the boat moved forward, hitting the mooring ball (a hollow float) with a resounding crack. I turned the wheel to try to get around it.

"Fuck," I heard Craig breathe as he leaned over to inspect the damage.

"Did anything break?" I said.

He looked up. "Go left," he said. I started turning the wheel. "Right now," he said, gesturing wildly. "Left. Left. Turn hard." Yanking a fender off one side, he ran to the other and held it against our boat to cushion the imminent blow against my new neighbor (Fritz had moved down the row) who, mercifully, was not there.

Soon we were free of the accursed space and moving slowly in the channel between two rows of boats. Craig joined me in the cockpit.

"I forgot the shifter went opposite of what you think," I said.

"You've got to remember that, Susan. It's crucial."

"Well, I'll remember it now. And I didn't know you meant turn *hard* left."

"Well, think about turning *around*, because we're about to run aground. It's shallow up ahead and narrow. You're going to have to make a Y-turn."

"Oh, God."

"Calm down," Craig said. "I'm going to teach you how to do it. Okay, throttle down and drive up close to the boats on your port side. That's left," he said.

"I know what port means, Craig," I snapped. But it's true that I sometimes got port and starboard mixed up. Stupid names, I thought (and still do), for left and right.

"Not too close, though," he said, standing near me, ready to grab the wheel. "Now turn all the way to starboard."

I obeyed, and the boat began to swing around its center in a wide arc.

"Okay," Craig said, "now hit reverse and turn the wheel hard over the other way and give it some gas." He watched. "More. Hit it. Hit it."

Heavy sailboats like *Honu* don't respond immediately to direction changes under power, and when they do, especially if you're wishy-washy about it, they sometimes fishtail as the water ripples unevenly past the rudder. This happened, and I panicked, jamming the gearshift back into forward with the accelerator open.

"What are you doing?" Craig said, yanking the fuel lever back.

"We were running into the boat behind us."

"No, we weren't. Do what I tell you, Susan, and everything will. . . ." He looked up. "Shit. We only missed that Beneteau by a few inches." He paused. "What are you thinking?"

"Your directions are confusing, Craig. You tell me to do things without explaining what to expect. Plus, I'm really nervous."

"I can see that." He sighed. "A Y-turn on a boat is the same as a Y-turn in a car. When you don't have room for a U-turn, you back and fill."

"Okay."

"And remember that when making sharp turns, the boat pivots around its center point. That's important. It's not like a car."

"Okay."

We were silent as I drove slowly past rows of boats toward the dock where the crane, looking like an oversized windup toy, waited. When I saw the situation, my heart nearly jumped overboard. A large powerboat was tied up on one side of the crane, a fishing boat on the other.

I would have to parallel park.

Two men from the boatyard walked over to watch, and a boat owner turned off his loud power tool, probably to better hear the swearing. Docking boats in tight spots is a spectator sport, especially in the rare case of a woman driving. I'd watched hundreds of landings over the years, and snickered with Craig over some spectacular failures. Payback time.

Henry's workers ambled over to the edge of the dock supposedly to catch our lines, but I figured they mostly wanted a better view of the crash. These were the classic dock jackals, still and silent, awaiting someone else's disaster. My hands shook, and sweat stung my eyes.

"Don't panic," Craig whispered. "Do exactly what I tell you. Trust me this time."

"Tell me what's going to happen ahead of time. Don't surprise me."

"Okay, here's how it works. . . ." This time he outlined the plan in my ear before we began. I understood and did exactly what he said. The boat slid smoothly to the dock. Craig tossed a line and jumped off with another in hand, and in seconds we had her tied up as if we did this every day. The disappointed men turned back to their work.

My knees felt weak and wobbly. "Congratulations," Craig said. "You did it."

"I did not. You did."

"Your hands were on the wheel," he said.

"That's a nice thing to say, but. . . . Thank you for helping me, Craig," I said.

"Hey, Susan," a voice called out behind us. "How did it go?"

We turned, and there stood Christine. I stared at her. "I thought we would walk to Ala Moana for dinner," I said to Craig. *Like we used to*, I thought. For years, the two of us had often walked from the boat harbor to the shopping center's food court for our evening meal.

"Sorry. Christine and I have a swimming lesson at San Souci," he said.

I couldn't decide if he was being cruel, dumb, or oblivious, or if my surge of emotion at Christine's appearance was justifiable hurt, unreasonable jealousy, or hormonal nutsiness. A, B, or C? All of the above, or none of the above? It didn't matter. Whatever Craig's intentions, Christine's aims, or my conclusions, the bottom line was the same: what I thought was going to be a good evening for Craig and me turned out to be a good evening for Craig and Christine. They would be happy. I would be miserable.

Uncomfortable with the tension, Christine walked her bike down the lane, pretending to look at boats.

"Well, you're all set," Craig said. "The yard men will take over from here. I'll see you later."

"I won't be home tonight," I said. "I'm staying on the boat."

We glared at each other.

"Fine," he said, lifting his bike off the boat with angry jerks.

And off they rode.

A few hours later, a yard worker, Ned, whose cap, clothes, and skin were splotched with paint, arrived to explain that the crane operator would raise Ned by harness to the upper third of each of the two masts, where he would secure a heavy canvas belt around them and their shrouds. After Ned came down, the crane would use the belt to lift the masts from the boat. (*Honu*'s masts are deck-stepped, meaning their bases sit on top of the deck rather than going through it to the keel, which is called keel-stepped. Deck-stepped masts are easier to take down than keel-stepped masts.)

Ned, about thirty years old, adjusted the harness around his legs and groin, and I watched him jump up and down. "Got to take care of the family jewels," he said with an impish smile. Ned lived on his sailboat and claimed to know boats backward and forward. He'd spent the previous ten years in the Coast Guard, where he worked on a Hawai'i-based buoy tender, a ship built specifically to service weather and navigation buoys throughout the region.

"We called that ship the 'Black Pig of Death,'" he said.

"That's an awful name for a boat," I said.

"Hey, people die on those ships, diving on buoys. This is a bad-ass place for any ship when the ocean has its hackles up." He paused. "Which is most of the time."

He was right. Hawai'i's northeast trade winds often blow for weeks, sometimes months, across thousands of miles of open ocean, creating walls of water so tall they can't support their own weight and spill over in thunderous crashes. Hawai'i's island mountains present obstacles for the offshore wind and waves, which squeeze through the gaps in the channels, accelerating the wind and building even steeper waves. It is not unusual to have thirty-knot winds and fifteen-foot seas in Hawai'i's channels. Sailors consider this a full-fledged storm in most places, but in Hawai'i, wind and seas like this are known as "strong trade wind conditions." Experienced sailors say that Hawai'i's channels present some of the roughest sea conditions in the world.

"I moved to Fanning when I first got out of the Coast Guard," Ned said. "I had that tropical island dream thing going."

Fanning, an atoll belonging to the island nation of Kiribati (pronounced *KEER-ib-bas*), was only a hundred or so miles from Palmyra. I perked up. "How was life on Fanning?" I said.

"Great, for a while. Then I got a local girl pregnant." He grinned sheepishly. "Oops."

Oops? How could this man have unprotected sex with an island woman he barely knew? Ned told me that his Fanning lover had the "usual reason" for getting pregnant, meaning marrying an American to gain U.S. citizenship.

There were no accidental—or intentional—children in my life. Being the oldest of four, the youngest born when I was seventeen, had a huge advantage. I learned early on how hard it is to raise kids, especially as a single parent, which had happened to my mother. As a result, at thirty, when I was still single, I gave myself the gift of a tubal ligation. When I met Craig two years later, he loved the fact I had made that decision alone, both because he liked my take-charge attitude and because, as the oldest of five, he too had decided as a teenager that he didn't want children.

"What happened?" I asked Ned.

"I have a son there now. Don't worry," he added quickly, "I send them money."

As if that's all there was to being a parent. I could practically feel my tied tubes smiling.

NED's legs dangled from his harness like a baby in a bouncy chair as the crane raised him about three stories to tie the lifting belts around the upper portions of *Honu*'s two masts. Back on deck, Ned helped me detach the forestay, unwieldy with the heavy furler threaded over it, and the seventeen other slack stays, which after turning them with my arthritic joints for ten hours the previous day felt like old pals. The stays dangled from the mast tops like the tentacles of a dead octopus. With a line, we secured the mass of suspended wires loosely to their respective masts and signaled to the crane driver that all was ready.

The crane picked up the looming masts, thirty and forty feet tall, as if they were balsa sticks on a model boat and laid them on sawhorses placed strategically in the boatyard for this purpose. In seconds, my mast-pulling chores were over.

The marina's work docks were not a great place for a lone woman to spend the night. When one of the nicer yard workers, who lived on his boat there, heard that I intended to sleep on *Honu* at the crane dock, he said, "Call out real loud if you have any trouble."

Wonderful. For the first time ever, I locked myself in the boat.

Craig arrived the next morning, as promised, to help me drive the boat into the slipway, a three-sided concrete docking stall made for boats to be hauled out of the water. Things seemed perfectly normal between us, as if Christine, counseling, and months of hurt feelings had never entered our lives.

"Good morning. How did the mast pulling go?" he said, examining the horizontal masts like sick patients.

Both the blessing and the curse of living with Craig was his aptitude for storing unpleasant experiences in the back files of his brain and slamming the drawer shut. This submersion of the negative made his job in emergency medicine bearable, and daily life with him pleasant and fun for the most part. But it also enabled him—and me—to shove dirt in those files and never clean it up.

His sunny greeting did not make me feel better. On days like that, I didn't know which of my problems with Craig were real and which ones I imagined. Hadn't he left angry the evening before? Hadn't I been fighting tears half the night? Were we becoming our parents, pretending everything was fine when everything was not? With no answer to these hard questions, I filed them and slammed the drawer shut. Again.

There's nothing like driving a sailboat into a tight space, with stern-faced men standing around watching, to get your mind off yourself. Craig spoke softly, directing me to the far side of the channel so I'd have time and space to adjust my aim at the opening. I was less nervous driving the boat this time, losing only two quarts of sweat instead of a gallon. He told me to speed up. My sweat glands apparently thought he meant them. "Faster," he said. "Or you're going to lose steerage."

While learning to drive a sailboat, a person's inclination is to drive excruciatingly slow, say, one mile per hour or less, to make an accidental hit more of a tap than a crash. But snail speed isn't the safest way to go, because a certain amount of water must pass the rudder (the vertical underwater blade at the rear) to turn the boat. It is possible, and common among novices, to go so slowly that the boat won't go where you steer it. Wind and currents further complicate matters.

I knew all this. It was one of the reasons I didn't know how to drive the boat. To do it right, you often had to gun the engine, and of course, when going fast, mistakes could become disasters. The few times I tried marina driving in the past, the ordeal felt like bumper cars from hell, and I quickly gave the wheel back to Craig.

But not this time. I sped up a tiny bit, but not enough, and the boat entered the slipway at an angle. The waiting workers saw this coming, caught Craig's expertly tossed lines (an art in itself), and were able to pull *Honu* straight.

"I came in crooked," I said, sweat dripping off my nose, into my ears, down my sides, and between my breasts.

"There's current here. You'll learn how to adjust for that."

I wished that boats, like cars, would just go where you pointed them.

Craig left for work, and soon a man drove a leggy steel frame the size of a small house to the slipway, where it straddled *Honu*. This machine, called a Travelift, looks and sounds like a roaring spider robot as it lifts boats from the water and wheels them to a work or storage site. Men passed heavy straps under *Honu*'s hull and fastened the ends to the Travelift's overhead beams. Thunderous motors pulled the straps taut, the boat rose from the water with a whalelike *whoosh*, and off they all roared into the boatyard, *Honu* swaying beneath like the prey of a giant Tinkertoy gone bad. The workers lowered the boat's lead-filled keel onto heavy wood blocks, propped the hull upright with padded stands, and left. This operation came off efficiently and skillfully, but that's not always the case. Travelift stories about straps breaking, braces failing, and boats crashing are boatyard legends.

Honu sat high and dry, looking oddly naked without her masts and rigging, and I stood next to her wondering what happened next. I went to see my boatyard ally, Henry, but he was distant this time, his manner abrupt, bordering on rude. He avoided eye contact throughout our meeting and left me sitting in his office for long minutes while he answered the phone or rang up a purchase. "Is everything okay?" I asked.

"Fine. We'll get the work started on your boat tomorrow."

Out in the yard, I climbed the metal ladder that workers had leaned against *Honu*'s side and stood on her bare deck, staring. The boat needed new standing rigging, meaning the wires that run from masts to deck, thereby keeping the masts standing. She also needed new running rigging, meaning the ropes—halyards, sheets, and lines—that "run" along the deck and control the sails. Henry and the rigger would take care of these heavy-duty tasks, but that was just the beginning. On today's list alone, I had to insulate the refrigerator, get an overfill protection valve installed on the propane tank, order new rubber water tanks (called bladders), and get the engine oil and fuel filters changed.

I also needed to research and buy a GPS, or Global Positioning System, the magical navigation device that tells sailors where they are at all times. This system revolutionized modern sailing because it eliminated the need to take sites with a sextant and make best-guess calculations, called dead reckoning, to figure out where you were. The GPS I planned to buy was similar to those in cars today but made for boats. A little TV screen at the wheel would show a figure of a boat representing *Honu* moving along on nautical maps, telling me my exact position. But I had been warned, as I went about investigating these machines, that just because I knew my exact longitude and latitude didn't mean the charts had been drawn correctly (some had not been updated since the 1800s), nor did it mean I was safe. Horror stories abound about container ships colliding with cruisers in shipping lanes and novices driving willy-nilly through commercial harbors. In such collisions, sailboats never win.

Honu also needed a new VHF radio for ship-to-ship communications, and a new inflatable dinghy for going ashore. Plus all those pumps to check or replace: the raw water intake pump, three bilge pumps, a freshwater pump, the air conditioning pump. . . . On and on the chores went, and as the day wore on, I wore out. And this was just organizing the list.

I went home and began searching the Internet for reviews of satellite phones, computerized charts, shortwave radios, and all the other electronic equipment I needed to update or install. Craig arrived from the E.R. while I was doing this. "How was your shift?" I said.

"Fine. How was the haul-out?"

"Fine."

He opened the newspaper. I stayed in my office and worked until I heard him go to bed. We had become our unpaired parents.

My days in the boatyard wore on. When I saw Craig, which was even rarer now since neither of us stayed home much, he patiently answered my boat questions. Mostly, though, he kept out of the boat work. I made some progress on my list, but little happened on Henry's end, and besides, he was never around. No work occurred on *Honu* the next day or the next, and I sat high in the cockpit watching the activity around me.

The boatyard was a wonderful place and an awful place. It was wonderful in that I saw all kinds of boats out of the water, their colorful bellies exposed like beached whales. When *Honu* came out, the yard workers power washed the marine growth off her bottom, unevenly blasting off layers of old paint and leaving her hull looking like a modern art painting. This struck me as so beautiful I took pictures.

Besides allowing people to see boats out of their element, boatyards also have an air of adventure about them, especially in Hawai'i, where sailors are coming from some faraway place, going to one, or dreaming about it. Oahu's boatyards are bustling places with continuous talk (some would call it bullshit) of murderous pirates, South Pacific paradises, and spectacular boat failures.

Work areas like this are also full of toxic substances and ear-splitting noise. Fiberglassing, and the grinding of fiberglass, are hellish jobs. Even watching someone else do it is hellish. Glass particles fill the air, settle on your skin, and in my case, created rashes that itched like mad but hurt when I touched them. One day I apparently inhaled some fiberglass particles and wheezed all night long. And the noise of the grinders' big motors, combined with the sound of their rough disks pulverizing hardened plastic, was enough to drive a person to drugs. The grease and oil that covered everyone in the boatyard made the flaking paint and flying fiberglass stick to hair, arms, and clothing. Oblivious workers picked up all that nasty stuff on the bottom of their boots and tracked it onto the deck and inside the cabins of my lovely boat.

Yet at the beginning of my third week in the yard, still almost nothing had been done. Henry had estimated the refit to take six weeks, but the halfway mark was coming up and they had barely started. When I explained this to Craig, he told me to assert myself. If he was managing *Honu*'s refit, he would hunt down Henry, have a man-to-man (surely a nose-to-nose) talk, and the work would get done. But the thought of demanding anything in that boatyard, of standing up to those judgmental men, especially the now-aloof Henry, made me queasy.

In the middle of that third week, I arrived at the yard and found that Ned had attached the new forestay to the mast but left the rest of the newly arrived rigging in its box. Being the workhorse of the standing rigging because it holds up the mast at the bow and supports the jib, the forestay needed a professional hand. When I questioned him about his experience with such things, Ned assured me that he was an expert rigger.

I climbed the ladder to the cockpit, found *Honu* deserted, and sat down on her dusty teak bench amid a whir of power tools on the boats around me. When I started the refit, I remembered that I had been worried about the workmen being rude. I worried people would talk me into buying things *Honu* didn't need. I worried I was too ignorant about boats to make sound decisions. I worried about where I would go to the bathroom, since the boatyard's one reeking, urine-splashed toilet didn't have a seat. Never once, however, did I worry that no one would show up to work on my boat.

"Hello? Permission to come aboard," a voice said from below.

I leaned over the side and saw Pierre, a harbor resident and boat worker I had known in passing for years. He stood shading his eyes with one hand and squinting into the morning sun.

"Come aboard," I said, and watched him climb the tall, trembling ladder. The top of his head bore short strands of gray hair, but the hair on the sides of his head he had dyed brown and grown long enough to sweep back over his ears. The wind was currently blowing this long hair backward, making it look like wispy wings.

Pierre stepped onto the deck and sat on the cockpit bench, strewn with tools and broken boat parts. His deeply tanned arms, neck, and face had the uneven color and leathery texture common to most longtime sailors. Pierre's skin and hair made him look older than his sixty-two years, but a trim, muscular body gave him a surprisingly youthful bearing. When my friend Abby met him, she loved his aristocratic face and aquiline nose, which hooked nearly to his upper lip. "You never mentioned that he's so . . . so *French*." The image of these two together made me smile, since Abby was six feet tall and curvaceous; Pierre was five foot two and weighed 125 pounds. I learned these numbers early in our acquaintance because he told them to me, stating often, "I'm just a little guy."

I wondered about the size of another of his body parts, too, because around his neck on a heavy gold chain hung a solid gold image of Tangaroa, the Cook Islands' god of the sea. In all depictions of this god, including Pierre's necklace, Tangaroa's penis hangs to his ankles.

"I've seen your boat sitting here with no one working on it," he said. He had emigrated from France to the United States forty years earlier yet still carried an unmistakable French accent.

Pierre's sweaty odor made it hard to sit next to him, and I pretended to tidy the cockpit as an excuse to settle on his upwind side. I explained my problem, and Pierre explained the boatyard's problem. "The place is bankrupt. I don't know this guy, Henry. He's only been here six months. I heard he's in Florida interviewing for jobs."

Florida? Some friend-in-the-boatyard Henry turned out to be. He was like one of those construction workers who tear up your kitchen for a remodeling job and never return. The old hormones began to sizzle, traveling down my nerves like a lighted fuse. The guy was lucky to be in Florida. I felt like beating him bloody.

"I'm trying to retire," Pierre said, "but I could help you out."

Pierre, who lived on his boat in the harbor, had for years been a free-lance boat worker. He knew *Honu*, a boat he had worked on in the past, because we hired him for the occasional boat repairs over the years. Everyone in the harbor knew Pierre. He had been a customer of the local outfitting stores for years and was exceptionally clever at making custom parts. We settled on an hourly wage, and the two of us made a list of items for me to buy and him to install: five Marelon sea cocks (plastic on-off valves), two new solar panels, a wind generator, a high-output alternator, navigation lights, a wind speed/point device, two six-volt golf cart batteries (called the house batteries) for lights and appliances, a twelve-volt battery for the starter. . . . The new list, two pages long, I added to my others.

A week passed with Pierre showing up each morning at nine and working until five in the afternoon. (Besides Henry, Ned had also disappeared, as had several other workers at the yard, apparently all laid off.) The boat began to change, and my spirits rose. But as we worked, the lists grew longer rather than shorter. In tearing the boat apart, we found additional parts and components that needed work. Some fixes uncovered problems that called for new systems entirely. The master circuit board needed new breakers. The fans worked only part of the time. All zippers on the dodger (windshield) were shot, and the bimini (cockpit awning) crackled with sun damage.

Almost every entry required hours of calling, driving, and Googling to get the right size and material. The listed items sprouted subcategories for gaskets, elbows, hoses, nuts, and bolts to make whatever system fit or work or stop leaking, and those subcategories gave birth to sub-subcategories. I had to buy grease guns and engine oil; fiberglass matt and epoxy resin; silicon spray and plumber's tape; gas cans, faucets, hoses, and couplings. And, in two separate, sobering moments, a new life raft and a man-overboard sling.

On one of my excursions, I bought a hundred-dollar Leatherman tool, a transformer toy for grown-ups that with a twist here or a spin there becomes a screwdriver, pliers, awl, or saw. I chose the biggest, beefiest one I could find. Years earlier I had bought a tiny Leatherman that I kept on the boat for crewing with Craig. The little knife had seemed just right for me at the time, but now it seemed insubstantial and girly. My new Leatherman had muscle, being so heavy in my pocket that it caused my shorts to droop on that side. I loved that manly knife. I didn't use half the tools in it, but carrying it around made me feel capable. It also suited my fluctuating hormones. *Call me captain*, I thought, hitching up my pants like a cowboy, *or I'll kill you.*

Of course, most of the time it was Pierre doing the work while I fetched materials that were sometimes so foreign to me that I didn't know what the clerk would hand me when I read him Pierre's request. I came to know Honolulu's industrial districts well. Diamond Head Sprinkler had the best variety of plastic plumbing parts; Pacific Ocean Producers sold UV-resistant wire ties; Marine Safety Equipment would service my emergency distress beacon, known as an EPIRB. Soon I could predict when I was about to drive around in congested Honolulu traffic. I would be kneeling next to Pierre in the filthy, sweltering boat, handing him things as I watched him drill, saw, crimp, or solder. Usually he was cheerful, humming a made-up tune as he worked. Suddenly the singing would stop. He would utter a curse, usually in English, but sometimes half-French, such as "fucking *merde*," and stare motionless at the recalcitrant part. "What's wrong?" I would say, before I learned it was better not to ask.

Often Pierre would be deep in thought, devising some solution, and wouldn't answer. If I pressed him, which I felt was my prerogative, I often regretted it. "I hate being bothered while I work," he would snap. Once he dumped a plastic bucket of my tools upside down on the floor, throwing wrenches here and there as he searched for the correct size. "Who keeps tools in a fucking *bucket?*" he said. I replaced the bucket with a toolbox.

Pierre was an excellent mechanic, electrician, and boat worker in general, but his tutoring skills were nil. "I'm not a teacher," he told me over and over, and indeed he was not. When he did offer an explanation, because he recognized that I must know some things to operate the boat, he often started in the middle. "If you need to bleed the fuel line, be sure to open the nut on the fuel pump," he once said.

"Where is it?" I asked.

"On the pump," he said, and bent back to work.

I let dozens of those kinds of things go, thinking that since I had new parts, the latest equipment, and a good mechanic, little could go wrong.

"We don't need these aluminum pieces," Pierre said one day as we attached the new shrouds (support wires) to the masts. "Take them back to the rigger for a refund."

"Henry has to return them."

He stopped working. "What does Henry have to do with it?"

"When I made the haul-out date, Henry told me he'd take care of the rigging."

"He ripped you off. He probably charged you a fortune for a phone call," he said. "Why didn't you ask someone about that before you made the deal?"

Henry had tricked me, disappeared before the job even got started, and Pierre was angry with *me*.

"I'm doing the best I can, Pierre. This is all new to me. At least I'm trying."

He stared at me for a moment and then went back to work. The next day, the four aluminum pieces were not where I left them. "I took them back and got you your refund," Pierre said when I asked. As he turned back to his work, he added, "They were a hundred dollars apiece."

I stood blinking in the flying fiberglass dust. What was I doing in this world of boats, cranes, tools, and engines where, next to everyone else, I was stupid and gullible? *Four hundred dollars?* Sweet Jesus. "Thank you," I said to his back.

"You're welcome."

Two, three, four weeks flew by, during which Pierre and I developed a love-hate relationship. No matter how hard I studied, concentrated, listened, and watched, I remained clumsy with tools and slow at grasping the problem or even the point. Often this was because I got thrust into the middle of a system without knowing its basics. For example, a broken oil pressure switch had nothing to do with oil pressure but rather, I learned from Pierre sniping at me, turned the alternator on and off. This refit felt like taking a calculus course without knowing algebra.

Working on the boat may have frustrated me, but my ignorance drove Pierre crazy. Besides that, we had almost nothing in common. Pierre's world consisted of bars, strippers, and schemes to get things free or cheap. My world contained Diet Coke, books, and wildlife.

Even so, Pierre sometimes surprised me with a conciliatory comment or a thoughtful present, such as a set of socket wrenches. You use socket wrenches for loosening and tightening nuts and bolts, and when he discovered that I didn't have any small enough to fit the smallest bolts, he presented me with the set as a gift.

"Thank you, Pierre," I said, even though I didn't know a socket set from a sock puppet at the time. "That was nice of you."

"They were cheap," he said. "And you're going to need them."

I am? I thought. *What for?*

Craig had always kept two big, beefy socket sets on the boat, which I used as needed, but I loved having my own set and made a point of keeping my smaller sockets clean and organized in their blue plastic box. Lined up in their little cradles, the socket heads reminded me of a mechanic's version of Russian nesting dolls.

In spite of Henry's and half the yard workers' absence, we finally "splashed" (got the boat back into the water). Pierre and I continued our work at the boat-yard's work dock, a place where trash floated in corners and drunks slept it off on the piers. When the time came to drive the boat into the work slip, I did a terrible job, my first time without Craig giving directions. The rear of the boat had a mind of its own regardless of where I pointed the bow. Pierre's instructional technique of yelling at me to slow down, back up, turn left, turn right, all while gesturing wildly, made me ten times more nervous than when I started. I got the boat close enough to the dock for Pierre to make a leap so wild he nearly fell in the water off the opposite side.

"I don't know how to drive the boat very well yet," I said, after we tied up.

"I noticed," he said.

Weeks ran into months, with Pierre working every weekday, me working seven days a week. I found parts and service, kept track of lists, and bought and organized tools. When Pierre and I were on the boat at the same time, I watched over his shoulder as close as I dared. We never had lunch together because Pierre didn't eat breakfast or lunch.

"People make too much fuss about food," he said, countering the French stereotype about fine cuisine.

Eventually, Pierre decided we didn't need the work dock anymore and said that the next day *Honu* could go back to her own slip.

Since it was obvious that the only way I would learn to handle the boat was to do it, I could not ask Pierre to maneuver *Honu* back to the slip. This time, though, I would have to *back* her in. I felt shaky and sick at the thought of it.

"How can I ever skipper this boat when I'm afraid of it?" I said to Craig that evening. Since I was now as busy as he was, we had been mostly ships in the night, exchanging only the bare necessities of daily life. We didn't know much about what the other was doing, but at least we stopped fighting, and that felt like progress.

He looked at me for a long moment. "Tomorrow," he said, "I'm going to give you a driving lesson."

And, oh, what a lesson it was. To say it forever changed my understanding—and comfort level—of boat driving is not to overstate the matter.

Instead of murmuring instructions I didn't understand, Craig took the time beforehand to explain some fundamentals, such as making Y-turns in tight spaces. This is similar to the back-and-forth Y-turn of a car but with one crucial difference: because a spinning propeller pushes water (called the "wash") against the rudder, which steers the boat, a sailboat in reverse insists on turning its stern either left or right, depending on which way its propeller turns. There is no standard direction in sailboat transmissions, so each skipper has to learn which way the propeller turns, how much influence it has on the rudder (here size matters), and how long in both time and distance it takes to overcome the wash.

Craig taught me that, when backing up, *Honu*'s propeller pushes her stern to the left (sailors say "she backs to port"). Knowing that, you take advantage of the directional spin and make it work for you. To make my Y-turn, I drove *Honu* as far to the left of the channel as I could and turned the wheel all the way to the right. It was quickly apparent that there wasn't enough space for *Honu* to make the complete turn, and that if I kept going like this, I would run into a moored boat. Under Craig's direction, I shifted into reverse, turned the wheel hard the other way, and waited for the boat to stop its forward movement and begin backing up. This takes a few seconds, but it can feel like an eternity as you watch your bow approach a crash. It was at this moment during my previous driving episode that I panicked. Now, trusting the laws of inertia and Craig's knowledge of the boat, I waited with breath held and knuckles white. And sure enough, *Honu* began to back up and straighten out. This gave me the room I needed to make the turn, and shifting back into forward, I easily finished the Y-turn.

I would have shouted for joy, except Craig advised me to repeat my elegant Y-turns until I had the feel of *Honu*'s forward momentum and backward propeller thrust. I did it over and over, and when I got comfortable with that, he showed me how to make double Y-turns, backing and filling in even narrower spaces. By the end of the lesson, I could turn that boat around in a space not much wider than the boat itself.

"I love this," I said, beaming. "Thank you."

"You did it yourself. You're a boat driver now," Craig said. This compliment felt so good that I nearly confused Craig the generous-with-praise teacher with Craig the loving-partner-I-missed-so-much. His phrases contained a genuine sweetness to them, but this was his nature. He would have said the exact same words, in the exact same tone, to Michele (my sister), Christine, or a guest on the boat. How I ached for some personal words from him.

Before my lesson was over, he showed me how long it took (far longer than I imagined) for the nearly twenty-thousand-pound vessel to slow down. I learned this by shifting into neutral with the boat going at different speeds. After that, he suggested I drive the boat backward around the harbor.

"Backward?" I said, thinking he was joking. He was not.

"If you can comfortably drive the boat backward," he said, "you can drive it forward anywhere." And so, much to the puzzlement and amazement of my fellow boat owners, I backed *Honu* up and down the rows of the Ala Wai Boat Harbor. Because driving in reverse seems so hard, few people do it. But I learned that day that this maneuver was not hard, just different. And Craig was right. After all that backing, going forward seemed easy. At the end of my lesson, I backed *Honu* into its slip as if I had done it a hundred times.

"Nice landing," Craig said. "Congratulations."

"Thank you," I said as we fastened the mooring lines. "You helped me so much."

"You did the driving, though," Craig said.

And this time I had.

MONTHS flew by with Pierre not only fixing or replacing mechanical parts and electrical equipment but also installing nonessential items—girl stuff, he would say good-naturedly—such as the clothes hooks and towel racks I silently slipped into his pile of parts. I also asked him to switch the gearshift, making

Forward push forward and Reverse reverse. I didn't ask Craig what he thought about that, and when I told him I had done it, he frowned in disapproval. I didn't care. The boat was mine, too. The last thing I needed, and Pierre agreed, was a crucial piece of equipment that worked the opposite of logic.

Pierre's arrival on the job created the whirlwind of activity I had expected from the start. I went home each evening filthy and exhausted. Slowly but surely, the refits—both *Honu*'s and my own—were under way.

8

I thought it would never happen, but finally *Honu* was put together enough for practice sailing. For my first venture into the ocean as captain, I chose for my crew two young women, Cari and Tracy, who both wanted to learn to sail. I had lived with Cari, a biologist, on Tern Island and had always looked forward to helping her band seabirds. She loved the species assigned to her, red-footed boobies, and carried on one-way conversations with them as she worked. "I'm sorry I scared you, sweetie," she'd say to a startled chick that had just pecked her arm to bleeding. "Look. I'm going to give you this pretty bracelet. You like it? I do."

Cari, waving with excitement about our upcoming adventure, hurried down the pier to hug me. Tracy, though, walked down the long dock with the grace of an athlete, a day pack slung over one shoulder. Tracy had a Lauren Bacall voice so loaded with sexual tension that when she spoke men stopped what they were doing to listen—even gay men. "That *voice*," my friend Scott said. "At first I thought she was putting it on, but it's real."

Cari and Tracy didn't know each other, but as marine biologists, both had spent most of their life on, in, or near the ocean. I liked these self-assured women and loved the fact that neither knew how to sail. I would have reliable helpers but still be the best sailor on the boat.

Standing on the pier that day, though, I didn't feel so cocky. The wind blew too hard, the boat looked too big, and I had never driven without Craig or Pierre directing. When things went wrong, as they so often did, those men had a lifetime of experience to help them figure it out, and they sometimes did so before I even knew there was a problem. "Hear that?" Craig would say to me. And before I knew what was happening, he had shut down the engine and was replacing a clogged fuel filter.

Dutifully, I checked the oil and water levels of my diesel engine (a Perkins 4-108, for those who care) and noticed a little tremor in my hand when trying to get the oil dipstick back in its hole. As Cari and Tracy boarded the boat and stowed their gear, I positioned myself behind the wheel and pushed the start button. Nothing happened. My big moment had arrived and I wasn't even going to get the boat out of the mooring. I pushed again, and the engine fired right up. This so overjoyed me that I didn't wonder why the starter took two tries to get going.

"Okay, let's go," I called out. "Throw off the lines." But we went nowhere. Tracy and Cari tossed the bow and stern lines overboard at the same time, and at that moment, a blast from Hawai'i's gusty trade winds rushed through the marina, pushing the boat sideways. In a panic, I hit the throttle and turned the wheel, causing the propeller to sever the slip's fixed nylon line (a floating rope that guides the boat in and out of the mooring). The sliced ends lay on the surface like two yellow sea snakes. A second later, *whack*, *Honu* hit the big white mooring ball in front of the bow. I gunned the engine, desperate to get past these lurking booby traps. "Watch the stern," Tracy shouted. I had forgotten that boats pivot around their center point. I straightened the wheel barely in time to avoid crashing *Honu*'s rear end into the neighbor's boat. Finally, we were clear of the slip.

"Glad that was easy," Cari said. I laughed, but my heart felt like a fist banging on a door. In my first two minutes as skipper, I'd given lousy cast-off instructions to my crew (I should have had them keep the windward lines taut until I had the boat moving), severed a line I needed, hit the mooring ball (again), and come within inches of crashing into another boat.

And then we did what women usually do when things go wrong: we apologized.

"I'm sorry I shouted at you about the stern," Tracy said.

"I'm sorry I didn't organize the castoff better," I said.

"I'm sorry I dropped the yellow rope," Cari said. She paused, smiling. "It doesn't matter, though. Because that was just practice."

These heartfelt apologies made us feel better, and with our graceless departure behind us, we motored out the channel. How I would back the boat into her space without the fixed yellow line to guide me I did not know, but I shooed the thought away to worry about later.

I explained to Tracy and Cari how to raise the mainsail. To keep the wind from filling the sail as it went up, thereby making the hoisting easier, I stayed

at the wheel and kept the boat aimed into the wind. My crew members did a
fine job of attaching the halyard and hoisting the main while hanging onto the
rocking boat, but something prevented the sail from going all the way to the
top of the mast.

"Okay, pull it back down," I called from the wheel. "Try it again."

Once more, the sail stopped a couple inches from the top. After a third
failed effort, I still could not see what was wrong. *How*, I wondered, *will I ever
be able to sail a boat offshore in the Pacific Ocean when I can't even get the mainsail
hoisted properly?* But who said I had to? Veteran sailors would be appalled over
flying such a slack sail—but they weren't on *Honu*.

"Leave it," I said of the recalcitrant sail. "It's good enough."

I unrolled the jib from its furler at the front of the boat, and off we went,
flying along in twenty knots of wind. "Flying along" on *Honu*, a thirty-seven-
footer, meant going six to seven knots, one knot being one nautical mile per
hour. Since a nautical mile is a little longer than a land mile, knots are a little
faster than the measurement we use for cars. Wind registering on the boat's
knot meter as twenty knots would register on land as twenty-three miles per
hour. That was a lot of wind for my first time sailing without Craig, but there
was no way I was going to cancel this maiden practice voyage.

Because the motion on a sailboat is all about where the wind and waves
(which usually travel in the same direction) hit the hull, turning the boat one
way or another creates vastly different rides. On *Honu*, and most sailboats, you
can tell precisely where the wind is coming from by looking at a little arrow at
the top of the mast. Known generally by its brand name, Windex, the red-
tipped arrow always points into the wind. Craig and other experienced sailors
don't need to look at the mast top to determine the wind direction because they
can steer by feeling it. For me, however, the Windex was an indispensable tool,
and I glanced up at it every few seconds.

We spent the afternoon experimenting with how the boat behaved going
different directions. First I tried "beating," the aptly named point of sail that
means sailing as close as you can to the direction of the wind and still make the
boat go. When beating, the wind and waves strike the boat on one side of the
bow. You know immediately if you steer too close to the wind, because the boat
stalls and you're dead in the water.

Beating is the most uncomfortable point of sail because the boat leans fairly
far to one side and stays there, tilting the entire vessel and everything in it and
on it. In addition, when the boat is pointed close to the wind, it's also pointed

close to the waves. The strikes of the oncoming waves cause the sloping boat to pitch back and forth like a hobby horse, and also to splash everyone and everything with salt water.

No one likes beating, and we three novices were no exception. Besides that, you need the mainsail to lie flat to beat (due to a law of physics called Bernoulli's principle), and mine looked like a baggy pillowcase. The little glitch with the mainsail, though, taught me a key point: even if I didn't do everything by the book, I could still sail.

After only ten minutes or so of beating, Cari started feeling seasick, and I "fell off," meaning I turned the boat a little away from the wind until it struck the boat between the bow and the center. Called "close reaching," this point of sail causes a little less jarring and slanting and spraying than beating, but not much.

Cari still felt nauseated, a common problem with beating and close reaching because, in addition to the ocean's motion, a tilted world causes more severe mismatches between a person's eyes and her balance sensors. It's this mismatch that causes motion sickness.

I fell off even more, explaining to Tracy and Cari that we were now sailing on a "beam reach," meaning the wind was hitting the side of the boat at about the middle, filling the sails and causing us to race along. Speedwise, a beam reach is great, but it can be unnerving because waves hitting the side of the boat make it roll from center to side. The rolls were such that day that, in order not to slide off our cockpit benches, we had to grab for something, anything, to hang onto until the leaded keel popped the boat back upright. I wished I had less than twenty knots of wind and eight-foot waves for my first day out. Although typical of Hawai'i, they were not what anyone would call relaxing sailing conditions. We weren't quite scared, but we weren't comfortable either.

Turning away from the wind some more, I sailed with the wind and waves striking *Honu* from behind the center, called "broad reaching." When broad reaching, the boat doesn't roll or pitch nearly as much, and we found the smoother motion a joy. With the wind and waves hitting *Honu*'s rear quarter, and her cockpit high and dry in the center, we felt like big babies being rocked in a cradle. Broad reaching is a good time to eat lunch.

My final turn had us "running downwind," with the wind directly behind the boat, hitting the stern. Sailing downwind provides the occupants with the smoothest motion, but it's rarely done for long, because it's hard to control. If you let the boat turn just a little too much, the wind catches the back of the huge mainsail and sends it and the boom (the pole supporting the bottom of the mainsail) shooting to the other side with a violent *bang*.

This happened. It's called an accidental jibe, and if you're standing in the wrong place when it occurs, the runaway boom can cause serious injury, hitting you in the head or even knocking you off the boat. Craig had several scars on his scalp from boom strikes during accidental jibes while racing.

Luckily, my accidental jibe was a whoosh of swinging sail rather than the crack of a runaway boom, and we were all sitting down. I took it as a cheap lesson. I learned the limits of downwind sailing without decapitating any of the crew.

Throughout the afternoon, we drew small amounts of blood on two shins and three fingers. Alex, a mutual friend of all three of us, had a theory about these kinds of injuries: if you found yourself bleeding and didn't know why, it meant you were having a good time. He was right. We had no idea how we had hurt ourselves, and were having so much fun we didn't care.

Up and down the Honolulu city front we sailed, enjoying the fluttery flight of the white terns and the elegant dives of the red-footed boobies that soared and fished around the boat. (The Marine Corps Base in Kaneohe Bay hosts a small colony of red-footed boobies.) Did we trim the sails correctly? No. Was the anchor wobbling loose on the bow? Yes. Did any of it matter? Not a bit. We took turns steering, fetched one another Diet Cokes, and laughed when the wind lifted the lettuce from our sandwiches and waves rocked the boat, knocking over our drinks. *Honu*, sleek and trim, cut the water as cleanly and smoothly as a sharp knife, and we advanced at a fine clip. I felt better than I had in months. *Here I am*, I thought, *a fifty-six-year-old woman who a few months earlier didn't know a finned keel from a forestay, skippering a fine vessel in gusty trade winds with an all-woman crew off a beautiful Hawaiian island. Call me Captain.*

I wished the day would never end, and not just because I felt button-bursting proud of our all-woman sailing team. No, when I reentered the harbor, I had to face the problem of parking the boat.

On the way back in, I explained to Tracy and Cari why we needed the yellow rope that now lay cut in half. In this type of boat mooring, the driver must back the boat straight to the dock between two neighboring boats, while a crew member maneuvers a boat hook over the side to snag bow lines attached to a floating mooring ball. Since this is a difficult move for even experienced boat handlers, Craig had installed a fixed-line system to make it easier. Swimming with a length of yellow polypropylene rope in his hand, he had tied one end to the mooring ball and the other to the dock. Once the crew member picked up this floating line with the boat hook, the driver could cut the engine and use a hand-over-hand technique on the line to guide the boat into position.

Both my athletic women crew members volunteered to dive off the boat, swim to the rope, and tie the propeller-cut ends together. Because I needed one person on the boat to handle lines, only one could go. A moment of silence passed, as they waited for me to decide. "Cari," I said. "You go." In the disappointment on Tracy's face, I had a fleeting vision of what lay ahead of me as captain: no matter how fair, some decisions would not be well received.

When we came to the slip, I slowed to a near stop and shifted into neutral. Cari stood on the aft rail, about eight feet above the water, and dove with the grace of a dolphin. She swam to the severed rope, tied the two pieces together, and hopped up onto the pier, smiling and waving. And a miracle occurred. Guided by the mended yellow line, I backed the boat in, Tracy retrieved the bow lines from the white float with the boat hook, and Cari tied the stern lines. In two minutes, without a word, we had the boat tied up like pros.

On the dock, Cari, Tracy, and I did what women do when things go well: we hugged. "That was fabulous, Susan," Cari said. "I learned so much."

"Compare our going out with our coming in," Tracy said, her velvety voice making everything all right. "We can do this."

After the women left, I stood on the pier gazing at *Honu*, so emotionally and physically spent that I wondered if I had enough energy to walk to my car.

"Nice boat," a passer-by said. "You handle her well."

Oh, how I loved that man.

"Thanks," I said. "I have a good crew."

When Craig got home that evening, I told him about my day, high points and lows. Only he knew how hard it had been for me, and his congratulations sounded sincere.

"Did you release the boom vang?" he said when I mentioned the problem with the mainsail. "The mainsail won't go all the way up with the vang cleated."

I knew the boom vang was a line with a block and cleat that connects the boom to the deck beneath the mast, but I didn't know its function. Craig explained that the vang applies downward pressure on the boom to counter the upward tension of the sail. After spending an afternoon skippering a boat with its mainsail resembling a loose-fitting bed sheet, I never forgot to check my dear vang again.

For the next several weeks, Pierre and I continued to work on the boat, and between repairing and adding new systems, I squeezed in other practice voyages.

Usually, to make retrieving them easier, I had my crew tie the mooring ball's bowlines to the floating, fixed yellow rope. Once, though, after a successful day sailing with a boatload of friends, one of those bowlines attached to the ball fell into the algae-green water of the slip and sank.

"Someone," I said, "needs to jump in and get that line."

This, I was learning, was one of the advantages of being captain—I could get others to do things that didn't appeal to me.

Tracy had been waiting for a moment like this since I had asked Cari to tie the severed yellow line weeks earlier. Without hesitation, Tracy stripped to her underwear and made a graceful dive. After handing up the fallen line, she climbed onto the dock and stepped onto the boat, her slim body gleaming and her triangle of dark pubic hair visible through her wet, white underpants.

My neighbors at the time were three friendly New Zealand men in their twenties delivering a catamaran from New Zealand to Vancouver. If Liam, the handsome, dreadlocked captain, wasn't smitten with Tracy after her stylish swimming performance (he struggled valiantly to not notice her subsequent attire), he most certainly was when he heard her speak. He invited her to tour the catamaran, and when we left *Honu* an hour later, Tracy was still inside. The next day, she set sail with Liam and his crew for Vancouver. I never saw her again.

There went a good crew member, I thought. But after she left, the image of Tracy's lithe young body and adventurous spirit stayed with me. In her, I saw myself in my early twenties, hitchhiking through Europe without a care in the world, running off as casually as Tracy had with any charming, good-looking guy. Now, like some lonely old woman standing on *Honu*'s deck, with aching arthritic hands and the heavy responsibility I felt in this sailboat undertaking, it would have been easy to think of my wild life in the late sixties and early seventies as the good old days. But I knew better. Even with menopause knocking down my door and my marriage in tatters, my glory days were right then and right there. I had my own boat and was going to sail it across a thousand miles of open ocean to an island paradise where I could perform the work that had become my life's joy. Regardless of what else happened, life doesn't get groovier than that.

By that time, I had other sailing companions. I had been preparing the boat for a Saturday afternoon practice sail with friends when one of them said, "I met these great guys who just moved here from San Francisco. They told me they wanted to learn to sail."

"Call them," I said.

When they got the call, Scott and Howard were halfway to Oahu's North Shore to go snorkeling. Later I joked that I could hear the screeching of their tires all the way to Honolulu as they made a U-turn back to the Ala Wai Harbor.

The three of us were an ideal match as skipper and crew. "We thought living in Hawai'i would be perfect if we just had a boat," Scott told me later. "But we did even better. We found a friend who had a boat."

Scott and Howard were so close as a couple that their first names seemed hyphenated: Scott-and-Howard. Scott had been a computer programmer before his retirement at thirty-nine (due to a stock bonanza). He had a knack for figuring out how things worked, especially electronics. Scott set up my GPS map system, got the satellite phone e-mail working, and installed a new radio/CD player. His exceptional talent for cooking (I had none) made him a perfect crew member, and I liked Scott's low-maintenance style. When he started losing his hair, he didn't go swoopy, take Rogaine, or grow one of those fringe ponytails. He shaved his head. Problem solved.

Howard had hair, and he liked it styled. When I knew him, he wore it short with a just-so flip-up in front. After one of our early sails together, I picked up my camera. "Howard," I said. "Smile."

"No pictures," he said. "My hair's a mess."

Scott and I laughed, and Howard let me shoot the photo. Of course, he looked terrific, sporty, like a born sailor standing at the helm.

Howard was not a born sailor, but he was a born planner, a huge help because orchestrating my practice voyages took time and effort to determine dates, invite friends, and buy food. The couple also pitched in with menial tasks, such as oiling seized tools, sorting spare parts, and scrubbing the rust-lined chain locker.

Scott often asked questions that required me to explain the names and functions of boat parts, and when I did not know, we looked up the subjects in books and on the Internet and learned together. In no time, Scott and Howard became my closest friends and best crew.

One day the three of us sailed to Ko Olina, a private marina on Oahu, with several other friends, all men. One of those was Alex, home from Palmyra for a few days to meet with his thesis committee (the group of people who supervised his dissertation progress) at the university.

Another of the men on board, Ken, had been a longtime ship captain with NOAA (pronounced *NO-ah*, meaning the National Oceanic and Atmospheric Administration, a scientific agency that monitors oceans and air). I was glad to have him along. This was to be my longest trip yet, about eight hours, and if something went wrong, I would welcome Ken's expertise.

The voyage would be a broad reach, the easiest way to sail in the blustery twenty- to twenty-five-knot trade winds typical of Oahu's south coast. This is called a Strong Breeze, or Force 6, according to a universal measure of sea conditions known to sailors as the Beaufort scale. Ranging from Force 0 (calm flat water) to Force 12 (hurricane), the invention of the Beaufort scale in 1805 standardized sea conditions, putting numbers to observations. In Force 6, for instance, the wind blows twenty-five to thirty land miles per hour with waves as tall as a one-story house, nine to thirteen feet. The often-illustrated charts that explain Beaufort scale measurements offer familiar examples to convey what these numbers mean. One chart says that in Force 6 wind, umbrellas are hard to control, empty garbage cans tip over, and overhead wires whistle.

Because of *Honu*'s wide beam and efficient hull shape, she surfs straight down big waves without turning and skidding sideways. This was a good thing on the way to Ko Olina because as the wind pushed *Honu* to the top of each wave, it usually broke in a spill of white foam, giving *Honu* a little shove down the other side.

Wind and waves most often come from the northeast in Hawai'i, because the northeast trade winds blow there about 70 percent of the time. If your general direction of travel is the same as the general direction of the wind, trade winds are a blessing. But in sailing, direction is everything. Trade winds, and the waves and currents they create, are often so strong that sailing against them can make it impossible for a boat to make any forward progress at all. You just plow into the punishing wind and waves, get wet, sick, and miserable, and go nowhere. I did not look forward to my upwind return.

When blowing hard enough for long enough, trade wind conditions can be storm-like and nerve-wracking no matter which direction you're going. Craig and I had several of our roughest trips ever on *Honu* going downwind in heavy trades.

About halfway through the trip, I noticed someone had led the jib sheet wrong. Good grief, I thought, do I have to keep an eye on every square inch of this boat at all times, and steer too?

"Scott," I said, "would you please relead the jib sheet through its turning block?"

"Sure," he said, standing, "if you say it in English."

"The jib sheet is the rope tied to the jib that runs back here to the cockpit," I said. "Look over the edge of the cockpit. See the brown turning block? The jib sheet is threaded the wrong way. You have to take it out, rethread it the opposite direction, and wrap it around the winch."

He uncleated the sheet and the jib began flapping furiously in all that wind, causing everyone on the boat to stop their conversation and look at me.

"We're good," I said. "The sail makes a big commotion when you uncleat it, but it won't hurt anything and needs to be led correctly. The sheet is rubbing a *puka* [*puka* means "hole" in Hawaiian, and in Hawai'i any hole of any kind is a *puka*] in my new dodger."

The cockpit's canvas windscreen is called the dodger because it's designed for people to sit behind and "dodge" ocean spray.

Scott did as I asked, and when we pulled the sail back to its proper position, called "sheeting in," it quieted down.

A while later Alex said, "Permission to go swimming, Captain?"

I stared at him. "You're joking, right?"

"No. It would feel good to get in the water."

We were a mile offshore, the wind was blowing like stink (a sailor expression), giant waves fell over themselves in whitecaps, and I had nine people to get to Ko Olina before dark. And Alex thought it would feel good to get in the water? In a rush of hormonal rage, I had the urge to shove him over the side. *See how this feels*, I thought—*PUSH*.

"Permission denied," I said.

"Really? Why?"

"It's too dangerous."

"But we could take down the sails, right?" he said. "And drift?"

"A boat drifts downwind a lot faster than a person in the water drifts downwind. The boat has mass, windage."

Alex looked longingly at the turbulent ocean. "We could put out a long safety line behind the boat. Or take turns."

This was so like Alex, not seeing the peril in his proposal, or the position he put me in when I had to keep saying no. It had simply occurred to him that it would be great fun to swim in this wild ocean. Estrogen replacement can only go so far, and this man was nearing the limit.

"Alex, it feels very wrong to me to let anyone get off the boat out here."

"Okay," he said, cheerfully. "Just thought I'd ask."

I was relieved he let it go, but the exchange troubled me. On the boat I had to decide what was right or wrong, safe or dangerous—and often I didn't know. If an insistent crew member pushed me to the wrong decision, someone could get killed. Yet if I was overly cautious, I could spoil a good time. Death or fun? On an afternoon cruise in Force 6 conditions in Hawai'i, the line between the two was a fine one.

As we arrived at the marina, I called the manager on the VHF radio for my slip assignment: row B, slip 20, he said, and gave me directions. I drove down the narrow row we all agreed must be B, but the signs weren't clear, and we soon realized that I was, in fact, driving down C. I would have to turn around. *No problem*, I thought, and drove calmly to the end of the row where I began making a tight Y-turn the way Craig taught me. I could see from the start it would have to be a double Y-turn, since the space was so small.

As I shifted into reverse and gunned the engine, Ken, the NOAA ship captain, startled me by shouting from the bow, "Look out, There's a boat right here."

"Where?" I said, thinking he could see some little dinghy I could not.

"The Beneteau. It's right here."

The Beneteau? *Well, of course the Beneteau is right there*, I thought. *That's why I'm backing up.*

"Turn, turn," shouted Ken. "More reverse. More reverse."

Scott and I looked at each other and shrugged. I finished the turn in good order and headed down the correct row to the guest slip, a narrow one between a concrete pier and a wide catamaran. *Honu* would fit, but just.

"It's going to be tight," Ken shouted back to me. "Real tight." He paused. "Slow down. Go left."

While learning to sail together, Scott and I had devised a system of hand signals and reserved yelling for emergencies. "Scott," I said, "would you please go to the bow and let me know what's happening?"

With a few silent signs from Scott, I eased the boat in, bumping neither the pier nor the catamaran, and stopped precisely where I wanted to. As people jumped off the boat to secure the lines, Scott patted me on the back.

When I straightened up from pulling the engine shutoff cable, Ken stood in the cockpit looking sheepish. "I'm sorry I shouted at you, Susan," he said. "I knew you were learning, and . . . well, I didn't know you could handle the boat so well."

"That's okay," I said. "A couple of months ago, I didn't know forward from reverse." (He thought I was joking.) "But I've been practicing."

"I feel terrible," he said. "Please forgive me."

"Of course, Ken. It's no big deal. Forget it."

He let it go, and we later became friends. But I remembered the incident vividly because it illustrated a crucial point: a boat can have only one captain.

9

$\mathscr{A}$FTER a few days at Ko Olina, Scott, Howard, Cari, and I were ready to take the leap across the Kaua'i Channel. At sixty-three miles, this is the longest distance between any of the main Hawaiian Islands. In 1796 the island of Kauai kept its independence because of this channel. When King Kamehameha, who had conquered the other main Hawaiian Islands, planned an invasion of Kaua'i, wind and waves overturned several canoes, forcing the king and his warriors back to Waianae. They did not try again.

Still, there's a big plus in sailing from Oahu to Kaua'i: like the Ko Olina trip, it's downwind all the way. Unlike the Ko Olina trip, however, Hawai'i's trade winds gradually weakened from twenty knots to ten, giving us a welcome break. After weeks of preparing the boat for the gale-force winds and the fearsome seas of the Kaua'i Channel, I didn't see any. The wind was strong enough to push us across but not so strong to scare us. The waves also behaved themselves, rolling beneath the boat without breaking. The swells were so quiet, and *Honu* scooted down them so smoothly, the cockpit felt like a porch swing on a summer day.

During our voyage along the Waianae Coast, the sun put on a pink and purple light show, while at the same time, the full moon appeared over the green mountaintops like a glowing piñata. Later that night, I watched blue-green twinkles come and go in the boat's wake like underwater meteor showers. The sparkles are made by tiny bioluminescent animals that contain a chemical reaction waiting to happen. When the boat jars each creature, the movement combines oxygen with a substance called luciferin that results in a flash of light. What this motion-caused light does for the organism isn't clear, but it must have some advantage, because countless species throughout the world's oceans make their own light when jostled.

With sighs of relief, we raised the mainsail to its full height, called "shaking out the reef." When it comes to sailing, "reef" has several meanings. *The* reef is the part of a sail rolled in or tied down to lessen the area exposed to the wind, and *to* reef is making it so. A reef is also a navigational hazard, such as a jutting rock or wall of coral that is noted as "DANGER" on nautical charts.

It's much easier to reef the mainsail in the marina when the boat is motionless than at sea where it's moving, and I often did it before I left. If the wind didn't necessitate a reefed mainsail, it was easy to shake out, meaning undo it. On *Honu*, you just untied the reefing lines and hauled up the rest of the sail with the halyard.

That done, we sat back to watch juvenile red-footed boobies circle the boat looking for a place to land.

Craig and I had a history with booby birds. Twenty years earlier, two juvenile red-footed boobies landed on the aft rail of *Honu* during our voyage from Costa Rica to Hawai'i. We were over a thousand miles offshore at the time and rolling in heavy seas. The young seabirds balanced there calmly for forty-eight hours, grooming their feathers by day, sleeping next to each other at night, and occasionally squabbling over rail space. Craig and I didn't know anything about seabirds at the time, and on the second day, we worried about the birds sitting there in the hot sun with no food or water. Craig placed a dish of precious freshwater on the deck beneath them, and I offered the pair bread crumbs and bananas. They suffered this indignity with curiosity, following our movements as if to say, "What can these people be thinking?" Later we learned that booby birds (and most other seabirds) drink seawater and eat fish and squid. Craig took a picture of me trying to feed the birds bread. We called the photo "Three Boobies on the Aft Deck."

No booby birds visited the boat this time, and I was glad. If they landed on *Honu* and Craig wasn't there, I would have felt sad that we weren't sharing the fun together. Even with a boatload of friends around me, with Craig absent I felt lonely.

The sky around the boat was bursting with other birds, and that helped divert my depressing thoughts. A red-tailed tropicbird thrilled me to my toes by flying close to the mast top to check it out. The feathers of both males and females are white, except for two ruby-red tail feathers as long as their bodies, about a foot-and-a-half. The tail feathers have no flight function; they're for decoration only. In one published study on the growth rate of these stunning feathers, Canadian biologists aptly call them "tail streamer ornaments." Tropicbird beaks are nearly cone shaped, heavy at the base and narrowing to a sharp point at the tip. The bills are so red that the bird seems to be wearing gaudy lipstick. Their banner tails and bright beaks give the birds an air of elegance, but there's nothing elegant about their calls. They sound to me like agitated goats—*braaaaawk, braaaaawk.* I had never before seen a red-tailed tropicbird in the main islands (they are common on Tern Island but not in Hawai'i proper) and felt a burst of pride. I had gotten myself to a good place.

A flock of wedge-tailed shearwaters skimmed inches above the water, rising and dipping with the waves in search of food. Hawai'i anglers look for offshore flocks, calling them "bird piles" because the birds sort of pile up as they hover and circle over schools of fish. As we gazed at them from *Honu*, the shearwaters found some fish, swooping and diving among large dark fins, tunas we thought, that were chasing smaller fish to the surface.

I feel sorry for small fish in the open ocean. They swim like mad to escape predators from below only to get picked off by predators from above. That's survival of the fittest for you, harsh but, in weeding out the weak, effective.

Also called natural selection, survival of the fittest is a key principle of evolution that makes our living planet what it is today. But it sure can be hard to watch in animals, and it's definitely hard to think about in terms of our own species. If humans followed Mother Nature's lead, we would leave disabled babies on forest floors to die. And then there are those of us who didn't multiply when we had the chance and go on to live far past the age that reproduction is possible. In biological terms, we are utter failures.

But at that moment I felt more successful than I had in ages. I had been readying the boat for offshore sailing for so many months that during those few hours of sailing along Oahu's west coast, all the work I did, the money I spent, and the hours I fretted were worth it. I may have lost my perfect life with Craig, but this new one had pluses. Good friends, marine life galore, a calm ocean, a glorious sky, the Hawaiian Islands, *my own sailboat.*

Still, I worried. This was my first channel crossing as captain, and being responsible for the welfare of everyone on board weighed heavily. I spent thousands of dollars on safety equipment I hoped never to use, yet one of my primary responsibilities required knowing where it was and how it worked.

Since we were sailing downwind, *Honu* could accidentally jibe, which meant the boom could come streaking across the cockpit without notice to smack people in the head or shove them overboard. Without Craig there, it would be up to me to administer first aid. A few drops of blood from a pokey cotter pin was one thing; a cracked skull was another.

On constant guard for wayward booms, I also wore myself out checking for leaks below the floorboards. All it would take was one burst hose or broken seacock to swamp the boat, and if I didn't plug it fast enough, *Honu* could sink within minutes.

I gave Scott, Howard, and Cari safely lectures about always wearing harnesses, turning off the gas, and conserving freshwater. They listened respectfully, but I didn't think any of them appreciated the gravity of onboard mistakes, especially in Hawai'i, where the islands are just drops of batter on a sixty-million-square-mile griddle. When one of the crew dropped the anchor, I held my breath, praying the chain would not leap off the windlass gear, wrap around a leg, and drag him or her to the ocean floor. My nose was also on duty. For cooking, we carried several gallons of propane, a gas heavier than air. An undetected leak could cause propane to settle in the bilge, the space below the floorboards where a little water always sloshed around, and the first spark of a bilge or water pump could ignite the gas and blow us to bits. *Safety, safety, safety* . . . this was my new mantra.

It had been Craig's, too, and I winced remembering how often his caution had irritated me. *Okay, okay,* I would think when he insisted on bathing strictly in seawater to conserve our freshwater stores. During his lectures about the explosive properties of gasoline and propane, I daydreamed, wondering what it was about these subjects he found so interesting. Now I knew. He was interested in keeping us alive. I would have called him on my cell phone to announce this revelation, but we had stopped calling each other.

At these times, the boat felt like a miniature *Titanic*, speeding toward unknowable disaster. Cruising sailboats have most of the systems we use in our houses, such as lights, faucets, refrigerators, computers, and toilets, as well as all the systems we depend on in our cars—engine, transmission, batteries, alternators. And on a sailboat, towering above everything, is a rat's nest of ropes, poles, and wires supporting flexing masts and heavy sheets of sailcloth. As if that isn't enough to keep track of, some components of these systems don't get along. Electrical circuits hate water, dissimilar metals eat each other up, and propellers and windmills wind up stray lines like yoyos. Sailors cram this mass of machinery into a small space, sprinkle it with salt, moisten, pound, and jostle it for hours, and then wonder why things go wrong.

Because *Honu* had an exceptional amount of storage space, I never worried about food, but having no watermaker, I worried about freshwater. If the boat were disabled and we had to drift for a long time, water could mean life or death. Howard turned on the water in the head to rinse his face. *Whir, whir,*

whir went the electric pump. Scott and I stared at each other. *Whir, whir, whir. . . .* Scott smiled, knowing I was fighting to keep quiet. *Whir, whir, whir, whir, whir, whir. . . .*

"Howard," I finally shouted. *"Turn off the water!"*

The pump stopped. "Sorry," he said, exiting the bathroom. "I didn't know we were short."

"We aren't. It's just . . . well, on a sailboat, letting freshwater run down the drain like that is not allowed."

He blinked and turned to Scott. "You didn't tell me she was a water Nazi."

We had a good laugh, but Howard was right. If I heard the pump running for more than five seconds, I'd jump up to interrogate the offender. "It's for pasta," Scott learned to call out so I would leave him alone in the galley. I probably went too far on water conservation. Or not. *Honu* carries 120 gallons, which is a lot, but if wasted, can go in a hurry. On the other hand, it was about 100 gallons more than we needed for that crossing. If the mast didn't fall down, if the rudder didn't fall off, if. . . .

One of my biggest headaches captaining a vessel was determining the line between prudence and paranoia. This was no menopause symptom—all skippers walk this shaky plank. At the start, I used Craig's tactics as my model, but things had changed since we had sailed together using a sextant to navigate and calling home via a single-sideband radio. The advent of GPS and satellite phones radically altered navigation and communication. Now if you're adrift, you can easily telephone for help, or if you're worried about a reef, you check your location on the GPS map. Still, people told me scary stories about over-confident skippers with all the modern gear ending up on the rocks or, worse, on the ocean floor.

On that wide channel crossing, though, a miracle occurred. After twenty-four hours of sailing, nothing broke, everyone stayed healthy, and the weather cooperated.

Proudly I orchestrated the anchoring of *Honu* among a dozen other boats in a calm corner of Hanalei Bay. From West Marine I had bought an eight-foot-long gray rubber dinghy, light enough that I could drag it high onto beaches alone and small enough that I could roll it up and stow it in the aft lazaret, a storage compartment at the back of a boat. Most sailors give their dinghy, also called a tender because it "tends" the bigger boat, a name that has something to do with the main boat. But I couldn't come up with anything clever, so I just called it "the dinghy" until something inspired me.

My three crew members had to go back to Oahu to work, but they would return the next weekend to help me sail back to Honolulu. With a foot pump, we inflated the little dinghy on the aft deck, dropped it over the stern where it landed on the water with a loud belly flop, and lowered my rusty one-horsepower motor onto the dinghy's wooden transom. Previously Scott named the outboard Bette Davis because it was cantankerous but tough and always came through in the end. (Craig had bought me the easy-to-lift outboard years earlier as a special gift so I could putter around by myself.) Sure enough, after a half-dozen pulls, the eggbeater of a motor started. My crew donned their day packs, and we climbed down the ladder on *Honu*'s transom to the waiting dinghy.

The weight of four adults in that little boat sank its edges near the water-line, but with the water glassy calm I could see—and dodge—each clump of coral and managed to keep the boat, and our bottoms, dry. My friends disem-barked on the nearby beach of the Hanalei Bay Resort, where they caught the shuttle to the airport. I waved good-bye and drove back to *Honu* alone in a light mist of rain.

The rain became a steady downpour that rinsed the salt off *Honu*'s decks. I rigged up the cockpit awning to collect it, not because I needed freshwater but to check that the catchment fittings on the new awning worked properly. (They did.) As rainwater dribbled through the clear hoses, I remembered similarly filling the tanks with Craig during a deluge in a Costa Rican anchorage. Later, when we discovered that rainwater had nearly filled our former rubber dinghy floating behind *Honu*, we used it to bathe. I took a picture of Craig soaking in the dinghy "bathtub," his head, chest, and arms covered in foamy shampoo. Through all those suds radiated his brilliant happy-to-be-alive smile.

At this fond memory, I reached for my phone and tapped in Craig's num-ber, a rare occasion these days.

"Congratulations," he said. "Being captain is pretty different from being a crew member, isn't it?"

An hour earlier I had been thinking the same thing, that skippering wasn't nearly as much fun as crewing. His tone, however, sounded accusing. *See the responsibility I had to shoulder alone all these years?*

To ask him what he meant would have risked starting a fight, so instead I mentioned a problem with the gasket on the fuel port, which he had a sugges-tion for fixing, and we said a chilly good-bye. That a conversation with Craig about my first channel crossing had spoiled my sense of victory made me feel incredibly low and, a moment later, furious. I decided not to call again.

That week I lived at anchor in one of the most beautiful bays in the world, relaxing on my gorgeously refit sailboat, which I had just skippered across the widest Hawaiian Island channel—and felt unbearably lonely. I went to bed alone, woke up alone, drank coffee alone. On my first morning, the sun lit up Kaua'i's Mount Waialeale *(why-AH-lay-AH-lay)*, a rare sight because, besides being 5,148 feet high, it's also the rainiest place on Earth—averaging 426 inches per year—and is usually cloaked in clouds and mist. (Honolulu averages about twenty inches per year.) The golden light of sunrise on that towering mass of jungle was breathtaking, but there was no one to hear me murmur, "Wow, look at that." I got out my camera and had to brush away tears to focus on the mountain, shaped like a bell curve.

The extent of my dependency on Craig, on his companionship, shocked me. All my life I had been critical of women who couldn't, or wouldn't, take one little step without a man holding their hand. But that hand-holding meant the man she loved was by her side. How I longed to see Craig's hand turning a socket wrench, hear him explain in too much detail the mechanics of an alternator, catch a whiff of his shampoo from those salt-and-pepper curls.

It was good that Scott, Howard, and Cari left me, I decided, because to sort out being lonely, I had to be alone. Unlike some days the past year when I felt blue for no discernable reason, at least in Hanalei Bay I could pinpoint the source of my sadness: I missed Craig profoundly. But how could I ever feel triumphant about my accomplishments when wrapped in a cocoon of loneliness? Independence, I was realizing, came at an enormous price.

I had a good cry, blew my nose, and gazed at the water, making a mental note of things that brought me joy regardless of Craig's presence or absence. First on the list that day was the lovely quiet of Hanalei Bay with the trade winds at rest. The boat rocked gently, and ripples of water kissed the hull with little splashes, sounding like a baby playing in a plastic tub.

I took a picture of my starboard neighbors' boat, an unusual-looking ketch named *Freedom.* My neighbors on the other side were a couple I met the week before in the Ala Wai Harbor back home, but I didn't want to visit them. I had told them my sailing plans—a few voyages and then Palmyra—but learned almost nothing about them except they were stoned on life. They were so in love with each other and so enamored with their six-month-old baby, the beauty of nature, the cosmos, and everything in between, I felt nearly dizzy with envy. It wasn't the baby—I had never wanted children, nor had Craig—but rather the rock-solid certainty the couple projected that they would spend their lives together. The certainty that I once had and lost.

They spotted me in the cockpit and called and motioned from their deck to come over. Sighing, I got in the dinghy and pulled the starter cord. Bette didn't usually like rain, but she was benevolent that morning and started right up. I motored over to see what these nice people wanted.

The flat turquoise water was so clear that I could see fish swimming below, and it took all my willpower to not stop the dinghy and jump in for a swim. But since the couple stood on their deck waiting, I puttered on, feeling both joy at being in that fabulous bay under its spectacular mountain, and misery over being there alone.

I didn't accept the couple's invitation to come aboard but held onto their boarding ladder while they told me about the two people aboard the *Freedom*, the boat on my other side that I had just photographed. Apparently, the owners were biologists who had arrived the day before from Palmyra.

That perked me right up. The atoll still seemed like an impossible distance away, but if those people could do it in a gaff-rigged (an old-fashioned design using sails with four corners) boat smaller than mine, so could I. Plus, they could tell me about the atoll, its residents, the anchorage, and—best of all, since they were biologists—the wildlife.

Off Bette and I went to visit *Freedom*, and this time I did accept the invitation to go aboard. The owners, Bill and Sharon, were a perky couple in their twenties. Bill talked nonstop about his boat, which he built, and its systems, which he installed, and how the two of them had worked for untold hours each week, year after year, living like paupers, spending every spare cent they had on Bill's dream of building a boat and sailing it across the Pacific. On and on and on, he talked.

As I sat there stifling a yawn, trying to appear interested, I kept an eye on Sharon. She reminded me of my former self, baking cookies while her husband and another captain—always a man in my cruising experience—discussed the charging capacity of their wind generators and the advantages of glass mat house batteries. This time I knew what Bill was talking about, but I didn't care. The boat, the design, the equipment, the dream. I shared none of it. What I wanted was the wildlife, and information on how to get to it. I broke in. Tell me about Palmyra, I said, hoping to learn what the lagoon looked like, if the coconut crabs stayed hidden or marched around in the open, if Palmyra's notorious rain allowed outdoor activity. Instead, here's all I learned from Bill and Sharon:

1. Alex was nice. (Knew that.)
2. Palmyra was beautiful. (Figured so.)

3. It took Sharon and Bill ten days to sail upwind from Palmyra to Hanalei Bay. (I understood that upwind sailing was tough but at the time did not appreciate the difficulty of ten steady, offshore days of it.)

Bill went back to talking about their well-designed boat and well-planned lives. I began to have uncharitable thoughts about these two nice people, and uncharitable thoughts about myself for resenting their togetherness. I planned a getaway with made-up excuses, worried that if I stayed much longer my wacked-out hormones would turn me into a werewolf and I'd go for their throats. Nevertheless, as Bette puttered me back to my boat, those dark thoughts fell away.

And so, to some extent, did the loneliness. *Here be paradise*, I thought. No wonder Hanalei Bay is the place of Pacific Island dreams. It's the home of that magic dragon Puff, and the area that Hollywood people chose for filming jungle movies such as *Raiders of the Lost Ark*, *Jurassic Park*, and a dozen more.

The mouth of Hanalei (pronounced *hah-nah-LAY*—Peter, Paul, and Mary had it wrong) Bay is about a mile wide, and inside lies a perfect crescent sand beach. Behind that, little forests of palm and ironwood trees stand among perfect island houses, some modest, some mansions, but all manicured as if posing for their big moment in the movies. Behind these houses, on charming lanes rather than plain old streets, rise massive mountains (Mount Waialeale being the big daddy), tall, wide, and deliciously green and lush. Nature has been working on the mountains of Kaua'i longer than the other main Hawaiian Islands, gouging out steep valleys with jutting ridges. A waterfall drops straight from the top of Waialeale, and with the mountaintop clear my first few days there—a rare occurrence—I got to gaze at it to my heart's content.

And content I came to be.

Each day upon waking at first light I would lie staring at the sky through the open hatch over my bed, listening to the snap, crackle, and pop of the snapping shrimp below. When Craig and I first lived on a sailboat in Hawai'i, we didn't know the origin of that distant popcorn-popping sound we heard whenever we were below deck. He thought it might have something to do with the fiberglass in the hull, but that didn't make sense because we often heard the same sound while snorkeling.

I was a student at the University of Hawai'i at the time, and one day my invertebrate zoology professor took the class on a field trip to the Diamond Head reef flats, where we turned over rocks to collect marine invertebrates.

These we took back to the lab and deposited in Petri dishes of seawater to examine and study. My dish contained a tan-colored, inch-long shrimp with one normal-sized claw and one enormous one. As the lab assistant instructed, I touched the big pincer with a pencil tip. *Snap* went the claw. I recognized the sound instantly—the popping mystery was over.

The creatures are called snapping shrimp (also pistol shrimp) because they use their one big claw to defend their mud burrows and also to stun passing prey with the jet of water resulting from the forceful closure of the claw. My local classmates, for whom these things were no big deal, laughed at my excitement over this discovery. But for me, every little detail I learned about the marine world, from upwelling currents to winter surf, from lantern fish to whale sharks, changed my life. Shrimp in holes make that noise? Amazing. Since then, the crackly chorus that fills the boat is, to my ears, a symphony of the sea.

How Craig and I loved the little snappers. When they were especially active, it sounded like a giant bowl of Rice Krispies in freshly added milk. "Listen," he would say, "the shrimp are having World War III down there tonight."

Craig was as thrilled as I was over marine wildlife. It was he who took me snorkeling the first time, renting the mask, snorkel, and fins at a Mexico marine preserve during our first year, and our first vacation, together. I was a confident swimmer in lakes and pools but had never put my face in the ocean.

"Trust me," he said, a phrase I would hear countless times in our life together. "You'll love this."

Craig helped me into the gear and held my hand as we flip-flopped like wounded frogs to the water's edge.

"What's that? And that? Look," I said as I bumbled along coughing, half drowned from inhaling seawater, half sick from swallowing it. Over the next hour I cut both knees and both elbows on coral heads, which because they are stinging animals make nasty sores, and broke out in giant hives where the black rubber mask and fins dug into my skin. And I loved every second. Craig didn't know the names of the fish and invertebrates, or care, but he knew more than me, which was nothing. I thought sea urchins were cactusy plants (they're animals) and moray eels were snakes (they're fish). I needed to get the facts. Soon after that trip, I bought my first little fish ID book.

While waiting out the week for my crew to return, I realized how little I now knew Craig. My mistake (the most recent one, at least) had been thinking that after years of devotion, Craig had quit the Twinship. But now, sitting alone at anchor in Hanalei Bay, I began to wonder if over the years our lives had taken a turn so gradual we hadn't noticed. Well, I hadn't noticed. It wasn't as obvious as a fork in the road, but more like a gentle curve that went on and on, and when it stopped, we were far from our original destination, that is, being best friends and helping each other through life. What bothered me most was why, if he saw it happening, didn't he tell me? Oh, that's right. He thought he did. Was I so self-absorbed that I could ignore something that important? Or had his message been so cryptic it was impossible to decipher?

After mulling this over for the millionth time, I dragged myself out of bed, made coffee, and sat in the cockpit to watch the sun once again astonish Kaua'i's mountains. And there it struck me: I was not alone in an empty cockpit on a lonely boat. Thousands of my dearest friends were right here with me. Snapping shrimp clicked greetings from burrows below, seabirds sent hellos from the sky above, and fish and dolphins swam circles around. This revelation reminded me of an exchange I had years earlier with one of my editors.

"You talk all the time about Hawai'i's humpback whales," he said, "but I've lived here all my life, and I've never seen one."

"To see whales, Roy," I said, "you have to look at the ocean."

For decades, I had been searching for, marveling over, and writing about marine creatures, and in the process, they had given my life direction and meaning. They still did. But to accept these gifts, I had to pay attention—to look at the ocean.

Later in the week, another new neighbor motored over in his dinghy. "Hope my generator isn't bothering you folks," he said. "I try not to run it too often, but I've got quite a few electrical things going on the boat."

I considered saying it wasn't *folks*, it was *folk*.

"Thanks for asking," I said, instead. "We're fine."

MY crew came back the next weekend, and those three fine human friends made me wonder how I could ever think I was alone in the world.

We rode around in my new dinghy, chatting over the roar of Bette the cranky outboard. A few of the bay's resident spinner dolphins sped over to accompany us. Their dorsal fins cut through the water, one behind the other, looking like the back of an undulating dragon. This might, some believe, be what ancient mariners called sea monsters and where the idea of Dragon Puff came from.

Spinners are considerably smaller than bottlenose dolphins (the species we usually see in marine parks), and these were small even for spinners, shorter than the eight-foot-long dinghy by two or three feet. They get their name from a habit of leaping clear of the water and turning 360 degrees on their tails, often three or four times, then landing on their sides with a splash. It's an astonishing animal ballet, and why they do it is a mystery. One dolphin biologist's hypothesis is that the splash landing signals to other members of the pod the location of the jumper, therefore marking the edge of the pod's safety zone. Sharks sometimes prey on weak or young dolphins, and there's protection within the group, where adult dolphins can gang up on sharks and drive them off. But why spin three or four times? No one knows for sure.

Another theory is that the dolphins are trying to shake off remoras, oceanic fish that suck big time. A remora sticks to its ride by using an oblong disk on top of its head that creates a powerful vacuum when pressed against a surface. Remoras aren't parasites. They're scavenging hitchhikers, eating their hosts' leftovers and skin parasites. Occasionally, remoras let go to grab a passing snack of fish or plankton and then restick to their host.

Eight species of remoras, also called sharksuckers, travel the world's oceans attached to the exteriors of sharks, rays, turtles, whales, dolphins, manatees, billfish, and ships. From one to three feet long, remoras have also been found attached to the *insides* of sharks' and rays' mouths and also in their gill cavities. (No wonder ancient Hawaiians thought remoras were shark offspring.) The largest remora, often attracted to sharks, is gray and grows to thirty-five inches long.

Large remoras' suction cups are so strong that in some parts of the world anglers tie a line around a remora's tail and let it swim. When it sticks to a fish or turtle, the angler carefully hauls in the remora and its unlucky host.

We humans can break a remora's strong suction with our hands, but dolphins don't have hands. They can, however, jump like gymnasts, making it possible that dolphins sometimes jump and spin to shake off remoras. High-resolution digital cameras with fast motor drives show even small remoras stuck to airborne dolphins.

But some researchers have another guess as to why spinners spin: because it's fun. Spinners and other dolphin species are famous for hitching rides on the bow waves of boats, as well as the wake of some whales, because surfing propels the dolphins forward with less effort. But since dolphins often leave their pods to sprint considerable distances toward whales and boats, their wave riding doesn't seem to conserve energy. Again, most researchers agree that wave riding for dolphins is playtime.

What cracked us up in Hanalei Bay was watching these sleek ocean racers try to ride the tiny bow wave Bette Davis made pushing the little rubber boat.

The dolphins swam so close to the dinghy we could have touched their gray, leathery backs, and the chuffing sound they made with each blowhole breath sounded like the stroke of an engine.

I surprised myself by not feeling sad that Craig wasn't there to witness the exceptional dolphin encounter. The fact was that although he would have loved it, this was my trip. My three mesmerized companions were happy and grateful to watch the show and leave the driving to me. I felt like a leader, their captain, and enjoyed it immensely.

There's nothing like being within petting distance of a pod of frolicking dolphins to inject some perspective into a person. The sight of those marine mammals having fun sent my blues flying like remoras off a spinning dolphin. At that moment, I saw myself for what I am: one smidgen of life among trillions of smidgeons of life, among trillions of planets circling trillions of stars burning in trillions of galaxies. And I was one happy smidgen. How silly to waste one second of this gift feeling otherwise.

Our dolphins were disgusted, we were sure, by our puny bow wave that barely gave them a lift. Between the dinghy's blunt nose and Bette's miniature propeller, we barely stirred the water. The spinners soon sprinted off to find a real boat to play with.

Later, we hauled the dinghy up the back of the boat with the mizzen halyard (the rope that pulls up the sail on the small mizzenmast), intending to lower the rubber boat onto the aft deck to deflate and stow it. But when the dinghy got to its highest point, the wind caught hold, swung it around the side of *Honu*, and smashed it into a solar panel, which I had forgotten to lower. *Honu*'s solar panels attached to the rail at the back of the boat, one on each side, flipping up to catch the sun or down to be out of the way. The panels were significant sources of energy for the boat's instruments and appliances, but not the only ones. I had three other means of generating electricity: a windmill, the engine alternator, and a generator that operated off the turning propeller shaft.

After hearing the crack of glass, we watched the panel's metal brace sink twenty-five feet to the ocean floor. It says a lot about the water of Hanalei Bay that we could clearly see the aluminum part lying in the white sand below.

The accident happened so fast, the four of us stood for a moment astonished. Quickly we dropped the dinghy to the deck.

"I'm really sorry," Scott said.

"That's all right," I said. "It's not your fault. Things break."

"Do you need that piece?" Cari said.

"I don't know. It might be easy to replace, or impossible."

"I'll get it," Cari said. "Can I?"

I nodded, grateful that she wanted to do it, and that she asked my permission before diving in. Cari stepped onto the aft rail, where she effortlessly and with barely a splash dove into the clear water. Diving twenty-five feet on one gulp of air is hard to do, but leaning over the side of the boat, we could see Cari's body turn wavy as she descended to the bottom and, in one quick motion, picked up the bracket. A moment later, she burst to the surface panting, smiling, and holding the piece up in the sunlight. We gave her three cheers. Later, Pierre and I replaced the old solar panels with new ones and changed their fastening system, which had grown loose with age. We didn't need the broken part after all, but I will always love Cari for retrieving it. I have it still.

To my mental list of captain's duties I added: before allowing any dinghy activity on the aft deck, lower the solar panels.

On this Hanalei voyage, I also learned that I had to be vigilant about navigation, even in calm weather, even when I was off watch, and even with a good GPS. I gave up *Honu*'s two sextants for three GPS machines—one main color unit, like a little TV mounted at the wheel, and two hand-held units for backup. The main sextant, which I learned how to use rather well sailing *Honu* to Hawai'i with Craig, sat on a bookcase in my office like the quaint antique it had become. But even though GPSs are a miracle of technology, you have to know how to read their symbols.

Motoring in calm water back to Honolulu from Hanalei (I got lucky that the trade winds quit), I woke at dawn to relieve Howard and Cari of their watch and found us off Barbers Point (also known as Kalaeloa), Oahu, entering a forbidden zone around the pipeline that Hawai'i's tankers use to pump oil ashore. To emphasize that absolutely no accidents can occur in this area and cause an oil spill, the fine for entering this zone is twenty-five thousand dollars. About this the Coast Guard is not kidding.

"Oh, no," I said as I leaped to turn off the autopilot. Spinning the wheel hard, I made a 180 degree turn and hit the throttle. "What? What?" Cari and Howard said. When I explained the situation, they looked sheepish. "We saw the circle on the GPS," they said, "but we didn't know what it meant." It wasn't their fault. I hadn't shown them how to decipher the symbols. (A press of a button explains what the circle means.) Lucky for me, it was six in the morning on a Sunday morning and our little slip over the line went unnoticed.

As we motored home to Honolulu that morning, the ocean turned so glassy that the reflection of the morning sun made the water look oily. Several bottle-nose dolphins, longer and thicker than the dainty spinners—bottlenoses can grow to thirteen feet long and weigh fourteen hundred pounds—shattered that ocean mirror when they bounded over to ride *Honu*'s bow wave, bigger than Bette's but small compared with the speedier powerboats. The clear-as-air water offered a perfect view of the big dolphins' distinct markings, including dozens of white scars that looked like propeller cuts crisscrossing the animals' backs and sides. But those slashes aren't from boats. Dolphins get into scraps with sharks, and also fight with each other, sometimes battling over females and occasionally killing the offspring of rivals. Females that lose infants usually become fertile again in one to two weeks, giving the slayer a chance to pass on his survival-of-the-fittest genes.

I stood at the very tip of the bow to watch the brawny yet graceful dolphins ride *Honu*'s wave. Years earlier, on an equally calm day at sea, Craig had pulled down the sails and climbed the mast to take pictures of a pod of dolphins frolicking in *Honu*'s bow wave, with me hanging over the bow watching. In one of those pictures, I'm waving up at him. A second later I lost my balance and nearly fell overboard. How we laughed.

I couldn't imagine that now. When had we stopped laughing?

10

CRAIG and I lived like two hamsters running on adjacent exercise wheels. Occasionally we got onto the same rhythm and talked to each other, but it was often in code, and sometimes in anger. I was still taking estrogen, progesterone, and antidepressants, but I felt out of sorts, as if I had done something wrong but couldn't remember what it was. I agreed with the recent change of terms from HRT, hormone replacement therapy, to simply HT, hormone therapy. Estrogen relieved some symptoms of menopause but did not replace everything I had lost, such as self-control.

Once while Craig and I were walking to the beach along a busy thoroughfare with no sidewalks, he, without a word, abruptly crossed the street and walked with the heavy traffic to his back rather than facing it, as we had been doing. When I joined him, I exploded.

"What's the matter with you? It's dangerous on this side. Why did you leave me?"

"Now you're telling me that I walk down the street wrong?"

"Yes. No. I just . . . oh, God. I don't know."

He stomped off ahead of me, our rare walk together spoiled.

The incident left me badly shaken. When the Twinship was abloom, Craig would never have crossed the street to walk away from me, and I would never have shouted at him with such venom. I knew my outbursts were hormone related, but since I had no warning they were coming, I couldn't avert them with reasoning. I regretted fighting with Craig horribly, thinking, *I've been invaded by an alien. Someone please shoot me.* I felt like the kid in *The Exorcist*, overpowered by forces of evil.

"The trades are supposed to build over the weekend," he said one morning at breakfast.

"Build" is sailor speak for increasing wind strength, but that term was not the code portion of his statement. No, this was how Craig told people his opinion when it was something negative. His observation about the trade winds meant, *I don't think you should sail to Kaneohe this weekend as you planned.*

Or not. It was possible that he was talking about the weather because he didn't have anything else to say to me. Either way, the comment depressed me because trying to figure out what he was thinking was exhausting. Most of the time I couldn't even figure out what *I* was thinking.

Whether his comment about the wind had hidden meaning or not, he was right that it was building. The trades had been amping up each day that week, which emphasized one enormous disadvantage of sailing: the difference between fun and fiasco is wind strength, and wind doesn't care about weekends, days off, or long-planned voyages. I had six friends who were counting on either sailing with me to Kaneohe Bay or meeting me there, and none could do it any other time.

Besides that, after the Kaua'i trip, Pierre discovered a faulty switch that meant that the engine's alternator had not been charging the house batteries properly. This was serious. If not fixed, it meant that I could lose power to my GPS, autopilot, refrigerator, and every other piece of electrical equipment on the boat. He replaced the switch, but the boat needed to be sailed to test the repair.

Honu needed this trial run to Kaneohe Bay to charge her batteries, and I needed *Honu* to sail away. With my marriage circling the drain, my body falling apart at the joints, and my mood swings ranging from homicidal to suicidal, I was more and more desperate to go to Palmyra. Living on Tern Island among the wildlife had been like taking a feel-good pill every day for four months, and I craved another fix. Also, I had recently received more details about my Palmyra job—fieldwork for an ant study—and in learning about those industrious little creatures, I had fallen in love with another animal family.

I knew that ants were part of a tree problem on the atoll but had not appreciated the reason until I went to a special meeting called by biologists at the U.S. Fish and Wildlife Service. There an entomologist named Peter who specialized in ant biology gave us a briefing on the Palmyra ant situation.

Ten kinds of ants thrive in Palmyra, he explained, all accidentally introduced to the atoll by stowing away on boats. Several of these ant species, in a behavior called farming, protect and transport living plant parasites called scale, hard-shelled insects about the size and color of a grain of rice (and so named because some species resemble fish scales), also accidentally introduced to Palmyra. The ants farm scale because the tiny insects eat the tree's sap and subsequently defecate a sticky sugar-rich substance called honeydew (nothing to do with the melon of the same name). Ants are crazy about honeydew.

This ant/scale relationship is a classic case of biological back scratching called symbiosis or mutualism. The scale insects get free rides to juicy new leaves, and the ants get a continual source of sweets. I thought this farming brilliant of the ants.

Peter, a soft-spoken man in his early thirties, in typical academic fashion, took his discipline so seriously that he did not crack one smile during his fairly lengthy talk about ants. Worker and soldier ants are all females, Peter explained, and as he talked, I imagined male ants hanging around the nest, showing off to the queen in hopes of getting lucky, while all the females were out working.

Ants, I thought, are as efficient as corals, which by hosting microscopic algae gardens in their cells, grow their own carbs. I wondered how I might get the subject of ants into a column about the ocean. They got to Palmyra on boats, but would that be too much of a stretch?

"You have a question, Susan?" Peter asked, seeing my quizzical expression.

"No, no. Just appreciating ants. They're amazing."

After Peter finished, another biologist explained that *Pisonia* trees had not evolved with ants or scale, and as a result, some of Palmyra's grand old trees, up to a hundred feet tall with trunks as big around as a compact car, had crashed to the ground. Too many scale insects, the theory went, were eating too many leaves.

More scale-laden trees seemed destined to fall, but before biologists could tackle the scale insects, they had to knock back the ants that farmed them. No one was thinking to eradicate ants in Palmyra—that was impossible. But if their populations could be dramatically reduced for a period of time, a scale-eating ladybug might be introduced to eat the leaf suckers and save the trees. With ant farming at its current high rate, the atoll's managers feared the ladybugs couldn't eat enough scale to keep the population in check. In addition, biologists were being extremely careful before introducing the nonnative ladybugs to Palmyra. One more alien species could add another buggy boxcar to this ecological train wreck.

A volunteer examining the root of a fallen *Pisonia* tree. Photo by Susan Scott.

My job, I learned at that meeting, would be to spread ant poison around three selected spots, with one similar control plot that had no poison, to see how long it took to stop the industrious little farmers, and for how long. All it took, then, was to count ants coming and going. Count ants. It sounded easy, as if all I needed to know I learned in first grade. I had done enough biology work, however, to know better. The actual counting of ants would be the culmination of months of hard work.

I did not answer Craig's comment about the trade winds building. He said no more about it, and after he left for work, I stared at his empty orange juice glass feeling equally drained. We had lost so much, I thought, fighting the tears that seemed to appear out of thin air like a cheap magic trick. Sick of feeling weepy, I forced myself to get ready for my trip from Honolulu to Kaneohe Bay, packing extra sunscreen and seasick medicine. For the voyage I would have two inexperienced crew members: Jan, a former refuge manager at Tern Island, and my brother-in-law, Joel. Because I knew the trip would be a rough eight hours mostly upwind, they would likely be green in more ways than boat skills. But we were going.

To get to Kaneohe Bay from Honolulu, I had to sail around Makapu'u Head, one of Oahu's most stunning sea cliffs. The wall of lava rock rises from the ocean like a Polynesian tiki god, its black face cracked and crinkled from eons of battering by water and wind. The trade winds speeding past the rock face create steep waves that explode like fireworks against the cliffs and reflect back to sea in choppy turmoil. The result is an ocean surface that looks like white hats bobbing in a cauldron of boiling blue soup. A similar wave-washed cove in nearby Hanauma Bay is called, aptly, Witches' Brew.

Honu heeled, shouldering her way upwind into Hawai'i's notorious channel waves. I watched the big ones rumble toward the boat, their tops falling over in avalanches of foamy power. To the uninitiated, it's a terrifying sound and sight, like meeting an eighteen-wheeler on the wrong side of a highway with no shoulder. "The boat is built for it," Craig had said, years earlier, when I got scared. "We're doing fine." Eventually, after seeing the boat plow through those waves over and over without rolling over, breaking up, or sinking, I relaxed, feeling grateful for my years of experience with such head-on collisions, and offered similar comfort to my right-on-schedule seasick crew members: "The boat is doing great; we're making good time." *Honu*'s bow rose smoothly up the front of each blue hill, punched through its breaking peak with a jolt and a splash, and slid unwavering down the other side into the trough. A second later, up the next wave face she climbed.

We hung onto winches, cleats, and cockpit fittings as *Honu* pushed into each pile of water. Over and over she did this in a manner and rhythm that made me proud. If the boat was making steady upwind progress—and I could see the progress because we slowly but surely passed Diamond Head—that meant I had the right sails up and trimmed correctly.

There's nothing like sailing upwind in big seas to make a person feel like a true mariner, but you pay for this accomplishment by getting marinated, because the collisions of boat and waves send clouds of seawater flying into the cockpit. Salt isn't dirty, and one or two mistings wouldn't be so bad, but when saltwater spray lands in the cockpit and on its inhabitants repeatedly, the water in it evaporates but the salt does not. And so it accumulates. Over time, the steering wheel looked and felt like the rim of a margarita glass, the cockpit teak turned crystally white, and my face and arms began to itch. Salt doesn't bother some people, but I don't like crackly eyebrows, the itchy sensation it gives my skin, or the stiffening effect it leaves on my hair. Salt spray clouds your sunglasses, but you can't wipe them off because the granules scratch lenses. And because salt also holds moisture, my cotton T-shirts and shorts felt heavy and damp. I daydreamed about sailing in the freshwater of the Great Lakes, where spray would feel more like a spring rain than a pickling solution.

Salt was going to be the least of anyone's worries on this trip, I knew. About 90 percent of humans get seasick, as do cats, dogs, and other land mammals, and the Kaiwi (pronounced *kah-EE-vee*) Channel often pushed that figure to the high nineties. Years earlier, Craig, three friends, and I planned a trip to Molokai. When it came time to depart, the trade winds were blowing twenty-five miles per hour with fifteen-foot seas, but since the voyage had been planned for months, we decided to go anyway. The constant bucking of *Honu* quickly drove our friends to the bunks below, but Craig and I stayed in the cockpit.

A few hours later, I went down to the head and found one of the women, Elizabeth, lying on the floor so seasick she was barely able to speak or move. I called up for Craig to come check on her.

"Elizabeth, this is supposed to be fun," Craig said. "We can go back. As soon as I turn the boat downwind, the motion will be much smoother."

"No," she said. "I don't want to spoil the trip for everyone."

"Are you sure?"

"Yes."

"Okay. Then tell me, what can I do for you?"

"Kill me," she whispered. "Please."

Craig declined. Instead, he handed her a powerful anti-nausea rectal suppository (to insert herself), which also had a sedative effect. She slept through nearly the entire Labor Day weekend.

But at least she tried. Some people in Hawai'i won't even attempt channel crossings. Years earlier, one of Craig's colleagues, Karen, who owned a sailboat in Honolulu told Craig that if he bought a boat, he could not sail it to Molokai.

Craig stared at her. "I can't?"

"Oh, no. The channels are way too rough here," Karen said. "What you do is hire someone to sail your boat across and you fly over."

This to a man who had raced sailboats competitively all over the world, sometimes in extreme conditions, and usually finished first. Later he rented another colleague's boat and crossed Hawai'i's channels over and over, impishly telling Karen afterward about the fun he had sailing to Maui, Lanai, and the Island of Hawai'i. She was not amused.

For me, responsibility seemed to be good seasick medicine. As the captain, I felt this common malady far less often than I had when sailing with Craig. Unfortunately, my two nonsailor friends weren't so fortunate. Jan lay in the cockpit grim faced and miserably nauseated. I had warned her about the violent motion and offered drugs when we left, but she refused, not wanting the drowsy feeling such drugs often induce. Besides that, she said something I heard often: she wanted to experience "real sailing." In Hawai'i's rough waters, though, that often turned out to be heaving over the side.

As Jan threw up over the aft rail, I asked if she wanted to turn back. Like Elizabeth, she said no, she didn't want to spoil the trip. Joel, not as sick but a true landlubber and more than a little anxious over the rough conditions, agreed that we should keep going.

To ease their misery, I started the motor, intending to use the engine to help us sail upwind faster. Once around Makapu'u Head, I could move closer to shore where the waters would be smoother. The engine started on the first try, but when I shifted into gear, it stalled. After several more false starts, my heart pounding with alarm, I dashed below deck to open the engine room doors and look around, praying that the problem would be something obvious. We use the term "room" for this space, but it's really a compartment. On *Honu*, the six-foot-long by four-foot-wide area that holds the engine and its entourage, such as pumps, filters, and a fright wig of wires and hoses, is large for a thirty-seven-foot boat, with access on all four sides, but it's not a place you walk around. Here you drape, squeeze, and wedge the necessary body parts into dark, greasy, and often sweltering spaces.

The boat pitched and rolled so wildly that it was hard to hold myself steady enough to even open the engine door latches. When I lifted my arm to switch on the light, I nearly went flying head first into the opposite wall. Hanging on for dear life, I managed to look around. Nothing obvious seemed broken, a depressing finding because I didn't know where to go from there.

I returned to the cockpit, wondering what on earth I was going to do, and how I was going to attend to it in those wild seas. At that moment, Jan, while throwing up, spotted a green rope trailing behind the boat. A line had snagged the propeller. No problem, I thought. That's something I can fix. Once I unwound the stray rope from the prop, my motor would be back in business.

The green rope turned out to be no stray piece of flotsam. It was the end of the main halyard, *Sir* Halyard, the line that hauls up the mainsail. In the boisterous seas, that traitorous rope had worked its way out of place at base of the mast, slithered across the deck, and fallen into the ocean, where it wrapped itself around the propeller shaft. There was no way to know how snarled it was without going down there and looking. In seas tumultuous enough to give a monk seal pause, I had to jump in and swim under the boat.

I dropped the sails (there was enough halyard left to work the main) to keep *Honu* from sailing off without me, but with no sails up, the boat bucked like a bronco, causing both my friends to be even sicker, and causing me to do everything one-handed, since I had to hang on with the other. I got out a long line, tied one end to the boat and the other around my waist, donned mask, snorkel, and fins, and jumped in the roiling water. That this didn't scare me half to death should have been a clue I was out of my mind, but I was so pumped up with adrenalin that, with no hesitation, I dove under the boat, unfazed by the danger of getting tangled up or being knocked unconscious by the kicking stern. The boat pitched back and forth like a demented rocking horse. This didn't scare me either, since years of scuba diving had taught me how to deal with wildly rising and falling boat ladders and hulls. (You hold one arm high so the force hits your hand, not your head.) In fact, I welcomed the feel of the cool water on my itchy skin.

Waves sort themselves by size into groups called sets, and since big waves travel faster than small waves, they march in formation: large sets are followed by medium sets, followed by small sets. Knowing how this pattern worked, I waited for a lull and in that relatively calm interval dove down to the propeller. It was like diving through Alice's looking glass. Wind and waves create commotion on the surface, but below the chaos, it was calm and quiet with rays of sunlight streaking through peaceful blue water. How often had I wished over that past year of misery with Craig and hormones that I could just go down there and live with the snails, whales, fish, and other creatures I loved.

Bad news awaited under the boat. By repeatedly putting the transmission into gear, and thus turning the propeller, I'd wrapped the main halyard around the shaft so tightly that the rope had rolled into a rocklike mass.

My friend Jan handed down my hefty Leatherman tool. The saw blade of the Leatherman was the perfect means of attacking the wrap, and I sawed like mad at that frozen rope, shocked that something made of fabric could be so solid. I couldn't hold my breath long enough to get through even one wrap.

At this rate, I thought, panting at the surface while holding onto the ladder as it yanked me up and down, I'll be here for days. Sawing while riding a pogo stick would not get the job done. If I could stay down there and keep cutting, I would have that rope off in five or ten minutes. I needed my scuba gear.

I climbed back on the boat, announcing to my friends that I was going to don my scuba gear and everything would be fine. They did not reply. Having succumbed to the furious and confused seas, what Jan and Joel most wanted to hear was that I had decided to call the Coast Guard to helicopter them off the boat. I raced below and hauled my air tank, regulator, and vest from below deck, one-handed and one at a time, up the companionway ladder to the heaving aft deck, and struggled into the gear alone. Jumping into the water with ten pounds of lead weights around my waist and a thirty-pound tank on my back was a daunting moment at the best of times, but it didn't bother me this time. I thought I knew what I was doing.

Checking my valves, hoses, belt, buckles, mask, snorkel, and fins (scuba divers remind me of *Star Trek*'s Borg drones), I stepped off the deck, plunged into the water with a huge splash, and again swam beneath the boat. This time I could breathe. With the Leatherman, I began making excellent progress cutting through the rope. Row after row of coiled line fell away while I comfortably inhaled and exhaled. Then the boat crashed down at an odd angle, clipping the edge of my mask and pushing it down to my chin. The blow also knocked the Leatherman from my hand, and in a split second it was gone.

As long as the mouthpiece, called a regulator, stays in a diver's mouth, a dive mask is not needed to breathe, or even to see. But you do need it to see clearly. Too close to give up, I replaced my mask over my eyes and nose, cleared it of water by snorting air into it (one of the first skills scuba divers learn), and went back to the pogo stick ladder where I shouted to Jan to hand down Craig's ancient and cherished rigging knife, a race prize he had won as a teenager. When I started sailing without Craig, I nicknamed the tool the "Sacred Knife," because it was a kind of totem for him, a symbol of his youth and sailing skills. If I lost that knife, I would have to find another one of any kind to kill myself with.

Unlike my lost Leatherman, though, Sacred Knife had a strap, which I tied to my wrist, and back under the boat I went, slicing back and forth into the green mass of stone-hard halyard. My arm ached after a few minutes of work—difficult when weightless and breathing through a hose—and I let out a silent cheer as four-inch pieces of line began to fall free from the shaft. Just when my arm muscles began trembling from the work of sawing while pressing, the last bit of halyard fell from the metal pole that turned the propeller. I climbed back on board, praying the halyard hadn't pulled so hard that it bent the shaft, a good possibility since I had jammed the transmission into forward gear several times before realizing the problem. Dripping wet, I dropped my Borg outfit to the cockpit floor, held my breath, and pushed the starter. It started. I held my breath again as I shifted into gear. The engine kept running and the boat moved forward normally. Thank you, *Honu.* Even my still-sick-and-scared friends shouted out hurrahs.

Soon after I freed the prop, *Honu* began rounding the headlands. In one short hour, we sailed far enough around Oahu that the trade winds struck us from behind, making the going smooth and fast. I was feeling great until that moment, but as I let out the sails for an easy broad reach, a cold fact struck me: I had not needed the motor at all. I could have left the line tangled around the prop, used the sails to reach the flat, calm waters of Kaneohe Bay, and there, sawed the halyard off the shaft in relative safety. My leaps from the boat off Makapuʻu Head, with inexperienced people on board while I got banged up underwater, had been foolish and dangerous and lengthened the the time they felt seasick.

I was not being hard on myself, as friends suggested when I told them that the whole episode had been one judgment error after another, but I knew I had made a mistake. I also knew someone else who would know. After sailing that stretch with Craig, not to mention about ten thousand other offshore miles with him, I should have known better. The more I thought about it, the more my big achievement became my big blunder.

I sailed into Kaneohe Bay bleeding from a dozen small propeller cuts on my hands and forearms. Once anchored, we inflated the dinghy and lowered Bette Davis to it, and I putted ashore to pick up four more friends. By the time we returned, my crew had recovered from their seasickness, and despite my protests, the Makapuʻu incident became an exciting sailing story.

Later at home, I told Craig what happened. Early in my story, he began nodding, deducing the bottom line—*I jumped off the boat*—before I got to it.

"I wouldn't have gone over the side out there," he said, not reproachfully, just stating a fact. "It would have been easy to sail into the bay and cut the halyard off there."

"I know that now," I said.

"It turned out okay. That's what's important. Plus you learned some things. Remember the time we were changing jibs and the sheets fell in the water, and the first thing I did was get to the gearshift so I could stop the prop from turning?"

I stared at him. I did not remember the incident. I didn't remember most of the potential boat disasters he talked about, because I had not been responsible for their outcome. When changing the sails, I didn't understand the consequences of the sheets falling overboard, and since my hands had not touched the gearshift, what he had done to save the propeller didn't register. Now that my hands were cut and scabby from sawing *my* halyard off *my* prop shaft, I would not make that mistake again. I had once been an operating room nurse, and at that moment I understood that the difference between crewing and captaining an offshore vessel was as different as watching surgery and performing it. You haven't done it until you've done it.

Craig had been multitasking again—reading something on his computer screen as I talked—and he barely looked up as we spoke. We were becoming one of those fading couples, so weary of trying to figure the other person out, and trying to make the relationship work, and wondering what to do when it didn't, that we were gradually, sadly, giving up.

He picked up a shiny new Leatherman knife from the table. "You got a present," he said. "Your friend Jan stopped by with this."

The Leatherman was a rung above the one I lost, containing even more tools—a wire stripper, a diamond-coated file—and bearing a green lanyard long enough to wrap several times around my wrist or even clip to a belt loop. The burly knife turned out to be too heavy to comfortably carry around in my pocket, but it didn't matter. That knife held a special place on the boat, and in my heart.

ONE bonus of writing a long-term newspaper column was that when I described my tribulations of learning to skipper a sailboat, I had a family of readers rooting for me. My mistake off Makapuʻu became easier to accept after I explained it in my column and several boaters e-mailed stories of their own struggles with rope-wrapped propellers. One woman, also a sailor, wrote that she had once been a passenger on an ocean-going cruise ship that accidentally wound a mooring line as thick as a man's thigh around its gargantuan propeller. It took several divers with underwater power saws all day to cut it off.

My favorite e-mail of encouragement came in two sentences that made me laugh: "I've been there and it's really hard. They make it look so easy on TV."

Craig's ho-hum reaction to my ordeals of learning to sail felt both good and bad. The good was that he was never critical of my bungles. He knew that when you learn by doing, mistakes will be made. I'm sure there were moments when he thought, *She didn't know that?* But he never let it show, nor did he ever question my equipment purchases or hiring decisions.

The bad feeling came when I could see that he wasn't interested enough in what happened to me or our boat to look up from his computer or the newspaper. This tuning out while reading was not new. (It's genetic—his parents and siblings do it, too.) It just hurt more now.

My readers were interested, though, and I soaked up their attention. Having them share their experiences so matter-of-factly showed me the value of viewing mishaps as lessons to learn from rather than reasons to kick myself.

A lot of people told me they wouldn't in a million years jump into the ocean off Makapuʻu Head for fear of sharks. Never once had sharks crossed my mind, because years earlier I had driven out my fear of what lurked below. I had been anxious about underwater creatures as a kid swimming in Wisconsin lakes, where running into a stick or leaf would startle me so much that I would stay out of the water the rest of the day. The ocean was far worse. When I began snorkeling in Hawaiʻi, if a piece of seaweed touched me I would nearly jump out of my skin.

"What are you afraid of?" Craig asked.

"I don't know," I said. "Boogeyfish."

That was the real reason, two months after we moved to Hawaiʻi, that I enrolled at the University of Hawaiʻi in Manoa to take courses in marine science. I wanted to learn what to worry about, and how to avoid it. Yet, the more I learned about marine life, the more impressed I became—and the more I wanted to know. Hydroids are *jellyfish* relatives? (They look like ferns.) Fish have air bags? (Called swim bladders, they regulate buoyancy.) The pink rocks are seaweed? (Some red algae contain calcium carbonate, the stuff of coral reefs.)

Soon sharks—the ultimate boogeyfish—became a nonissue for me. After studying sharks in books, diving with them, and later writing about them, I convinced myself that worrying about a shark attack was about as reasonable as worrying about an asteroid crash. On one Australian beach notorious for shark attacks, one swimmer out of thirty *million* has been bitten by a shark.

Statistics like that don't dispel a terror of sharks for many people, thanks to the film *Jaws* and Discovery Channel's annual Shark Week, but they work for me. And so sharks didn't worry me that day off Makapu'u. Eventually, neither did my ill-advised leap over the rail. No amount of reading, talking, or watching others (or TV) would have made an impression on me like that dive off my boat in rough waters. From that day on, I walked the deck's perimeter checking that every line was secure before starting the engine. I also learned to trust my sails. In a bad spot, they would always get me somewhere else.

If, that is, I had sails.

11

I knew that Craig and Christine had not excluded me from everything they did—I had excluded myself. At restaurants, they talked about clip-in pedals, the merits of carb loading, and the variation of strokes in freestyle swimming. The only thing more boring than watching them work out was listening to them talk about it. Even so, seeing Craig jog, pedal, fix flats, swim, laugh, chat, share food, and drive off with Christine in her red convertible sports car felt like a stab in the gut each time it happened. As a result, I used *Honu* as a haven, a cozy refuge where I could sit below deck rather than drive home and imagine various scenarios for the future: my old life as it had been with Craig; a new life with Craig in which we were separate but equal; my life as a captain sailing *Honu* to exotic places, alone or with crew. More often than not, after Pierre and I finished our day's work, I would clean up the mess and spend the night on the boat.

The transient dock of the Ala Wai Boat Harbor, however, wasn't a great place for a woman to live alone. The lock on the gate had been vandalized so often that state harbor managers had given up fixing it, and as a result, *Honu*'s row, on the outskirts of the main harbor, had become a haven for drug dealers, the homeless, and people who, in a better world, would have been locked up. Fritz, the scary transient sailor, still lived nearby, and his anger toward me had grown over time. Each day, as he passed *Honu*, he deliberately stomped and glared to make his hostility known. Alone on my boat, I felt vulnerable and defenseless.

Another threat came from Popeye, the nickname I had given my alcoholic neighbor. Popeye drank so much whiskey straight from the bottle that dribbles from his mouth had permanently colored his gray beard a streaky brown. He was so drunk so often that he couldn't climb the ladder from his main salon to his cockpit. I knew this because when someone spoke to him, he would reply from below, bellowing obscenities.

With Popeye's boat so close to *Honu* that gusts of wind made our fenders touch, I could hear most conversations. Two middle-aged men, one recently released from prison (I heard them shouting about his prison term), hung around Popeye's boat. A typical conversation went like this: "Hey, motherfucker, I'm fucking coming aboard." "The fuck you are. Go fuck yourself." After the men boarded the boat, which they always did no matter what Popeye said, a stream of bone-thin people with gray-tinged skin arrived and departed like ghosts with telling regularity. Once I even glimpsed a handful of wrinkled green bills pass from one emaciated hand to another.

Popeye's acquaintances were clearly dealers of crystal methamphetamine, a horrible drug that can turn normal people into homicidal maniacs. Hawai'i is notorious for its crystal meth manufacture and use, and the grisly crimes people commit after smoking it. News stories of a baby thrown off a freeway overpass, a teenager torching his house and burning his mother and aunt to death, and an elderly woman, out for an early morning walk, murdered and tossed in a dumpster were ever present in my mind.

One night, noise and scuffling shot up so loudly from Popeye's main salon that it woke me from a sound sleep. Popeye, coughing horribly, shouted, "I'll kill you, you fucking motherfucker." Just as I was about to call 911, the commotion stopped.

The next day, I went to the harbor mistress and complained, but she could not relocate *Honu*. The falling-apart harbor was full. And to evict Popeye and his buddies was easier said than done in a state facility. As she and I discussed possibilities—moving Popeye's boat to the work dock, calling the police—Popeye's friend the ex-con walked in. He shot us a vicious glare and stormed out.

Had he followed me? "Don't move them," I said. "They'll know I complained and I'll be even more afraid of them."

I stayed home for the next few days, grumpy at being frightened away from my own boat. Would a man have been so intimidated by that pathetic bunch? I didn't know. I did know the awful meth stories, however, and believed that laying low for a few days was the smart thing to do.

At home, Craig and I were as polite to each other as if we had just met. It felt wonderful. This behavior wasn't just an eye-opener—it was a jaw-dropper. When had we stopped treating each other with the common courtesy we afford casual acquaintances, strangers even? I loved him thanking me for doing the laundry, something I had done for us both since day one, and when I asked him if he would help me carry in a load of groceries, I asked with a please and, after he graciously did so, ended with a thank-you. How gradually we had slipped into taking one another for granted. No matter what happened to us in the future, I promised myself I would never drop such basic civility to him—or anyone—ever again.

When Pierre called to say he had finished making a titanium fastener for the new wind generator and wanted to meet me at *Honu*, I asked Craig to go with me. I wanted my menacing neighbors to know I had an imposing husband around, even though he was rarely there. Craig agreed. We arrived to yellow crime-scene tape encircling Popeye's boat. The hatches were closed, the companionway locked.

"You missed all the excitement," Pierre said in greeting. "Your neighbor died on his boat last night."

I was shocked, but not surprised. "How did he die?"

"Who knows with that bunch?" Pierre said, shrugging.

Pierre left to make an adjustment to the windmill fitting. "Do you think Popeye was murdered?" I said to Craig.

"He probably drank himself to death," he said.

"Still," I said, "dead on the boat is pretty spooky."

Almost nothing is spooky to Craig. "These people aren't after you," he said. "Besides, you've got your drawbridge [the block-and-pulley boarding system I made allowed me to haul the plank up behind me once I got aboard], and no one can get aboard *Honu* without it."

He was right. Even at the best of times, with stools and fender steps as boosters, *Honu* was a tough boat to step onto because of her so-called high freeboard, the distance from the waterline to the rail. Boarding her from the water was impossible without a ladder, and from a dinghy it was nearly impossible, especially if the owners didn't want her boarded. Years earlier, several rowdy teenage boys from Niʻihau had approached *Honu* in a motorboat, demanding booze (that privately owned Hawaiian island is dry). We had none, we said (true), and when the boys threatened to come aboard to look for themselves, all Craig had to do was move to the rail and stare down at the kids' vulnerable heads and shoulders, which barely reached the deck. They left immediately.

Popeye's ex-con friend arrived, his eyes bloodshot, clothes rumpled. He paced the dock a few seconds, staring at the police tape around Popeye's deck.

"Hello," the man said to Craig and me as we drank coffee in *Honu*'s cockpit. The disheveled man stood near my lowered gangplank but made no move to step onto it. Nautical protocol dictates that no one, even friends, board someone's boat without asking permission.

Craig and I murmured chilly hellos. We did not invite him aboard.

"Did you know Victor died last night?" he said.

I never knew Popeye's real name. "I heard."

"Let me tell you something," he said, addressing me.

Please don't, I thought.

"Before he died, Victor wrote down on a piece of paper that I could have his boat. He willed it to me. It says so on the paper. He signed it."

I looked at Craig. He gave me an I-don't-know-what-to-say shrug.

"You don't believe me?" the man said. "When I come aboard last night, Victor was laying in the bunk real drunk and all. Then he gave me the paper that said I could have the boat, and I fell asleep, and when I woke up, I left." He paused. "I didn't know he was sick. I thought he was just passed out."

The man stared at me, at Craig, at the yellow tape, and at me again, obviously trying to decide if he should step over something that said, "DO NOT ENTER. POLICE SCENE" with two witnesses ten feet away. He decided against it.

"I'll be back," he growled. "This is *my* boat."

Craig didn't think that the man had threatened me, or that he killed Popeye, believing instead that the yellow-skinned, big-bellied drinker had likely died from alcoholic cirrhosis. Okay, maybe this guy had not murdered Victor-Popeye, but if he used crystal meth—and his rotten teeth and pasty skin suggested that he did—the potential was there.

I must get this boat out of this harbor, I thought.

Since eighth grade I had spurred myself on by saying, "Something will happen." It was a variation of Scarlett O'Hara's "I'll think about that tomorrow" and was similar to one of Craig's favorites, "Things will become clear." As an attitude, it sounds passive, but to me it meant forge on. Carry on. Think about problems another time. I traveled to a lot of places in life riding this train of thought, and now I practically chanted it as I worked like a crazy woman, which was how I regarded myself, on the boat. It worked. Something did happen.

A week later, I looked up, and there stood my dear friend Alex, who was supposed to be working on research in Palmyra.

We had been e-mailing often. He knew I had no crew, and unless I found someone fast, the Palmyra voyage was off. My adventure would be over before it began.

"Alex," I said, exchanging bear hugs. "What are you doing home?"

"There was an empty seat on the supply plane."

"How long are you here for?" I said, delighted to see him.

"That depends," he said, grinning, bursting to blurt it out, "if you have room for a crew member to Palmyra."

I was dumbfounded. "What are you saying?"

"I have time to sail with you to Palmyra. I can be your crew."

This was wonderful news. Alex had one outstanding qualification for crewing for me to Palmyra: we were best friends. I didn't have a girlfriend as good as Alex. I didn't have a dozen experienced offshore sailors volunteering to sail to Palmyra with me either, but if I had, I would still have chosen Alex. Sailing with someone who understood who I was during this tough time of life meant more to me than whether the person knew a sheet from a halyard. And mechanically, he was better than me. He may not have known much about sailboats, but he did not have to chant to himself *righty-tighty, lefty-loosey* just to turn a screw.

Craig had met Alex but didn't know him well, nor did he know that Alex and I had hashed over just about every detail of our personal lives when we worked together on Tern Island. My friendship with Alex wasn't a secret—I talked about Alex freely—but since Craig and I weren't discussing anything personal anymore, he didn't know how much Alex meant to me.

When I told Craig the news, he said, "I wish you had someone with sailing experience."

"Alex is competent and strong and not afraid of the ocean," I said. "I've seen him handle Tern's powerboats in extreme conditions."

"Does he know anything about sailboats?"

"No. But he's smart. He'll learn fast."

"I wish you had one more person with some offshore sailing experience."

I wished it, too, but not as much as Craig did. I was so happy to have Alex as my first mate, it felt like the perfect solution to my crew problem, especially since anyone else who crewed for me needed to be accepted as a Palmyra volunteer and commit to a four-month stint of hard work in an isolated atoll.

"Well," Craig said after a long, thoughtful gaze at me, "I guess you've got your crew."

PERMISSION to anchor in the lagoons or harbors at any National Wildlife Refuge, even as a volunteer worker, is never easy. The remote areas are among the few havens left for wildlife to reproduce and live in peace, and managers take that seriously. To get approval to live on *Honu* in Palmyra's lagoon for four months would have been difficult at any time but was even harder when I applied because the atoll was in a period of transition.

As a tiny atoll (less than a square mile of land) lying halfway between the main Hawaiian Islands and American Samoa, with nothing but thousands of miles of open ocean between, Palmyra had never been a seat of stability. Practically everyone but the *menehunes* (little people in Hawaiian mythology) had laid claim to Palmyra's splotches of land and their surrounding reefs.

In 1859, Dr. Gerrit P. Judd of the brig *Josephine* declared possession of the atoll for the United States and the American Guano Company, even though no guano existed on the islands. (The islands' dense vegetation used the guano as its own fertilizer as fast as the birds dropped it.) Three years later, in 1862 King Kamehameha IV pronounced Palmyra part of the Kingdom of Hawai'i. Unaware of the king's assertion, a British sailing captain in 1889 claimed the atoll for the United Kingdom. Nine years later, in 1898, when President McKinley annexed the Territory of Hawai'i to the United States, he specifically included Palmyra Atoll. The U.S. Navy commandeered the atoll to use as a base during World War II. But when Hawai'i became a state in 1959, Palmyra Atoll, abandoned by the military after the war, was left out.

During all this declaring, petitioning, and seizing, Palmyra remained privately owned. You could buy and sell Hawaiian islands in those days, and people did just that with Palmyra. Beginning in 1862, one man sold his share of the atoll to another, who willed it to his wife, who sold it to a judge, who sold it, in 1922, to the Hawai'i-based Fullard-Leo family. The family planted coconut palms there and established the Palmyra Copra Company.

Hawai'i residents feel a kind of cousin-kinship with Palmyra, and most were horrified at the end of the 1990s to hear potential buyers discussing the atoll's possibility as a casino site or a nuclear waste dump. The owners, still the Fullard-Leo family, refused to sell to those entities, holding out until the Nature Conservancy could raise the lowered asking price of thirty million dollars. The Nature Conservancy came up with the money in 2000 and bought the land. In 2001, the U.S. secretary of the interior declared Palmyra Atoll a National Wildlife Refuge.

Thereafter, the refuge was (and still is) comanaged by the private Nature Conservancy and the federal U.S. Fish and Wildlife Service. Add to that mixed bag ten universities and research foundations, known as the Palmyra Atoll Research Consortium, contributing funds to use Palmyra as a research station. Each of the above groups has its own executive mandates, financial obligations, and visions for the atoll. Throw in a few personal agendas and some individuals asking for favors, and establishing the protocols about who could go where, for how long, and for how much money became a monumental task.

Because Palmyra policies were still evolving, people were nervous about my application as a volunteer there. If I wanted to sail to and work in Palmyra, I was told, I had to promise to do whatever anyone asked of me. I agreed. Happily. Yet even with my vows to work hard, obey rules, and keep a low profile, some U.S. Fish and Wildlife Service managers in Honolulu had reservations. How could they let a volunteer work for Fish and Wildlife in Palmyra when they had no Fish and Wildlife employee there yet? Who would be my supervisor? What would happen if I got hurt? Hit a reef? Behaved badly?

Besides that, government workers are wary of journalists, fearing skewed interpretations of activities. But I sympathized with the well-intentioned people experimenting with public/private alliances to create and run refuges. More significant, I have my own approach to helping save wildlife, and it's not digging up scandal. For me, watching and working with marine animals are as delightful as opening my closet door to discover ET in there wearing my clothes. I try in my columns to share the joy of those connections, and with joy comes caring.

Also of interest to me during the months of *Honu*'s refit was the surge in sensationalist media coverage of plastic pollution, with reports that it was killing everything from albatrosses to zooxanthellae (the algae in corals). What was often described as a "Texas-sized garbage patch" in the Pacific Ocean—something people imagined as a dense mass of junk that ships could scoop up and cart away—was more accurately characterized as countless plastic objects broken into billions of tiny pellets. The widespread reports of a floating dump left countless people thinking that the ocean is one big trash-strewn petroleum pit with nothing left in it to care about. It's not so. Places like Palmyra prove it. I had to get there, though, to make my case.

Because of my precarious position, I made a point of not asking many questions as I sat in the federal building's Remote Refuges office near downtown

Honolulu with the biologist managing the U.S. Fish and Wildlife side of Palmyra.

"The Nature Conservancy and Fish and Wildlife are separate entities at Palmyra," Roger said, "and it's TNC's camp. They pay for everything there. They're already doing us a lot of favors, and we have to be careful not to take advantage. Therefore, you can't use any of TNC's facilities ashore."

"Okay," I said. It took effort to keep exasperation from my voice because he had already told me this several times over the past few months. "I understand."

"You'll have to eat all your meals on the boat," Roger continued. "Can you carry enough food for that long?"

"Yes."

"Are you sure? Because you won't be able to eat TNC's food. They bought it. They flew it there. They hire people to cook it. It's for their guests and workers, not ours."

"I'm sure," I said.

Roger clearly didn't believe me, but I was confident in *Honu*'s storage capacity. She's large for a thirty-seven-foot boat, wide in the middle with tall sides. This so-called freeboard has a lot to do with a boat's interior living space. The higher the freeboard, the larger the cabins. Tall men can walk around inside with headroom to spare, and the boat has cupboards (called lockers on boats) inside cupboards. Along walls, under bunks, and inside desks, the lockers on *Honu* are so extensive you can lose items for months at a time. I once lost an iron—a clothes-pressing iron—for six months.

"Maybe I can convince TNC to let you ship a tub or two of food on their barge," Roger said.

I did not need to ship food. "Thank you. But it's not necessary."

"Does your boat have a holding tank? Because you can't flush any waste overboard in refuge waters."

He meant did *Honu* have a specially designed container for storing the contents of the toilet. A holding tank, which complies with state governing authorities, is the method of dealing with a boat toilet. Some marinas have pump-out facilities for holding tanks, but it is also legal to empty a holding tank into the open ocean if the vessel is three miles or more from shore. This is acceptable because disgusting sewage to humans is nutritious food to many marine organisms.

"It has a Coast Guard–approved holding tank," I said.

"You'll have to drive outside the fringing reef each week to empty it."

He meant that every week I must move my safely anchored boat from the calm lagoon to the open ocean and back again. To do that, Alex and I would haul up the anchor and its two hundred feet of chain, drive the boat several miles into the open ocean, where conditions are usually rough, and hand pump the holding tank into deep water. Then we would drive back into the lagoon, use the depth finder to locate the one small anchoring spot there, drop Bruce (my anchor has its brand name "Bruce" stamped into its metal base), and dive on it to make sure it had dug in well enough to hold the boat. If not, which was often the case in hard-bottom anchorages such as the one there, I would have to anchor all over again.

"People live there," I said. "They must have toilets."

"They have an outhouse."

"But I can't use it?"

"Right."

I said nothing. Roger and I stared at one another. I wished he was joking. He was not. "That's just how it is. The facilities are not ours to use."

"Okay. I won't use their outhouse."

He paused and smiled. "You'll be working for us forty hours a week," he said. "Here's the volunteer agreement. It's the same one you've signed before."

Forty hours was low for Fish and Wildlife—my previous agreements with them at Tern Island in French Frigate Shoals had been for forty-eight-hour weeks—but I knew from past stints with this agency that this would be no vacation. Chronically short of funding, the service had their volunteers pay in sweat—and often in blood since bites and cuts were all in a day's work—for the privilege of living and working in a National Wildlife Refuge.

For animal lovers like me, the rewards were well worth it. Because Hawai'i's wildlife evolved with no land predators, most of the animals are fearless, loveable, and often laughable. For instance, a curious young albatross once untied my shoelaces while I stood talking. One evening, I watched a wedge-tailed shearwater flip-flop down a long hall on its big webbed feet, pass my open bedroom door, and turn straight into the bathroom, as if that had been its urgent destination. During a morning walk, I found so many turtle hatchlings heading the wrong way (inland) that I had to put them in the pockets of my cargo shorts to carry them all to safety. Oh, the joy of having your pockets full of baby sea turtles. Working in a remote Hawai'i wildlife refuge was as close to being Dr. Doolittle as a person can get.

As I waited for Roger to fill out my indenture papers, I looked at the hands that lay in my lap. The lumpy, crooked fingers, formerly so long and slender that all my life people asked me if I played the piano, were now balking at the simplest task, such as pulling lids off yogurt containers. The backs of my hands were changing too, blue veins showing clearly beneath thinning, brown-spotted skin. *These hands can't be mine*, I thought. *They belong to some old lady.*

"We're having a meeting in ten minutes about the *Pisonia* problem," Roger said, looking at his watch. "The entomologist designing the ant study will be there. You should attend too."

We settled back in our chairs to wait. "Did you hear I got married?" Roger said.

I met Roger ten years earlier when he was a volunteer biologist for Fish and Wildlife. He was the kind of guy who mapped out a life route and stuck to it. Roger's plan after college had been to work as a volunteer for the U.S. Fish and Wildlife Service, and then travel around the world until a position opened and they hired him. That accomplished, he would get married and have some kids.

All went according to schedule until he turned forty and still had not met the mother of his future children. Roger signed up with an Internet dating service and went to extraordinary lengths in search of a mate, even flying to the mainland for promising-sounding dates. His doggedness paid off. He had recently married a nice woman who already had three small children.

As Roger talked about his well-organized life, I thought about the differences between Craig and Roger. While each considered himself the undisputed captain of his own life ship, Craig's course lacked compass points. When an opportunity presented itself, he would happily veer off to see what happened. But even as a free-wheeler exploring the world, Craig stuck to several nonnegotiables: his career had to be stimulating, his partner independent and childless, and his exercise vigorous, frequent, and outdoors.

"All you want to do is work and work out?" I had shouted at him once during a fight over his Ironman training.

"Yes," he said. "It's not complicated."

Oh, for such certainty. Compared with Roger and Craig, I lived in a pinball machine, ringing, flashing, and tilting as I bounced between men, cities, jobs, and dreams. As a young woman, I had no idea what I wanted or how to find out.

With Craig, my feverish search for a good life had ended. I found, in him, peace of mind.

Now I had to find it in myself.

"INSTANT family," Roger said, beaming as he opened his wallet to show me a picture of his new wife and kids.

"Congratulations," I said.

A flush of happiness spread over Roger's narrow face, his scalp pinking up through thinning blond hair. He rattled off the name and age of each child.

"This is good?" I said.

"Yes. There aren't any decisions to make. It's done. We've got three kids."

I, too, felt a flush of happiness. I may have lived in a hit-and-miss world, but my surgical sterilization had been no wild whim. Growing up with an unhappy, drinking, low-income mother and three siblings, I knew well the dark side of raising and supporting children. By the age of eighteen, I was sick to death of shitty diapers and snotty noses and decided to do something different with my life—not something important, necessarily, but something interesting. As I looked at the pictures of Roger's three stepchildren, I had no regrets.

The jury was still out, though, for Craig. He said he didn't want children, and he claimed that my proactive move on the matter was one of the things that attracted him to me. But during one of our volunteer medical trips to Bangladesh, he had fallen in love with a malnourished six-year-old boy. Little Johney (that's how he spelled his name) had two club feet, but that barely slowed him down. He played, strutted, and fought valiantly when kids made fun of him, all the while standing on the sides of his ankles. This abnormal stance would work for only so long. As children with club feet grow, their weight eventually damages the ankle bones beyond repair. The only medical option at that point is amputation with prostheses.

"I'm not leaving him that way," Craig said, eyes brimming with tears as Johney, also in tears, waved good-bye to us. Craig was a seasoned E.R. doctor. His eyes rarely brimmed with tears.

It took a year to make the arrangements, but we went back for Johney and brought him to Honolulu's Shriners Hospital for Children. Orthopedic surgeons operated on his feet, inserting through his frail ankles and legs a series of pins and rods that would have brought Hercules to his knees. Not Johney. The following year was long and painful as Johney, wheelchair bound, bravely bore the torture of having the pins through his bones moved daily to straighten his feet. He stayed with us on weekends when he was well enough to leave the hospital and lived with us for several months after he was discharged.

During that time, Craig, even when exhausted from work, played with Johney each and every day, taking him to video arcades and movies and buying him anything he wanted. When it was time for Johney to go home to his parents, both Craig and Johney hugged, moped, and cried. "You can come back," I heard Craig tell the boy one day. "For the summers. Maybe you can go to school here."

"Craig," I said later, "how is this going to work? I know you love Johney, but it's me who went grocery shopping and cooked the meals he liked, bought him clothes, did his laundry, enrolled him in classes, cleaned up after him. Who's going to do that if he lives with us again?"

"I will."

"You'll quit your job?"

He said nothing. Of course he would not quit the job he loved. He was angry with me for no longer wanting to take care of this child (who was not an orphan—his parents offered to let us keep him for the boy's sake) and frustrated that he couldn't do it on his own. Mostly, though, he was heartbroken over having to say good-bye to a little boy he loved and who loved him back equally. I loved Johney, too, but not in the same way as Craig. He wanted to be Johney's father. I was content as his auntie.

The charming Johney went home to his parents, and we became a special aunt and uncle, visiting him each year in Bangladesh. But after the little boy left, Craig remained angry, and I remained defiant. The Twinship had changed during Johney's year with us—children do that to couples—but I could see nothing to do about it. I did not want to adopt a child for myself and could not do it for someone else. Not even Craig.

FISH and Wildlife granted me permission to go to the refuge as long as I provided my own transportation, purchased my own food, used only the boat's bathroom, and did fieldwork for the ant study for three to four months, depending on setup time and preliminary results. If this didn't take forty hours each week, I agreed to make up the time banding seabird chicks and performing other Fish and Wildlife chores, such as data entry and supply organizing. That refuge managers can load the work on like this and still have waiting lists of eager volunteers shows how desirable these remote island preserves are to biologists. It's heaven with blisters.

A mature coconut crab carrying a coconut. Photo by Susan Scott.

At the ant meeting, I learned that in addition to conducting the ant study, I was to help Alex glue radio transmitters to hermit and other land crabs. This would monitor how the ant poison affected the nontarget species, such as the plucky crabs that skittered all over the island. "Of course," one senior biologist said, almost as afterthought, "you'll have to remove the coconut crabs from your study sites before you spread the ant poison."

Remove the coconut crabs? Aside from my rundown marriage and worn-out body, the main reason I wanted to go to Palmyra was to see the world's largest land invertebrate, the coconut crab. Part of my fascination with this creature was my fear of it. Alex had sent me a short video of one of these giant crustaceans dragging a machete—a big one—down a path. Mature coconut crabs, also called robber crabs for their habit of carrying off anything bearing the scent of coconut, have bodies the size of Chihuahuas and leg spans up to four feet across. What attracted and terrified me about these crustaceans was the fact that they bear two enormous front claws, one for cutting and one for tearing. These miniature hedge shears are strong enough to open a green coconut, a task I can't do even with axe-like tools made for the job.

"How does one remove coconut crabs from one's study sites?" I said.

"You pick them up and carry them to the other side of the island," the biologist said.

Pick them up? I thought as I left the Fish and Wildlife office. I didn't mind some cuts and bruises in my wildlife work, but the claws of coconut crabs can remove fingers from hands. I knew how to hold regular crabs from the back of the shells without getting pinched and had safely picked up hundreds of sharp-beaked seabirds, but I could not imagine myself being brave enough or strong enough to catch a coconut crab and carry it around.

The thought occurred to me that this stint in Palmyra could make me even more depressed if I couldn't handle the work. I shooed the thought away. Whatever my failings might be, Palmyra would provide unique material for my newspaper columns, which I would send via satellite phone. Besides that, I knew from experience that no matter how I imagined the place or the work, I would be wrong.

Of course, I might also be wrong about the trip's subsequent benefits to my relationship with Craig, to taking a break from our marriage, to being a sailboat captain. But if this wasn't a move forward, at least it was a move. Something would happen.

12

$\mathcal{G}$ET a gun," my neighbor Paula said, sipping white wine. "You can buy them at Sports Authority. I saw them there in a glass case."

"I'm not buying a gun. Palmyra is a wildlife refuge full of birds and crabs. There are only a few people there."

"Exactly my point," she said. "What if pirates show up?"

Paula wasn't alone in her fear of pirates. The media coverage of boats being hijacked off the coasts of Somalia, Columbia, and Indonesia had the public, and many of my friends, imagining the high seas to be full of murdering thieves. My research into the topic found a pirate attack on the way to Palmyra about as likely as that of a great white shark, both predators being regional and, within their regions, rare. Some offshore areas were riskier than others, but the part of the Pacific where I was going was not one of them. At least not now. The past was another story.

It's fitting that an atoll so remote and empty of people would also carry stories of pirates and buried treasure. In 1816, a Spanish pirate ship named *Esperanza* wrecked on the reefs of Palmyra. Somehow, the crew managed to lug their plunder of Incan temple gold ashore and bury it beneath a palm grove. After a year of being stranded, the thieves built three rafts, climbed aboard, and set out. Two of the rafts were never seen again, but an American whaling vessel picked up the third. The sole survivor on that raft lived long enough to tell his tale and then died. No treasure has ever been found in Palmyra.

"There are no pirates where I'm going," I said.

"You're a woman alone on a boat. You need a gun."

"I'm not alone. I'll have Alex."

"One young biologist. What's he going to do on a desert island where who-knows-what can happen? Get him a gun, too."

"Palmyra is hardly a desert island. It's a scientific research station in a marine sanctuary. People live there to protect the animals."

Paula was not an outdoor person, and my scheme to sail off to a remote atoll in the Pacific seemed to her dangerous, difficult, and entirely unnecessary.

"Why sail a thousand miles to see marine life anyway?" she said. "Haven't you got anything left here to write about?"

"Of course," I said. "I have millions of things to write about in Hawai'i. But the wildlife in Palmyra is different. I need to see it."

"Susan," she said, "I'm worried about you."

If she's this worried about me now, I thought, *wait until she hears about the Palmyra murders.*

This grisly crime had been a big news story in Hawai'i when it happened in 1974, and it resurfaced in 1991 when Vincent Bugliosi published a book about the murder trial called *And the Sea Will Tell*. On the run from the law, a man named Buck Walker sailed with his girlfriend from Hawai'i to Palmyra, where he met, murdered, and dismembered a San Diego couple, Mac and Muff Graham, who were living on their sailboat at anchor in Palmyra's lagoon. Walker and his companion stole the dead couple's boat, far nicer than their own, and sailed it back to Honolulu, where people immediately recognized it. The couple was arrested. Walker claimed the boat's owners drowned in a dinghy accident, but later Muff's chopped up, blowtorched body washed up in a sea chest on a beach in Palmyra's lagoon. Walker got life in prison; the girlfriend was found not guilty.

That's all most people knew about Palmyra, and after my intentions to sail there became public in my newspaper column, people I met at parties, on beach walks, and even at the West Marine store warned me. "Be careful," they said in dramatic tones. "That's where that couple got murdered on their boat."

I had my own concerns about sailing to Palmyra, but pirates and murder were not among them. Paula had been right, of course. With a suspicious death and blatant drug dealing occurring three feet from my boat in Waikiki, I knew that living on *Honu* alone could be scary. But I also knew from working on Tern Island and from Alex's e-mails that Palmyra was a haven for naturalists, not killers. I was far more likely to be killed in my own city marina.

As for guns on boats, Paula's unwavering conviction that guns were a good thing reminded me of a Dutch sailor Craig and I met years earlier in Costa Rica. The man and his girlfriend had been sailing their catamaran past Colombia on their way to Panama. Because tales of pirates in the area frightened them, the couple took down their radar reflector and sailed without lights. Their

VHF radio had broken earlier, but they didn't much care. They didn't think they needed it at sea.

Their precautions were justified, they thought, when one dark night lights appeared on the horizon from the direction of the Colombian coast. The lights grew bigger and brighter with alarming speed, and as the mystery boat drew close, all the sailor could think about were stories of Colombian drug dealers shooting people and throwing them overboard so they could steal their sailboat to smuggle drugs. The man got out his gun and aimed the loaded weapon with shaky hands, prepared to shoot. The powerboat with its blinding spotlights drew alongside the catamaran, but just as the man's finger began to tighten on the trigger, a voice boomed from a loudspeaker. "This is the United States Coast Guard—prepare to be boarded."

The Coast Guard sailors also held loaded guns. Since the catamaran had been sailing with no lights and their calls went unanswered (given the cruisers' radio was down), the Coast Guard thought it was a drug runner. They had come close to killing each other.

Such recollections depressed me, but not because of the near tragedy. Since Craig and I didn't go on trips together anymore and had different friends and activities at home, we would have no more shared stories, and that for me had been a large part of the fun of being a long-term couple. Now when I thought of past tales, like the Dutchman on the catamaran, I grieved almost as if Craig had died. No one else would ever know or care about my past experiences like he did. Craig had been such an integral part of my existence for so long that I couldn't separate the life I led from the man I shared it with.

During the refit, I found at the bottom of a remote locker a few of the nautical charts we had used while sailing from Connecticut to Hawai'i. The notes and numbers on the charts in Craig's handwriting conjured up visions of Craig and me in the middle of the ocean singing our hearts out to my pathetic guitar playing, listening to *The Hobbit* on cassette tapes, eating popcorn while listening to NBA playoffs on the shortwave radio thousands of miles offshore. Tears filled my eyes. We had been so good together. I became so angry with him for spoiling my sweet memories, and so hurt that he was now making memories with someone else, that I crushed the charts to my chest, marched to the nearest dumpster, and hurled them in. I would buy my own charts, I promised myself, and from now on the handwriting on them would be mine.

ONE evening Paula, who lived in our condominium complex, invited Craig and me to her country club, and while we were eating, the subject of the thirty-year-old Palmyra murders of Mac and Muff Graham came up. Again she urged me to buy a gun. When I refused, she appealed to Craig.

"She's got one," he said.

I stared at him. "I do?"

"Yes. It has six big red bullets."

"Ah, the flare gun." This orange plastic pistol, made for shooting distress flares into the sky, looks so much like a toy that I smiled at the thought of using it to defend myself. Still, a gun was a gun.

"Would a flare kill someone?" I said.

"At close range," Craig said, "I believe it would."

"There, Paula, see? I'm all set."

She thought about this. "Okay, Susan, keep that gun under the cushion in the . . . the place where you drive."

"The cockpit."

"Yes, there. And keep it loaded with all six bullets."

"They're flares. Flare guns only hold one flare at a time."

"Buy six of those guns, then, and load them all. Put them somewhere you can grab them in a hurry." She paused. "Buy some marinated artichokes, too. I'll give you a recipe."

I was sailing to Palmyra. The thought thrilled me to my toes one minute and frightened me into a cold sweat the next. I didn't dwell on my fear, though, because the preparation of the boat consumed me. Alex and I worked day and night on the final details of the voyage. One day, Craig sailed with us a few miles offshore to show Alex and me how to use the sea anchor, an underwater parachute-type device that stabilized the boat in a storm, essentially stopping it from moving forward or, in hurricane conditions, from rolling over. Craig and I had carried this emergency "brake," fussy with all its lines and fabric, on *Honu* for decades but never had to use it. I prayed that Alex and I would not have to use it either.

Once we were back in the marina, Craig went home, and Alex and I hosed the salt water off the sea anchor, which lay on the dock looking like a miniature white parachute. We stared at the canvas drying in the hot sun. "Will you remember how to rig this up?" I said.

"Maybe," he said. "You?"

"Maybe. But, then, we did it in flat seas and no wind with Craig directing."

I asked Alex to buy a barrel of diesel and arrange to ship it to Palmyra on a barge transporting construction material for a cabin-building project there.

This was a just-in-case measure. If we got becalmed during the voyage and had to use the engine, we could top off the fuel tank for the trip home.

He also bought fishing gear, since I don't like to fish and had no hooks, lines, or rods on the boat. I eat fish occasionally, but I don't kill fish. It's hypocritical, yes, but beating an animal to death as it fights for its life on the deck of my boat is not something I do if I can avoid it. Craig felt the same. Years earlier while sailing from Costa Rica to Hawai'i, a thirty-five-day voyage, we caught a mahimahi. Craig held the head of the magnificent male fish (the steep forehead is distinct in males) on the deck with one hand and, with a knife in the other, sliced through the spinal cord, giving the thrashing animal a quick death. The humane killing, though, gave us no comfort. Mahimahi are famous for their brilliant colors, golden on the sides and flashing blues and greens on the back and head. In grieving silence we watched those iridescent colors of life fade to the yellowish grays of death.

We ate the fish, but the unpleasant memory of killing it spoiled the meals. "I don't want to fish anymore," Craig said.

"Me either," I said.

We agreed that we would put out a line only if we were desperate for food. It was the last time either of us ever fished.

U.S. Fish and Wildlife Service officials continued to remind me that I was not allowed to eat the Nature Conservancy's food or use any of their facilities, and I spent days shopping, cramming my yellow VW Beetle full of groceries and loading them onto the boat. I did not, however, buy more flare guns, or guns of any kind, even though countless people suggested it. I had no experience handling firearms and didn't want to learn. Flare guns were enough for me.

Not knowing how much food I would need, I felt it better to err on the heavy side, cramming every locker with canned vegetables, cake mixes, and staples like flour, yeast, sugar, and pasta. Fretting over the possibility that I still might raid the Nature Conservancy pantry and embarrass Fish and Wildlife, Roger arranged for me to ship two large plastic containers of food on the barge with Alex's drum of diesel fuel. Back to the bulk-item grocery store I went, pushing more overflowing carts.

"I don't know what I'm going to do with all this food," I said to Alex as he helped me stow.

"Don't worry. We'll eat it."

"We?" I said. Because of a previous arrangement with Nature Conservancy, the camp provided Alex's meals and lodging (and outhouse privileges) while he conducted his studies.

"You thought I was going to let you eat by yourself on the boat for four months? I would never do that."

Tears stung my eyes. "Thank you," I said.

In the middle of all this activity, Pierre and I worked long hours, including weekends, to install the last systems on the boat. We mounted a wind generator on the mizzenmast, fitted a new wind speed instrument on the main mast, and replaced the leaky, greasy stuffing box—which I hated because I could never get it adjusted correctly—with a new device called a packless shaft seal, known as a PSS.

Sailors talk a lot about their stuffing boxes and shaft seals because these devices plug the large hole in the boat made by the inboard transmission's propeller shaft. This is not your average hole in the bottom, like the ones that drain the sinks or flush the toilet. Those holes are fitted with devices known as through-hull fittings that are designed to hold valves, also referred to as seacocks—those pesky cocks again—which open and close the holes. As a result, holes in boats are usually referred to simply as through-hulls, as in "*Honu* has nine through-hulls."

The hole for the shaft is another story. On boats with inboard engines, a sturdy metal shaft connects the transmission inside the boat through a hole in the hull to the propeller outside the boat. Seawater wants to rush into the hole around the shaft, and if the hole isn't sealed properly, the boat sinks, and fast. But you can't pack anything tight around the shaft, or put a valve on it, because the shaft turns—in *Honu*, up to a thousand revolutions per minute. A too-tight seal causes friction that impedes the shaft and burns it up. A too-loose seal leaks seawater, sometimes at an alarming rate.

Honu's old stuffing box bore no resemblance to a box. Around the one-inch-diameter shaft, several round nuts enclosed a hollow place, called a packing gland, into which one stuffed strips of Teflon-impregnated cloth that allowed the shaft to turn freely but stopped water from leaking in. (Shaft, box, nuts, glands—the system sounded like grade-school sex talk.) I never could quite envision how the thing worked, and adjusting it, which I had to do often to either loosen the nuts to cool the shaft or tighten the nuts to slow the leak, required a huge wrench that hurt my arthritic hands to pick up, much less use. "Hand me the Channellock," Pierre said to me when we were replacing the stuffing box with the new and better PSS.

"What's a Channellock?"

He gave me a look of disgust and jabbed a finger at the tool. "That."

"Oh. I thought that was a pipe wrench."

"Jesus, you've been using the thing for six months and you still don't know its name?"

Pierre was becoming more cantankerous as my launch date grew near, worried, I suspected, about my skippering skills. Going from Alex to Pierre to Craig was like juggling a teddy bear, a jackknife, and a Rubik's Cube. Spending the morning with huggy, open-book Alex left me wide open for a slash of criticism from Pierre.

Later that day, Craig broadsided me with one of his cryptic comments. "Ed and Linda [California acquaintances] have taken separate vacations for years," he said out of the blue.

"What?" I said.

"When he goes windsurfing in the gorge, she visits her family back east."

"And?" I stared at him.

"I'm just saying it works for them," he said, and walked out the door.

When Craig had said, *I do talk to you, but you don't listen,* apparently this is what he meant.

At the boat the next day, I searched for a place in the captain's cabin to stash my cases of Diet Coke and opened the locker that held Craig's clothes for the last twenty years. *Okay,* I thought, *if he doesn't want to sail with me anymore, there's no need to keep his clothes on the boat.* As I began pulling T-shirts, shorts, and underwear from the locker and piling them on the floor, his scent wafted to my nose. How I loved that smell. Twenty-five years previously, when I met Craig in a hospital recovery room, his heady, sexy, male smell had punched right through the strong odor of surgical anesthesia and made me dizzy with desire. As he pulled off his blue surgical hood and said hello with a big sunny smile, I had only one thought: I must touch this man or die. To me, Craig's man smell was the best drug in the world.

Detox time. I stuffed those pheromone-laden clothes into a black plastic bag, tied it tight, and dumped it in the trunk of my car.

So much to do. For years we kept a small library on the boat. I pared the books to the ones I really wanted to read, such as *Treasure Island* and *The Sex Lives of Cannibals* (a hilarious memoir of a year in the South Pacific nation of Kiribati, by J. Maarten Troost), and gave up the ones I thought I should read but never did, such as *The Odyssey* and *Moby Dick.* Scott helped me set up an e-mail system on my new satellite phone, and Howard burned onto CDs Bill Clinton's autobiography, *My Life,* read by Bill himself, for Alex and me to listen to during our seven-day passage. My sister helped me make backup copies of everything on my laptop, which would be the boat's main computer for e-mail, navigation programs, and writing my columns. We were so close to leaving that I daydreamed about Palmyra all day long, its rainbow reefs sparkling through crystal clear water, puppyish seabirds, cheeky crabs . . . my Shangri-La.

Alex called. "I'm at the Fish and Wildlife office," he said. "Bad news."

"What?"

"They're thinking of not letting you go."

I was too shocked to speak, but I should not have been. Thanks to Roger, I knew my position as a Fish and Wildlife volunteer was weak, and that the service did not have a refuge manager, or even a paid employee, living on Palmyra yet. Alex, a former employee, had quit to return to school, so he was now considered a volunteer. Even TNC's onsite manager, Luke, who ran the camp and the human aspects of Cooper Island, had no authority over wildlife, other islands, or reefs. That would be the Fish and Wildlife manager's job. When they hired one.

Although Roger had given me the job, and we had signed the papers, now some higher up Fish and Wildlife individuals were vacillating. "They're afraid that if they let you sail, and work at Palmyra," Alex said, "and don't let other volunteers do it later, it will look like favoritism."

Up, down. Up, down. If my hormones weren't driving me crazy, bureaucracy was. A bumper sticker I'd seen around my neighborhood came to mind. *WARNING: I'm out of estrogen and I have a gun.* Mine was a flare gun, but still.

"I'm coming over there," I said.

"Um, I don't think that's a good idea," Alex said. "Let me talk to them."

I took a deep breath. "Okay, tell them this: I am sailing to Palmyra whether I work for them or not. I'll take the time ordinary cruisers get to anchor in the lagoon. And once I'm there, I might have some boat repair issues that will cause me to stay a little longer."

Alex thought for a moment. "If you can't stay for the four months, I won't be able to sail back to Honolulu with you."

"I'll figure something out. *I'm going.*"

"Maybe one of the other TNC volunteers can crew for you on the return trip. I'll send an e-mail and ask."

"Okay. But whatever they say, you and I are sailing to Palmyra. Next week."

I continued my feverish preparation, going from deliriously happy to gutter-level depressed, and sleeping so poorly that each morning I could barely move a limb. I felt like a tired old workhorse dragging a too-heavy load day after day after day. The refit would never be finished; the paperwork would never get done. My mood swings, again at high throttle despite hormone replacement, threatened to mutiny my own command. This trip, I kept thinking, had been doomed from the get-go. My motivations seemed wrong. Sure, I wanted to see Palmyra and work with the wildlife there, but was that a cover for the urge I had to run away and hide? If so, was that so terrible? As usual, I had no answers.

Alex's e-mails got some positive responses, and he assured me that there were several workers on Palmyra who would love the adventure of sailing with me to Honolulu.

Just as we got that settled, someone in the U.S. Fish and Wildlife Service reversed the no-go decision. I don't know who, or why, or how high or low in the chain of command this occurred, but I wasn't about to ask. Suddenly, I had permission to sail to Palmyra, live on my boat in the lagoon for four months, and work for them after all.

I felt like one of the ants I was going to Palmyra to study (and kill). As an individual, I had a job to do that was, in the small picture, important. From the federal government's perspective, though, I was a bug in the sugar bowl that could be squashed, or not, at the whim of unknown workers in a vast bureaucracy.

THE night before our hard-earned and long-awaited launch day, the notorious northeast trade winds came on hard. When I got to the boat that morning, the halyards hammered the aluminum masts like dinner bells, and *Honu*'s rails rubbed against the late Popeye-Victor's boat, still wearing its now-bedraggled lei of crime tape. Having your boat bouncing in its mooring the day before a long, offshore trip is not an auspicious beginning, but I was not about to waver, not then.

"We'll tough it out," Alex and I agreed on the phone.

Then the boat began heeling (leaning to one side) in the slip, and the national weather service upgraded "gusty trade wind conditions" to "small craft advisory." The strong trades continued building, gusting to thirty-five knots with twenty-foot seas in the channels. Thirty knots of wind can knock a person down. This is Force 7 on the Beaufort scale, called a Moderate Gale, but conditions that day hammered on the door of Force 8, known as a Fresh Gale.

Craig and I had once sailed downwind in Force 8 conditions for four days when approaching the Panama Canal from the Caribbean Sea. The wind during that memorable passage had blown a steady forty knots with gusts higher, and the waves grew so tall that when *Honu* was in the troughs, the waves looked from down there to be nearly mast high—four to five stories above the water's surface. The storm had come on after we left Curaçao, and at that point there was no turning back and no port to run to.

That voyage was one of the few times I have ever seen Craig worried, but with nothing to be done but sail, he sailed. And he did it with impressive skill, respectful of the tremendous forces of nature bearing down on us, while remaining alert to *Honu*'s strengths and weaknesses. Using his sailing harness to tie himself to the mast, Craig took down the triple-reefed mainsail. Back in the cockpit, he furled the jib so far that we joked (later) about sailing under handkerchief alone. Once he rolled in the entire jib to check a turning block, and the boat sailed just fine at four to five knots under bare poles, the nautical term for no sails up.

When *Honu* was in the troughs, the monster waves behind us broke with a terrifying roar, their white water rushing downward toward the boat like river rapids. But with the autopilot driving like a champ, and the boat sailing as she was built to, *Honu* scooted straight up the next mountain of water in plenty of time to escape the deluge from behind. Over the top we went, and straight down the next wave.

Hour after hour, we hung on in the cockpit, getting wet with salt spray while waiting to see if those monster breaking waves would swamp us from behind, called getting "pooped." (The poop deck in old sailing ships was located at the rear of the boat.) They never did.

On the second day, the sights, sounds, and salt became so unnerving that we moved below to the main cabin and kept watch from there, peering out the companionway every fifteen minutes or so to make sure nothing had changed. After four days, the wind stopped as if someone flipped a switch, and the ordeal seemed like a bad dream.

Whenever anyone asked Craig and me if we had any storms while sailing *Honu* home to Hawai'i, those four unnerving days immediately came to mind.

I had no intention of living that nightmare again, especially without Craig. I called off Alex's and my departure for Palmyra.

I had been given a reprieve. And reprieve is exactly how I viewed it, because I was scared to death to leave. After all this preparation, all this practice, all this money (about fifty thousand dollars over ten months), I didn't want to go. A lot. I declared that we would wait. The rigging howled in agreement.

It being December, I spent the day wandering Honolulu alone, seeking comfort in the Christmas crowds and trying to savor restaurant meals. After all, I would soon have to cook everything I ate.

Another day passed, but the gale did not. My sister and other women friends took turns taking me to lunch and presenting me with thoughtful gifts such as chocolates, candles, earrings, and hats.

Another day came and went. Everyone, including Craig, told me I was wise to be waiting for safer weather. But I felt far from wise. Beneath my bold talk, and extensive preparation, I was lonely and afraid. *What was I thinking? I can't do this.* My mood fell as low as the fenders that swung from *Honu*'s rails.

Alex called. "Susan, we have to talk." His voice sounded as strained as I felt. "I know it's still windy, but I can't take one more day of waiting," he paused. "To be honest, my courage is failing. I'm starting to think about flying back to Palmyra. There's an unexpected seat on this week's plane."

I surprised both Alex and myself by replying, "We leave tomorrow."

When I told Craig, he said, "It's still blowing hard. The seas are going to be really big by now."

I remembered those freight-car waves from other trips, but thinking about rough sea conditions and being in them are two different things. "I know, but the wind can stay strong around Oahu for weeks at a time. And if Alex flies back to Palmyra, the trip is off, and I can't let that happen." I didn't mention that we were both losing our nerve.

"I would wait another day or two," he said

What to do? I knew Craig was right. You never leave in a storm if you don't have to. Still, a common occurrence among potential offshore sailors is planning, organizing, and working on the boat for years and never actually leaving. Nautical folk singer Eileen Quinn even wrote a song about it called "Tomorrow I'll Go Cruising." You can always find an excuse for not shoving off.

But that was not the song of this captain. "I'm leaving in the morning," I said.

Craig stared at me, his look conflicted. No one knew better than he how savage the seas were likely to be in this weather, yet he knew I was under pressure to go and respected my decision.

"It's your trip," he said, "your call."

Alex arrived at eight in the morning to the continued symphony of a hundred halyards in concert with their masts. Because no one else dared take their boats out in this weather, Alex walked alone, the only soul striding down the pier under the gray, turbulent skies.

Craig met us at the boat, and with him at the stern and Alex at the bow, I drove the boat, even in that gusting wind, out of the tricky slip and around the corner to the fuel dock without a hitch. Ironic, I thought. Just when I'm getting the hang of driving in marinas, I'm heading to sea where a skipper needs entirely different boat-handling skills.

Family and friends stood waiting at the fuel dock to bid us bon voyage. Michele brought giant, colorful fish balloons that the wind beat against the mast and tangled in the rigging. Others brought leis, their delicate flowers wilting in the wild weather. We filled *Honu*'s fuel tanks with diesel and topped up the gas cans for Bette Davis. There was no more putting it off. Craig and Pierre made the final rounds of the boat with me, checking rigging, securing halyards, and coiling lines. Craig and I hugged and looked for long seconds into each other's eyes. I had no idea how he felt about me leaving, why we were having trouble living together, or if he would be there when, and if, I returned. *Who is this man?* I wondered.

"Good-bye, Craig. I'll call you when we get there."

"Good luck, Susan," he said, and jumped off the boat.

So formal we had become, each using the other's first names instead of the usual Twinoid. Craig's face was drawn and serious. Whatever else might be on his mind, he was worried about me sailing this boat offshore, especially leaving in wretched weather. He knew that there would be no help in the open ocean, and not much at Palmyra either. I had learned a lot during the refit and on my practice trips, but as far as sailboat handling and repairs went, he and I both knew I had only graduated from preschool to kindergarten. "Good luck," he said, again.

"Bon voyage," my friends and family called cheerfully, as though Alex and I were going on a Carnival cruise. They threw mooring lines to the boat and kisses to me. "Safe trip!"

Because *Honu* was still in the lee of Oahu, and therefore protected from the full force of the wind by the island's towering mountains, it felt like we were out for a dinner cruise. I was glad for the moment of peace, because that look in Craig's eyes haunted me. *What,* I wondered, *does he want?*

"Men want two things," my friend Paula said weeks earlier as we sat on her lanai discussing the question. "Sex and to be left alone."

"Sex and solitude? That's it?"

"I didn't say solitude. That's different. They want to be left alone about everyday things. Especially doctors. I know. I married one once."

Paula handed me a Perrier and poured herself a glass of wine. "How many times have you been married?" I said.

"I don't care to say," she said, with a wave of her hand. "Listen," she went on, "men don't want to come home and hear how the plumber didn't fix the toilet right, or how much the car repair is going to cost. They hate that stuff. They want to come in the door, get a kiss hello, and sit down to read the newspaper. If you have sex with them that night, they had a great day."

"Should I wear Saran Wrap at the door, too?"

"I didn't say be a sex slave. Just do it when you feel like it, don't bug him, and he'll be happy."

What kind of companionship is that? I wondered. *For either of us?* "You don't think there's more to men than that?"

"Of course there is. They just don't want to talk about it."

"But how do you know what they're feeling?" I said.

"Jesus. Never ask men about their feelings. You can tell how they feel by how they act. Women talk. Men act."

I remembered thinking at the time that her theory maybe made sense for other men, but I had thought Craig was different, that he wanted to share his important feelings with me, that I knew everything about him, and that he wanted to know everything about me. When I looked back at the dock now, though, I saw a stranger.

I steered *Honu* into the wind, and Alex hauled up the mainsail. After turning the boat downwind, we unrolled the jib, and in a few brief minutes, the outer buoys of the Ala Wai Channel were behind us.

With the wind pushing the port (left) side of the boat between its center and rear, we scooted along at a broad reach. This point of sail gets the nickname "sleigh ride" because a sailboat's motion resembles that of a sleigh gliding through snowy woods. *Honu* broad reached through our wavy wilderness like a racehorse, moving with grace up and down the slopes of the liquid hills.

Alex stood on the aft deck gazing back toward the city, and I engaged the autopilot so I could join him. "Say good-bye," he said.

The wave peaks offered breathtaking views of Honolulu, rising as if from a crack between Oahu's jungle mountains and the Pacific Ocean. From our vantage point, the island looked like a fairytale kingdom surrounded by a blue moat, complete with fantastic creatures swimming, flying, floating, and crawling. None were visible at the moment, but that's the charm of the ocean. Whether I can see the animals or not, I know they're there, an entire spectrum of life perfectly at home in a world as deadly to us humans as Mars.

Our vistas were brief, however, because after the boat rounded the crest of each smooth wave, it plunged down the other side like a toboggan on ice. At the bottom, sandwiched between two solid walls of water supported, impossibly, only by wind, the boat would hesitate for a second. And then, as if taking a deep breath, my lovely *Honu* began climbing the next hill, leaving my panic in the trough behind. The boat sailed downwind so briskly, so forcefully, that returning to the harbor now would now be like paddling up a waterfall. There was no stopping and no going back.

We glided along with astonishing speed for the small amount of sail flying. At the dock, Craig had put a triple reef in the mainsail, making it smaller by two-thirds and thereby vastly diminishing its power. Lashed down like that, the sail looked bound and gagged, but in those stormy conditions, restraints seemed fitting. With strong wind from the rear, full mainsails can, in one quick jerk, rip boom hardware from the deck or, worst case, a skipper's head from her neck. The jib, however, was safe up there at the bow. We eased the jib sheets, and the sail billowed off *Honu*'s right front side like a giant throw pillow.

The cockpit, in the center of the boat, remained high and dry, the motion neither jerky nor jarring. I sighed with relief. Aside from those disturbing seconds in the valleys of the waves, leaving in such strong trade winds didn't seem so ill-advised after all.

The jangle of my cell phone, the last call it would receive for months, startled me.

"We can still see a little bit of white from the top of your sails," said a cheery voice. "Bon Voyage. Good luck."

It was Scott, not Craig, who thought to call me for a final farewell. I didn't care. I suddenly had a hundred more important things to worry about besides who called me and who didn't. All my attention focused on watching the masts in the marina disappear. The city receded with alarming speed, the skyscrapers shrinking until they looked like hazy stacks of gray Lego blocks. Finally the mountains, too, sank into the sea.

"Gone," I said, shocked at how quickly my island vanished. When you live in the hustle and bustle of Oahu, it's easy to forget how tiny and isolated the islands of Hawai'i are.

At sea, we felt it acutely. Out there, *Honu* felt like nothing more than a fragile dish floating in the middle of an endless ocean. The next land, Palmyra Atoll, was a thousand miles away, and even that was only a handful of acres. The danger in what we were doing hit me hard. How alone we were. How minuscule. Never had I felt so small and vulnerable.

For a last, long peaceful moment, Alex and I gazed at Oahu's towering Koʻolau mountains, which had stood as barriers to the full fury of the open ocean's wind and waves. When *Honu* sailed beyond the last of the island's protection, the ocean clobbered us.

13

WIND that had whistled now howled, making such an unnerving wail through the rigging that it sounded faster than the twenty-five knots we saw on the anemometer. And it was faster. When sailing downwind, you add the boat's speed, about seven knots, to the reading, making the real wind closer to thirty-one or thirty-two knots. It takes effort to walk against this much wind, a Moderate Gale, or Force 7 on the Beaufort scale. At Force 7 those umbrellas that are hard to control at Force 6 turn inside out, heavy tree branches move, and sailboat captains become hypersensitive to every sound and movement on the boat. Force 7 winds exert tremendous force on the gear, tempting sails to tear, wires to break, and masts to fall down.

The farther we sailed from the island, the harder the wind blew and the bigger the waves rose. The rounded swells rose to unstable peaks that couldn't support their own weight and spilled over in white rage. Some waves smacked *Honu*'s side, striking the middle-to-rear quarter with shocking blows that rolled us sideways. Single-hulled sailboats such as *Honu* (known as monohulls) have rounded sides and bottoms, and when wind and waves push hard on one side just so, the boat rolls like a half-empty bleach bottle. In most conditions (hurricanes being the awful exception), the leaded keel hanging below the boat stops a monohull from turning so far on its side that the boat swamps.

Still, in the powerful wind and wave conditions Alex and I faced, *Honu* sometimes rolled far enough to make us grab for anything fastened down, as we watched the water splash the rail. In the first of those revolting rolls, hanging on with my knobby knuckles, I wondered why any sane person would climb into a giant jug and point it out to sea.

With the trade winds building for the past week, some waves humped up to twenty feet tall, and foam from their breaking tops blew off in streaks. *Bang*!

A wave hit the hull sounding like someone whacked a wall with a baseball bat. Sometimes, in a flash of panic, I was sure we hit a log or a container lost from a ship, both considered offshore hazards because their masses float below the waterline and you can't see them. I've heard countless stories over the years of boats sinking after reportedly hitting whales, but in many cases, the sailors never saw the whale. Whale collisions do occasionally occur, but it's more likely that the boat hit a container, tree trunk, or other floating object as *big* as a whale.

We hit nothing. The big bangs were waves bashing the side of the boat. When the track of a wave and the direction of the boat intersected at exactly the wrong moment, *wham*. The water struck the side with such force that, rather than roll, the entire boat—rigging, sails, and cabinetry below—shuddered from the blow. Craig called this jarring crash the "brick wall phenomenon," because it felt like you hit one.

Almost immediately, my autopilot, an Alpha 3000 model that we affectionately called Alphie, started slipping, the mechanism being unable to consistently steer the course through the barrage of blows. This was terrible news because, unlike humans, an electronic autopilot never gets tired or bored, doesn't care about rain and salt (its mechanisms are protected inside the boat), and doggedly sticks to a set direction. Over the years, Craig and I had found that, in many conditions, we could not steer a course as well as the autopilot.

Taking the wheel ourselves, and feeling how hard it was to drive, Alex and I decided (wished) the autopilot was not having a mechanical failure. We convinced ourselves that the conditions were simply too rough for the machine to handle. In a cobwebby corner of my mind, I knew that in the past Alphie had steered just fine in conditions rougher than this, but I swatted the thought away. With only two of us to drive, an autopilot failure in any condition would turn the voyage into an exhausting stand-at-the-wheel marathon. And even though I had a spare autopilot, called an Autohelm, a simpler device that attached to the wheel in the cockpit, I had never assembled it or set it in motion.

Alex and I got nauseated about the same time, not vomiting but unable to think about anything else. *If I start to throw up, can I make it below to the toilet, or should I go for the side of the boat?* We took our seasick tablets and sat silent in the cockpit, waiting the sour thirty minutes it took for the medication to stop our stomachs from churning.

After watching and listening to the boat strain for half an hour, I decided that even with the mainsail as small as it could get, it was still more than we needed.

"Let's reef the jib and get rid of the main," I said. "It will slow us down and lighten the load on Alphie. That will help with the motion, too."

Some sailors resist such reefing and braking, but I was happy to hobble the boat, not only to help Alphie drive but also for the sake of the ride. When sailing isn't fun anymore, a good captain does what it takes to make the experience less miserable.

Alex leaped to the task, clipping the leash of his sailing harness to a safety line that ran the length of the boat. Sailing harnesses are vests of sturdy red webbing that close with heavy, stainless steel clasps. Each harness clips to a five-foot-long leash that the sailor fastens to anything bolted to the boat. Not all sailors wear harnesses, but in 1986, when Craig and I sailed *Honu* from Connecticut to Hawai'i, we agreed that, once offshore, in calm seas or not, everyone sitting in *Honu*'s cockpit would wear a harness. One of us falling overboard without the other knowing had been our worst nightmare. Now it was Alex's and my nightmare.

"Swear to me you will always wear your harness and never, ever go on deck without telling me," I said to him shortly after we left. "Not even one toe out of the cockpit if I'm not watching you." If he went over the side, the leash would keep him attached to the boat, but unless I released the sails to stop us, it could drag him in the water like a hooked tuna until he drowned. Alex promised to be vigilant, and I promised, too.

Even with the harness around his chest and the leash attached to the deck, his first step from the cockpit sent my heart to my throat. If he slipped and went over the side, *I was the only one who could save his life*. It didn't matter how many times I had crewed for Craig, or how many practice voyages I made around Hawai'i, skippering a sailboat out of sight of land in the middle of Pacific Ocean fury weighed on me like nothing before. I had prepared for everything except the emotional burden of the role. Nor had I thought I would be so scared.

Alex moved forward in a crouch, gripping the lifelines that line the deck and adjusting his gait to the boat's motion. Just as he reached the mast and stood up, a beast of a wave rushed the boat, rolling it farther than it had rolled before and at a slightly different angle. I had been standing to watch Alex and saw the wave coming. I gripped the binnacle (the support at the wheel made for gripping).

"Hang on," I called, but my cry might have been inside my head. I couldn't separate the wind's shriek from my own.

Alex wrapped his arms around the mast in a bear hug. The wave hit. The boat rolled so far that the motion lifted his bare feet off the deck, causing his legs to flap in the wind like a yacht club pennant.

Once he gets back in the cockpit, I thought, *I will never, ever let him go out on the deck again.*

A moment later, the boat leveled and Alex regained his footing.

"Wrap your leash around the mast," I yelled.

He did this, and released the mainsail's halyard. The sail threw a temper tantrum typical of loose canvas in high winds, but Alex managed to pull the thumping, whacking material down. At the same time, I hauled in the mainsheet to still the boom and secure it in the center of the cockpit.

With Alex at the mast and me standing on the cockpit bench in front of the wheel, we worked together to lash the thrashing mainsail to the boom, using red sail ties that I had custom ordered with "Honu" printed in white letters.

In the past, my priorities on the boat had been making it cute and cozy, leaving Craig with the responsibility of maintaining and sailing it. But that day in the nightmarish ocean, as I wrestled with my mainsail and worried about keeping my friend alive, with salt in my eyes and bile in my throat while stubbing my toes bloody, I no longer cared whether the webbing I used to tie the sails was fire engine red or Caribbean blue. That life was gone.

His dangerous job done, Alex made his way back to the cockpit hand over hand on the lifelines. After he climbed in and refastened his leash to the binnacle, I felt such relief to have him safely back on the bench with me that I clutched his arm with both hands.

"My God, Alex, I will never in my life forget the sight of you dangling from the mast like that," I said. "It nearly stopped my heart beating. Until this wind lightens up, you aren't leaving this cockpit again."

"Is that an order, Captain?"

"Yes."

"Promise?"

"Promise. From here on, we do everything from inside the cockpit or leave it for later."

I had Alex (from the cockpit) roll in a bit more of the jib until Alphie drove normally again. We had to cut the boat's speed to under five knots to do that, but I didn't care. It might be slow, but we were still moving forward in a boat that was neither sinking nor swamping, and we were safe in the cockpit. That was enough progress for me.

There is no help in the open ocean. In worst-case scenarios, if you're lucky, you get a life-or-death rescue. I carried an EPIRB—emergency position-indicating radio beacon—that when activated would signal a satellite to send *Honu*'s location to the U.S. Coast Guard, which would organize a search and rescue with vessels in the vicinity. The rescuer could be a fishing boat, cargo ship, or another recreational vessel, and it might take days for them to arrive. EPIRBs are marvelous inventions that prevent shipwrecked people from drifting around for weeks or months in life rafts. If you activate your EPIRB, though, you have made the decision to abandon your vessel, even if it's still afloat, because help will come only to save lives. No towing or repairs are considered.

Because night was closing in, I had to evaluate the possibilities and deal with them while we could still see. I watched Alphie regularly turn the wheel back and forth, checked the GPS map, and decided that, if nothing changed, the autopilot was working well enough to keep us on course for the night. Alex and I tested the waterproof strobe lights on our sailing harnesses, half blinding ourselves with their flashes. Falling overboard was bad enough in the daytime when the person on the boat could see the person in the water. But at night, the only hope of a rescue would come in spotting those pulses of light in the tumultuous sea.

Night fell as if an executioner's hood dropped over our heads. In tropical latitudes, the sun plummets past the horizon as if it has fallen in a hole, making twilight time almost nonexistent. There was light, and then there was none. And I mean none. This was not your average night at sea with moon grinning and stars winking. It was the blackest night I had ever experienced. The moon, in its new phase, cast no light at all for the entire night, and dense clouds obscured the usual glimmer of starlight that causes the surface of the sea to sparkle.

Our inability to see beyond the boat's rails would have been bad enough, but the roar of waves charging toward the hull like attacking soldiers unnerved me even more. Unsure when the hits would come, I found myself bracing and relaxing at the wrong times, hanging on until my hands ached and then loosening my grip only to go flying off the bench. Squalls passed overhead every twenty minutes or so, pummeling us with sideways rain. Even in tropical latitudes, strong nighttime wind blowing on wet face, hands, and feet sucks away body heat. It had not occurred to me to buy neoprene gloves or rubber boots, and socks would have been soaked in minutes. So in addition to being wet and salty, we were cold.

"We might as well try and get some sleep," I said to Alex. "Go below. I'll take first watch."

Honu's main salon sofa converts into a comfortable double bed that is visible from the companionway, the opening between the cockpit above and the cabin below. "Companionway" always seemed like an odd name for the entrance to a boat's interior, because there is nothing companionable about it. It's an opening in the deck with a set of six steps steeper than a normal staircase, but not quite as upright as a ladder, and stainless steel railings on both sides. Craig and I called the double bed at the foot of the companionway a sea berth, because the person on watch in the cockpit can get the attention of the person sleeping in that bed with a shout. With only two people on an offshore passage, *Honu*'s forward and aft cabins were off-limits for sleeping. If the watch person had a problem, the person in either of the two cabins was too far away to hear a call for help.

"You go ahead," he said. "I'm wide awake."

As captain, it was my responsibility to take the hardest job first, but I wasn't sure which was worse: to lie below and listen to the waves bash the hull, or sit outside and imagine the wind ripping the rig off the deck. I checked my watch. Time crept at starfish pace. Only five minutes had passed since my last check. Alex dawdled, half-heartedly trying to convince me to go below first, as I half-heartedly tried to convince him to go. Neither of us thought we would fall asleep with every creak and groan sounding like *Honu* was splitting open and every sharp turn on a wave making us fear that Alphie had died. But more than that, neither of us wanted to be alone.

It was then that the mother of all flying fish soared across the cockpit, nearly stabbing Alex in the eye.

When the two of us leaned over that edge of the cockpit and discovered that the sputtering animal on the deck was not a seabird but a flying fish, a rush of satisfaction swept through me. Here we were, two people no more significant to this angry ocean than two bits of nanoplankton, looking at another bit of nanoplankton (the fish) that, through a cosmic fluke, lay in dire straits on the deck of my boat. What were the odds of a yellowfin tuna or spotted dolphin lunging to eat a twelve-inch-long flying fish, and it leaping at least six feet above the water to escape, only to whiz pass Alex's ear and land on the narrow deck behind him? Pretty low.

Because I had never seen a *malolo* (flying fish) that large, I wanted to look it over and write about the extraordinary fish and its journey to my deck. Big-hearted Alex, on the other hand, saw in the stranded creature a fellow life form experiencing pain and fear and thought only to relieve its suffering. For a significant second, it struck me that this voyage was not an escape but, rather, the peak of my existence, the place I had been heading for all my life. As frightened and miserable as I felt, I had never felt so alive, been so *there.*

I watched Alex pick up the marooned *malolo* and return it home. That he did it so quickly, and with so much empathy, made me realize without a doubt that he was the best crew member I could have chosen for this momentous journey. I would never again have a first voyage offshore as captain, and would never have another friend like Alex to share it with.

These thoughts passed through my racing mind in an instant, of course, because I also realized that if the fish I so admired had soared an inch or two to the left, Alex might be dead. It was not okay to sit back and thank my lucky stars that Alex hadn't been killed, because a glaring issue remained: *What else could kill him? Could kill me?* Paranoia struck. I jumped up to look for things I might have forgotten to do. *Could the boat be leaking in a place I hadn't checked? Did I smell propane? Were Alphie's gears grinding? How do you launch the life raft again?* Black nights and rough seas spawn boogeymen galore, and they swarmed into my cockpit like Blackbeard's pirates.

"Alex, please. Go stretch out," I said, releashing myself back to the wheel. "Even if you can't sleep, it's silly for the two of us to sit here all night. I'll worry plenty for us both, believe me."

He agreed, and it was then that I watched him strip to his shorts and stretch out in the sea berth. For the next five minutes or two hours (the two felt the same), I sat in the cockpit wondering, *Was I a perverted old lady for ogling my young friend?* Maybe so. I had no idea how to behave anymore. But with each glance at the prone figure lying in the dim cabin below, I began to notice something else. Alex was the same age as Craig had been when we met. Hadn't I, only a few weeks earlier, been sitting on the floor inhaling Craig's pheromones from his moldy old clothes? Out there in the black, cold, wet cockpit, just thinking about him conjured up his intoxicating scent. I recalled the first time we went snorkeling and how his muscled body looked so perfectly proportionate, so exquisitely masculine, and how, twenty-five years later, his Ironman training had gotten him back into shape.

I was not ogling but comparing. Alex's maleness reminded me of all I missed and had lost. I adored my husband, who after all those years was still the only man I wanted. Looking at Alex brought Craig back to me, not only in my senses but also in *Honu* and the oceans we had so often sailed together. Under the endless horizons of those endless seas, this sailboat had molded us together like nothing else could. If, when I returned, Craig and I continued to pass each other by, so be it. It was only by a fluke of fate that we found each other in the first place. At that moment, even while terrified, even while worrying that I had failed to do something important on the boat, I felt enormously lucky to have had those years with Craig.

I also felt enormously grateful to be right where I was, and who I was: a fifty-six-year-old woman skippering her own sailboat through a Pacific Ocean storm with a dear friend and adept crew member. People dream of having such an adventure at sea. I was doing it.

14

$\mathcal{N}$ONSAILING friends and readers often ask me two questions about being at sea. The most common one, mostly from women, is how you go to the bathroom on a boat. To me it seems like an odd question, because nearly all boats big enough to cross oceans have bathrooms similar to the ones we have at home, complete with toilet, sink, and shower. Not everyone knows that, though, and besides, women want details from another woman. Do you have to squat over a bucket? If there's a toilet, how do you sit there when the boat is bouncing all over the place? Is toilet paper allowed? And so forth.

Honu has a functioning bathroom, called the "head" on boats, so, no, you do not have to balance over a bucket. Even so, *using* the toilet in a pitching, rolling boat is practically an art.

In rough seas, I wait as long as I can stand it before climbing down the heaving ladder and lurching past the main instrument panel, which is loaded with hair-trigger on/off switches. Here attention must be paid. If an elbow or hip bumps those switches, even lightly, you can accidentally deactivate one or more of the boat systems that you really do not want deactivated, such as the bilge pump or GPS. During my practice voyages I had several moments of panic when the boat inexplicably began turning in circles after someone inadvertently turned off the autopilot.

Once I've passed the poorly located control board, I struggle through the narrow bathroom door and close it tight, making sure the latch is secure since it tends to fly open on its own. I don't much care about that, but it embarrasses my male crew members, so I remind myself to be careful. Inside, I drag down my shorts with one hand while holding onto the edge of the sink with the other (the sailor's rule in rough seas is *one hand for you, one hand for the boat*), sit on the toilet, and brace myself there by extending both legs and placing my feet flat against the opposite wall.

Almost all boat toilets have seawater flush systems. Some are electric, but on *Honu* you have to draw in and push out seawater with the up-and-down movement of a hand pump.

Toilet paper is allowed, but you can't throw it in the toilet because it clogs the hoses, and since these are stinky inside and attach to holes in the bottom of the boat, clearing them is not something you want to do, especially at sea. When we bought *Honu*, a brass sign above the toilet said: "Please do not put anything in this toilet unless you have eaten it first." The sign remains.

Since flushing even small amounts of toilet paper can block hoses, I tell everyone on my boat they must never, ever drop any kind of paper or trash in the bowl, emphasizing that if they forget, the offender has to fish it out. If the item is not retrieved, I explain, we'll be reduced to the dreaded bucket for the rest of the trip. This notion is revolting enough that the toilet never gets clogged.

The problem becomes what to do with used toilet paper. Plastic bags in the waste basket work, except that the full ones have to be stored on the boat or shaken over the side, because no plastic should ever be thrown in the ocean. Since both options are high on the yuck scale, I line the head's wastebasket with a cone of newspaper. The person in charge of cleaning the head that day closes the top of the cone and throws the whole works over the side. Both newspaper and toilet paper degrade quickly in the open ocean.

But that first night on the trip to Palmyra, relieving myself on the boat at sea was a misnomer, because by the time I finished, a new urgency arrived: being closed up in the sweltering, heaving little bathroom made me horribly nauseated. With each visit, after pulling my clothes back on one-handed and pumping the toilet handle the twenty times it took to thoroughly flush seawater through the hoses, I staggered past the instrument panel, raced up the ladder, and collapsed in the cockpit for the hour or so it took my stomach to recover. By then, if I was drinking the recommended amount of water for tropical heat, I had to go again.

And then there are men. Most simply walk to the back of the boat and pee off the stern. Watching them do that—and I did have to watch, at least from the corner of my eye, to make sure my male crew members hadn't fallen overboard—I had honest to God penis envy.

Human urine, by the way, is sterile and 95 percent water. The rest consists of nitrogen, sodium, potassium, and other chemicals, all of which occur naturally in seawater. Sailors urinating and defecating (human feces are nutrients to countless marine organisms) in the open ocean pollutes it about as much as Earth's communication satellites pollute the Milky Way. Like most pollution, it's a matter of concentration.

THE winds and seas died down after that first long night, but only like an earthquake dies down to its aftershocks. The conditions dropped from Force 7 to Force 6, and we still faced walls of water twelve to fifteen feet high and heard the twenty- to twenty-five-knot winds whistling in the wires. But the ocean had baptized us the day before, and although Alex and I didn't consider the sailing exactly restful, at least we believed we would live. In fact, not having drowned or become hysterical after our first terrifying night at sea, the two of us gained confidence. I remembered my friend Cari's words: *We can do this.* The conditions hadn't changed all that much, but sunshine made a huge difference. The sun's soft yellow rays turning the morning clouds pink felt as good as rising to the surface from a sea cave and gasping that first breath of air.

Since we rode up and down on waves of seasickness, neither of us felt like cooking. I was too queasy to want coffee, but by noon a caffeine-withdrawal headache gave me the energy to boil some water on the propane stove and stir up a cup of instant coffee. The headache went away, and soon Alex and I were puttering around like sea turtles: short bursts of activity separated by long periods of rest. The boat jerked in rhythm to the smallest swells and rocked to its side in the biggest, making any activity, even lounging in the cockpit, physical work involving hands grabbing rails and feet and legs bracing against bulkheads. It was an odd kind of exertion—not enough to make me feel like I had any exercise but enough to tire me out. On long passages, most people lose weight without trying, a phenomenon well known among sailors, and another topic of interest to my friends. For those trying to shed a few extra pounds, this seems like magic: lie around, eat whatever and as much as you want, and arrive at your destination ten pounds lighter.

We tried my new shortwave radio but got no reception. Craig had been able to tune in several stations on the old model (long broken), and my failure irritated me. Could I do *anything* without him? I didn't know if the problem was the radio, the time of day, or my own ineptitude. I soon gave up. Besides, Alex and I were salty, greasy, and stinky after that first day and night at sea and didn't care about connecting with civilization. Most of the time we sat gazing at the ocean zombie-like, sleepy from being unable to drop off the previous night, spacey from scopolamine, and tired from the energy it took to hang on in the cockpit. There was no marine life to watch. The deep blue of tropical waters is beautiful to behold, but that lovely color means the water is low in algae, and algae are at the bottom of the marine food web. A blue ocean, therefore, means water that's low in nutrients and therefore doesn't support much visible life.

Once we knew that the boat was doing fine, the warm sun felt so good on our skin that we took turns bathing on the aft deck, upending buckets of cool seawater over our heads and rinsing the salt off with a cup (and only a cup) of freshwater. After changing our damp, grungy clothes, we tidied the boat. I was unwavering about hygiene, in both body and boat, believing cleanliness had a direct relationship to the captain and crew's state of mind. This proved to be true. We felt much better afterward.

We each slept soundly the next night when off watch, and the next day, the wind and seas dropped another notch. Some excitement occurred as I was pulling in the jib and saw its slack line (known as the lazy sheet) pull out of its block and drop over the side like a snake striking prey. I sail with the transmission in neutral, because the forward motion of the boat causes the propeller to spin, thus turning a large alternator that murmurs like a deep and distant voice. These alternators, called prop generators, provide an efficient way of getting free electricity while sailing. Having one also means that the propeller is always turning.

The lesson I learned about lines in the water from the Makapu'u propeller incident had been seared into my brain, and when the jib sheet fell into the water, I raced for the gearshift and pulled it into reverse, stopping the prop before it wound up the dangling line. (In reverse gear with the engine off, *Honu*'s propeller does not spin.) It occurred to me that if I hadn't had the rope-on-a-prop experience, I would never have acted so quickly, and one of us would have had to dive under the boat, a dark thought out there in the open ocean. My vigilance was beginning to make the boat's rhythm, motion, sounds, sights, and smells as much a part of me as my own heartbeat. *Honu* and I had to travel, work, and breathe together whether in twenty feet or twenty thousand feet of water. If I didn't pay attention, I was acutely aware, we could also die together.

The prolonged trade wind conditions made the seas rough by coastal standards, but after sailing across Hawai'i's channels with Craig for years, I had come to consider such boisterous wind and waves almost normal. Alphie the autopilot apparently thought so, too, because it drove perfectly in the diminishing swells, leaving Alex and me free to do what sailors do on boats offshore.

And that's the second question friends and readers ask me most often about offshore voyaging: What do you do all day? Sleep, for one thing. With only two people to keep night watch, we were up half the night, and would be every night until we arrived. We also cooked, sort of. Because we felt hungry in the cockpit but nauseated when moving about below deck for more than a few minutes, "cooking" often involved gathering finger food from the galley, such as Goldfish crackers and beef jerky, and carrying it to the cockpit. Occasionally, a feast occurred when one of us made peanut butter and jelly sandwiches or got truly energetic and boiled water for saimin noodles.

We had brought audio books, music, and movies to use on each of our personal computers and CD players (MP3 players were not common at the time), but plugging headsets into our ears seemed too antisocial. As old friends, Alex and I didn't have to talk to be comfortable and often remained silent for hours on end, but when one of us felt like sharing a thought, earbuds prevented it. Instead, we preferred to let Bill Clinton read us his life story on the boat's CD player, which broadcast over four loudspeakers. To make the book last longer, we rationed ourselves to one hour-long CD at a time.

Besides sleeping, reading, and listening to audio entertainment, sailors also spend a lot of time staring at the ocean. This became one of Alex's and my favorite pastimes. We spent hours sitting next to each other in silence, watching the wind whip the water into swirling blue-and-white parfaits that rolled under and around the boat. The rhythm of those always moving, always rumbling waves hypnotized me. In their momentum, I drifted into a state of consciousness I never experienced anywhere else. My brain became a clean slate. It was meditation without effort, serenity without drugs.

Some sailors get addicted to these periods of harmony with the sea and set out time and again on long offshore passages, not to go anywhere in particular but to get their fix. I had communed with nature in this way on plenty of my passages with Craig, but as skipper, my stoner intervals were all too brief. After an hour or so spacing out in the cockpit with Alex, my awareness snapped back with a jolt, giving me that stomach-turning feeling you get after sleeping through an alarm set for an important meeting. Up I jumped from the cockpit cushion, dashing below to lift the floorboards and check my through-hulls.

That's the other thing skippers and crew do all day: check gear and fix what's broken.

I started my checks with the propeller shaft that had caused me so much grief in the past. Cool to the touch and dry. Perfect. Forward I swayed, examining the seacocks, donning a headlamp to peer into the engine compartment and inspecting the freshwater tanks for leaks. All seemed fine until I arrived in the forward cabin, looked into a floor space that had never before leaked, and found more than a gallon of seawater sloshing around. I knew it was seawater because I tasted it, a tactic I learned from Craig. (In the middle of the night one time in the marina, I stepped from our bunk into ankle deep water. "There's water all over the floor!" I called out in alarm, and Craig, from a dead sleep, said, "Taste it.") If a leak is freshwater, that's good news because it's coming from the inside and can't sink the boat. If it's seawater you've got a problem, maybe serious.

Quickly, I pulled spare sails, tarps, and blankets from the storage space beneath the V-berth where the leak seemed to be originating. The gear at the bottom of the locker was sopping wet, yet even after I dumped the dripping mess onto my lovely teak floor and bailed a bucketful of seawater from the bin, I could not see how it was getting in. This didn't qualify as an emergency, but a seawater leak at sea, in a new place, puzzled me and demanded investigation. I needed some advice.

I entered Craig's number in my new satellite phone, not knowing if he would be terse or cryptic, or even cold, given our silent parting. Seconds later his cell phone rang. I loved this new telephone technology, a far cry from the old days when people relayed messages, if they were lucky, through single-sideband marine operators and ham radio enthusiasts. Except for the occasional cutout when the signal switched satellites, the satellite phone worked as well as my cell phone—clear reception, no static, no delay.

He answered on the first ring. "Susan. How are you? What's happening?"

That he sounded so happy, so relieved, to hear from me was a big surprise, and for a few seconds I was speechless. I had been gone only two days, but something had changed. For the first time in ages, I heard the old concern, the genuine caring, in his voice.

"I'm fine," I said. "We're good."

"I've been following the weather. Are you getting pasted out there?"

"We did yesterday and last night, but the boat did well. The seas and wind are better now. Not exactly calm, but manageable."

"Good work, Captain. You're doing a great job."

"I have a couple of questions about the boat."

"Okay. Shoot."

We discussed *Honu*'s leak like, well, like two skippers talking boats. The leak was a puzzle to him, too. The bailing would be a pain, and the leak required monitoring, but since it wasn't big enough to sink the boat, he advised me to wait until I got to Palmyra to track it down.

"Don't worry," he said. "This is what happens to boats when they sit for so long. Caulking dries out, gaskets get cracked. A leak here and there is normal."

"I wish it had happened when I was still at home."

"You didn't have seas like this at home."

"Right. Thanks for the advice. I wasn't sure what to do."

"You're doing a fine job," he said. After all those years of skippering the boat with a semi-interested first mate, Craig could now talk captain to captain. We were beginning to speak the same language.

"How are *you* doing?" I asked. "What's happening there?"

His hesitation told me that he and Christine were probably planning a race somewhere. "Not much," he said. "Busy." Our mutual language was nautical only. If we weren't talking about boats, we weren't talking. We said our good-byes and hung up.

That evening while I was on first watch, Alex ascended to the cockpit to report a strong diesel smell in the main cabin, an odor that made him profoundly nauseated. He remained in the cockpit taking deep breaths while I went below to investigate. I lifted the teak floorboard (called the "sole") beneath the companionway ladder to look at the fuel port, seven inches in diameter, in the top of the fifty-gallon fiberglass tank. Pierre and I had replaced the old, leaking aluminum cover with a plastic one, but the gasket sealant we used had gradually come unstuck during the storm, making the leak far worse than it had ever been. Under the boat's violent motion, diesel fuel slapped the underside of the lid, oozed through the gap, and rolled under the sole of the main cabin, wasting fuel and stinking up the boat.

We covered the oozing port with plastic bags and tried fashioning gaskets out of cut-up hoses. Alex helped as much as he could, but every few minutes he had to rush to the cockpit for fresh air. Nothing worked. For the second time in a few hours, I called Craig. The sound of his hello made me want to say *I love you. Why am I out here without you?*

"Hi," I said. "Me again. We're fine. But remember the fuel port Pierre replaced?"

Again, he was upbeat and chatty. "Diesel isn't flammable," he said. "It might smell up the boat, but the leak isn't dangerous. One of two things will happen. You'll either use the engine and the fuel level will drop and stop sloshing. Or it will leak enough for the level to drop and stop sloshing."

The fuel leak might not have been dangerous, but it disabled my one and only crew member. "Alex can't use the sea berth or the galley with the smell so strong," I said. "I'll have to try to soak it up with the white pads."

"I'm sorry this is happening to you," Craig said. "Those leaks are bad luck. It's not your fault."

"Thanks for saying that."

"I mean it. You're doing a fine job under tough circumstances."

The oily fuel had run beneath the floor boards in hard-to-reach places, and I had to lie on my stomach to adequately push the thick petroleum-absorbing pads into and around corners. I packed the leaking lid with the pads and changed them often, storing the soaked ones in heavy black garbage bags. It was nasty work, but it didn't nauseate me as it did Alex, who began to wretch almost immediately when he tried to help.

"I'm really sorry," he said over and over.

"Alex, it's not your fault. Stay in the cockpit. Don't worry. I'm fine," I said. And I *was* fine. It was my boat that was leaking, and I had to deal with it. I couldn't expect Alex to do a job that made him sick, nor could I ask him not to use the sea bunk or the galley.

The two leaks had me on my hands and knees often in the rolling boat. Either I worked with sponges, rags, and buckets to clean up the mess they made, or I was down there checking to see if they had changed from a pain to a peril. Each time I climbed the ladder back to the cockpit, my skin and clothes bore some disgusting blend of salt water, diesel fuel, and dirt. Between tending the actual leaks, I continued scouting for new ones. Call me captain? I felt more like a scullery maid.

We had no moon on our second night, but the clouds gradually dissipated, and that meant no more drenching squalls. It also meant stars. With no competition from cities, and no moon or cloud cover, the twinkling stars felt like fairy dust sprinkling light on the water for us to see the white wave tops. So bright did the Milky Way shine that night that it looked like a real path, a shimmering road meandering to some place magic. As I lay in the cockpit looking up, I remembered a black T-shirt Craig once bought me when I was struggling with an organic chemistry class. The shirt pictured the Milky Way in white, with a little arrow and the words "You are here." That night, I had never been more *here*. I might not have been sure of my destination, but at least the journey had begun.

We took two- to three-hour watches, wrapped in sleeping bags, leaning against big pillows, and listening to audio books and music. Alphie the auto-pilot had been working fairly well, but the occasional rambunctious wave pushed it momentarily off course, almost as if Alphie dozed off for a moment. I did not know what that meant mechanically, but before I could worry about it, the machine would perk up and go back to work.

Over the next few days, the wind gradually died down and the seas grew flatter. *Such is sailing*, I thought. *First we get our doors blown off, and now, even with all the sails up, we aren't going anywhere.* Except I didn't have all the sails up. There was one more—the spinnaker—but I had never flown it and didn't know how.

In windy Hawai'i, we so rarely used this enormous sail that I had seen it up only a couple of times. I called Craig a third time to get instructions on how to fly *Honu*'s big, billowing spinnaker off the bow.

This time, it wasn't just the sound of his voice I found comforting. I was engrossed in the details of what he was saying. It was my job to get the spinnaker rigged and flying, and also to take it down, no small task when the wind comes up. But throughout Craig's upbeat and lengthy explanation—how he loved talking sailboats when I was truly paying attention—the spinnaker gradually ceased to be an option. The wind dropped to a whisper and quit. We were suddenly becalmed, a welcome relief from the way the trip started.

With no wind, we could motor along at six to seven knots using *Honu*'s powerful engine, which would have the bonus of lowering the level of the leaking diesel fuel. After pulling down all the sails, I tried to start the engine by pushing the starter button. Nothing happened. Not a click, a groan, or even a shudder of defeat. During the refit, I told Pierre about the starter occasionally playing dead, and he looked over its connections and found no obvious problem. Every time he tried, it started right up. Clearly, there was something wrong in the wires or the starter itself, but the on-again-off-again performance made it nearly impossible to track down. This is a common problem in starters because they contain an electrical device (enclosed in a metal box bolted to the starter) called a solenoid that sometimes jams.

"What do you think is wrong with it?" I asked Pierre after he finished checking the connections.

"Probably a sticky solenoid. But it's working now," he said. "If it doesn't turn the engine over, hit it with a hammer."

He was not joking. Even my sailboat engine repair book, which used photos of *Honu*'s exact model engine and starter as examples, said of a hesitating starter, "First try hitting it [the solenoid] with a hammer."

Now I was at sea with plenty of fuel and an engine that would not start. "What's wrong with it?" Alex said, as I tried the starter again.

I don't know, I wanted to shout.

"Sometimes it takes a few tries," I said. "It's got *menehunes* in it." (In Hawai'i you can blame everything from lost car keys to a sticky starter solenoid on these mythical little people.)

I was beginning to realize that no matter how hard I worked to prepare, no matter how many experts I hired or books I read, there would always be events on this sailboat that were out of my control. If the starter started the engine, we go. If it failed to start the engine, okay, I had to fix it. If the autopilot died, all right, I would dig out the spare and figure out how it worked. *Go with the flow* never felt more pertinent. As I sat watching the heaving (but not breaking) swells, it occurred to me that all I needed to know about marriage, menopause, aging, friendship, careers, love, life, and death, I could learn from *Honu*.

The engine started on the next try. Its droning sounded wrong out there in the watery wilderness, and its heat made us sweat in the galley and sea berth even with all the hatches open, a luxury we had not been able to afford in the rough seas. Alphie liked motoring through smooth water, though, and worked consistently. I was immensely relieved.

Honu's engine always leaked a little oil—the nature, Pierre explained, of old-style diesel engines. After we motored for twenty-four hours, however, I noticed an unusual amount of oil soaking the white petroleum catch pads (the same type I used to soak up the diesel fuel) I had placed in the pan beneath the engine. Removing the dripping two-foot by two-foot squares, which as long as we motored got soaked with black oil, became another of my grubby chores, turning my nail beds filthy, my skin a diseased gray, and my clothes permanently stained.

To top off these fluid woes, I discovered that my stash of Diet Cokes in the aft cabin had banged together in their locker so hard that three had exploded. While cleaning that up, I learned that Diet Coke was only part of the liquid problem back there. The rudder packing had begun to leak seawater. Good lord. My lovely, high-end French sailboat was beginning to feel like the *African Queen*.

So as *Honu* motored, Alex and I took turns mopping and sopping, bailing and pailing. As the engine burned fuel, the level in the tank lowered and the diesel leak stopped almost completely, making Alex a happy man.

With each new leak and chore, my appreciation of how hard Craig had labored on this boat, how reliably, rose another notch. I had helped him with such chores, but helping the person in charge was a far cry from being the person in charge. While sailing with Craig, if I felt seasick or exhausted, he excused me, graciously with no guilt trips, leaving me free to take a nap. I now appreciated the price of such courtesy. Captains don't get many naps.

That night at sea I missed Craig far more than I had in the past months. Even during the refit with Pierre, even when Craig was traveling with Christine or working nights and weekends, he was still *there* in my life. But he was not *here* on this boat.

That's what got me in trouble, I decided that night. When it came to growing old, I had depended on the Twinship. Craig, I knew, would love me no matter how old I got, as I did him. But the refit showed me that it didn't matter what Craig or anyone else thought about me aging. What mattered was what *I* thought about it. And the problem with deciding this during menopause—especially during a year when a young woman had moved in with us—was that I could not separate rational thought from hormone confusion. My brain and body seemed to have parted company. With the periods of composure that estrogen replacement and antidepressants helped me gain, I considered myself an upbeat, high-energy woman with places to go, friends to make, and goals to achieve. Yet with its wrinkles, spots, and twisted joints, not to mention the occasional out-of-the-blue rage and frightening forgetfulness, my body was turning me into an old crone whom people ignored, or even disliked, without even knowing me. Who was the real me?

When I brought up this uncomfortable straddling of two worlds to my counselor (who had become my singles counselor, Craig having dropped out), he told me about a male client in his fifties who was tired of dating younger women because they all wanted children and he did not. When the counselor asked him why he didn't date women his own age, the man said, "Because they remind me of my grandmother."

The counselor and I stared at each other. "This is not helping me, Martin," I said.

"I'm just telling you that that's how some men in their fifties think about some women in their fifties," he said.

"But what does that mean, 'they remind me of my grandmother'? Is it about sex?"

"Susan, everything is about sex."

I knew that. Hadn't I, nearly paralyzed with fear, eyeballed Alex and a moment later gotten dizzy with desire over the smell of Craig's pheromones? Simply the *memory* of Craig's scent had been all it took to get me going. You don't have to be a biologist to know that from aphids to zebras, life is about sex, and we humans are right up there oozing hormones with the rest of Earth's creatures. No wonder women feel lousy during menopause. Besides the physical decline and mental confusion, we're getting the first inklings of nature's cruel message: *You, my dear, are toast.*

There's nothing like skippering a sailboat offshore for getting your mind off life's hard questions. At sea the days and nights ran together, and as Alex and I watched the GPS at the wheel tick off the miles, we worried less and laughed more, working on small projects in random order according to our moods. Alex rewired a corroded connection to the engine room light and whipped the ends of several ropes. ("Whipping" is tying nylon thread in a particular way around the ends to keep them from fraying.) We both fashioned new gaskets for the diesel tank (without success), and I scrubbed floors until I looked like Cinderella before the ball.

When boat repairs and maintenance were taken care of, I stared at the water thinking about everything and nothing, a state of mind that's like a cross between a mescaline trip and a frontal lobotomy. Often, my thoughts contained some kind of food theme. My brain would get going on a subject, such as how much canned fruit we had left, and examine it to absurdity. *Apples and oranges and peaches, oh my.* I once discovered two hours had passed and all I had decided was that we should eat the last of the bananas today.

Other times, I couldn't think about anything at all. The moving water felt like a dream, where everything visible—the boat, the water, the sky—was in constant motion but nothing ever changed. With the horizon always the same blue line in the distance, it seemed as if we weren't moving toward anything, least of all forward. The sameness of the rhythm made me feel as if *Honu* floated on a saltwater treadmill. Sometimes a wayward wave would give the boat a sharp slap, startle me back to the planet, and leave me with earthly cravings. *Must have gummy worms.*

Always, though, the ocean went on about its business, indifferent to my little boat, not caring whether it floated like a cork on its surface or rolled around in pieces a mile down on its floor. The Pacific Ocean sent its waves swaggering endlessly on like living entities, either rising tall and spilling over in a lather or arching their backs in nonchalant shrugs and rolling on. I loved the apathy of the sea. Since I was nothing to it, I could reinvent myself, start over with any definition of who I was. But later. *Too hard to think about right now.*

One night as Alex prepared to relieve me on night watch, out of the void a cruise ship crept up behind us, the huge vessel rapidly growing larger and larger. This was no subtle approach. The ship had enough lights around its multiple decks to illuminate Maui. It was also big enough to crush us to splinters and never even feel the hit. Did the helmsman see *Honu?*

VHF radios intimidated me, but Alex had often used such radios at Tern Island. I handed him the mike.

"Call them," I said. "Make sure they know we're here."

"Why do I have to call?" he said. "It's your boat. You do it."

I had just given an order to my first mate—and he refused. But he was right. It had not been very captainy of me to turn over the radio communications. I should do it myself.

Having to talk over the radio, though, felt like getting called on in class when I hadn't done the assignment and having my stammering answer broadcast over the PA system. All vessels at sea monitor channel 16, the hailing or emergency channel, making the call oh so public. Even after you agree on another channel for a conversation, anyone listening can tune in and eavesdrop. (I knew that because I often did it, garnering information about weather and anchorages without having to talk.) Besides that, these radios are on speakers, so anyone in the pilot house or on the bridge can listen to you sputter the wrong compass points—"We're northwest of you . . . I mean *south*west. No, south*east.* You're northwest of *us*"—or make up weird words for the official radio alphabet. In my nervousness I have in the past turned Alpha, Bravo, Charlie into Apple, Broken, Cargo. And I often forgot to say "over" at the end of mangled sentences.

"You have more practice from Tern Island than I do," I said. "Please."

"I don't know what to say."

"Ask if they see us. We have to make sure they see us."

Getting run over by a big ship is a universal fear among offshore sailors. Alex hesitated and took the mike.

"This is the sailing vessel *Honu* calling the cruise ship behind us. Do you see us? Over."

A voice with a heavy Russian accent came back immediately. "This is the *Norvegian Wang*. Do not worry. We have been vatching you on radar for a long time."

He meant the *Norwegian Wind*, an enormous cruise ship that frequented Honolulu Harbor, but his accent made "wind" sound like "wang," and we started laughing. It was hysterical laughter, far too much for the silly joke, but hilarious to us in our nervousness. Wiping his eyes and snorting as he got himself under control, Alex told Captain Wang we were heading for Palmyra, and he informed us they were bound for Fanning, an atoll about 150 miles southeast of Palmyra. Suddenly, I wanted very much to be the one talking to the cruise ship captain. I was the captain of *Honu*. I should be the one telling him about my boat and destination.

Too late. The ship passed quickly. It was a mile away according to our GPS map, but even so, it loomed over us like a twenty-story dragon breathing white fire. We bid a silent good-bye to the Good Ship Wang and were once again alone in that enormous dark ocean.

I knew that the open ocean in tropical latitudes is a marine desert, but the sea heard my yearning for marine life, and next morning we had our first offshore visitors: two pilot whales headed toward *Honu*, apparently swimming over to check us out.

Pilot whales are easy to identify from a boat. They have all-black bodies and distinct round foreheads that protrude beyond the mouth, giving them a cute egghead appearance. Their scientific name, *Globicephala*, means "globe head" and refers to the whales' well-defined, bulbous-shaped foreheads. In some areas, fishermen refer to these whales with the charming nickname of potheads.

The little twenty-foot-long whales that passed the boat were short-finned pilot whales, a warm-water member of the dolphin family. (Whales are one large category with multiple divisions, the dolphin family being one.) Short-finned pilot whales' front flippers are about one-sixth their body length. The only other pilot whales in the world are long-finned pilot whales with fins about one-fourth their body length. Both species live in kin-based groups, but the long-finned ones prefer the cold waters of the North Atlantic and Southern Ocean.

Pilot whales got the name "pilot" from the probably false belief that a single member leads the pod, even to death on a beach. Another source says that the term "pilot" came from the notion that the whales will guide fishermen to a catch. This might be partially true since pilot whales sometimes swim with schools of herring, tuna, and the whales' favorite food, squid.

A fact I love about short-finned pilot whales is that the females go through menopause and beyond. This was discovered in 1984 after researchers examined 298 bodies of short-finned pilot whales that had been killed for food in Japan. By using growth layers in teeth to determine each whale's age, the scientists learned that female pilot whales stop reproducing at thirty-six years of age. Their ovaries wither, yet they live nearly thirty more years, to about sixty-five. Male pilot whales don't live much past forty.

One biological explanation for life after menopause is the grandmother hypothesis, a theory that older females help younger relatives raise their offspring. Like people, pilot whales also live in genetically related family groups. And here's some food for thought (boomers take heart): female pilot whales continue to copulate long after their ovaries quit. This, researchers speculate, may help stabilize the pod by reducing fighting among lusty males and keeping them from wandering to other pods looking for love.

In the ocean you can't pick out these go-getting grandmothers from other pod members, but just seeing those two pilot whales checking out *Honu* made me feel good. In the world of mammals, we aging women are not alone.

Pilot whales, I decided, would be my *aumakua* (*ow-ma-KOO-ah*), or guardian spirit, a concept in Hawaiian mythology in which each human family has one or more animal type looking out for them. In Hawai'i, the appearance of one's *aumakua* is taken as an omen of good or bad, depending, I guess, on how your day is going. Because the voyage was finally going well, I took the pilot whales' sighting as a positive sign.

Pilot whales, larger than bottlenose dolphins but smaller than humpback whales, are common in waters off the Hawaiian Islands, where fifteen to fifty sometimes swim shoulder to shoulder to round up a meal of squid and small fish. It's hard to have a chorus line of two, though, and our whales swam far apart. They also kept their distance, never coming close enough for a good photo. What were those two little whales doing way out there, I wondered? Where were they going in such a hurry? We would never know. Seconds after we spotted them, they disappeared.

This was our one big wildlife highlight in that vast tropical ocean. Coral reefs, which get a lot of press over their teeming marine life, grow only in shallow coastal areas, not much past a hundred feet deep, which is as far down as sunlight penetrates. The absence of marine life reminded me that tropical off-shore waters are the oceans' deserts. As is true of all deserts, amazing animals live there, but they're far apart and hard to find.

SOMETIMES during a watch I listened to a bon voyage gift, a creepy audio book about a serial killer stalking women, and regretted it. I didn't need help generating bad dreams. My sleep was already fitful, with one ear always listening for trouble. A new sound, a familiar one that changed pitch, or the smallest alteration of the boat's motion had me bolting up to the cockpit to see what was wrong. That I was becoming as alert as Craig to the boat's vital signs gave me little consolation. It just made me tired.

On one of those black nights, I stayed in the cockpit after my watch and enjoyed a meteor shower with Alex. We oohed and aahed over the shooting stars like kids on the Fourth of July. Afterward, we sat opposite one another in the cockpit talking quietly about his girlfriend, a young woman currently working for the Nature Conservancy in Palmyra. The affair started out bright and sparkly, but the fireworks fizzled, and he felt sad about it. By the time Alex and I arrived at Palmyra, this woman's volunteer term would soon be over. He had to end the affair before she left the atoll, and although she knew it was coming, he worried that she would not take it well. In fact, Alex felt awful about all his failed relationships. And as a smart, softhearted, and attractive man, he had plenty. He worked in a field with lots of single women at remote outposts, and they didn't hesitate to hop into bed with him. The problem was that he fell in love with nearly every one.

"What are you looking for, exactly?" I said.

"A soul mate," he said. "I don't want to spend my life alone, and I don't want love affairs. I want to be half of a couple."

I offered more details about my struggles with Craig, Christine, and hormone therapy. Even if Christine had never entered our lives, I said, Craig and I had been heading for trouble. I had become too dependent, expecting him to solve my aging and career problems, and he had protested by clamming up and working out. Alex nodded. He had traveled the path of relationship road kill more times than he cared to remember and understood the frustration.

Agewise, we seemed an odd pair with our twenty-five-year difference, but overall, our friendship made sense: he was a young man desperately trying to find a life partner, and I was an older woman desperately trying to keep one. Also, we had run away to sea together.

One afternoon we sat watching a light breeze wrinkle the ocean's surface. This was a sign to turn off the motor and haul up the sails. "How about if go for a swim first?"

"No," I said immediately. "I don't want you off the boat."

"But it's still calm. I just want to get wet."

I sighed, not wanting to do it, but not wanting to be a killjoy either. Years earlier, in windier conditions off Costa Rica, Craig and I swam behind the very slowly moving boat, but the decision had been his, and I trusted his judgment. Craig allowed himself to play with his boats as well as work with them.

"Okay," I said, "but we put out a long line, *and* you tie your leash to the ladder. No swimming off."

I turned off Alphie and the motor, tied a hundred-foot-long floating line off the rear cleat, and held my breath as Alex eased himself down the stern ladder. After clipping his harness leash around the ladder's frame, he immersed himself, grasped the bottom rung with both hands, and as the light wind pushed the hull, let his body drift in the deep blue bottomless water. Jesus, there were those long legs dangling off the boat again.

"That's it," I said, after about thirty seconds. "Get back up here."

"It's feels great," he called from the water.

"Alex, please. Come in. You're scaring me."

He climbed back to the deck, dripping and grinning. "That was great," he said. "Try it. Just do a quick dip."

I hadn't planned on it, but ordering myself to lighten up, I donned my harness. It did feel good to lower myself in the ocean and let the water rinse the sweat off my sticky skin. But I was so concerned about getting separated from the boat that I scrambled back on board in seconds, happy to have the deck beneath my feet and Alex safely in the cockpit. Still, I did it. I took a sea bath.

On day five, the light wind increased to twenty knots and the seas rose accordingly. Soon, up went the wind and waves another notch. It seemed as if the Pacific Ocean had two speeds: dead and overdrive. We furled the jib a little at a time until it was rolled up completely and sailed with only the mainsail, which we eventually triple reefed. The wind gusted to thirty-five knots and the waves rose steadily to about fifteen feet. The boat bucked and pitched and heaved until we, too, were feeling like heaving. We dropped the mainsail and flew only the jib to see if the ride got any smoother. It was the same either way, not quite as bad as that first night, but only because daylight allowed us to see those barreling waves. Also, we now had some experience.

Up and down, in and out went the sails. Since we weren't sure what worked best for the boat in these squally conditions (or, to be truthful, in any conditions), we tried all combinations. Just when we were satisfied that the boat was sailing its best, conditions would change. A container ship, silent as a shooting star and big as a planet, passed only a mile or so behind *Honu*, scaring us into scheduling a more formal watch during the day. Container ships can sink you in bright sunlight just as quickly as on dark nights.

Honu had entered a notorious zone of unstable weather called the Intertropical Convergence Zone, or ITCZ, that encircles Earth on both sides of the equator. The key word here is "convergence" because it's where the northern and southern trade winds meet, forcing hot, humid air up. This is the recipe for thunderheads, and the ITCZ cooked them up one right after another. When the angry dark clouds couldn't hold one more drop of water, they burst open like water balloons, exploding rain at thirty to forty miles per hour.

But not constantly. Sailors of old called this zone the "doldrums" because, between thunderstorms, wind could be nonexistent, temperatures sweltering, and the boat dead in the water. This is where the Ancient Mariner stalled when his painted ship drifted upon a painted ocean. Our painting, though, felt more like a still from *Victory at Sea*. The wind varied between strong and very strong.

I had imagined the ITCZ as an endless ceiling of sooty clouds, but instead, the bright blue sky was pocked with black thunderheads that patrolled the area like enemy battleships. Rain fell around us in veils, and the changing wind direction caused the waves to abandon formation. Mountains collapsed to foothills that flattened to plains that rose to mountains. The wind confused the water, and in its bewilderment, it attacked *Honu* from all sides. We rocked side to side, pitched forward and backward, and heaved up and down, sometimes, it seemed, all at the same time. All this motion started and stopped with such unsettling inconsistency that I wasn't sure if I should launch the life raft or take a nap.

Sailors of all eras dreaded the ITCZ because you must zigzag around its thunderstorms when you can, and when you can't, you have to push through. Or run from them. Pierre, who had crossed the ITCZ nine times, advised that I not try to shorten my sails and bash through the tempests but rather, when one appeared that I couldn't drive around, turn the boat and run downwind. The storm would speed past in a half hour or so, he said, and I could then resume course. It sounded like a good tactic. Too bad I never got the chance to try it out.

Alex and I hung on in the cockpit as the wind swirled, the seas churned, and *Honu* flew downwind. I felt more confident than when I started out five days earlier, cocky even. *I'm prepared*, I thought. *I'm tougher now.* We estimated *Honu* would arrive in Palmyra in two days. I may not be able to fly a spinnaker, I thought, but I'm getting this boat to the atoll in good order.

And then, with one little Champaign cork pop, *Honu*'s forestay broke at the top of the mast.

15

I stared bug-eyed. My sparkling new jib no longer flew off the starboard bow like a billowing banner of downwind sailing. Instead, it drooped over the life-lines like so much wet laundry. The bottom of the sail remained attached to the bow, but its middle and top had fallen flat on the surface of the wind-swept sea and lay jerking in the breaking waves.

I had been sitting on the left side of the cockpit when the odd *pop* occurred. A second later, *Honu* rolled to her right, suddenly elevating me to the high side of a teeter-totter. The canvas shade over the cockpit (the bimini) obscured my view of the boat's starboard side, but I didn't need to see it to know disaster had struck. The boat's tilt was unlike anything I had ever experienced, the slant sickeningly wrong, like the angle of a broken collarbone or a dislocated hip. From his view on the starboard side, Alex saw the problem.

"The jib fell down," he said with childlike wonder. Since Alex hadn't been around sailboats much, I thought he must mean that the jib ripped or a rope failed. Jibs don't just fall down.

This one did. Unlike the typical jib-hoisting systems found on most sail-boats, where you hauled the jib to the mast top with a rope called the jib hal-yard and left it there, *Honu* had an unusual French mechanism: when the halyard reached the top, the sail snapped into a fitting that locked it in place and released the halyard. You lowered the now-free halyard with a line called a messenger and secured it to the mast. It was a simple system that Craig and I both liked, but it had a huge disadvantage. If the forestay broke at the mast top, a rare event that is always a catastrophe, the jib and its furler had no halyard—no rope—holding it up, and the whole works would fall down.

The whole works did fall down, the whole works in this case being the furler, jib, and forestay.

I hadn't paid much attention to the forestay during the refit because I never actually saw the wire, it being completely covered by the furler. And with the pulley working well, I rolled and unrolled my jib without giving the backbone of the whole system, the forestay, any thought whatsoever. At that moment, however, that wire (still obscured inside the furler), became the center of my universe.

Having a forestay fail on a sailboat is like having the front guy-wire break on a tent, or a support beam fall down in your living room. The tent, the ceiling, or in a sailboat's case, the mast, may or may not collapse, but if it doesn't fall right away, you know it will soon.

On *Honu*, the weight of all that gear—sail, forestay, and furler—had bent a stainless steel stanchion (the posts supporting the life lines), and the sprawl of it all caused the boat to lean far to its starboard side. Too far. It wouldn't take much more to dip the rail underwater. The turbulent waves could swamp the boat. This possibility so terrified me, I thought, *We're going to die.*

The forestay and its gear, looking massive in its state of collapse, was now attached to the boat by only one fitting at the bow, held on by a large cotter pin I had found nearly impossible to remove during the refit. Something (unknown at the time) had given way at the top of the mast, and now the front part of the boat was empty. The unnatural space on the foredeck looked so odd that it seemed as if someone had knocked out *Honu*'s front teeth.

The sight paralyzed me, broken forestays being an unknown. No stay had ever let go when I was sailing with Craig. I didn't know what such a failure looked like or what to do about it. All I knew was that when a stay breaks, the mast falls.

Amazingly, *Honu*'s mast still stood, but it wobbled horribly. A scraping sound came from above, and I looked up to see the backstay, the usually taut wire supporting the mast from the rear, floppy and banging against the spinning blades of the windmill. The boat's motion in the rough seas was jerking the mast backward, another sickening sight, as it would not jerk for long. Without support from the bow, it would fall over backward, crashing onto the cockpit—and us—like a toppled tree.

We cast off the jib's sheets to ease the boat's alarming tilt, but the sudden lack of tension on the sail only caused the fallen gear to sag even lower over the side. Crawling to the bow, we saw that the aluminum furler and sail remained firmly attached to the finger-thick forestay, which remained firmly attached to the boat.

"I have a bolt cutter. Can you cut it?" I said.

Craig had bought the tool twenty years earlier "to cut a stay" he said. The four-word phrase he left unsaid—*in case of emergency*—had not registered with me. Until that moment, the wide-handled, three-foot-long device seemed like a nuisance on the boat, something that cluttered up the tool locker. Now the bolt cutter felt like the holy grail of sailboat tools, a blessing of Craig's foresight.

"I think it's easier to pull the cotter pin," Alex said, kneeling next to the stainless steel fitting, called a toggle, that still fastened the bottom of the forestay and furler to the bow. With the rest of the rig dragging heavily in the stormy seas, the boat leaned so hard to the starboard side and pitched so wildly from bow to stern that we had to hang onto the lifelines with both hands and jam our feet in the gutters below the rails just to stay on deck. One misplaced limb and over the side we would go.

Pulling the hefty cotter pin was beyond my strength. I had enough trouble straightening out the much smaller bobby-pin-sized cotter pins, and this was the biggest on the boat, two inches long and thick as a key ring. And it was holding an enormous load.

"Can you do it?" I said.

"I think so."

I ran below to get him a screwdriver, Vice-Grips, and needle-nose pliers, only barely catching myself from a fall when I slipped on a step going down the companionway. The pitching, rolling, heaving boat in the choppy seas had been bad enough with sails up to stabilize the motion. Now it felt as if we were hurtling over speed bumps in a car with four flats.

Alex sat on the bow and wedged his legs into the bars of the stainless steel railing called the pulpit. When he began straightening the bent prongs of the cotter pin with his young, male hands, so much stronger than mine, so intact, a bitter thought struck me: *At one time in my life, I might have been able to do that. No more. The time had passed. From here on, I would always need help. If I lived. If I was nuts enough to sail offshore again.*

Using the tools without visible effort, and in slow motion (it seemed) on the angled deck, Alex bent and began to tug the beefy pin from the toggle holding the wire to the boat.

One of the jib lines fell in the water, squirming like a white tentacle searching for something, such as my propeller, to strangle. My memory of diving under the boat off Makapuʻu to cut that stray line again flashed on like a neon sign. I scrambled back to the cockpit to shift the transmission from neutral to reverse. The prop stopped spinning.

Finally, Alex was able to pull the pin from the toggle, and *whomp*, the remainder of *Honu*'s jib, furler, and forestay dropped the rest of the way over the side and lay flat in the water. The release of all that weight on the rail caused the boat to level off, but that offered little relief. It was so windy now that, free of its burden and with no sails up, *Honu* pitched like a rodeo horse. Alex and I looked like rodeo riders, too, since we had to hang on with one hand while we worked with the other. When I looked up, to my astonishment, Alex stood at the rail gripping the tail end of the jib sheet. This was the massive forestay, furler, and jib's last tether, connected to *Honu* only by Alex's right hand, the left one being busy holding his body aboard the boat.

"I can't hold it much longer," he said, his muscles straining against the gear heaving in the fifteen-foot waves.

For a second, I couldn't understand what he was saying. The line he held in his hand should have been wrapped around the winch and cleated off in the cockpit. But in our earlier efforts to level the boat, one of us had cast it off.

"What should I do?" Alex yelled, his whole body leaning against the tugging sail.

I don't know, I wanted to scream. In our frightened state, it never occurred to either of us to simply rewrap the line around its winch, a quick and easy way to secure it.

The sail, flat and heaving upon the ocean's surface, jerked Alex's entire body as a breaking wave crashed onto the jib's heavy furler and forestay. Could the two of us haul that much gear into the boat in this weather? If we did, then what? The sail was still threaded onto its aluminum furler, five feet longer than the entire boat. How would we deal with this unwieldy mass of metal, wire, and cloth? A gust of wind rocked the mast back again, and the whirling windmill, mounted on the smaller mizzenmast behind the cockpit, hit the sagging backstay and scoured it with fast-turning blades. The horrible clank and clatter of blades against wire sounded like a warning alarm: *Red alert—the mast is going to fall down.*

"Let it go," I said.

Alex opened his hand, and we watched, horrified, as the line he had been holding dropped into the sea. For a second, the sparkling white triangle of sail lay flat on the water's surface, looking like a huge manta ray belly up. A heartbeat later, it began its mile-long descent, the white cloth turning turquoise, pastel blue, dark blue. Like a kraken, the sea monster of ancient lore, the ocean swallowed that enormous chunk of gear—jib, forestay, and furler. In one great greedy gulp, it was gone.

A shot of panic swept through me. What had I done? When I got to Palmyra, if we could make it there, *Honu* would need serious fixing, but now I had no gear to fix. *I had thrown it away.*

But with the mast jerking and the backstay clanging its warning, there was no time for second thoughts.

"We've got to stabilize the mast," I said.

This may have been Alex's first offshore voyage on a sailboat, but he had spent a lot of his life jury-rigging gear in field camps and repairing systems on power boats. He knew what to do. We had to secure the mast at the bow with the jib or spinnaker halyard. This was no brilliant innovation on our part. The sailing world is loaded with stories about saving masts (or trying to) with halyards. *Honu*'s spinnaker halyard was rarely used but remained ready to go, being fastened on the side of the mast.

Having a specific task to perform forced me to focus, and that calmed me considerably. *Slow, deep breath.*

"Fasten the spinnaker halyard to the bow," I shouted. "I'll winch from the cockpit."

Alex clipped the heavy halyard to the deck plate at the bow while I led the other end from the mast to the cockpit. The angle was such that the halyard lay hard against the canvas dodger that worked so well keeping waves and spray out of the cockpit. In an hour, the halyard would saw through the canvas and the dodger would be in shreds. Making my way hand over hand on the pitching boat to the tool locker below, I found a turning block and brought it up. Together, Alex and I fastened it to the sail track that ran along the deck outside the cockpit, away from the dodger. We worked as a team—not as two old salts but as two novices fighting fear to function to the best of our ability. Sometimes we talked and made mutual decisions; other times we worked in silence using instincts and best guesses.

The new angle worked. I wrapped the halyard around the large cockpit winch, inserted the winch handle, and cranked. "Tighter," Alex shouted, kneeling on the deck at the bow so he could look up at the mast. I turned the winch handle with all my strength. "More," he said, watching the mast's angle. "More."

I cranked until the halyard, our makeshift forestay, twanged like a guitar string. My God, what if this broke too? "Let's add the other halyard," I shouted from the cockpit to bow. "As a backup."

We repeated our efforts with a second halyard, which I tightened on another winch to twanging strength. While I could not see the mast's angle from where I worked, the towering aluminum pole stopped its unnerving shudder.

"That's it," Alex called, shading the sun from his eyes with his hand as he looked up. "We're good."

Leaving the cockpit, I crawled to the front of the bouncing boat, where I skinned my knees raw on the rough nonskid deck. Securing the mast did nothing for the boat's wild motion (we needed sails up to regain stability), and even on hands and knees, I had to hang on simply to look up. Rigged properly, the top half of the mast was supposed to lean back a bit, but at that moment, its ramrod straight position was a beautiful thing. It wobbled no more.

We crept back to the cockpit and sat down, staring at each other wide-eyed, dry mouthed, and speechless. The wind screamed. The waves bashed. Could we fly sails from a jury-rigged mast? How far were we from Palmyra? I didn't have enough fuel left to motor there and did not know the alternatives. *Honu* pitched and rolled to no rhythm. We hung on.

"Holy shit," Alex said.

"Exactly," I said.

But I knew what to do next.

Alex watched in silence as I retrieved the satellite phone from the nav station below, carried it to cockpit, and dialed Craig's cell number. I prayed he was not in the E.R. sewing up a moray eel bite or removing a fishbone from a tonsil. I waited, breathless, as Craig's phone rang, trying to think of the message I might leave if he didn't answer. *Hi, it's me. We're fine but, um, there's a problem. Call me.*

"Hello, Captain," Craig said, seeing the call was from me. "How's it going?" His voice sounded as sweet as it did the first year we lived together. In those days he would call during a busy day at the hospital just to tell me he loved me. I opened my mouth to calmly explain that the boat was disabled, but we were uninjured and afloat.

Instead I blurted, "Oh, Craig. The forestay broke."

A few beats passed, unusual for Craig, who is rarely taken by surprise and never at a loss for words. Then, in a voice that might have been asking if I had paid this month's electric bill, he said, "Is the mast still standing?" The bigger the emergency, the softer and calmer became Craig's tone. The strategy worked well to calm people in the E.R., but at home it often angered me because the tone sounded like he was making light of my problems, or didn't care. At that moment, however, hearing him so composed was as good as taking a valium.

"Yes," I said, taking a deep breath. "We managed to get a halyard on the bow. Two, actually."

"Oh. Then you're going to be fine."

I nearly laughed at this standard E.R. doctor phrase. So good to hear his voice. "The jib and furler went over the side with the stay."

"Where did the stay break?"

"At the top of the mast."

"It's attached at the bow?"

"Not anymore. All that gear hanging off the side leaned the boat too far over. We had to let it go."

Another long silence, no doubt digesting the fact that all that gear was gone. "Are you both okay?" he said.

A wave slapped the bow as *Honu* scooted down a wave from behind, and the collision nearly jerked the phone from my hand.

"Yes. Just scared."

"The boat is afloat. You saved the mast, and you have a rudder. No worries."

No worries. Craig would say that to a patient with a shark still attached to the person's leg. Still, I loved the security of having my expert-sailor husband tell me that this major boat failure was manageable.

I explained the situation: low on diesel fuel, no sails up, riding the roller coaster of ten- to fifteen-foot waves in the ITCZ. Our past voyages had never taken Craig and me through this zone, and the area was unknown to him. I felt a teensy glimmer of pride describing the circumstances, discussing options.

He told me which sails he would fly in which locations. "I think the mast can support the mainsail, if you triple reef it." On day five, we had done just that, shortening the sail to make it as small as possible, leaving up only a tablecloth length of fabric. "The wind will push the sail and the mast forward because you're going downwind."

"Not always," I said. "The squalls are coming at us from every direction."

"Well, I'm not there to see the conditions. I can tell you what I know about jury-rigging techniques, but you have to decide which sails to put up and where. You're the captain. You know the sea state, and you know the boat."

I sat silent for a moment, the rocking of my world having nothing to do with the boat's motion. Whatever happened from here on, success or failure, was up to me. Craig was right. At the moment, I knew the wind directions, the waves, and the boat's fitness better than he. The decisions had to be mine.

He finished his list of suggestions.

"I'll call you back," I said.

At the rear of the boat, we hoisted the little mizzen sail up the small (but intact) secondary mast. At mid-deck, we prepared to hoist *Honu*'s tiny, never-before-used storm jib off the baby stay, a wire about half the length of all the others, hence the name. It was this short stay, not found on all sailboats, plus the wind pushing from behind that had kept the mast standing long enough for us to fasten the halyards into a temporary forestay. I barely noticed the baby stay before, but now I spoke to it, *a wire*, as if it were a real baby: "You brave little darling. How big and strong you are."

Craig and I had never flown *Honu*'s storm jib, and when I dragged it from its dusty locker, I discovered it had no clips (called hanks) to attach it to the baby stay. Small shackles should work, I thought, shackles being the sailboat version of safety pins. I lurched to the front of the boat to the spare parts locker, got out my rigging box, and—hallelujah—found enough shackles to do the job.

I decided to fly the two tiny sails but not the mainsail. The last thing I wanted was to tempt the mast to fall down. Better to be underpowered and go slow. But speed turned out to be the least of our problems. With distribution of the two small sails so unbalanced, and the wind and waves so forceful, Alphie refused to turn the wheel even an inch. Ordinarily the autopilot pushed and pulled a device called the steering quadrant, a compact mechanism that attached to, and turned, the rudder. Apparently, something in it had finally let go.

Another mechanical failure, but this one left me calm. Autopilots are labor-saving devices not crucial to the boat floating or the mast standing. And at least I knew where to go to troubleshoot. The motor arm lay at the rear of the boat, underneath the plywood boards of my bed.

"We have to look at the autopilot," I said. "It might be something simple that's come undone."

Alex and I clutched our way down the lurching companionway ladder and made our way to my bed in the aft cabin. The untended boat threw me against the instrument panel, and I had to stop to check which bells and whistles I set off (none). While continuing my way aft, another big wave rolled the boat, and

I plopped with a thud into a sitting position on the settee as if I had just arrived for a cup of tea. Being below deck in such violent, random motion would normally have had me throwing up in every basin, bowl, and trash can, but apparently my stomach got the message that this was no time to be fussy. I felt no nausea at all.

Alphie consisted of aluminum tubes, hydraulic rods, and electric wires in a space beneath my mattress. I tore up the bed, heaving blankets, sheets, pillows, and several hatch boards to the floor. When I kneeled over the exposed machinery, the motion tipped me into the hole beneath, bruising my arms and banging my head. I ended up half-sitting, half-lying on the edge so I could look down with Alex, bent and braced opposite me.

"Go to the cockpit and turn Alphie's dial left and right," I said. "I'll watch to see what happens."

Alex unfolded his long legs from the small space and headed toward the companionway, his body slamming back and forth against the walls like an out-of-control skateboarder. I stared at the two-foot-long aluminum arm that was supposed to move back and forth as it turned the wheel. The motor whirred softly each time Alex worked the controls, but the arm did not move. We switched places with the same results and then examined the entire autopilot system together, searching for wires loose or parts dangling. Everything looked intact.

That was the extent of our "repair." Alex had never seen the device, and all I knew about the Alpha 3000 was its location.

Back to the spare parts locker. I dug out the old autopilot, a cylindrical contraption called an Autohelm that attached to the wheel in the cockpit. Years earlier, this simple machine had driven *Honu* from Connecticut all the way to Hawai'i. I lugged it to the wheel, where we set it up with cheery optimism—I had a spare autopilot—only to find that its glory days were over. It would not work. But I remembered: *Honu* had a *spare* spare autopilot. Stumbling back down the companionway, I burrowed deeper into the parts locker again and retrieved the second old Autohelm. We set it up. It, too, was dead.

Frantically, Alex and I looked for loose connections on the two identical Autohelm motors, each about the size of a large can of peaches. Both appeared intact on the outside, which meant that we had to open the black, waterproof canisters, which had not been made for easy opening. Alex took the wheel while I banged around below and located a container of miniature screwdrivers, called a jeweler's set. Like a bad horror film involving telekinesis, the boat's rocking and rolling slid sockets from their cubbies, upended jars of bolts, and sent screwdrivers and pliers airborne. Because the pandemonium had caused me to misplace, for the zillionth time, my reading glasses, I could barely see the tips of the tiny screwdrivers, let alone the heads of the autopilot's screws.

"I'll drive, you screw," I said, so frustrated at not being able to see up close anymore that I had to force myself not to behave like Pierre and, with a curse, throw something.

"It's really hard to steer," he said, as he turned the driving over to me.

I knew the sail arrangement was not ideal, but steering *Honu* in those big waves and howling wind felt like driving a tractor-trailer with a blowout. In two seconds, the wheel jerked from my grip and the boat turned straight into the wind and stalled, pitching violently again like a seesaw. Both Autohelms flipped off the cockpit bench and landed on the floor, which surely didn't do them any good.

"Give me a minute to get the feel of it," I said.

As Alex gathered the gear from the floor, I wrestled *Honu* back on course. I had to glue my eyes to the compass while gripping the lurching wheel to stay on the course to Palmyra. Inside the black canisters, Alex found several loose wires.

"Can you fix them?" I said, squinting (without success) to see the ends.

"They need soldering," he said, barely able to hold the disordered mess of spaghetti still enough to examine.

"I've never soldered," I said.

"I have," he said. "I'll try."

Once again we switched places and I stumbled below, this time to fetch the soldering gun and solder. Craig had saved the old autopilots for years, because like every veteran captain, he had a just-in-case mentality regarding spare parts. That foresight had saved the day, and possibly our lives, more than a few times, but the "save-it-for-parts" approach resulted in an odd assortment of junk that would make a hoarder blush. During the refit I had organized the pieces, assuming they worked or Craig would not have saved them, so at least I knew what I had and where it was located. But a harsh new lesson awaited. Before I considered a spare a spare, I had to check that it actually worked. When Craig decided to save those autopilots twenty years earlier, their motors ran. No more.

Between me hauling out half the boat's tool boxes and spare parts, and the sea flinging us like an orca tossing a seal (killer whales sometimes play with their food), the cabins below deck looked like the boat had rolled over. Only in the movies does a boat's wild motion stop or turn to a gentle sway when a person goes below deck. Every slam to the bow and roll to the side opened unfastened lockers, setting hammers and wrenches free. Some tools took to the air, bashing my arms and legs. Even the teakettle went AWOL, rolling off the stove and landing in the sink of dirty dishes.

I struggled up the companionway ladder with one hand, the soldering gun and solder in the other, lay them down on the floor of the cockpit, and took the defiant wheel from Alex. In one way, the driving was active and exciting, and in another way, it was horrible and exhausting. Soon it became deadly boring, because the only way I could maintain course was to stare at the compass. In those confused seas with all the wrong sails up, *Honu*, unless forced, refused to go in the direction we needed to go. Even a quick glance up to watch Alex or look at a wave threw the boat off course. My arm muscles, not used to performing the back-and-forth motion I needed to steer, quickly grew tired, and that gave me a jolt of reality. Even if we got one of the autopilots working, it would never be able to drive in these conditions. And how long could I keep this up?

Alex was on his own with all the tools we had out. I tried not to gasp aloud as irreplaceable screws leaped from his hands like Mexican jumping beans and disappeared under the slatted floorboards Craig and I had nicknamed the "swamp" because retrieving anything—screws, washers, buttons, potato chips— was so hard we just left them there. Since Alex was unable to hold everything while soldering, he kept stopping his delicate red hot soldering of minuscule wires to catch objects in midair.

The autopilot disaster was enough frustration to have us cursing like, well, sailors. We had the presence of mind, though, to laugh over some of our goofy swearword combinations, such as "shitsucker" or "fuckslam." Still, in the end, all three autopilots remained stone cold dead.

Alex took the wheel again so I could call Craig. I told him the problem. He said, "I don't have any more ideas other than what you've already done. I never had any of those autopilots fail. I never had a forestay break either." He paused. "I'm sorry this is happening to you. It's a run of really bad luck," he said.

"I should have tested the spare autopilots before I left," I said.

"I never tested them either, Susan."

"Well, it doesn't matter now," I said. "No autopilot could ever steer the boat in these conditions. Alex and I will have to drive."

"If you maintain the course you're on, you should be able to make Palmyra in three days. And if for some reason you can't steer, which is extremely unlikely, Samoa is directly downwind from you."

Great comfort in that, I thought. Samoa was twenty-five hundred miles of open ocean away.

"Why wouldn't I be able to steer?"

"If the rudder fails in some way, you can't steer the boat."

That would make the forestay failure look like kid stuff. I told Craig about the slow leak I had discovered at the rubber post, the place where the rudder enters the hull.

"Well, I can't see it," he said. "What do you think?"

"It seems minor. It's not getting worse," I said, making a mental note to check the rudder area more often.

Craig continued. "*If* you were adrift, *Honu* would get close enough to Pago Pago [American Samoa's main town] to get towed in. There's help there. But you'll make Palmyra. I know you can do it. You're doing great."

"*Honu* might not agree. The boat feels awfully broken."

"It's not your fault, Susan. You did all the right things. And you saved the mast. That's huge. We never had a stay break when we sailed together, but when it happened on your first trip you got the boat leveled out and those halyards attached in good order. I'm proud of you. Truly."

I felt a little better over this heartfelt comment, but it didn't last long when I remembered how far we still had to go. Also, Alex deserved credit, too. "Alex did a lot. He's been super."

"I'm glad you have him. But you're *Honu*'s skipper, and you're doing a good job of it." He paused. "Call me often," he said. "I'm thinking of you."

"Thanks. Don't worry. We'll be okay."

"Day or night. Anytime. Call me."

He sounded like my old Craig. Ironically, with the boat disabled, I felt more in control than I had in ages. By steering my own ship (a little too literally at that point), I had taken a giant step toward taking the helm of my own life. In the midst of all that turmoil, I knew Craig would always be there for me, even when *there* was not *here*. We were apart, but together, I told myself. Of course our relationship was changing. We as individuals were changing. No longer were we two kids goofy in love, and in lust, in a basement waterbed playing twins, saying that together we could take on the world. We *had* taken on the world, and done pretty well. Now we were aging adults facing the hard facts of our bodies slowing down, of collecting age-related maladies, of not being seen as, or feeling like, sexual beings. I had no idea how life would be when Craig and I lived together again, but whatever happened, that had been love in Craig's voice on the satellite phone. The Twinship might have been hit by a truck, but it still had a pulse.

I hung up feeling grateful and lucky that I had such an extraordinary partner. *You're on your own*, he was telling me, *but I'm here when you need me.*

Despite our already-tired arms and aching backs, Alex thought the two of us driving would be no big deal, and in normal circumstances, he would have been mostly right. We had only some three hundred miles to go to reach Palmyra, and two people could certainly manage to drive a sailboat for that long, about seventy-two hours, we guessed, since we were going three to four miles per hour. We were supposedly sailing downwind, but again, this was the ITCZ, and passing squalls caused the wind to change direction and the seas to batter us from odd angles. Add to that the sails being grossly unbalanced, and the driving became harder work than I dreamed possible. It took two aching hands gripped on the wheel, and all of my attention on the compass, to maintain course.

As the hours passed, it got harder. Every fifteen minutes or so, I would lose concentration and the bow veered, making sharp left or right turns. If I didn't correct it immediately, *Honu* in seconds rounded up into the wind and stalled.

The ITCZ also clobbered us with black curtains of rain strung erratically between us and Palmyra. At night, my wet clothes made me feel cold enough that I got chicken skin, a Hawai'i term for goose bumps. I donned full foul weather gear as I had our first night out, but that turned out to be overkill at ten degrees north of the equator. Then I was wet from sweating inside the bib overalls and jacket.

After the first hour steering, my arms and hands ached worse than ever before. We agreed on two-hour shifts, secured our harnesses to the binnacle, and set our resolve.

Sometimes I made my shifts almost unbearable by going over and over the gear failures, wondering what I might have done to prevent them, considering ways I might have saved the sail and furler, and then worrying about how I was going to replace them. I knew this was useless and self-defeating, but it was hard to think straight out there in the middle of the Pacific on a busted boat, especially at night.

The steering marathon kept us wet, salty, dirty, and tired. The worst of it was the salt burning my eyes and the body odor wafting from the neck of my yellow rain jacket. The scent was new to me—not the usual salty odor of physical labor but a sour smell of anxiety and fear. Were the halyards strong enough? Would the mast keep standing? If it fell, would we drift past Palmyra? If the rudder failed, could the wind and currents take the boat somewhere other than Samoa? I checked the halyards supporting the mast each time Alex and I changed shifts, but only during the day. No roaming the deck in the dark.

The next evening when Alex came up from below to relieve me, I was so glad to see him I nearly burst into tears. My back ached from the stance at the wheel. Stuffing cockpit cushions between my sore backside and the hard cockpit bench had not helped.

"How you doing?" he said.

"Good," I lied. "I'm fine."

"Then you probably don't want this," he said, smiling as he produced a cheese sandwich, fat with lettuce and tomatoes. It reminded me of all those sandwiches I had handed a grateful Craig when he was steering the boat in rough conditions. How good it felt to have a thoughtful crew member.

When Alex took the wheel, I ate with shaky hands. Having concentrated so hard on driving, I had forgotten to eat.

Nights were harder by far. Alex often drove longer than his two hours, taking two and a half or sometimes three-hour shifts. I realized the enormous cost of this gift when I tried to return it, that extra half hour being a constant battle to keep my eyes open and my hands tight on the wheel. Each time I looked at the clock, sure that extra half hour had elapsed, only five minutes had gone by.

As the minutes plodded to hours, the steering became more demanding and more dull, a killer combination. One night I did not wake up when Alex called down for me to take my shift. No matter how loudly he called, I did not stir. In desperation, he threw a flashlight. It hit my leg, and I bolted up, heart pounding, sure we were sinking. "I'm really sorry," he said. "It was my last resort."

I called Craig several times, not to ask questions but to let him know we were forging on. He encouraged me like a sports coach. "You're making good time." "The boat will be fine." "I know you can do this." During my calls, I gave him our latitude and longitude readings so he could follow our progress on Google Earth. (That's what we said, but we both knew that he needed our position in case he had to tell searchers where we were when we last spoke.) Hearing his voice was almost as good as taking a shower or getting a nap, but since the pick-me-up didn't last long after we hung up, I often stayed on the phone for twenty or thirty minutes. At $1.20 per minute, this quickly added up to hundreds of dollars, but Craig never tried to hurry the calls, nor did he ever once mention the cost. He seemed to like the phone calls as much as I did, because he often prolonged them by talking about the weather in Hawai'i—so uniform that there is no word for "weather" in the Hawaiian language—or the latest politics in Washington, which I had not cared about at home and certainly didn't care about out there in the middle of nowhere. I listened intently, happy for the contact.

Craig quickly figured out what replacement parts *Honu* needed and made arrangements I could never have made from the boat. He had already rush-ordered a new sail from Hong Kong, had a furler and forestay in the works from the local rigging company, and bought a new autopilot that would arrive in Honolulu by second-day delivery. This was typical of Craig's generosity (and expertise in sailboats), but I never took it for granted and thanked him often.

Craig also thoughtfully e-mailed the manager on Palmyra to let him know that *Honu* was disabled and that we might need help. I believed I had saved enough fuel for motoring the final miles into the lagoon, but I had little idea how much diesel the final push would take. *Honu* might need a tow.

As the strong winds and pounding waves wore me down, I became a ghost, stiff with salt and floaty with fatigue. By midmorning of our third day of driving, the eighth out of Honolulu, I was steering when Alex, bleary, climbed the companionway steps and plunked down in the cockpit. He squinted at the horizon ahead, jumped up, and hurried to the foredeck.

"Land ho!" he shouted. He made his way back to the cockpit. "We made it. We're there."

I strained to see what he saw in the distance. It looked like blades of grass sprouting on the water.

A moment later, a branch bearing a few green leaves floated past. "I feel like Noah at the end of the flood," I said.

"That's one of your trees," Alex said. "It's a *Pisonia* branch." The native trees I had come there to help save.

Frigatebirds began circling the boat. More boughs drifted past. The "grass" grew taller by the minute, and soon I saw that the "blades" were the tops of massive, towering trees. I was so excited and exhausted that I half expected to see a dove with an olive branch land on my boom.

Alex and I gave each other a hug, during which time *Honu* made a quick turn upwind that knocked us both to sitting on the cockpit bench. We got up laughing and cheering like a couple of football players who had just scored a winning touchdown.

As Alex steered the boat back on course, I turned on the VHF radio to announce our impending arrival.

This time, I did the talking.

16

$\mathscr{A}$s we limped toward Palmyra, now only ten miles away, I remembered how I had imagined my arrival in the atoll: dropping *Honu*'s crisp new sails, the engine leaping to life when I pushed the starter, driving proudly down a well-marked channel. Inside the calm, sparkling lagoon, I would stop my finely tuned boat in the turquoise waters and drop my anchor in soft white sand. Curious terns would balance on my booms. Booby birds would rest on my rails.

Instead, I felt more like a ragged, eye-patched sailor staggering into port. With the bow missing its rigging, a blanket-sized storm sail at the boat's center, the mainsail wrapped sloppily around the boom, and the little mizzen sail quivering over the aft deck, *Honu* resembled a do-it-yourself kit assembled by the nautically challenged. The boat had not been designed for this odd sail placement, and the instant my mind wandered, the bow of the unbalanced boat lurched off course like a willful two-year-old.

I could not roll up my jib because it, and its rolling mechanism, now lay with the lantern fish a mile down on the ocean floor. At least, I thought, I had storm and mizzen sails to take down. Most cruising sailboats have neither a mizzenmast nor a baby stay to fly emergency sails *from*.

Before you relinquish sail power, though, you need to have the engine running. I pushed the start button.

Silence.

Another push. Except for the thuds of my heart, nothing.

Another try. Dead.

Sailing upwind in a narrow channel is difficult at the best of times, but with the boat jury-rigged, I couldn't even consider it. I needed the engine to get into the lagoon. Tears brimmed my eyes when I pushed the button for the third time and nothing happened.

"Please work," I whispered to the solenoid gods and, taking a deep breath, tried again. On the fourth push, the engine fired up with a roar as if the system hadn't misbehaved at all. That starter was going to get a time out one day soon—with a big fat hammer.

Most atoll lagoons consist of a white sand floor covered with water so clear and shallow that its bright turquoise color turns the clouds pastel blue. *Honu* was within a half mile of Palmyra's lagoon, but for reasons unclear, the clouds above remained white and puffy without a hint of that comforting blue lagoon. Another Palmyra fantasy down the drain. And as for that well-marked channel that led inside the lagoon? The World War II–era markers were long gone, and coral heads booby-trapped the approach. I steered as Alex, who had traveled to Palmyra by ship several times and knew the entrance well, watched from the bow.

"The reef extends pretty far to the west here," he shouted over the drone of the engine. "Turn more. More. There's a coral head on your right. The entrance is over there. It's hard to see. There aren't any pilings. No, don't go there. It's shallow just inside."

Because coral tends to grow between an atoll's islands, a big problem with sailing a boat into atoll lagoons is locating an opening deep enough for a keel to pass through. Palmyra didn't have a natural passage into its lagoon wide enough or deep enough for big boats (*Honu* needed only six feet of water to get in, but big naval vessels require fifteen feet or more), so at the beginning of World War II, the U.S. Navy brought in dynamite and blasted out reef and sand, creating a channel twenty feet deep and a hundred feet wide from the open ocean into the lagoon.

In the aerial photos Alex e-mailed me when I was still in Honolulu, the channel looked obvious, its depth showing nearly black next to the pale sand shallows. But the dredging had been done in the early 1940s, and after the Navy departed, mounds of sand drifted wherever there were openings, making the edges of the passage hard to distinguish from the perspective of a sailboat's deck. Besides that, the nautical chart of the atoll was a quarter mile off the GPS reading, making my GPS map, an instrument I usually relied upon, useless for near-atoll navigating. The only guidance systems I had into Palmyra's lagoon from miles of surrounding reefs were Alex's recollections, a depth finder, and my two bloodshot eyes.

I was conservative, following Alex's advice about where to steer. When Craig and I had sailed *Honu* through the Caribbean and Pacific, we were shocked by the number of wrecked sailboats that lay on beaches next to clearly marked channels. Exhaustion can make even brilliant sailors stupid.

As if reading my mind, Alex said, "About ten years ago, a sailboat hit the reef out here. A nice French one, a Beneteau. It washed onto the north beach. I'll show it to you later."

Oh, my aching eyeballs. If I wasn't careful, I could make that two nice French boats washed onto the north beach.

For an hour that felt like a day, I dodged the submerged coral heads surrounding the atoll as we made our way toward the only opening into the lagoon.

"Hard right now," Alex called from the bow. "Narrow here, straighten her out. Whoa. Left, left." (We rarely used the terms "port" and "starboard" since it required thought and "left" and "right" did not.)

It felt as though the islands were the center of a mirage, their treetops always remaining the same distance away.

"Last one," Alex called out. "Bear right."

Finally, *Honu* glided into the mouth of the channel that led to the lagoon.

After days of fighting the weather of the Intertropical Convergence Zone, Palmyra's entrance channel felt like a paved highway, silent and smooth. Since over the years shifting underwater sand had claimed the edges of the channel, I took no chance running aground and drove down the middle, where dark blue meant deep water. I had little room for error and thanked heaven my engine started. If I had to beat (sail) up the narrow passage, each course would last only a minute or two before I would have to tack again. On both sides of the centerline, the navy blue faded like color chips on a paint card until there was no blue at all, just clear water, only inches deep, sparkling over cream-colored sand.

And that was it for sand. I was accustomed to the blinding white islands of Hawai'i's northwest atolls, such as my treasured Tern Island, where albatrosses and other seabirds walked and nested on acres of ivory-colored flats. At Tern, a stint without supplies could kill you quickly for lack of freshwater. Palmyra's islands, though, being in the rainy equatorial zone, looked like dinner plates overflowing with salad greens, sand showing only on the rims. Bushes, ferns, trees, and vines grew to the waterline in most places, elbowing one another aside to get their place in the sun. The most determined of the coconut palms leaned far over the water. Their bending crowns looked like bows of welcome.

Nor was the color of the lagoon turquoise, as it had been at Tern Island. It was olive green and murky. No one knew if this water color was natural for the lagoon or if it was the result of the normal flow of water being drastically altered for decades, because in addition to the entrance channel, the Navy had also dredged the lagoon to accommodate ships. Now I understood why the clouds didn't reflect the blue color of the lagoon: it wasn't blue.

With the exploded and excavated coral, navy workers built runways, roads, and a land bridge called a causeway that in connecting islands had stretched across the entire lagoon. Other marine structures—piers, pilings, and seaplane ramps—further transformed Palmyra's original shape, resulting in three areas known as West Lagoon, Central Lagoon, and East Lagoon. With no mainte-nance, the causeway and other navy alterations had been crumbling for years, allowing the three bodies of water to gradually merge. But they weren't there yet.

In the aerial picture, the atoll's shape reminded me, vaguely, of the shape of the ants I was there to study. The insects have two antennae up front and three body segments: head, middle (thorax), and rear end (abdomen). (We mammals call the middle of our bodies our abdomens, but in ants, crabs, and other arthropods, the abdomen is the last section at the rear.) At the west end of the atoll I pictured the edges of the deep channel *Honu* had just entered as the two antennae. The ant's head was West Lagoon (1.4 miles long by 1 mile wide); the middle, Central Lagoon (a mile long by half a mile wide); and the rear end East Lagoon (1.2 miles long by 1 mile wide).

Because the islands and their surrounding reefs absorbed the shocks of the open-ocean wind and waves, the boat cut through the glassy channel water like a great whale, leaving a broad V in its wake. So braced was I against the rolling of the boat at sea that the abrupt lack of motion nearly knocked me over. I also nearly fell over with relief at entering a lagoon where I was inside and protected rather than outside and exposed.

In the lee of the atoll, my skin felt warm and damp, like I'd been licked all over by a big friendly dog, as soon I would be. A breeze made the 90-degree air comfortable, but whiffs of rotting leaves told of steamy heat, and sooty terns announced that, as usual, they were wide awake. "Wide-awakes" is a nickname for these raucous seabirds because they never sleep. Their shrieks in nesting colonies go at high volume twenty-four hours a day, seven days a week.

The sound of a motorboat startled me.

"Look. They're coming out to meet us," Alex said, pointing.

Speeding toward us in one of the atoll's two small powerboats was Luke, the Nature Conservancy's camp manager, and seven of the current twelve residents. Dadu, the last of the abandoned dogs in Palmyra, rode on the bow like a furry figurehead. I was so moved that all these people, including the dog, had motored down the channel, probably a mile from their camp and pier, to escort us in that I had to take deep breaths to stop a sob from escaping my throat.

At the same time, the realization that I was safe in Palmyra's lagoon, that my offshore peril was over, that I would soon lie down in a still and silent boat without having to listen and worry and bail and plug, had the same effect on me as a sleeping pill. My thrill energy had been used up. I felt so drugged I thought I might be dreaming, but the effort it took to smile, and the ache in my steering-weary arm as I waved hello, made it real enough.

"Hello," I called out.

Even my cheeks felt tired. I watched Alex wave to his almost-ex-girlfriend as the boat drew near us. He looked like I felt: greasy hair, red eyes, droopy shoulders. I took some satisfaction in the fact that he, at twenty-nine, appeared to be as beaten up as I did at fifty-six—so much for envying his youth. I had forgotten that even the young sometimes get used up and look like crap.

When two other greeters showed up at the boat, though, I perked right up. A pair of black-tipped reef sharks, each about four feet long, emerged at *Honu*'s bow, parted, and swam one on each side, as if ushering the boat into the lagoon. Their simultaneous appearance and coordinated placement made the little sharks seem like ads for a theme park.

In terms of weight, sharks make up about half the fish in the Palmyra area, a good sign of a healthy coral reef. Because anglers have caught and killed most of the sharks on most of the world's reefs, including the main Hawaiian Islands, this shark escort was a first for me and thrilled me to my toes. The nonaggressive black-tipped reef sharks were easy to identify because they wear their name tags on their backs: the tops of their back and tail fins looked as if they've been dipped in black paint. Most sharks, including this species, have gray bodies, but these two had oddly light skin, creamy with a greenish tinge. Their pale backs, an inch or so underwater with dorsal and caudal fins breaking the surface, seemed to glow in the dark green water as they kept pace with the boat.

Luke sped ahead and docked his powerboat at the pier off the camp, while I drove the hundred yards or so to anchor off the shoreline.

The channel and West Lagoon were, and still are, the only areas deep enough to accommodate small ships and sailboats. I would go no farther in *Honu* than the spot I dropped my anchor, and that spot was the one and only place in the atoll to anchor a sailboat.

Most atoll lagoons have soft sand bottoms, but Palmyra's West Lagoon, about one square mile in area, had been excavated to seventy-some feet deep throughout by the Navy and therefore had an unnaturally hard, flat bottom. That, combined with the depth and opacity of the water, made finding a secure anchorage in the lagoon nearly impossible. The only spot suitable was near an underwater hill (called a berm) thirty-five feet deep and about two hundred yards off the camp. Alex thought he could locate the narrow berm, but with no buoys or floats to mark the spot, he had difficulty. It took great effort to focus on Alex's instructions of where to drive because as he tried to locate the berm by triangulating off trees, piers, and buildings on land, I had to watch the depth finder for the one or two seconds it detected the shallow place. I wondered if this voyage would ever end. I felt like an ancient menopausal mariner cursed to sail forever.

Back and forth I drove for thirty agonizing minutes, watching the digital readout of the depth finder, a sonar device installed under the hull. The silent gage flashed discouraging numbers: seventy-two feet, sixty-eight, seventy-one, seventy-six. Finally: thirty-five. We dropped the anchor, but not in the right place because the boat dragged backward when I reversed gears to test it. After several tries, the anchor seemed set, but into what I did not know. The boat stopped moving, and at the moment, that was enough for me.

We stood at the rail, staring at the water. "There's a no-swimming policy in the anchorage," Alex said. "The sharks can see us, but we can't see them."

He meant gray reef sharks, not the black-tipped reef sharks that greeted us. Grays aren't normally aggressive toward humans, but the species can be prickly about their territory. If you get in their space, and they don't like it for some reason, the sharks arch their bodies sideways. This signal is not subtle, and when we saw it on Tern Island, we swimmers either went back the way we came or got out of the water. The sharks were satisfied with that and went back to their business of finding fish to eat.

The murky water of West Lagoon, however, was going to make us blind to shark warnings. I stared into the cloudy water. The bottom rung of the boat's boarding ladder, about four feet below the waterline, was not visible. Still, more than anything in the world I wanted to drop my aching, stinking, exhausted body in that murky, shark-filled lagoon.

"Can we just get wet?"

He laughed. "You go first." Alex shared my attitude about sharks. Attacks are so rare they aren't worth thinking about, and if a shark did eat me, so be it. At least I would die doing something I loved.

We counted to three and, fully clothed, jumped at the same time. Our plunge from the rail frightened the little escort sharks at the surface, and they disappeared with a splash. Taking some deep breaths, Alex and I took turns free diving to glimpse the anchor. It lay on its side on the hard-packed sand. Not ideal but good enough. If there were sharks down there, they behaved like sharks usually do and kept their distance.

When I climbed back on deck, several of the island's residents—Nature Conservancy employees and volunteers—had paddled out in kayaks to meet the crazy middle-aged woman who had sailed to Palmyra with Alex, whom they all knew. I gave them a tour of the cabins, not caring that the interior was strewn with foul-smelling clothes, half-eaten food, and grease-covered tools.

The plunge had been as refreshing as a nap, but the rebound was fleeting. As we sat in the cockpit, the visitors talked too fast and too loud. *Welcome to Palmyra how are you feeling we were worried about you what happened to the boat. . . .* After being at sea for eight days, mostly silent and now energy drained, I felt a sensory overload. I could barely talk, let alone sort out names, faces, and jobs. I did notice, however, that a couple of the volunteers were, if not as old as me, at least in the ballpark. I had expected to be the old lady among a bunch of twenty-somethings. It felt comforting to have some comrades-in-aging.

The visitors noticed my frequent blinking, said their good-byes, and paddled back to camp, taking Alex with them. I was grateful for the solitude and grabbed the satellite phone to call Craig, not thinking twice about it. We had been talking so frequently, discussing so many issues affecting *Honu*, it once again seemed normal to call him. We might be communicating only about a sailboat, but we were communicating. Offered a positive moment, I grabbed hold and gave it a hug.

"I'm in," I said. "Safe and sound. *Honu* is anchored."

"Congratulations. Excellent skippering job."

"It was more of an adventure than I thought it would be. I wasn't sailing one day before things started going wrong."

"And you still got there." He paused. "That forestay should never have broken. Someone screwed up big time."

"I thought I was ready, but I wasn't ready for that."

"No one is. That's what makes offshore sailing so hard. The problems are never what you expect, and it's something different each time."

I remembered his hesitation when I announced my intention to sail to Palmyra, his warning that equipment can break when a boat is sailed hard, that a skipper has to think on her feet, to improvise. I didn't get it at the time. I figured I could head off failure by replacing everything replaceable beforehand, having experts install the new systems, and testing them on interisland trips. But brand-new cars break down. Computers crash right out of the box. And those things don't get blown around, shaken, and sprinkled with salt water. Of course stuff often breaks on boats.

Forestays, however, do not, at least not very often. I didn't realize what a rare catastrophe this was until much later when sailors asked me if I had any problems while sailing from Hawai'i to Palmyra.

"Well, my forestay broke," I say.

"Your *forestay?* My God. What did you do?"

Every time an exchange like this happens—and it does, time and again—I smile inwardly, remembering the whole terrifying incident and how well Alex and I dealt with it.

On the satellite phone, Craig explained his difficulties getting my gear replacements. "Pierre is helping a lot. He feels responsible. He thinks he should have checked that forestay fitting before the yardmen covered it with the furler."

"What do you think?"

"I think shit happens."

Craig had discovered that a new forestay and furler were too heavy and bulky for the small plane that flew to Palmyra, so he convinced the Nature Conservancy managers in Honolulu to let him load the new gear onto a barge rented by the Conservancy and heading for Palmyra by hired tugboat. He had to hurry. The tug and barge were preparing to leave. The exact date had not been set, but managers told him it was going within a week. As he talked about the arrangements, it dawned on me what he was saying: I would have to assemble the forestay and furler myself, and *install it on the boat.* There was no way I could do such a massive job so crucial to the integrity of the rig. Such critical repairs were for experts.

"I bought you a Harken furler," Craig said. "It's highly rated."

During his racing days, Craig had known the Harken brothers when they were starting their now-famous sailboat hardware company. Most sailors knew the Harken name, and I did too, but that's all I knew.

"Craig, I don't even know what another furler looks like or how it works, let alone how to replace one. I've never even climbed the mast."

"I know," he said, quietly.

"Maybe Pierre can come here with the new gear," I said. "Would you ask the Nature Conservancy people if he can ride on the tug when it comes with the barge? Oh, and ask Pierre, too."

Craig apparently had similar thoughts. "Good idea," he said. "I'll do it."

"Thanks. And, Craig? In the past I wouldn't have known how much work all this is for you, but I do now. I appreciate everything you're doing. Truly."

"You're in circumstances beyond your control, Susan. Of course, I'm going to help you."

"Every cell in my body thanks you, Craig. I mean it."

"You're welcome," he said.

As formal as our words sounded, we might have been brokering a real estate deal. I didn't care. At least we were brokering.

CONSERVING freshwater on the boat was no longer necessary since I was now in a rain forest and could collect all the water I could store. After taking a heavenly shower in *Honu*'s head, I closed the hatch over my bed, covered it with dark green cockpit cushions, and lay down in my bunk. The room turned eerily quiet since closed-up sailboats are nearly soundproof as well as waterproof. In the dark cabin at noontime, I felt like a vampire beneath her coffin lid and fell into a deep and dreamless sleep.

Several hours later, groggy but anxious to get off the boat, I inflated the dinghy and began the ten-minute row to the pier. (For such a short trip, Bette Davis was too unpredictable to use, sometimes taking a dozen pulls to start and occasionally stalling in midtrip.) A small splashing sound caused me to turn around, and I saw I was about to run into a white bed sheet that I guessed had blown off a clothesline and into the lagoon and was now twisting underwater as it sank. But this was no bed sheet. My rubber boat stopped just feet from two manta rays turning summersaults, their white undersides flashing bright as they flapped their broad pectoral fins. The movement reminded me of the way we as kids used our bodies to make snow angels.

The rays had no fear of my little dinghy and stayed close enough for me to reach out and touch them. Such animal indifference to people is a hallmark of wildlife refuges, since the creatures that live there have learned that humans aren't anything to worry about. Rather, they see us as one species among many, all sharing space in our search for food, shelter, and mates. To feel like one of the creature crowd is the main reason I spend so much energy and money getting to nature preserves. In areas where animals view humans as harmless and, at best, as allies, I get a glimpse of what the world would be like if we didn't hunt, hurt, or harass the other life forms on our planet. That's not the real world, I know. We exist in a food chain, after all, and some people will always tease, bully, and kill animals for fun. But sanctuaries give me peace of mind. Living in harmony with wildlife may not be most humans' first instinct, but refuges prove that it's possible.

A little pat on the rays' fins would have been safe—the white-bellied manta rays with jet black backs have no teeth or tail stingers—but I didn't want to startle them and spoil their dining. As I drifted in the nutrient-rich lagoon, the rays continued their plankton sifting, swimming forward as they sucked water into their gaping mouths. To direct tiny drifting animals toward their open jaws, the rays flapped paddle-shaped fins called palps, one on each side of the mouth. The busy feeding reminded me of a toddler shoveling food into her mouth with mittened hands.

I had been in Palmyra only a few hours and already I had two firsts: a shark escort for *Honu*, and a ray escort for my dinghy. I sailed there precisely for such extraordinary encounters, and as if whistled for, they came. Black-tipped reef sharks and manta rays swimming close had thrilled me in other marine sanctuaries, but this time was different. Having sailed my own boat there under my own captaincy made me feel as if these marine residents belonged in my life, and I in theirs. The anticipation of what Palmyra held in store gave me a rush of childlike happiness similar to that of a long-ago Christmas morning when I woke to find the red bicycle that my mother had convinced me was far too much to ask. There *is* a Santa.

As I watched the two gentle giants, about eight feet across (some species grow to twenty-two feet), tumble into the depths of the lagoon, I finished rowing to the camp's small boat pier, a modern structure on plastic floats that stood in stark contrast to the huge steel-sided World War II cargo pier covered in rust beside it.

Alex met me as I tied up the dinghy and introduced me formally to Luke, the camp manager, who led me to an enormous platform tent. The staff used the interior as a kitchen and the porch as a dining area that seated about twenty people on plastic chairs at folding tables. From a whirring ice machine similar to the ones in hotel corridors, Luke scooped two glasses of cubes and filled them with water from one of several refrigerators.

The Fish and Wildlife managers in Honolulu had warned me so often to lay low around Nature Conservancy employees that I reminded myself to listen only, and not talk. Luke motioned to a chair. I sat, preparing to promise to never use the camp's facilities, to eat my own food on my boat at all times, and to remember that I was neither a volunteer nor an employee of the Nature Conservancy.

17

$\mathscr{F}$IRST off, I want you to eat in the dining room with us," he said.

"You mean bring my meals in from the boat?"

"No. I mean share the meals we prepare here three times a day. I know they told you that you couldn't eat with us, but there are too few people here to live separately, and it just creates an us-versus-them mentality."

I was so shocked that all I could do was gape. *Honu*'s lockers bulged at the seams with canned milk, freeze-dried soups, boxed macaroni and cheese, and a hundred other food items that would last for months, if not years. All that planning, shopping, and cramming, plus two large bins of food still coming on the barge, left me with enough food on the boat to sail around Cape Horn with a side trip to Antarctica. I sat there blinking, digesting the news.

"What? You don't want to eat ashore?" Luke said.

"No, no. I mean, yes, I do. Thank you," I said. "That's very nice of you."

"You'll have access to everything everyone else here has," he went on. "Food, kayaks, showers, DVDs, whatever."

"What about the outhouse?" I said.

"What about it?"

"Can I use it?"

He laughed. "Of course you can use it. You can use anything you want. The only thing I ask is that you help out once in a while with kitchen cleanup. We rotate the chores on a calendar." He smiled. "Welcome to Palmyra."

Luke watched my face as I reimagined my vision of life on Palmyra for the next several months. "I'm the manager here," he said with a shrug. "I run the place the way I see fit."

I shouldn't have been surprised. This is how things often go in remote biological field stations. Managers in cities make rules and set policies that don't always work in far-flung camps where people of various ages, educations, and personalities have to live together. Most onsite managers do their best to toe the company line, but in the end, they do what works.

Luke leaned back in his chair, and a smile softened his craggy face.

"Melissa [his wife] and I sailed here, too. I felt for you out there with no forestay, but you saved your mast, and that's what counts. I don't help with boat repairs here, but I approved the loading of your gear on the barge, so don't worry about getting it here."

A barge coming to the atoll within two weeks of my arrival was a stroke of luck on my part. Barges did not normally come to Palmyra. Food and supplies were either flown in on a chartered airplane at great expense or transported aboard a federal research vessel that visited only once every year or two. But during my time in Palmyra, the Nature Conservancy was by chance remodeling its camp, replacing a couple dozen failing platform tents with wooden cabins and small buildings. Currently, workers in Honolulu were packing building materials onto a barge, and in another week, a tugboat pulling the barge would set off for Palmyra. This was the deadline Craig was rushing to meet. Since roller furlers are not stock items, he had to have the one he chose for *Honu* shipped express from the U.S. mainland to Honolulu. Our concern was that the furler would not arrive in time for him to get it on the barge.

If I didn't get replacement parts, I didn't know what would happen. A month earlier I would have panicked over such uncertainty, but already Palmyra had started working its magic. Every minute I spent fretting about the boat was one less minute I spent appreciating one of the most spectacular marine wilderness areas left on Earth. I made a decision. Whenever a worry about the furler, barge, or boat repairs wiggled into my consciousness, I would replace it with the image of those graceful, gliding manta rays.

My conversation with Luke, who in supervising the building of a new camp in that distant atoll had a hundred details to attend to, was over. With a wave of his hand, he invited me to check out the camp and make myself at home. I felt like a puppy finding the backyard gate open.

Palmyra's camp was larger than I had imagined, occupying about a square block on the lagoon side of Cooper Island, the largest of the atoll's approximately twenty-five islets. Military personnel had in the 1940s occupied other islands of the atoll, but now Cooper, with an area just over a third of a square mile, was the only island inhabited by humans—not many, though, and not the same ones for very long. Depending on job descriptions, contract lengths, and research projects, Palmyra's population varied between four and twenty-something.

When I arrived, a couple of cabins had been finished. They were large enough for two single beds and two small tables and had a hobbit-house character about them, the outside walls painted a dark green that blended with the surrounding forest. As cozy as the cabins were, I preferred the old khaki-colored platform tents. Sagging under the weight of fallen wet leaves and splotched with nature's graffiti of black mold, they had the classic look of a nineteenth-century camp occupied by English explorers. As an adolescent, I had loved the story of the intrepid reporter Henry Stanley finding the long missing and presumed dead medical missionary David Livingstone in a remote African jungle, and uttering the famous phrase, "Dr. Livingstone, I presume?" Surrounded by an equally exotic jungle, Palmyra's decaying tents appealed to my childhood sense of adventure.

About twenty buildings and tents stood scattered throughout the camp, many half hidden by foliage, but Palmyra's humans and structures were not my prime areas of interest. As if answering my unasked question, *Where are all those crabs Alex e-mailed me about?*, a bright red hermit crab tootled across my path like a windup toy.

In most crab species, a jointed crust covers the outside of the entire body, protecting the soft muscles, tissue, and organs within. (The biological term "crustacean" comes from the Latin *crusta* for crust.) The hermit crab stands apart from other crabs in that only the forward part of the body—head, legs, and pincers—bears this crusty armor. The rear end of a hermit crab is soft, making it an easy target for predators. To protect this vulnerable body part, the hermit crab searches for an empty seashell on the beach or ocean floor and backs in, coiling its "naked" spiraled tail deep inside.

I had seen countless hermit crabs in tide pools and on coral reefs in my travels, and occasionally I had seen fingernail-sized hermits skittering across sand and among pebbles. Never, though, had I seen a hermit crab as large, colorful, or charming as the one before me. The creature looked like a jumbo strawberry with legs, its top dipped in swirls of white chocolate.

I squatted to stare at the crab that in its snail shell was about the size of a mandarin orange. The creature stared back with two black eyes set like polished jewels on bright red stalks. Below the eyes waved four antennae, the sensory organs crabs use to smell, touch, and taste their surroundings. A dimpled red crust covered the crab's other front parts—a curved back and six jointed legs,

Strawberry hermit crabs at the compost heap. Photo by Susan Scott.

including two leading pincers—all of which spilled from the opening of the creature's adopted home, a cream-colored snail shell called a turban because it resembles a swirling headdress. The crab peeking out of its snail shell reminded me of a soldier emerging from an armored tank, radar on, weapons ready.

Frozen in place, the crab seemed to be weighing its options: run for cover, keep on walking, or duck inside its turban shell and hide. After a few seconds, the teacup warrior apparently decided I was just another of those tall but harmless aliens with the big feet, and off it ambled into the woods.

After my first glimpse of a strawberry (their common name) hermit crab, I saw the red fists everywhere, clambering over fallen logs, rummaging through piles of brown leaves, climbing branches of verdant bushes, and hiding beneath rocks large and small. Some crabs made their way into the jungle foliage, and I found them tucked deep inside their shells sleeping in the damp cradles of bird's-nest ferns. Fronds in this fern family grow up and out from a central cuplike point, that being the "bird's nest" of the name. These common houseplants are native to, and abundant in, Palmyra, where they thrive in the high humidity. Strawberry hermit crabs snoozing in these living nests reminded me of a Hawai'i book on ferns titled *What Are Fronds For?* The crabs knew the answer: for naps.

The hermit crabs strode around like they owned the place, and in numbers they do. Anywhere between fifty thousand and one hundred thousand—they're hard to count because they roam—live on Palmyra's islands, a land mass totaling nine-tenths of a square mile. One theory as to why Palmyra hosts an exceptionally large population of hermit crabs is that the U.S. Navy's digging and dredging of lagoons and island beaches in the 1940s exposed seashells normally sunk or buried and therefore previously unavailable to the land crabs. Since the number of available seashells limits hermit crab populations, the extra turban shells caused a housing boom. With crab food (any plant or animal, dead or dying) abundant in the fertile atoll, and crabs recycling their seashell homes generation after generation, the population stays high.

I fell in love instantly with the busy crabs, and the crabs seemed to love humans too, or at least they loved our food. During my exploration of the camp, I came across a compost pile behind the kitchen tent where hundreds of hermits crawled over and around one another like Pac-Man characters. Hermit (and most other) crabs are crackerjack recyclers of organic material, and the camp's compost pile was nirvana for the pocket-sized scavengers. Having found heaven in a heap, the crabs swarmed through the garbage, shoveling moldy bread, mushy bananas, and rotting meat into their mouths with their heavy front pincers. The so-called compost pile didn't produce much compost, but it sure hosted a lot of happy crabs.

Most of Palmyra's hermit crabs were of the red species, but about a tenth of the population looked like plums rather than strawberries, their wine-colored bodies smoother and longer by an inch or so than their red cousins. Because of the size difference, many of the purple crabs lived in too-small turban shells with bodies bulging out of their adopted homes like kids wearing last year's jackets.

For me, the crabs were sprinkles of glitter over an enchanted kingdom. When I could tear my eyes from the strolling strawberries and rambling plums, I saw that someone had painted images of geckoes on the sides of old buildings and drawn airplanes soaring on outhouse walls. Cheery white and yellow fishing floats guided walkers down paths, and from a twenty-foot-tall tree hung items that had washed up on the atoll's beaches, such as flip-flops, plastic toys, and fish net floats. I later learned that Luke's artistic wife, Melissa, viewed marine debris as I did, not as trash to be dumped into garbage bags but as colorful art material that could make a camp feel homey.

I was surprised to find a dive tent equipped with a high-speed compressor and enough first-rate scuba apparatus to outfit the *Calypso*, Jacques Cousteau's famous ship. Most equipment in remote field stations had the beat-up look of the overused and often repaired. This top-quality gear reminded me that in the world of ocean research, Palmyra was a precious gem. When scientists came to study the atoll's sixteen thousand acres of coral reefs, they would be well equipped.

Beyond that, a tent holding kayak racks sheltered a dozen or more kayaks in a variety of colors and models, another sign of a well-appointed workplace. I also found washing machines, dryers, hot showers, a walk-in freezer, five re-frigerators, and two free-standing ice makers. The luxury of it all amazed me. At home, I had been so immersed in refitting the boat, and so sure that the Palmyra camp would be off-limits to me, that I never asked what facilities the camp possessed.

One aging tin-roofed wooden building had the words "Palmyra Yacht Club" painted in white over black mold and green algae on its outside wall. Inside, a DVD player had been connected to a large monitor positioned in front of several rows of lawn chairs. A diesel generator whirred in a building behind, providing electricity for lights, computers, power tools, kitchen aids, and apparently, video watching. Besides its well-stocked DVD collection, the Palmyra Yacht Club contained a decades-old trading library with floor-to-ceiling shelves of musty books by authors ranging from Danielle Steel to Jean-Paul Sartre. There I found five copies of lawyer Vincent Bugliosi's *And the Sea Will Tell*, an account of the Mac and Muff Graham murders that so stigmatized Palmyra a dozen people had told me to buy a gun. Bugliosi's true story of the trial of Buck Walker and his girlfriend, the two accused of murdering the wealthy couple, was made into a TV movie in 1991 and became as important to the world's true crime aficionados as the crabs and coral reefs were to the world's biologists and nature lovers.

All this, combined with gourmet meals and fine wine (Melissa had been a chef in a four-star restaurant), made the camp look and feel like a playground for the privileged. And it often was. Luke and Melissa had been hired, along with several assistants, to maintain the camp and to feed and take care of the Nature Con-servancy's guests, some of whom had donated millions of dollars toward the purchase of Palmyra. The camp was also being designed to host scientists from various institutions and universities that contributed financially to the camp's up-keep. When those people came to visit, the workers rolled out the red crab carpet.

Alex appeared while I was crouched over a long line of red hermit crabs trailing one behind the other into the forest. "They look like they're having a parade," I said.

Having lived on Palmyra for months while studying the relationships among the long-ago introduced rats, several native crab species, and a wide variety of vegetation, Alex had become an authority on all three: Palmyra's rats, crabs, and plants.

"They're going to the ocean," he explained of the hermit crab conga line, "to lay their eggs."

Before visiting Palmyra, my experience with hermit crabs had been almost exclusively with underwater species. Although strawberry hermit crabs have adapted to life on land, they have oceanic beginnings. Female strawberry hermit crabs deposit their fertilized eggs near the shoreline. The eggs hatch in the ocean, and the current-propelled baby crabs spend, like so many of us, their youth adrift. Several molts later, the youngsters swim ashore and scurry about the beach looking for empty snail shells. This house hunting is urgent. Until they find a suitable shell—large enough to hide inside but small enough to carry—the tiny crabs are easy *pupus* for seabirds, shorebirds, and larger crabs. (In Hawaiian, the word *pupu* means snail, and in modern Hawai'i, *pupu* means appetizer or a light meal.)

Hermit crabs never kill a snail to get its shell but will fight with other hermit crabs to get a shell the aggressor deems superior. I never saw a totally naked hermit crab looking for a shell, but on Cooper Island's north beach I did see crabs in snail shells attacking other crabs in snail shells. The shells looked the same size to me, but apparently not to the crabs.

Once a hermit crab finds a shell to call home, it backs its soft, narrow rear end, called its abdomen, into the empty chamber. Located on the abdomen are two pairs of small rear legs that press against the shell's inner walls to help the crab hold its body inside. Tiny scales on the legs provide traction for gripping the shell's inner smooth surface.

A hermit crab protects itself at the open end of its mobile home by withdrawing inside when threatened and positioning one or both of its pincers over the shell's opening. This effectively slams the "door" shut when danger lurks.

Alex and I had switched roles since our sailing adventure. As a PhD candidate, he qualified as a University of Hawai'i researcher, and that was one of

Palmyra's supporting institutions. He had also been a long-term Fish and Wildlife employee and knew the ropes of the agency far better than I did. On land, therefore, I followed Alex's lead. The boat in the lagoon, however, was mine to manage, and there, Alex, as first mate, would do what I asked of him.

Besides those varying positions, I was a volunteer for the U.S. Fish and Wildlife Service, a guest of the Nature Conservancy, and my work partner was a friend who treated me as an equal. That left me in the enviable position of having no real boss on Palmyra. Honolulu managers who knew me trusted that I would carry out my assigned work, repair the boat that brought me there, and sail away, leaving the atoll a better place than when I arrived.

THE purpose of the Palmyra ant study was to learn what kind of ant poison knocked back the ants and for how long. Alex and I didn't have to scout for ants. At least seven species nested and roamed just about everywhere throughout the atoll's islands. We did, however, have to scout for places to conduct the study. Study protocol called for us to choose four locations, called plots, each with mature *Pisonia* trees growing in them but each far enough from one another that there would be no question we were dealing with separate ants and separate nests. To begin our site scouting, Alex suggested I walk with him while he checked his research sites on Cooper Island because he knew an area that hosted about a dozen *Pisonia* trees. It might be a good spot, he thought, to create our control.

A "control" in a scientific study is an area that the researchers leave alone for comparison purposes, treating it the same as the experimental areas, except the control is not subjected to the experiment. The control can be thought of as the norm, crucial to a sound study because you must have data from an unaltered sample with which to contrast the altered ones.

According to procedures agreed upon at our Fish and Wildlife meetings in Honolulu, Alex and I were to measure four plots with similar vegetation, each fifty by fifty yards, spaced throughout the atoll. In the middle of each of those areas, we would measure a fifteen by fifteen yard square space and there stick in the ground twenty plastic flags on wire posts an equal distance apart. Every day that I visited a plot, I would place an inch-square piece of paper containing a fresh dab of peanut butter and a splash of corn syrup, an ant banquet, at the base of the twenty flagged spots. Fifteen minutes later, I was to count the number of ants feasting on each square of paper.

After a week or so of this, Alex would help me sprinkle ant poison throughout the fifty-yard-square areas of three of the four plots, leaving the control plot poison-free. I would continue to count the ants daily, and in this way we would learn if all, or only a fraction, of the ants in the plot had been killed, how long it took for another species to move in to the territory, and how long it took for the dominant species to rebound. These facts all needed to be known before ladybugs could be introduced to Palmyra to eat the scale insects farmed by the ants.

"This is the only island people are allowed on now," Alex said as we started walking toward the center of Cooper. "When Palmyra became a National Wildlife Refuge, Fish and Wildlife made the other islands off-limits for anyone except official researchers."

"You mean no one in the camp can go to any of the other islands even though they live here?"

"In theory. The Nature Conservancy manager goes where he needs to," Alex said. "And you and I can go anywhere Fish and Wildlife work takes us. We can invite Nature Conservancy workers to come along if they volunteer to help us, but otherwise they're limited to Cooper."

This you-can't-go-here-but-I-can order cleared up some of the mixed messages I had been getting about my work and living arrangements in Palmyra. The Nature Conservancy had purchased all but one tiny island of Palmyra Atoll from the family that had owned it for decades. (The family kept ownership of Home Island, built by the Navy in the 1940s.) Soon after its thirty million dollar purchase, the Nature Conservancy donated all of the atoll except Cooper Island, the largest of the atoll's island, to the U.S. Fish and Wildlife Service, which promptly made its part, including the surrounding waters to twelve miles, a National Wildlife Refuge.

In retaining ownership of Cooper Island, the Nature Conservancy had the right to make its own rules there, and although all parties involved were well intentioned, this created management issues. The Nature Conservancy wasn't crazy about doling out its hard-won private donations to support employees of the cash-strapped U.S. Fish and Wildlife Service, and Fish and Wildlife managers weren't, in turn, inclined to give special privileges to wealthy donors. Even so, considering the complexity of the issues involved in jointly governing such a remote atoll, Palmyra was getting the protection the plants and animals there needed and deserved.

A person could get around Cooper Island on foot in an hour or so, but its towering coconut palms, giant *Pisonia* trees, and dense undergrowth of ferns, philodendrons, and other tropical plants slowed the walking, making the island feel larger than its one mile length and quarter-mile width.

Alex, over six feet tall with a stride to match, took off into the forest so fast that I had to trot to keep up with him. Because much of the atoll had in the distant past been a copra (dried coconut meat) farm, many of its trees were coconut palms. Wherever their umbrellalike canopies shaded the ground, the undergrowth was sparse, but this didn't mean the going was easy. Fallen coconuts—some hard and green, others cracked and brown—lay everywhere, some so concealed by ferns, grasses, and creeping vines that a walk in the woods was more like a stumble through a toy room. The coconuts I could see were bad enough, but those under fallen fronds and braided philodendrons rotated beneath my feet and sent me flailing in whichever direction they rolled.

Then there was the weather. When people told me that Palmyra averaged 180 inches of rain per year, it hadn't meant much. Now, though, as I thrashed through palms so lush that their canopies transformed the forest floor into dark shadows on this bright day, I got the message. Given the tiniest bit of encouragement, seeds in Palmyra seemed to erupt rather than sprout, the plants quickly sending out shoots, roots, fronds, tendrils, stems, vines, and branches to stake their claim on limited land. It seemed like *Little Shop of Horrors*, Palmyra style.

The copious fruits and seeds of all this growth made Palmyra's forest floor a paradise for crabs, but marginal real estate for ground-nesting seabirds. From my experience working on the dry, sandy islands of Hawai'i's northwest atolls, where seabirds are sitting almost everywhere you go, Cooper Island by comparison seemed nearly empty of birds. It was a false illusion. Because Palmyra's forest canopies leave few spaces for the birds to fly through, and flourishing plants filled most of the ground space, the seabirds with feet able to perch on branches—red-footed boobies, frigatebirds, black noddies, and white terns—made their nests high in the towering trees. Palmyra's red-footed booby population is second only to the Galapagos, but you rarely see those birds in Palmyra. They stay high in their havens.

Even with egg-and-chick-eating rats a constant threat, some ground nesters managed to find open spaces, defend their nests, and successfully raise offspring. If a person knew where to look (and had Alex as a guide), you could find brown and masked booby parents on spits of causeway land and red-tailed tropicbirds tucked under bushes sitting on eggs. While stumbling after Alex, I heard the distant screech of sooty terns, another ground-nesting seabird, and several cries of bristle-thighed curlews, a relatively rare migratory shorebird.

As I lifted my legs high and walked in zigzags to avoid surprises on the ground, I heard a muffled thud in the distance, and then another, like boots dropped on a wooden floor. A moment later, a green coconut fell so close I felt the whoosh of its velocity as it passed my shoulder. The mature coconut, weighing about ten pounds, hit the damp ground with a loud thump.

"Jesus. That thing nearly killed me," I said, staring at the coconut cannonball lying next to my foot. I looked up. The closely packed coconuts on these old plantation palms looked like green bowling balls hanging on strings.

"We're supposed to wear hard hats when we're in the forest," Alex said. "They're in the office."

"Does anyone wear them?"

"No. They're too hot."

I decided to consider death by coconut the same as death by shark bite or death by flying fish. They are rare occurrences that could kill me in a second, but if one did get me, at least I would have died following my heart.

At the moment, I could die following Alex. With his long legs and little boy excitement over showing me the site of our future control plot, he kept pulling ahead of my high-stepping gait, and I lost sight of him.

"Alex, slow down," I called out after he disappeared for the third time. But with the wind whistling through the trees, waves breaking against the atoll's coral reefs, and sooty terns shrieking somewhere across the island, he didn't hear me.

Feeling alone and abandoned, I stopped to catch my breath, inhaling the coconut-scented air laced with the musty odor of rotting leaves—soil in the making. But standing still, I realized I wasn't alone at all. If the rustling, skitters, and quivers of the ferns were any clues, I was Snow White with a hundred thousand dwarves.

Strawberry and purple hermit crabs have excellent senses of smell, hearing, and sight, and as I stood there, crabs emerged from fallen branches, fern nests, and cracks in tree trunks to check out the scents and sounds of the human in their midst. The creatures may have loved chowing down at the camp's compost pile, but their hub was here in the jungle. Sticks and leaves crackled as the crabs, most active at night, emerged from their siestas. Yet even while moving, the crimson crabs in their off-white snail shells blended so well in the shadows of the massive trees that I could barely see them. I felt I was in a Dr. Seuss story, a human Horton in Whoville.

As I stood there alone in the shadows, I also felt a little spooked. The trees murmuring, the surf pounding, and the crabs crunching through the underbrush conjured up the ghosts of the murdered sailors Mac and Muff Graham. I didn't dwell on this gruesome story (unlike several acquaintances, who knew nothing else about Palmyra), but when horrific violence occurs in such a beautiful and peaceful place, it lingers in people's minds. It lingered in mine that day as I stood under a blackening sky in the foliage-dark jungle, feeling deserted by Alex. Still exhausted from the boat-steering ordeal of our voyage, unsure of the direction of the potential control site, and more than a little annoyed with Alex for leaving me, I half expected the bony hand of Mac Graham to suddenly appear on my shoulder.

The couple reminded me so much of Craig and me during our sailing trips together—exploring atolls, anchoring in remote places, meeting unusual people—that I thought often of the Grahams while I lived in Palmyra. From their home city of San Diego, the Grahams, a forty-three-year-old retired naval officer, Malcolm (Mac), and his forty-two-year-old wife, Eleanor (Muff), sailed to Honolulu in 1974 on their immaculate thirty-eight-foot ketch, *Sea Wind.* The couple spent several months in Honolulu getting ready for a long, leisurely stay in Palmyra. During that time, our neighbors in the Ala Wai Boat Harbor became friends with the Grahams. Apparently this was easy, because whenever the subject of Palmyra came up, our neighbors grew pensive, saying, "We missed them after the *Sea Wind* left. The Grahams were such nice people."

According to most accounts, the couple's kindness was why, once settled in Palmyra, they became acquainted with another sailing couple, Wesley (Buck) Walker, thirty-six, and Stephanie Stearns, twenty-eight, who were living on a battered, poorly equipped sailboat with two pit bulls. When Stephanie and Buck (a former marijuana grower on the run from the law) grew low on food, the Grahams shared some of theirs, occasionally inviting the younger couple to the *Sea Wind* for meals.

In August of 1974, the twice weekly ham radio reports that Mac routinely sent to a friend stopped. A few months later, Buck and Stephanie showed up in Honolulu on a lavender boat that had obviously been hand painted. If Buck and Stephanie were trying to disguise the *Sea Wind*, they were not going to succeed, because color means little in identifying a sailboat. When observing a vessel, sailors see its hull shape, note the deck layout, and remember its rig. Rarely do they recall the color of the hull.

Buck and Stephanie, arrested almost immediately, claimed that the Grahams' inflatable dinghy had capsized while the couple was fishing, and the two drowned, despite both being strong swimmers. Oh, and Mac had said that if anything ever happened to him and Muff, Buck and Stephanie could have the *Sea Wind*. No one believed this outlandish story, but without bodies, it was impossible to prove foul play, and the couple were convicted only of boat theft. Several years later, though, a South African sailor anchored in Palmyra's lagoon found an old sea chest containing bones. Forensic investigators determined that the bones, cut with a blow torch to fit into the chest, were those of Muff Graham.

Stephanie got off on an insanity plea, but Buck got life in prison in 1985, and parole in 2007. A couple years later, a stroke sent him to a nursing home, where he died, still claiming his innocence. Mac's body was never found.

The memory of that couple's tragic end made me appreciate that, although Craig and I had been having problems over the past two years, at least we were alive to *have* problems.

I plopped down on a log to wait for Alex and watched the antics of the hermit crabs, which had no compunctions about climbing on top of each other's shells, or scrambling up flimsy branches that drooped precariously under the crabs' weight. While climbing, a hermit crab would sometimes lose balance and tuck and tumble, rolling like a croquet ball to a stop. This seemed to neither hurt the crab nor deter it in its mission, whatever that might be. A few seconds later, out popped a head and two alert black eyes on their stumpy red stems, and off the creature crawled in search of a meal, a mate, a shell, or a nap. I never knew which. The crabs engaged in all pursuits with equal enthusiasm.

How elegant and simple the crabs' lives seemed. How grateful I felt that these creatures let me watch them go about their business. Silently I thanked the Nature Conservancy and the U.S. Fish and Wildlife Service for making Palmyra a sanctuary and for letting me work there.

By the time Alex appeared out of the gloom, the ghosts had vanished and my anger at him for leaving me had cooled. Such was the power of simply sitting down in a forest to watch, listen, and absorb its life. It was like getting shot with a tranquilizer dart.

"I lost you," I said to Alex when he arrived. "I didn't know where to go."

"Oh, I'm sorry," he said, surprised. "I guess I got excited about visiting my sites."

Alex's natural sweetness and youthful enthusiasm made it impossible to stay mad at him. Besides that, a strawberry hermit crab with a big hole in its snail shell caught my attention as it puttered past.

"Look," I said, picking up the crab. "This one has a skylight." We peered into the *puka* of the broken shell, wondering if the crab knew that its soft, pink backside was exposed.

Because they need bigger shells as they grow, Palmyra's hermit crabs recycled their turban shells often, fighting bigger crabs for bigger shells and leaving the smaller castoffs for smaller crabs. With baby crabs constantly coming ashore to make the islands of Palmyra their terrestrial homes, and turban snails less numerous than hermit crabs, empty snail shells were in short supply. It was a hand-me-down system that had gone on for decades, and many shells contained chips, cracks, and *pukas* in their tops and sides.

"Watch out," Alex said. "That big pincer can give you a nasty blood blister."

He showed me how to safely hold the crab. You keep your fingers as far from the opening of the shell as possible, and with the other hand tap on the crab's "door" claw. I learned that safety didn't last long. When I first picked up the crab, it ducked as deep into its shell as it could go, using its front claws as French doors, slammed shut and locked. Tapping on those claws with my finger told the crab that danger still lurked outside, and the creature stayed withdrawn. But hermit crabs are successful, in part, because they're bold and curious—good traits for scavenging—and after a minute or two, the hiding crustacean couldn't resist opening its claws a crack and poking its eyes out to see what was happening.

After about thirty seconds to a minute, the crab's snappish front claws began to unlock. (Crabs that have outgrown their shells are more exposed and unlock their claws more quickly.) When my crab saw it was being held by a monster, it reached for my thumb and tried to pinch me. *Put me down right now,* the little David seemed to be demanding. Being a smart Goliath, I put the crab down. It scurried away as if late for an appointment, a crustacean version of Alice's rabbit.

While I studied (some would say played with) the hermit crabs, Alex disappeared again. Even half-running, I couldn't catch up and lost him again. Sweating and alone, I stood in the forest, more exasperated than angry. What a *boy* he was being, running like a reebok through the jungle just because he could. Having lived on the atoll for months doing his crab/plant/rat research, Alex seemed to know every tree and shrub, but I had no idea where I was, what direction I should go to get back to camp, or how long it would take.

Craig would never do this to me, I thought, as I stood there panting. All those years we hiked together, he either let me lead or slowed to my pace. As I waited for Alex to come looking for me, if it occurred to him to do so, I realized that for Alex and Craig, hiking with me must be similar to how I felt while taking my eighty-year-old aunt for a walk around the block. After I got her home to rest, I went out for some real exercise. Like Alex was doing with his dashes through the forest. Like Craig did with Christine in their races.

For the first time since Christine entered our lives, it made sense to me that Craig should have a workout partner besides me. Not only could I not keep up with him, I didn't want to. I liked hiking, but for most of the Twinship, Craig and I had done our trekking and climbing together, he slowing down for me, and me picking up my pace as much as I could for him. Still, I would never come close to being the athlete he was, and now, after years of holding back, he had found a friend who could keep up and wanted to race. I, however, was perfectly happy sitting in the woods watching crabs. Clearly, it was time for each of us to assume our own speed.

Alex appeared, a small stream of blood running from his elbow down his forearm. The sight of his abrasion made me to look down, and I saw that I, too, was bleeding from various scrapes and scratches received while tripping over vines and avoiding rolling coconuts. In addition, I had multiple bruises from falling into things on the boat. As usual, I hadn't felt the minor injuries when they occurred, but over the eight-day voyage my arms and legs had developed so many contusions that I looked like I had a clotting disorder.

The difficulty of all I was doing showed on my skin like Girl Scout merit badges. I felt proud that I earned my red and purple marks doing something besides setting tables and making beds, the skills for which I had once earned real Girl Scout badges.

For the first time since I arrived in Palmyra, a rush of euphoria tickled me. Alex had run off because he was sure I would be fine on my own. And I was. *You take care of your responsibilities*, he was saying, *and I'll take care of mine*. One thing I loved about my friendship with Alex: it was never boring.

The coconut palm grove on Cooper Island had been planted in a past-century attempt to farm copra, but as we walked, we left the coconut-strewn plantation behind and entered a stand of *Pisonia* trees, the species we had come to save.

My first sight of Palmyra's *Pisonia* trees, the nobility of the atoll's native plants, showed me instantly what the urgency to save them was all about. The largest of those still standing rose a hundred feet, the base of their shallow root systems as big around as King Arthur's round table. Near the smooth gray trunks of the mature trees grew stands of young *Pisonia* offspring with slim branches holding baby leaves up to see the sun. But all was not well. Amid the grove, several five- to ten-story trees had fallen and lay on the ground at unnatural angles, like boxcars derailed. Sandy soil clung to ten-foot-high tangles of exposed roots, and bright green leaves that would soon wither and die rose from robust-looking boughs.

The majestic trees standing silent amid their newly fallen comrades made me want to pet the living trunks and whisper: "Hang in there. Help is coming."

Walking among the *Pisonia* was slower than moving through the palms, because the dense green leaves darkened the forest floor even more than the wide shady palms. And then there were the fallen giants to make our way around, too big and branchy to climb over or step through.

Alex and I walked around the area, noting that black ants marched up and down nearly all the healthy-looking trunks. Using our feet to measure an area about fifty yards square, we tied orange plastic strips at the edges.

That established the required control plot, but because it was the only suitable *Pisonia* stand left on Cooper Island, our three experimental plots, in which we would eventually sprinkle the ant poison, had to be elsewhere. Alex knew of three areas on Eastern Island that would likely meet the study criteria. Since Eastern was separated from Cooper by three lagoons, we would have to go there by kayak.

18

I spent my first night on the boat in the lagoon having nightmares. Blasts of wind blew rain sideways beneath the awning over my bed, forcing me to close the overhead hatch. The cabin grew hot and humid. *Honu* swung back and forth on her anchor chain in a wide arc, and I lay in my bunk listening to the steel links drag over the hard-packed lagoon floor, clunking like the chains of Marley's ghost.

I got up, donned a foul weather jacket over my T-shirt, and went to the bow to check the anchor. You can't, of course, actually see an anchor lying on the ocean floor at night (or even most days), but skippers still go out on windy nights to "check the anchor." What we are really doing is judging the conditions, which often sound worse than they are when you're lying in your bunk below. Rain soaked my hair and beat my bare legs as I watched the boat pull against the chain. The angle of the chain to the water's surface is all you can see, but if the chain jerks at the water line when the boat tugs, it means the anchor is hopping along the seafloor. The chain did not jerk. Besides that, once I stood on the deck I could feel the wind, and although gusty, it wasn't as strong as it sounded from my cabin.

The atoll's high humidity had turned the previous sunny day into a sauna, but the nighttime wind and rain left me feeling as if I had wandered into the camp's walk-in fridge. I went back to bed with wet hair and cold feet and, shivering with cold, climbed under my covers.

A dozen times in the night I sat up and looked through my cabin window at the moonlit pier to see if the boat was moving backward. It was not, but the eerie rattling of the heavy chain made it sound as if it the anchor was slipping. When I finally dropped off, I had boat-crashing nightmares so vivid I woke myself with my own shouts.

I wasn't the only sailboat captain to sleep poorly at Palmyra. The first was Captain Edmund Fanning, an American explorer and trader in fur seal skins who recorded the existence of the atoll but did not go ashore. In 1798, Fanning and his sealing crew of twenty-seven crossed the Pacific on the ship *Betsy*. One night Fanning awoke in his cabin with a sense of foreboding. Another account says Captain Fanning had a premonition delivered in a dream that something was wrong. Whether a notion or a nightmare, a feeling of unease had to be the norm for those early explorers. Any captain in his right mind would be worried while sailing at night in uncharted waters pocked with ship-shattering reefs.

Fanning woke three times, took this restlessness as a warning, and issued orders to reduce sail and slow the fast-moving ship. In the light of morning, Fanning saw breakers ahead. Due to the boat's reduced speed, the captain was able to avoid hitting sharp coral reefs surrounding several low-lying islands. Edmund Fanning neither landed nor gave the atoll a name, choosing instead to get some distance between his ship and the shallow reefs.

Four years later, in 1802, an American ship, *Palmyra*, skippered by a Captain Sawle, did land on one of the atoll's islets, but unintentionally. A storm blew the ship ashore. Through enormous good luck, the vessel remained intact, and when the weather cleared, Sawle was able to sail away. He named the atoll after his ship.

I had read these sailing accounts in the comfort of my home on Oahu, and although the explorers' feats impressed me, they hadn't meant much. Now, though, having navigated my own boat—with charts and with someone who knew the area—through Palmyra's maze of coral heads, the stories came alive. In my pitch-black cabin, I could practically smell the sweat on the captains' musty uniforms and hear the men's hoarse shouts as their wooden ships bobbed and rolled in the black unknown. I also shared their bad dreams. Even safely inside the lagoon, and dog tired, the unnerving scrape of the chain links on the hard seafloor made my first night in Palmyra a long one. My body may have reached the destination of my dreams, but my brain sailed on.

When the next morning *Honu* seemed to be in the same spot, I ordered myself to stop worrying about the anchor dragging. The holding ground might be marginal, but the anchor had stayed put all night in windy conditions. For heaven's sake, I was inside a lagoon surrounded by islands surrounded by reef. What could go wrong?

As much as I wanted to go ashore and get to work with Alex on the other three ant plots, my first duty was to straighten up the mess we had made inside

Honu. Sailboats are like dorm rooms. It's possible to make them look tidy, but it's constant work keeping them that way. When *Honu* was Craig's and my only home, we lived under what we called the T-shirt rule, a directive that applied to all clothes, tools, toys, and gear. If you buy a new one, you must get rid of an old one. This was hard enough for Craig and me, who didn't have many belongings, but the limited space was incomprehensible to most people. My mother once sent me my deceased grandmother's three-foot-tall, twenty-pound table lamp with a shade the size of your average umbrella. We farmed out such gifts to friends who lived in real houses and in that way managed to keep our volume low and our stuff stowed.

Even so, a simple project like having guests for coffee could bring chaos to *Honu*'s compact living quarters, and Alex and I had just completed a colossal project: sailing to Palmyra on an incapacitated boat. For seventy-two hours we upended cushions and bedding to get into lockers; threw blankets, T-shirts, and foul weather gear on the floor; piled crusty bowls and greasy pots in the sink; dug out tools and left them out. As a result, the cabins looked like we had sailed through a hurricane.

As I worked replacing socket wrenches and handles in their proper cradles, Alex arrived in his kayak. "I came to help clean," he said.

"Thanks for the offer," I said. "But I'll trade you. How about current cleaning for future fixing?"

Alex was not a natural-born cleaner, and the look of relief on his face made me smile. We cut a deal. I would get *Honu*'s interior shipshape, and he would help me track down the seawater leak at the bow. But later. At the moment, we both needed time alone.

I coiled lines, folded and stowed the storm jib, wiped oil from my engine catch pan, washed encrusted oatmeal from spoons, and gathered sweaty sheets, salty jackets, and grease-stained T-shirts. It was a pleasure doing chores on the motionless boat in the glassy calm lagoon after eight days at sea. When the morning sky darkened with an oncoming squall, I set up *Honu*'s rain-collecting system, a slackened awning with fittings for hoses. The clouds galloped across the atoll, dumping rain with the intensity of a buffalo herd plunging over a cliff. Rugs of rain fell from both sides of the canvas awning tent that stretched over the cockpit, and water streamed down my clear collection hoses as if someone had turned on a faucet. In thirty minutes *Honu*'s 120-gallon freshwater tanks were brim full. Well, that took care of one concern. While at Palmyra, I could use freshwater with abandon, a nearly unheard-of luxury on a sailboat with no water maker.

The squall passed as quickly as it arrived, and in minutes the sun again blazed in a sky so blue it looked like frosting on a tropical-themed cake. I could practically hear the jungle whirring as its leaves set to work on their photosynthesis projects. In biology, plants are called primary producers because they're the first link in the food chain that supports nearly all life on Earth. Standing on the deck in that equatorial sun, I felt proud to be part of the team helping Palmyra's giant *Pisonia* trees survive to carry on their mission of life.

AFTER the rain stopped, I opened the boat's three overhead hatches. Viewing this as an invitation, a dozen or so wasps flew in, drifting through the cabins like tiny hummingbirds in search of nectar. But it wasn't nectar these insects were after. The wasps, all females, were mud daubers looking for places to build their mud nests and lay their eggs.

Alex and Luke both warned me that these one-inch-long wasps would get inside the boat, but they neglected to mention that the wasps looked like the ballerinas of insects, flying and hovering in black-and-yellow tutus with their long legs dangling below. Mud daubers are not aggressive like their yellow jacket cousins but will sting if provoked, meaning if you try to shoo them out of your boat.

I installed the Velcro-and-mesh nets Scott had kindly sewn for *Honu*'s hatches and directed the wasps, gently with a towel, one at a time, toward the large mosquito net I hung over the companionway. Once they banged into the net wall, I removed the clothespins at the opening and let each wasp fly out. It took about thirty minutes to get the dozen wasps out of the cabins, but that didn't discourage them. They buzzed around *Honu*'s masts, booms, and sails as if answering ads for free apartments.

Why these insects flew a hundred yards offshore, probably a hundred miles in wasp distance, rather than raise their offspring on land where there was ample food and mud, was a mystery to us all. But sailboats have countless nooks and crannies, and for some reason, Palmyra's mud daubers loved to set up housekeeping in them.

To discourage the little homemakers, I stuffed plastic bags in the obvious openings on the boat's exterior, and as I did so, another approaching storm blackened the sky. The ITCZ (Intertropical Convergence Zone) is the perfect place for a menopausal captain, I thought, as I ran to close my overhead hatches. The weather here is as unpredictable as my moods. I got the hatches closed as the rain started falling. This time it hammered the awnings so furiously that water splashed inside the cockpit, and I had to go below to stay dry. The furious rain sounded like a thousand tiny woodpeckers pecking *Honu*'s deck to bits. The hits reminded me to walk from cabin to cabin to check places where the boat had formerly leaked.

On sailboats, seawater leaks and rain leaks are not always in the same places. Waves hitting the boat push water up, and sometimes in, but a moving deck doesn't allow seawater to puddle up. Rain falls from above, of course, and if the boat is moored or at anchor, water pools on the still deck and sneaks in at places that are dry at sea.

The freshwater leaks were worse than ever. Rain slipped through cracks in teak rails, seeped around loosened deck fittings, and ran down wires whose sealers had given up sealing. A V-berth leak soaked pillows on the port side, a starboard leak trickled water onto my precious books, and old leaks in the head and the aft cabin vanity had reverted to their previous soppy behavior. Oh, and the bases of both masts had started up again, leaving puddles on the teak floor.

This wasn't good news, but it didn't surprise me. All boats spring leaks here and there. After all, they sit in the water year after year, get pummeled by rain and waves, and have dozens of joints, seams, and deck fittings. When you use a boat often, you notice a leak and fix it. *Honu* had sat neglected for years, and in the process had come unglued.

I had come unglued, too, over the years. In depending upon Craig to fix everything that ailed me (an easy attitude to slip into when living with a person who fixes people for a living), I had neglected my own basic maintenance. Now *Honu* and I were in the same pickle. *To stay in good shape*, I thought, digging out spare towels, *this boat and I had to keep moving.*

I found a wet spot on the outside edge of my cabin's double bed, but not the kind that had been there during Craig's and my better days. The puddle came from water dripping through a leak where the solar panel wire led through the deck to the battery bank. I laid a terrycloth rug on the spot and, staring at it, sighed. Instead of a man, I now slept with a bath mat.

When the clouds cleared, I stuffed my stinking laundry into the lost jib's crisp new sail bag, feeling sad that it had been demoted so early in its career to such a low rank. The bag was so full I had to shoulder it through the companionway, but once on the deck I saw that I could not drop it to the dinghy as planned, because the dinghy now contained an inch of rainwater. Back I went to get a plastic bowl, a tool I used daily thereafter to bail the dinghy.

When I returned, I stopped and stared at the sunny, now tranquil lagoon and the lush jungle surrounding it. A rush of satisfaction swept over me. I had done something I once thought impossible: I sailed *Honu* to Palmyra without Craig.

At that moment, I felt not like the person I had been over the last couple of years—helpless as a seahorse stranded on a beach—but much more like the woman Craig had fallen in love with, a competent and confident person who looked forward to the future. And on the satellite phone, Craig was the man I had always loved. When I had a problem with the boat, he was there for me without hesitation or reserve, yet he never bossed me. This was the Craig who was proud of me, and said so, and was standing ready if I needed help. We might not be talking about our innermost feelings, but who said we had to? At least for now, this worked.

It took me ten minutes to bail the dinghy and, since I had anchored *Honu* a hundred yards from the dock, another ten minutes to row ashore. After tying my inflatable boat to the new small boat pier built by the Nature Conservancy, I began to meet the island's few residents, all either hired by or accepted as volunteers by Nature Conservancy managers to help run the camp. Since I had been nearly comatose during these workers' visit to the boat the day before, this felt like our first meeting.

The camp on Palmyra's Cooper Island was not your average field station, either in appearance or in personnel. The Nature Conservancy hired the staff there specifically to take care of the Nature Conservancy people, who included hired employees, multimillion dollar donors, and conservation-minded volunteers of widely varying backgrounds. Visitors also included researchers, and while I was there, a team of construction workers had been hired and flown there to remodel the camp. During my stay, the fewest number of residents on Cooper Island was eight, including Alex and me, and the most twenty-eight when construction was in full swing.

Besides the Nature Conservancy providing cabins, a screened kitchen and dining room, flush toilets, offices, and a research laboratory, all in various stages of building that year, the organization also offered donors and scientists laundry service, satellite Internet, fine meals, wine and cocktails, scuba diving expeditions, and transportation by boat, kayak, and bicycle. Since the Nature Conservancy's continued existence depended on charitable contributions, the mission of the cushy camp was to give wealthy benefactors and scientists from research institutions insight, in comfort, into the value of Palmyra as a wildlife refuge and research platform. The idea was that this would encourage individuals and institutions to donate more cash to the cause.

It was tricky business, because accommodating the organization's target group—philanthropists and grant-writing researchers—required months of planning and a potful of money, and the Nature Conservancy couldn't afford to take care of anyone who happened to show up at the remote outpost, such as ocean-weary sailors. The Nature Conservancy and Fish and Wildlife Service agreed to allow offshore sailors one week of anchoring time in the lagoon, but no repair assistance or food supplements were provided, and exploring was limited to Cooper Island only. That arrangement continues to this day.

As for Alex and me, a deal had been made. The U.S. Fish and Wildlife Service would pay the Nature Conservancy a daily fee for Alex's meals and lodging, and I was to provide my own on the boat. In theory. Clearly, each manager had his or her own method of running the remote camp, a particularly complicated job during this transition period. Of the twenty-eight or so people coming and going on chartered supply planes, five were paid Nature Conservancy employees with various backgrounds, and about ten were construction workers. Another five to ten people (the number changed with plane arrivals) living at the camp were Nature Conservancy volunteers who had offered to help with the building projects. One man, a mathematician, had experience building Habitat for Humanity houses. One was a dentist, another had a degree in political science, another in physics. Their common bond, with one another as well as with Alex and me, was loving wilderness enough that, to get to live in it, they were willing to work for free.

To make managing this diverse bunch even stickier, a team of researchers from the University of California was scheduled to arrive in a month. On top of that, in sail two Fish and Wildlife volunteers on a disabled boat.

A person practically needed a PhD in psychology to supervise the range of personalities at Palmyra that winter, but that's true of most research stations. Such camps need mechanics who see beauty in a crab, biologists who appreciate the elegance of diesel generators, and volunteers willing to put aside their graduate degrees to pull weeds.

Luke had a tough job in managing the rapidly changing camp that year, but when he welcomed me to the family, he meant it. The little settlement on the edge of an island in the middle of nowhere was a tiny village that enacted its own rules and decided its own protocols. While I was there, the place had the feel of a benign dictatorship with Luke as leader, Melissa and her helpers as domestic workers, and the others as worker bees. All of them welcomed Alex and me warmly, but since our research had nothing to do with their daily work of building, food service, and machine maintenance, we did not spend our days with them and therefore were not core members of the clan. I had, I felt, the perfect position in the camp: accepted yet peripheral.

Our other three ant plots didn't come as easy as the first.

Alex knew the flora of the atoll better than most of us know our own backyards and chose for our potential study sites three areas on Eastern Island, the farthest one from Cooper Island, where we lived. Stands of native *Pisonia* trees thrived on Eastern Island, and also, as in our control plot, some trees there had recently fallen.

"How far is Eastern?" I asked, as Alex and I packed our two kayaks with gear, intending to scout, measure, and flag the study sites.

"A half-hour paddle, maybe forty-five minutes," he said. "It's upwind and upcurrent." He smiled. "Coming home is easy."

I knew that smile. Upwind and upcurrent meant that kayaking to Eastern was going to feel like jogging up a boulder-strewn mountain. But kayaking across Palmyra's stunning lagoons was a privilege few people in the world would ever enjoy, and I told myself to appreciate the experience, no matter how grueling. I reminded myself, too, that Alex didn't wait for people slower or weaker than himself, so it didn't surprise me when he took off at a clip, leaving me to fend for myself.

I knew how to paddle a kayak, but paddling against fifteen-mile-per-hour wind and two-mile-per-hour current required muscles I hadn't used in some time, and I grew tired fast. By the time I approached the eroded opening, called the "cut" because it sliced through the crumbling Navy-built causeway separating the second and third lagoon, I could not see Alex ahead. I had paddled over a mile, and the muscles of my arms and shoulders ached and burned. Besides that, sitting in the hard plastic kayak hurt my back and numbed my bottom.

At the gap my heart sank. Alex had failed to mention that this narrow passage, the hardest part, ran like rapids, the adverse current flowing strong and deep between two walls of coral. I could see him far ahead, already across the third lagoon and closing in on Eastern Island. His muscles in machine mode, he hadn't noticed my kayak disappear behind him. I took a deep breath, aimed toward the cut, and paddled like mad to one side, where the current is weakest. But propelling the kayak forward as fast as I could didn't get me through, and when I stopped, panting and aching, the rushing rapids and steady wind spit me back like a watermelon seed.

After catching my breath, I tried again. *Ptui.* The white water pitched me back again. As I sat in my kayak drifting with alarming speed back where I came from, I thought Alex was thoughtless and mean, leaving me so far behind. Here I was in a new place, on my first kayak trip in years, lost in an overpowering current, and he hadn't given me so much as a glance over his shoulder.

I jerked tight the straps on my reef-walking sandals, paddled to the far side of the cut's coral wall, and jumped into the fast-moving water in the place that looked shallowest. The water was mid-thigh deep, and I could stand in the current, barely, if I leaned forward and set my foot down firmly with each step. Grabbing the bow line, I towed the kayak behind me, allowing my feet to shuffle over the rough bottom one painstaking step at a time, sometimes stubbing my toes on sharp rocks, while walking gradually into deeper water. At the center of the cut, the water rose to my waist and the current nearly toppled me as the kayak bumped and twisted at the end of its tow line. I clutched at little coral outcrops in the wall, abrading my fingers here, scraping my elbows there, and continued making slow progress forward. After what seemed an hour but was more likely fifteen minutes, I passed the narrow center, and the current eased. The water level dropped, too. A few steps later, I jumped into the kayak and paddled like mad.

I'd made it, but there was one more lagoon to cross. My arms felt like they weighed forty pounds each, and several times I had to get out and drag the kayak over and around coral heads too shallow or too dense to paddle around. By the time I tied my little green boat next to Alex's red one, he had already disappeared in the woods to inspect and record data at his study sites. When it came to research design and information gathering on the effects rats had on crabs and native plants, Alex was a careful and responsible scientist. But traveling to his study spots was another story. He made his way to his locations with all the excitement of a kid on the morning of his tenth birthday.

I dug out my water bottle, took a long drink, and surveyed the cuts and scrapes on my hands, elbows, and feet. Nothing serious. While I stood knee deep in the water, resting my sore arms, shoulders, back, and legs, several black-tipped reef sharks, curious as crows, swam over to see if I might be something to eat. In that shallow water, I could now see the advantage of the sharks' creamy white color. Their bodies blended well with the lagoon's sandy bottom.

But there was no hiding those black-topped dorsal fins cutting the water in the characteristic upside-down V shape that shouted, *I am a shark, and here I come.*

"I can see you, you rascals," I said to the two- to three-foot-long sharks, as several hovered a few yards from my legs. I took a deep breath and basked in the high that had come from strenuous exercise and from outwitting the wind and currents. Sharks? Big deal. I stomped my foot lightly and the sharks bolted, gone in an instant.

What a grand experience, playing with sharks. Now I loved Alex for leaving me alone to fend for myself, to figure out a way to make things work. Unwittingly, he had forced me to take another step toward independence. And suddenly there he was on the shoreline, hurrying toward me with a concerned expression, as if he had just remembered that someone else had been kayaking through the lagoons with him.

"Did you have any trouble getting through the cut?" he said. "The current was strong today."

"I'm only bleeding in two places," I said, smiling.

Rested and rehydrated, we scouted and marked the second of our future study sites in the center of the long, narrow island and paddled our kayaks to both ends to choose the last two. In each case, we measured and flagged the areas to be poisoned (fifty yards square), and the areas inside these in which I would count ants (fifteen yards square).

Mission accomplished, at least for now. I had gotten myself upwind and upcurrent under my own power to one of the most beautiful and remote places in the world. And there was a bonus. The towering *Pisonia* trees of Eastern Island protected the shoreline from the wind, creating a calm, clear turquoise pool where more manta rays turned somersaults in their search for plankton. So numerous and unafraid were these big harmless fish, I had to paddle around them because they neither dived nor detoured at the approach of an advancing kayak.

Another bonus to working on Eastern Island was getting to know fiddler crabs, one- to two-inch-wide crabs that dug their holes in expanses of white sand flats located in several areas off the island. The teasers sat at the edges of their holes by the thousands, but I couldn't get a good look at one, even when I moved as slowly as possible. Because Palmyra's bristle-thighed curlews and other shorebirds eat fiddler crabs, they're quick to hide, and the slightest movement caused the crabs to duck into their perfectly round holes.

After I passed, though, the crabs would pop up behind me, a behavior that caused crabs to be all around me but never nearby. It felt as if I was playing the toddlers' game Whac-a-Mole. You can never win. But we could win this one because we had hands, cheating, I'm sure, from the crabs' point of view. To give me a close look at Palmyra's fiddler crabs, Alex dug one out.

Male fiddler crabs have one enormous pincer that doesn't pinch. The claw is for courting displays only. Our male crab's bright red claw was so large— nearly as big as its entire body—it looked front heavy, like it might fall on its face from the weight of it. The name "fiddler" supposedly comes from the male crabs' eating motion. As it draws food to its mouth with the working smaller front claw, it looks like a bow passing back and forth over the large claw, the "fiddle."

The crab's two eyes were gray bulbs atop pink stalks probably half as tall as the crab was wide, handy for peeking out to see if the coast was clear of shorebirds. Across the crab's black back, nature had tattooed a yellow butterfly.

"You will be an ambassador for your species," I said to the crab as I photographed it sitting quietly in Alex's palm. "People are going to love your outfit." The Hawaiian Islands host no fiddler crabs, but they're close relatives of the ghost crabs we commonly see on Hawai'i's beaches. After taking pictures, we returned the crab to the sand, where in seconds it dug a new hole and disappeared.

During those first weeks in Palmyra I felt as if I were walking in and out of a theater showing a great movie. While immersed in the world of sharks, rays, crabs, and trees, my problems seemed so remote they were nearly nonexistent. But climbing the ladder to the deck of my boat or opening a chilly e-mail from Craig reminded me that I still had a broken forestay, aching joints, and a husband who may or may not be there when I got home. How I longed to stay forever inside the magic multiplex of nature.

Back at the Cooper Island camp, Alex and I used an old shack (torn down now) as a combined lab and office, complete with electricity and plank desks for laptops, specimen jars, and books. A satellite e-mail system in the shack allowed us to send data, reports, and questions to Fish and Wildlife biologists and managers in Honolulu.

Because Alex's expertise on Palmyra's plant and animal life put him in charge of the ant study, I became the official fieldworker, so-called because that person goes into the "field" collecting whatever data the study requires. Between his doctoral research and Fish and Wildlife tasks, Alex didn't have enough hours in a day. To give him as much time as possible, I would do whatever parts of the ant study I could do alone. We had weeks of planning, organizing, and testing before ant poisoning could occur, and during that time, I wanted to learn as much as I could about ants.

All the atoll's ant species were aliens that had arrived as stowaways over the years on boats and inside containers. Tiny red ants marched in long lines in the shower rooms. Much bigger black ones called big-headed ants followed one another through the dining tent vacuuming up crumbs. And middle-sized crazy ants, so-called because they run in circles and zigzags, foraged along the camp's paths. The crazy ants' movements were so erratic that my eyes could barely follow one individual. "Crazy" behavior seemed a better strategy for evading predators, I thought, than running in straight lines like lemmings over a ledge.

Still, the system of laying down biochemical signals that say "follow me," "run in circles," or "attack" obviously works well for these social insects. In mass, the world's some twelve thousand ant species constitute ten to fifteen percent of all land animals. One acre of land in the Amazon rain forest contains over three million ants. A supercolony in Hokkaido, Japan, was discovered to have 306 million worker ants and 1 million queens in forty-five thousand interconnected nests. Ants are predators, scavengers, herbivores, and farmers, turning more soil than earthworms. Like humans, these insects have multiplied and conquered Earth. Also like humans, when introduced to territory with defenseless plants and animals, they eventually destroy their own resource.

The more I learned about ants, the more I admired their collective power, and as I walked around Cooper Island, I imagined ant cities, subways, and apartments humming with life below. I began to feel a little bad about killing ants but stopped that train of thought. I agreed with Alex that all living creatures have a right to exist, but when we humans upset the balance of nature, such as introducing ants and scale insects—unnatural parasites in Palmyra—to native species, it's our duty to try to make it right.

To count ants, I had to learn to tell one kind from another, since the study targeted only those that farmed scale. I learned ant biology from E. O. Wilson's Pulitzer Prize–winning book *The Ants*, which I brought with me on the boat, and also from Peter, the ant expert in Honolulu. He explained by e-mail how to identify each species, and I went around the atoll collecting ants in jars by their color, size, and behavior. Still, even with the ant book and Peter, it was hard to identify the smaller species. Alex and I asked Fish and Wildlife for a microscope, and to our amazement (because it was an additional expense), the Honolulu managers sent a new one on the next plane.

Microscopes have always been among my favorite biology tools, and I set this one up in a corner of our office shed to examine ants, scale, and anything else I found that might be interesting, such as the brown spots called spores (reproductive bodies) on the underside of fern fronds. To share the fun, I carted the microscope and my specimens to the dining room, a common gathering place.

"Look," I said to anyone passing. "You can see the ants up close. And the scale. Here's a spore. See?"

Most people took polite glances, but I was the only one enamored with this miniscule universe. "I never knew anyone could get so excited about ants," Luke said one day after I implored him to check out a big-headed ant I had mounted under the lens. "We should call you Ant Susan."

From that day on, he and most others there did call me that.

I quickly learned to identify the two ant species that farmed scale in Palmyra: big-headed ants and crazy ants. Peter, the entomologist who had designed the study, politely answered my questions by e-mail but had no sense of humor about his subject. When I sent him ant jokes ("Oops, there goes another rubber tree plant"), he never replied.

Our tumbledown shed grew homier by the day as we arranged space for the microscope and pounded nails in walls for hanging day packs and clothing. Crazy about the smell of peanut butter, rats moved into the makeshift office, as well as several red and purple hermit crabs, which licked sweat from our kicked-off sandals. Alex and I spent long hours in the shed working out the details of the study, creating timetables, methods, and contingency plans. This was biology work at its best and worst. The best was that the managers in Honolulu were being meticulous about gathering data before even thinking about introducing an alien species (ladybugs) to kill another alien species (scale) in a wildlife refuge. The science was sound, the methods made sense, and Alex and I were good at it.

The worst was that the agency doing it was flat broke. The U.S. Fish and Wildlife Service has never been well funded, but federal administrators had cut funds to such a minimum that some departments barely functioned. Honolulu managers had had no choice but to have volunteers conduct this fieldwork, and once it was done, if ladybugs were deemed appropriate, no one knew if there would be money to buy them. I was told that the water and soil samples I was to collect would sit on a shelf somewhere until the funds were found to analyze them, which might be never.

Still, making this study as scientifically precise as we could was the first step toward saving the grand *Pisonia* trees falling at our feet, and Alex and I took it seriously.

And those giant trees really were falling, if not exactly at our feet, at least in our near vicinity, sometimes with almost no warning. One day while flagging one of our Eastern Island ant plots, an alarming creaking noise arose. It started as a low moan and increased in seconds to a high-pitched screech. We stopped working to look around, but before we could register what was happening, an ear-splitting crash, accompanied by an alarming crackling and crunching, shattered the forest peace. We dropped our tapes and stakes and ran toward the sound, stopping in a clearing near the beach to stare. A healthy-looking sixty- to seventy-foot-tall *Pisonia* tree, its bushy leaves still green and shiny, had toppled. The tree's flat expanse of exposed roots was nearly twice as tall as Alex.

Another day, I paddled alone to one of our flagged ant plots on Eastern Island and couldn't find it. *How could I be lost?* I wondered. *I've been here several times, and the island isn't that big.* But I was not lost. The neighborhood had changed dramatically after an enormous *Pisonia* tree crashed across our well-marked path. Tangles of leafy branches poked up everywhere, and two red-footed booby chicks lay among them, killed in the fall. I sat on the fallen trunk for a long, sobering moment. If I had been on this path, which I soon would be several times a week, I would have been crushed by the species I was sent there to save.

Now there was one movie I didn't want to see.

19

$\mathcal{A}$ LEX and I were ready to begin work at the four ant study sites. Each plot had both young and old *Pisonia* trees, all crawling with ants that nurtured the scale that killed the trees. In some areas, dozens of dead trees lay like collapsed columns, a forest sacked and pillaged by an army we could barely see. We measured and flagged the areas to be poisoned (fifty yards square), and the areas inside these in which I would count ants (fifteen yards square).

To count ants systematically at each plot, I was to cut twenty one-inch paper squares from index cards, drop a dab of peanut butter and a dribble of corn syrup on each, and lay them on the ground at precise places marked with plastic flags on wire posts. After fifteen minutes, about the time it took me to drop, dribble, and distribute all the baited squares, I would walk around and count the ants on each of the twenty white papers. Afterward, each paper had to be collected and thrown away, since a new, clean paper was to be used each time. That done in one plot, I would pack my gear into plastic containers that fit on the back of my green kayak and paddle to the next plot to repeat the procedure.

To provide researchers with before-poison data to compare with after-poison data, I had to conduct weeks of counts at each of the four plots before we spread the poison on the three Eastern Island sites.

It all seemed straightforward enough. But since the study involved messing with nature, it had complications, and complications of complications.

Because you can't change procedures once a study is started, we needed (as do most researchers) to plan and perform pilot studies, or trials, before launching the real thing. Pilot studies reveal the snags in proposed methods and show how solutions work—or how and why they don't. A test study also gives the fieldworker, me in this case, practice for the real thing.

During one early pilot, I laid out squares of ant bait and soon learned that plenty of animals besides ants were wild about peanut butter and corn syrup. Everyone involved expected this, but what surprised us was the speed with which the nonstudy subjects horned in.

The strawberry hermit crabs, for instance, viewed the ant bait as complimentary *pupus* and raced for them just minutes after I put them down.

"You are so busted," I said to a strawberry hermit crab chowing down on one of my corn syrup papers the first time I tried to count ants. "But adorable," I added, because when I picked up the crab, its sticky legs and shell reminded me of a toddler caught raiding the cookie jar.

Walking to a more distant paper, I picked up a scurrying crab, and when it slammed shut its pincer door, I saw it was brown with peanut butter. Caught red-handed—and red-clawed.

I had already determined that the dominant ants in all my plots were a species called big-headed ants. The worker ants of this species looked like your average black sidewalk ants, not big-headed at all. But I met their namesake early on when a crab approached a baited paper already full of ants. When the crab began stealing the ants' bonanza, the ants surprised me by running away. In seconds, I saw that the worker ants weren't exactly running away. They had gone to call in the marines.

Big-headed ants are named after their soldiers, which have heads so oversized they look like they're wearing tiny black football helmets. And they have big teeth to match, which were murder on other ant species but too small to hurt me (or any human), and certainly not the armored hermit crabs.

Even so, those big-headed soldiers charged to do battle like Samurai warriors. Some swarmed over the crab, and others took up posts trying to guard the peanut butter/corn syrup patch. Neither tactic worked. The crab's crusty exterior shell protected it from ant bites, and the crab, seemingly oblivious, continued eating. But although the ants were losing the war, they couldn't stop fighting. Like professional soldiers everywhere, the big-headed warriors' mission in life was to attack anything that threatened the well-being of the nest, in this case a thief stealing a windfall of fat and sugar. I admired the ants' valiant efforts at attacking a creature hundreds of times their size. In this, crabs and ants are comrades in arms.

I picked up the little hermit bandit, careful to keep my fingers on the back of the crab's snail shell, placed it in a white bucket, and headed back to my other stations. There I found an arthropod war, with hermit crabs pushing and shoving each other to get at the peanut butter/corn syrup cards, many of which were already eaten clean, and big-headed soldier ants fighting their losing battles.

Back in Honolulu, we had wondered how long it would take the crabs to get to these aromatic freebies, and now we knew: only minutes. Clearly, since we wanted ants to eat at the bait cards unimpeded, I would have to collect all the hermit crabs in the vicinity.

The next day, before putting out the food in my control plot, I picked up all the crabs I could find—about fifty—and deposited them in five-gallon buckets. Surely, I thought, I can set out the bait and count ants in my fifteen-minute time window before more distant crabs pick up the scent of peanut butter and come running.

The crabs I placed in the bucket were hell-bent on escaping, and although they could not climb the smooth sides, they scrambled on top of each other, making unstable piles that toppled with a clatter as their turban shells clacked against the hard plastic. This didn't hurt the crabs since they tucked deep into their snail shells when they fell. Almost immediately, the thwarted climbers emerged and began another summit attempt.

It took me a day to estimate by sight how many crabs I could add per bucket. Too many and the crabs quickly formed a hill, allowing the ones at the top to reach the edge and make fearless leaps to the ground. The escapees did not run to hide. They ran to the peanut butter. Only a few crabs to a bucket meant that the crabs couldn't get out, but I had to paddle a dozen bulky buckets from plot to plot and carry them around my bait sites.

Alex suggested that since we were collecting hermit crabs in the same areas each day, we make a harmless mark on the tops of their snail shells to see where they went, since no one knew if they stayed in one small area or roamed their entire island. (These land crabs don't swim between islands.) I added a handful of marking pens to my study box, and for several days Alex and I marked the shells of the hermies we collected in the study plots, using a different color and symbol each day. On Valentine's Day we drew red hearts on the hermies' shells in the Cooper Island control plot, and for a month or so afterward (rain eventually washed the hearts off), camp residents found walking Valentines in all parts of the island. Through this, we learned that the strawberry hermit crabs are not territorial but, rather, wander from shore to shore of their home island in their search for food.

Collecting hermit crabs helped preserve my bait for only a week or so, because even though I was careful to collect and remove my bait papers as soon as

I could (they stayed out in each plot for about twenty minutes), peanut butter and corn syrup often dribbled off the sides, and the scents lingered in the plots. Like the compost heap crowds, more crabs began hanging around the study sites. Soon, even after beating the bushes to find and collect crabs, I could barely turn my back before another popped out from nowhere and scampered toward my bait. Besides that, hauling five-gallon buckets in my kayak turned out to be unwieldy and time-consuming.

Just when it was becoming clear that collecting crabs was not going to solve my problem, rats joined the feast. It took the more isolated rats of Eastern Island longer than the camp rats on Cooper to get over their shyness in my presence, but after a few days, the scent of peanut butter became so irresistible that the rats began to show themselves in broad daylight. (This bold behavior suggested that the rat population was enormous.)

One day, I came back to my ant supply box near my kayak to find a gray rat standing on top of the closed peanut butter jar, its dainty pink paws held at its chest like a puppy begging a treat. Wild rats in wildlife preserves are considered pests of the worst kind, and they certainly were on Palmyra, where their population had gone unchecked for decades. But rats also make good pets for good reasons: they're intelligent, friendly, and cute. My sister once had three black-and-white pet rats that entertained us endlessly, sitting on our shoulders, running up our shirt sleeves, and nibbling snacks from our hands.

Having had no predators on Eastern Island, the dark gray rats (common name: black rats) had an air of innocence about them as they peeked at us from under logs and behind ferns. I felt great affection for the Eastern Island rats, as did Alex. Some days we would sit motionless and watch a rat walk right up to a bait card and begin licking peanut butter with its pink tongue as it watched us with intelligent black eyes. It seemed as if the rat was saying, *You will never catch me.* And it was right. The second we moved, the rat was gone.

I would find a way to outwit the wily rats of Palmyra, but not before another species crawled in to help themselves to the treats.

ONE day at lunch before we set out to monitor the ant plots, Alex appeared in the dining room and asked if I wanted to walk with him to another of his study sites on a part of Cooper Island I had not yet seen. "We can take Dadu," he said. "He likes to go for walks." Dadu roamed freely, yet if any of us said, "Dadu, want to go for a walk?" the dog behaved as if he had been stuck indoors all day. As predicted, Dadu jumped for joy at the offer, and off we went.

Dadu was what I call a uni-dog, the kind of universal mutt you see around the world in communities where humans leave dogs to survive and breed on their own. These highly adaptable mongrels are brown and smaller than coyotes but bigger than beagles. The description fit Dadu perfectly. Years earlier, someone had abandoned three such mixed-breed dogs on Palmyra, and Dadu was the last survivor. The other two were buried in tiny graves with painted markers. Dadu didn't miss his pack buddies, though, because they had not been buddies, I was told. For reasons known only to the dogs, Dadu's two companions had not liked him. The dogs snapped and snarled at Dadu if he ventured too close. Having heard the stories, I attributed the scars on his body to dog fights. But I soon learned that not all of his bites were from dogs.

Dadu loped with us like any pet dog on a walk in the woods, but when Alex and I reached the end of the island, Dadu suddenly went crazy, yelping, running, and leaping straight into the water. With the tide out, the water in the corner of the bay came to the dog's belly, causing Dadu to half run, half swim in the clear shallow water.

"What on earth is he doing?" I said.

"Chasing a shark," Alex said.

We stood at the shoreline watching a black-tipped dorsal fin weave back and forth in panic as the dog closed in, driving the two- to three-foot-long shark toward the mud beach.

"When no one was here to feed them, the dogs ate sharks. This is one of the shallow places he can corner them."

"Does he catch them?" I said.

"Rarely. And if he does, the shark isn't usually injured. See these scars? Dadu is the one who gets injured."

"Can we stop him?"

"No. He won't come when you call him, and he won't walk on a leash. He shouldn't be here, but since he's lived in Palmyra all his life, he's been grandfathered into the refuge."

I felt sick watching the dog drive the frantic little shark back and forth in the shallows with all the determination of a border collie rounding up sheep. It was an enormous relief to see the shark make a sharp turn, race toward deep water, and escape.

Dadu rejoined us at the shoreline, shook the salt water off his fur and onto us, and sat down panting, his pink tongue hanging out with the exertion. Dadu gazed up at Alex with a happy dog smile on his face.

"Does Dadu chase the crabs?" I asked.

"No. I'm sure they taught him some painful lessons. The cats leave the crabs alone too."

Passing boaters had abandoned two house cats, also grandfathered in. The camp's animal lovers treated the grateful animals like war orphans. During my time in Palmyra, I often saw workers moving boxes and gear in a little wagon with the two felines riding atop like Egyptian temple cats.

After I left Alex that day, I realized how much the camp pets illustrated a key aspect of wildlife refuges at Palmyra in particular, and throughout the world in general: nearly every place on the planet has been affected by humans. We've altered some areas more than others, but few spots on Earth remain pristine. As a result, when creating protected habitat for native plants and animals, conservationists must look beyond human alterations and make the best of what's left, working with land owners, the military, long-time residents, and everyone else with interest in regions intended to become endangered species habitat.

Palmyra is a typical example of such compromise. On some websites, the atoll is advertised as "one of the last pristine tropical reefs in American waters." This gives many people a false impression, because although some reefs surrounding Palmyra are indeed pristine, many are not, nor are any of the islands.

"Pristine?" scoffed a blogger who had been to Palmyra. "Hardly." What he meant was that for over a century, people altered the atoll to suit their purposes, such as using it as a fishing camp, copra plantation, haven for offshore sailors, and military base.

But the fish-processing hut (the current Palmyra Yacht Club), coconut palms, and cruising boats were mere drops in the bucket compared with what I would observe over the next months regarding the alterations the U.S. Navy brought to the atoll's islands and coral reefs between 1940 and 1945.

Before the Pearl Harbor attack, the base was planned as an aerial supply route to Canton Island and the Society Islands' Bora Bora. On December 24, 1941, a Japanese submarine surfaced offshore and fired at a dredging barge in Palmyra. Navy men fired back, and the attacker took off. This was Palmyra's only assault, but the men stationed at the atoll—around two thousand at a time, totaling six thousand from 1940 to 1946—got busy. Through blasting and dredging, they deepened the natural channel into West Lagoon and piled the dredged coral, sand, and soil nearby, creating five new islands named Sand, Home, Leslie, Ainsley, and Dudley Islands. Workers also dredged West and

Central Lagoons, clearing away sand banks and other areas too shallow for naval vessels. As a result of all this exploding and heaping, during the World War II years Palmyra's land area doubled.

Deepening and widening the channel and digging out the lagoons also caused stronger current flow, dropping the lagoons' water levels and changing their natural shapes.

Construction continued at what must have been a feverish pace. Navy men erected more than a hundred buildings, five runways, several wharves, fuel tanks, pipelines, and living quarters, including a hundred-thousand-gallon rain catchment system that provides freshwater to Palmyra's human inhabitants to this day. And the Navy wasn't done. Workers proceeded to join all the major islands of the atoll by building a continuous roadway in a ring, covering reef flats and filling channels between islands with sand, coral, and soil to make land bridges called causeways. It was through a gap in one of these washing-away causeways that I paddled my kayak to and from the Eastern Island ant plots.

Even though war never truly arrived in Palmyra, the place looked as if battles had been fought there, because the Navy left Palmyra a junkyard when it left, abandoning boats, planes, trucks, tons of gear, and nearly all the buildings. They even left their dishes. It was common for people working in the islands to find, wedged in the soil, heavy white coffee cups of 1940s vintage and silverware with "USN" stamped into the handle. (Because it's a National Wildlife Refuge, these and all objects found in Palmyra are not to be taken from the atoll.)

I never found any small items, but I did, along with everyone else, see and explore innumerable buildings, all inhabited by the spirits of people who lived there waiting for attacks that never came.

Some men stationed on the atoll felt bad luck lurked there and called it the Palmyra curse, an expression attributed to "old salts in the Pacific." In one incident, a U.S. patrol plane crashed near the base, but after extensive searching, no trace of it was ever found. Another pilot had trouble finding Cooper Island, and residents heard the plane slam into the ocean. Rescuers "didn't get to the poor guy fast enough," an officer reported. "Sharks found him first." In another airplane tragedy, a plane took off, and for no discernable reason, said the astonished ground crew, the pilot turned south instead of north, the direction of his destination. No one ever saw the plane again.

Civilians also entertained eerie thoughts about Palmyra. "Can an entire island be haunted or cursed?" asks one Internet site (www.strangemag.com), created by a man who seems to wish it were true. In his account, the source of a book called *The Curse of Palmyra Island*, Curt Rowlett relates incidents of "nautical high weirdness" (as opposed, apparently, to nautical low weirdness) on Palmyra and a "supernatural pattern of disaster and near-disaster associated with the place" that includes, of course, the killing and dismemberment of Muff (and most likely Mac) Graham. It's no stretch that someone would get the creeps from that tale. Every time I paddled my kayak across the serene spot where the two boats had been anchored, I thought of the unfortunate Grahams and their murderous neighbor.

"I had a foreboding feeling about the island," testified a yachtsman at Walker's 1977 piracy trial. "It was more than that it was a ghost-type island. . . . It seemed to be an unfriendly place to be. I've been on a number of atolls, but Palmyra was different. I can't put my finger on specifically why, but it was not an island that I enjoyed being on."

Another sailor who also testified at the trial said, "The island is a very threatening place. It is a hostile place. I wrote in my log: 'Palmyra, a world removed from time, the place where even vinyl rots. I have never seen vinyl rot anywhere else.'"

Of course vinyl rots there, I thought when I read this. Lush with bacteria, simmering in equatorial heat, and doused several times a day with tropical downpours, Palmyra wrote the recipe for rot.

One of the spookiest structures I encountered was a still-furnished military hospital, built in the 1940s to receive wounded soldiers. Because the war in the Pacific ended before that became necessary, the hospital was never used. To enter the building, as was true of many other abandoned structures on Palmyra, you had to part, with both hands, philodendrons and other thick vines that grew on the roof and spilled over the doorways like string curtains made of leaves instead of beads.

The hospital had no windows, being built as a bunker with a curved concrete roof, and was pitch black inside. I wore a headlamp when I went in, but that illuminated only one item at a time: a stack of metal beds with rusty springs, a white medicine cabinet with glass doors on rusty hinges. The bright beam of light made the rooms' corners even blacker, since my eyes couldn't adjust to the darkness, and I shuffled my feet to avoid tripping over unseen hazards. Doors creaked and banged in the wind, and rainwater dripped cavelike onto concrete floors.

Once I heard a rhythmic clicking sound that made me want to whirl around and call out "Who's there?" But I knew who was there: crabs. In nearly all the long-deserted buildings, crabs roamed the rooms, their hard exoskeletons tapping the concrete like the walking canes of blind pedestrians. The sounds reminded me of the dots and dashes of Morse code—L.E.T.M.E.O.U.T. the crabs seemed to signal. As I stood in that old building listening to crabs knock and water drip, I wondered what Craig would have made of this relic of a hospital. A wave of grief swept over me as I realized that I would never know. The part of my life where we shared everything was over.

Only one naval runway on Cooper was still functional, but it had shrunk to about half its original width due to foliage gradually reclaiming the cracked concrete on both sides. On one side of the runway, backed into dense bushes of *naupaka* (the Hawaiian name for a common succulent native throughout the tropical Pacific, scientific name *Scaevola*), rested a World War II airplane, its propeller and wings scarred with corrosion and most openings in its body sprouting vegetation. The former fighting machine looked forlorn sitting there, reduced as it was to its role as a rain forest flower pot.

Keeping the runway operational and safe for the small planes (chartered by the Nature Conservancy) that flew to Palmyra was an ongoing chore and a major concern for atoll managers. With no emergency services available, accidents had to be avoided at all costs.

With the Navy came rats, believed to have been accidentally introduced to Palmyra in the 1940s aboard vessels and inside containers. The transplanted rats discovered paradise in the equatorial atoll: a warm climate with no predators except a few people and their pets, and ample food in crabs, bird eggs, chicks, coconuts, and seeds. With such bounty, the rats reproduced like, well, rats. *Rattus rattus*, also called the black rat or ship rat, reaches sexual maturity at three months of age, and given enough food, each female can give birth to an average of forty offspring per year. The super-successful mammals swim well and eventually overran every island of the atoll.

Usually rats are nocturnal and wary, but the rats on Palmyra were so numerous and unafraid that they ventured out during the day. When Alex and I opened the door to our barely standing office shack where we worked on details of the ant study, it was common to hear, over the groans of the rusty hinges, the scritching of tiny toenails on cement as our resident rats ran into cracks and crevices. They didn't hide for long. While we worked on the computer or peered into the microscope, twitching whiskers and pink sniffing noses began to appear in the wall holes. Usually that was all I saw of the rats while working in the office, but I could hear them rummaging around in their concealed dens. Sometimes, I even heard, or imagined I heard, baby rats squeaking for their mothers' milk.

When we left the office and clicked off the one light bulb hanging from the ceiling, the rats emerged on search-and-destroy missions. We knew this from the damage caused by their notorious teeth. One afternoon, early on in the ant work, I left several large jars of peanut butter on the desk, thinking that since they were uncracked they were safe. The next morning, though, I found the plastic lid of one jar gnawed mostly through. I rescued my ant bait just in time, sealing all the jars of peanut butter and bottles of corn syrup inside heavy plastic bins.

I soon got used to the sound of skittering feet, and the sight of furry rear ends and trailing tails, as the rats scurried for cover when I walked into the room. I also learned to empty every crumb of food from my backpack after a day's work and to hang it high on a nail to keep it from those sharp and efficient teeth. Once I found a hole chewed in a shirt pocket that I had draped on a chair back. Vigilance was vital.

In the camp, people tried to protect their food and belongings by sprinkling rat poison around the perimeter. No one liked poison in the refuge, but the workers had tried using live cage traps and liked those even less, because you had to carry the trapped and terrified mammal to the shoreline and hold it underwater until the rat drowned, gasping and struggling to the bitter end. The poisoning seemed more humane, and although it didn't reduce the number of rats overall, it kept them, mostly, out of people's tents and Melissa's well-equipped and superscrubbed kitchen.

I felt sorry for the rats on Palmyra, and of course, so did Alex. We saw them often during the ant study, and sometimes talked to them, explaining we understood that it wasn't their fault they were there and thriving. Even so, the rats were so destructive to so many species, you could barely call the place a refuge. The rats' unchecked scavenging of the islands' plants, seeds, crabs, birds, and eggs was a disaster to all of the atoll's species, native and nonnative alike. One of Alex's main areas of research was the effects the rats had on Palmyra's flora and fauna. If rats were eradicated from the atoll, an enormous undertaking being considered at the time, what would be the ecological consequences? It was possible—probable, I thought—that through his determination to understand the relationships between the plants and animals of Palmyra, Alex would one day be instrumental in bringing about a positive new balance of nature to the atoll.

BEFORE I sailed to Palmyra, I had often wondered how workers coped with the heavy rain there, but the showers, it turned out, were a blessing. It rained nearly every day, but rarely all day. The occasional black cloud raced to the atoll, delivered its load of water, and hurried on, leaving me wet, cool, and refreshed. During my first weeks there I learned to mostly ignore the rain like everyone else and walked around in downpours while continuing my work. After a deluge, the sun and wind usually dried my lightweight clothes quickly, except for underpants and bra, which stayed wet and stuck to my skin. There in the tropical rainforest, underwear seemed like the work of the devil, and along with most others in the camp, I soon stopped wearing it.

The Nature Conservancy kept the two ice machines running continually. Even so, the ice bins were often empty by day's end because working in the equatorial heat (averaging 85 degrees Fahrenheit) and humidity (averaging 80 percent or more) made everyone crave water, the colder the better. Palmyra's temperatures and humidity often ran higher than in Hawai'i, but the heat was not the miserable kind in which you can get no relief. Although the smallest labor made me sweat, gusty winds acted like giant fans that cooled me when I sat in the shade. I found Palmyra to be surprisingly comfortable most of the time, but exerting the least bit of effort in that muggy climate, especially in the sun, made me as soaking wet as if I had jumped in the lagoon. No one had to remind me to drink water. I was nearly always thirsty and downed about a gallon of water each day.

Walking around naked, or nearly so, was never okay in the camp, but as long as people arrived dressed and left with clothes on, skinny dipping at the camp's swimming hole, a picture of paradise at the island's edge where palm trees lined a clear pool, was acceptable. My first visit to the pool came one sultry afternoon before dinner when the wind had stopped and an unrelenting sun turned the island into a sweat lodge. Most of the other camp members had the same idea.

Being careful not to look at one another's nakedness, we women dropped our clothes on the bank and waded in up to our necks, our self-consciousness over excess weight, saggy breasts, and all those other bodily "defects" women feel cursed with quickly and safely submerged. Not the men. Someone had knotted a rope and tied it in such a way that people could swing high over the pool and drop in near the deep middle. The men were delighted to shed their shorts, grab the rope, and swing back and forth over the pool like Tarzan wannabes. None of the women were bold enough body-wise to swing, but the men, naked as blue jays, flew over our heads with shouts of glee. With their thighs clamped tight around the rope, the guys' testicles got trapped behind their legs like squashed kiwi fruits, and the sight caused us women to giggle like a bunch of schoolgirls.

The fun ended when the cooks left to finish their dinner preparations and I rowed back to the boat to change clothes. In minutes, my swimming euphoria vanished and I was crying. How I missed Craig. *I'm unlovable and unloved and deserve it*, I thought. *I'm sitting here alone on this boat in this atoll because I was a bad partner.*

After I finished shedding my tears in great, gulping sobs, I recalled a story a friend told me years earlier. She and another woman friend went skiing in Colorado, and that evening they sat in a hot tub, talking about the day. Suddenly, Marge, in her mid-fifties, burst into tears.

"Marge, my God, what's wrong?" Gail said.

Sobbing, Marge replied, "I'm a terrible person."

Gail waited to hear the story, to find out what Marge, whom everyone thought was an exceptionally good person, had done that was so bad. But there was no story. She couldn't explain it. Marge felt awful about herself, even wondering if she deserved to go on living. When later Gail and I, both in our early forties, discussed this incident, we agreed that although Marge was of menopause age, and talked of hot flashes and other symptoms, there must have been something else going on. We didn't get it. No one gets it when it's happening to someone else, even a sister or best friend. Menopause is so personal, and so different for individual women, that when it happens to us we're each on our own.

Marge, I heard later, got on HRT and felt better. I felt better on it, too, but not normal. The estrogen stopped my physical symptoms but had not stopped these sudden outbursts of emotion. I didn't mind a good cry now and again, but tears for no particular reason were unnerving. Sure, I was alone in Palmyra, and I did miss Craig, but was I really abandoned and unloved? I did not know. Not knowing what was real, what I imagined, or what I caused myself was a living nightmare. Alfred Hitchcock's *Psycho* should have been a story about menopause.

I went below deck to blow my nose and stared at the wrinkled, sun-spotted, red-faced woman who looked back at me from my cabin mirror, a lovely piece of custom-made art framed in stained-glass turtles. Like Grandma Mary, I wondered, *Who in the world is that old lady?* Unlike Grandma Mary, though, I decided to keep my turtle mirror and embrace my aging face and body with the same mind-set I accepted Palmyra Atoll's history of human usage. We may not be pristine, this atoll and me, but in us there is still the beauty of life.

That evening, after we residents finished Melissa's fine calamari dinner with tossed salad, scalloped potatoes, steamed carrots, and homemade apple pie, Dadu wandered into the dining room wet and shivering. Because short-haired Dadu sometimes got cold in the evenings when rain soaked his fur, one of the repeat volunteers made him a fleece jacket with a hood. I put this coat on the shaking dog, and while petting and talking to the grateful animal—adorable, I thought, in his flowery outfit—one of the chronically grumpy construction workers walked in.

"That dog looks ridiculous," he snapped. "Take that off of him."

"He was chilly," I said, thinking the man was joking.

"Chilly," he sneered. "It's not cold here. And dogs don't wear clothes. *Get it off.*" The tone astonished me, but when I looked up, I saw that the worker's eyes were bloodshot and slightly unfocused. Having grown up around alcoholics, I knew enough to shut up and disappear when a drinking person got mean. I removed Dadu's sweater, folded it neatly, and strolled past the unsteady, glowering man.

Forever forgetting to bring my flashlight from the boat, I stumbled toward my dinghy in total darkness, barely making out the white plastic floats (lost from fish nets) that Melissa had collected from the beaches and placed along the edges of the path. As I walked on, I became oddly elated, as if I had hit the jackpot in a slot machine. How good it felt to simply stand up and walk away from behavior I did not like. I don't know why this seemed like such a grand revelation out there in the wilderness, but at that moment I knew one thing that was going to happen when I got home: I was going to stop fighting with Craig, see what happened next, and evolve.

Of course, I knew that life wasn't always that simple, but I didn't stop to ponder. I was sick of pondering and tired of mourning. I felt that something had been resolved by my calm exit, and by my decision to continue exiting from distressing situations, and left it at that.

On the boat that moonless evening, the wind stopped completely. I lay back in the cockpit gazing at the stars in a sky so clear and a lagoon so glassy that Orion, Pleiades, and billions of stars with no names glittered on the water's surface. Loving my own personal *Starry Night*, I moved to the deck for a better view and noticed a circular white glow like a foul ball hit out of the Milky Way. I got out the binoculars and star books and leaned against the mast to identify this fuzzy round thing in the sky. It was the Magellanic Clouds, two galaxies so close together from Earth's point of view that they look like one. Named after explorer Ferdinand Magellan, the chalky spot is visible only from, or near, the southern hemisphere.

In Palmyra, about 350 miles north of the Equator, the galaxies hang at a comfortable viewing angle, a choice spot in my celestial gallery. Gazing at those galaxies from the deck of my own boat gave me such a rush of pleasure that I let out a whoop of joy out there all by myself. If, lying on my own sailboat in the lagoon of a fabulous atoll, I could pick out and bask in the glow of the Magellanic Clouds, I must be doing something right.

20

"W̶HAT part of the forestay failed exactly?" Craig asked me on the phone.

"I don't know. It broke at the top of the mast, and I haven't been up there to look yet."

He paused. "You're going up the mast?"

I had always been afraid to climb that forty-eight-foot-tall aluminum pole rising, and usually swaying, over the solid deck. With Craig's help, I had once gotten about a quarter of the way up, but the sight of all the gear below that could skewer me if I fell scared me so much that I clambered back down. In truth, I hadn't tried very hard. What was the point? If something needed fixing up there, Craig would do it.

One of the rare days we finished early with the ant plot work, Alex, a rock climber, volunteered to go up, but to understand the fix, I had to see the failure. Alex could climb later if I found some task up there beyond my strength. The first climb was my job.

Alex helped me dig out the long-buried bosun's chair, used only once by Pierre. The term "chair" was wishful thinking. Bosun's chairs come in all models and prices, the more expensive ones being something with a hard bench you can actually sit upon. Not having had any experience with these mast-climbing devices, however, I bought a cheap one, which was just a canvas sling that goes around your bottom and between your legs, connecting at the belly with a heavy ring made for fastening a halyard.

On most boats, a person on the deck has to, with great effort and care, haul the person in the bosun's chair up the mast, like hoisting a sail, except harder. *Honu*, however, had come with mast steps installed. The steps were somewhat like the horizontal posts that stick out from the sides of telephone poles but with one difference: the outside of each of *Honu*'s steps bent up and angled back to fasten to the mast, creating a well-attached little triangle for the toe of your shoe.

Even so, climbing *Honu*'s mast wasn't entirely easy. The steps began above the boom, requiring some creative scrambling to get to the first step, nor do they go all the way to the top. Someone on the deck has to haul the climber up the last few feet by halyard. As an added precaution, the rule on *Honu* had always been that besides the bosun's chair, the climber also had to wear a sailing harness, clipping its leash around the mast while ascending, and also while parked at the top.

When the boat is under way, this four-story climb is perilous and petrifying because a swinging mast top at sea looks and feels like an upside-down pendulum. It's less frightening in a slip or at anchor but still demands all your attention. Ripples in the water that barely rock the hull send the mast top swinging like a metronome.

Having never climbed the mast, I hadn't given much thought to *Honu*'s little aluminum steps. Now I felt like tying red bows on each of those glorious metal rungs. When going up a sailboat mast, any foothold is a gift.

We made a plan: I would support most of my own weight on the small steps while Alex kept the halyard on the bosun's chair taut to check an accidental slip.

I put on my sailing harness, took a deep breath, and forced myself to the mast base. Stepping into the bosun's chair felt like I was donning a giant diaper, another safety I may wish I had if I got any more scared.

"You don't have to do this, you know," Alex said, seeing my hesitation. "I'm more than happy to go up."

"Thanks. But I need to do this."

"Okay, then," he said. "Up you go."

My sweaty palms slipped on the mast's winches as I clambered gracelessly onto the main boom. And up I climbed, one toehold and sweaty handhold at a time. In moments, I was standing on the spreaders, those horizontal bars that make a sailboat mast look like a giant cross. You can stand fairly comfortably on *Honu*'s spreaders, getting a solid stance by hanging onto the mast.

"I'm stopping for a rest," I called down to Alex, who looked up anxiously.

While I gazed down at him, an amazing thing happened. My fear turned to exhilaration. It was fantastic seeing *Honu* from above. This time, her stanchions, winches, and windlass didn't look like piercing weapons, because I understood each device's function. Now the deck hardware seemed like old friends, assistants helping me get this boat where I wanted to go.

Standing on the spreaders reminded me of the out-of-body experiences people describe, the kind where you're floating above your real life. Except I really *was* floating—well, suspended—above my real life. *Why had I ever wasted money and risked my health with drugs and alcohol?* I thought. *To get high, all I had to do was climb a mast.*

"Are you okay?" Alex called out.

"I'm fine," I called down. "Look where I am. Halfway up and not scared at all."

He gave me two thumbs up, and I continued climbing.

The higher I got, the smaller *Honu*'s deck grew, and the more expansive became my view of the lagoon and its surrounding islands. When I had gone up as far as I could go on my own, Alex hoisted me the rest of the way, about four more feet to the top. Once I was there, he cleated off the halyard, and I tied myself to the mast with my leash. I felt comfortable—as comfortable as anyone can feel while hanging with all your weight in a crotch-jamming bosun's chair. The only way I could fall now would be if the mast fell too, and with the jib and spinnaker halyards still supporting it from the bow, and the other shrouds secure, I felt safe.

This gave me a moment to sit back in my diaper and gaze about. I hadn't brought my camera, but I didn't have to. My eyes took the photos. The images of the boat and the atoll from the top of my mast burned into memory while I watched with perfect clarity the black, kite-shaped manta rays glide near the lagoon's green surface as they shoveled plankton-loaded water into their mouths.

The lagoon was glassy calm at that moment, and the boat remained perfectly still—until Alex walked from the base of the mast to *Honu*'s bow. This caused a motion almost imperceptible on deck, but the nearly five-story mast swayed, making me feel like a bug on a blade of grass. It was a small swing as these things go, but the movement gave me a hint of what it must have been like during our voyages in the big waves of the open ocean when Craig had climbed the mast to fix a fitting.

From that height the Cooper camp, perched along the shoreline with its charming huts, looked like a South Pacific version of the hobbits' shire. The trees were so tall and dense, I couldn't see the ocean on the opposite side of Cooper Island, but I could hear the roar of the surf breaking against the atoll's fringing reef. So protected were we inside Palmyra's lagoon, it was easy to forget that the atoll was only a dollop of dirt in the middle of the Pacific Ocean.

The author attaching the new forestay and furler to *Honu*'s mast top.

During my view on high, it shocked me to see how small the boat looked. No wonder out there in the open ocean I felt like a speck. I'm a speck *on* a speck. The biggest surprise, though, came in my lack of fear—no, delight—at being at the top of a wiggly sailboat mast. I had avoided climbing this mast for years, but once I forced myself to do it, I loved it. I wasn't sure if my courage levels had changed, or if in opening myself up to new opportunities I was finding hidden strengths and untapped pleasures. It didn't matter. The moment was all I had and all I cared about, and it was excellent.

"How is it up there?" Alex called.

"Sorry. I'm not coming down. I'm going to live up here."

Oh, how I loved being tied to the tippy top of my own mast, which I had somehow managed to keep standing, harbored in the atoll of my dreams. At this distance from land, and this height above the water, the unobstructed views of Palmyra's lush green islands in that manta/shark/fish-filled lagoon were so beautiful I got a little misty.

"Hey, Captain," Alex shouted. "My turn."

I almost forgot I had a job to do. "I just need to check this fitting."

I examined the dangling hardware, called a toggle, that had once held the forestay. *Good God*, I thought, *this piddly little thing is all that holds the jib, the furler, and the forestay up here?* One stainless steel connector—a three-inch piece of metal no bigger than your average dog biscuit, currently hanging loose—was the only difference between the mast standing up and the mast falling down? I'd not seen this connection when the gear was lying on sawhorses at the yard, because it had been inside the lengthy furler, which now lay at the bottom of the sea. Now with the furler gone, I could see that the top of the forestay wire had pulled out cleanly from the toggle. That must have been the pop we heard when it fell. *How does that happen?* I wondered. The toggle looked neither broken nor defective.

With tools I'd loaded in the bosun's chair's side pockets, I pulled the cotter pin from the toggle to free it and dropped the hefty metal piece in my pocket.

"Ready to come down," I called to Alex, who walked back from the bow to the mast, where he uncleated the halyard. (Smart sailors don't stand under a mast when someone is aloft for fear of getting hit on the head by a dropped tool. People have died that way.)

My descent felt like backing down a tall ladder. With the steps and two safety lines holding me, I felt safe, happy, and triumphant. To my list of life-altering events, which at this point contained doorknobs and hermit crabs, I added mast climbing.

Later, I called Craig. "I got the toggle. Getting up the mast was easier than I thought. It was amazing and beautiful up there."

"Congratulations. I hope you never have to do it at sea, but if you do, now you know how. How did the piece fail?"

"I don't know. It looks fine."

"Send it back on the plane with the autopilot. I'll pick them up at the airport."

"I can hardly believe that this small chunk of metal is the only thing holding up all that gear under all that force," I said.

"On a sailboat there are a lot of things like that," he said. "Sobering, isn't it?"

I sent the piece home and days later got an infuriating diagnosis. Craig had shown it to a marine surveyor, who said the fitting (a Norseman, for those who know rigging techniques) had been put together improperly—grossly improperly—and simply slipped out. Ned, the chirpy know-it-all who told me he was an expert at these kinds of fittings, and everything else nautical, didn't have a clue what he was doing. "That jerk," I said, when Craig told me this on the phone. "He told me Norseman fittings were his specialty."

"He lied. Done right, those fittings are stronger than the stays themselves."

"Why didn't it fail when I was home? That's why I did all those test sails."

"The trade winds never came on hard when you were sailing here, and you motored a lot."

"The trip to Ko Olina was windy," I said. "And so was the one to Kaneohe Bay."

"I don't know why it didn't give way sooner, Susan. These things just happen. Maybe your other trips were too short to yank it free. You and Alex were sailing in strong wind for days."

I never thought I would have wished a major boat part had broken in one of Hawai'i's channels, but I did now.

"Do we have any recourse?" I said.

"The marine surveyor says we do. It was clearly done wrong. The yard was responsible. They should pay."

But with the boatyard bankrupt, Henry had taken a job somewhere in Florida, and Ned had moved to the Midwest. The new owners didn't know Henry, Ned, or *Honu* and didn't care what happened before they were there. We were out six thousand dollars.

Craig employed his usual philosophy about such losses—shit happens—and I loved him for it. His job in the E.R. gave him a daily look at what matters (debilitating illness and death) and what doesn't (everything else). This forestay failure was unfortunate, he thought, but Alex and I weren't hurt, we had the money to fix it, and the whole thing was a learning experience. Some days I felt awful about taking our boat on my own, barely knowing what I was doing, and then asking Craig for enormous amounts of help. I told him that on the satellite phone, and he sent me this e-mail: "If it makes you feel better, in the Sydney-Hobart race the two front runners (hundred-foot boats) had to pull out. One lost its keel, and capsized and the other 'wrinkled' its deck when it fell off a wave. This is another way of saying it nearly broke in half. Don't worry about the boat. Enjoy Palmyra."

Craig's unflappable approach to life—don't sweat the small stuff and it's all small stuff—worked well for him, and usually I found it inspiring. Sometimes, though, I couldn't muster up the self-discipline to view my problems as small stuff, and at those times his dispassionate reaction to them—and me—was exasperating. Life is just not that rational, that scientific. I knew he loved me, but would it kill him to show a little sympathy and affection when I was hurting or worried or confused?

This time, though, his practical point of view worked well regarding the boat failure. His race boat story did make me feel better.

THE tug *American Islander* arrived, its belching black smokestack as misplaced in Palmyra's lagoon as a coal car on a passenger train. Yet the sight of it tied up at the old Navy dock felt like a hug from home. Five days earlier, that boat, a familiar one around the main islands, had been sitting in Honolulu Harbor. *If I got on this tug*, I thought as I stared at it through my cabin window, *I could be home in four or five days*. I didn't consider doing that, but knowing it was possible made me feel less homesick.

But homesick for what? Despair washed over me, and my heart felt as heavy as *Honu*'s anchor lying on the lagoon floor. Everything important to me back there—my partner, my home, my peace of mind—was gone. Closing the curtain, I sat on my cabin sofa next to Craig's first valentine to me, a Raggedy Ann doll (now age twenty-five) with a hand-stitched red heart containing the words "I love you." I wanted to rip that doll's head off.

Wait, I thought, opening the curtains and staring at the tug. *Were my furler and other gear on the tug?* The furler Craig had worked like mad to buy, assemble, and load on time? Surely these efforts were a sign that he still wanted to be my partner. The question was: what kind of partner was I? Were my fears real, or was the menopause monster I decided a day earlier I could ignore wailing on me again?

I had to do something. Anything. I washed my face and rowed the dinghy toward the tug for a closer look.

The wharf was held together by ribbed sheets of metal so old and rusty that pieces curled out here and there like tiny sabers. Captains of normal boats didn't dock there for fear of getting holes in their hulls, but tugboats aren't normal boats. Black tires line their rails, and their steel hulls are tougher than the docks themselves. Without hesitation, the tug captain parked at the poky pier, and in minutes the crew of three had the boat and the barge tied up and ready to unload.

Pierre had declined to come. I knew in e-mails from Craig that Pierre had been vacillating, but the full impact of him not being on that tug struck like a blow. It was now, without a doubt, up to me to assemble the furler and install it along with the forestay. God help me. I was still mumbling "clockwise tightens" and struggling with flashlight batteries. Alex volunteered to help, promising to devote a whole weekend to it. Neither of us had any idea how to assemble a furler, or even what it looked like in pieces, but the gear, Craig said, came with a well-written manual, and we would send pictures home of the finished installation.

I stopped caring that Pierre didn't want to help me. It was time to learn how to fix my own boat.

I was useless helping unload the barge, which took forklifts, trucks, and backs much stronger than mine to lift and haul the construction materials into an aluminum-walled warehouse. My own gear (two plastic bins of food and the furler), small in comparison, was not in sight. Intending to return later to look for it, I rowed back to the boat and spent most of the day scrunched up inside the chain locker and crawling under the V-berth looking for my seawater leak. Alex said if I cleaned out the area and found the problem, he would apply the epoxy paste to seal it up. This was a good deal for me since I'm allergic to epoxy catalyst, and it's a messy job besides. For hours I worked in the chain locker, dragging the spare anchor and chain out with great effort and scouring thirty years of rust and salt off the locker's walls, rim, and floor with a wire brush to find the crack. I could see a dark spot on the inside where seawater stained the teak, but could not find a fissure or fault on the outside. It had to be something obvious—I'd emptied two buckets of seawater from there after only eight days at sea. Now it was dry as a bone and I couldn't see a place to put a patch.

Smeared with wet rust, I climbed out of the chain locker and plopped down on the deck. More than anything, even the forestay breaking, my failure to find the leak gave me a worse sense of defeat than I had felt in months. My trouble-shooting skills were pathetic. What was beneath the anchor well? I had no idea. Could that much water get into a crack so small I couldn't even see it? I didn't know. Was the leak somewhere else completely? Maybe.

As I worked, more and more questions arose. With this boat, I felt like each step forward set me two steps back.

Alex paddled out and found me sulking on the deck. "How's it going?" he said.

"I can't find the goddamn fucking leak."

He stared at me for a long moment and said, so softly, so carefully, that I had to smile, "Want me to take a look?"

"Yes. Please."

He examined the walls and bottom of the now-clean compartment. "I could run a bead of epoxy along this seam," he said.

"I don't see a crack in it."

"I don't either, but it's worth a try since it's empty and you cleaned it up so well."

I sighed. "Okay."

"Are you all right?"

"Frustrated."

When he finished applying the epoxy, which I was sure did not address the problem, I said, "While you're here, would you mind looking at the starter's electrical contacts with me? Pierre and I went over them back home, but something is wrong in there. I need to check them again."

Alex had been on his way to a remote part of the lagoon to monitor one of his study stations, but he had never refused to help me, and I'm sure he sensed that this would not be a good time to start.

We located the starter's electrical contacts. They all looked clean and shiny—no corrosion, rust, or bare wires. Still, we scrubbed them thoroughly with a wire brush and baking soda solution and put them back together. It started right up.

"Success," Alex said, smiling.

"The contacts weren't corroded."

"Maybe there was a loose connection that's fixed now."

I shrugged, not knowing if we had fixed the short in the starter or the leak in the V-berth. But at least we eliminated some possibilities. This, I was learning, was the nature of repairs in general, and boats in particular. You chip away at options until you hit the right one.

Maybe that applied to marriage malfunctions as well.

The tug-and-barge unloading went on and on. For three days the tug captain, his crew of three, and all the Nature Conservancy workers unloaded the barge using the tug's crane and the island's forklift, pickup truck, bicycles, wagons, and handcarts. Watching the workers going back and forth from dock to camp reminded me of the ants that I continued to catch, mount, and examine in the microscope. Humans have a lot in common with ants in our tireless building of homes and moving of material. As individuals, an ant or person doesn't have much impact on the planet, but in groups, look out.

When it comes to altering Earth's environment, ants and humans are as mighty as Thor's hammer.

Before the tug left Honolulu, Craig e-mailed that he had dropped off the furler and forestay at the Nature Conservancy's loading dock but had not actually seen them go onto the barge. Until I saw the gear, then, I wasn't sure it was there. During the unloading work I asked a volunteer if he'd seen my furler in the huge pile of building materials, but he didn't know a roller furler from a fairy tern and had no idea.

I worried about my jib, too. The replacement from Hong Kong, supposedly in the mail to Hawai'i, was small as sails go. Rolled up tight, it would fit into a bag about the size of a king-sized pillow case. But bulk was not the problem. Luke had promised to squeeze the thirty-pound jib onto one of the flights, but each cargo load to Palmyra had been so close to the small plane's weight limit that items were continually being off-loaded for a later date.

On day three of barge unloading, Luke stopped at the Fish and Wildlife office shed and poked his head in the door. "Susan, I thought you'd like to know that your drum of diesel arrived, and so did your food containers." He paused, pretending to scratch his head. "Let's see, there was something else for you too. . . ." He smiled. "Something heavy in a long box."

As island manager hosting a woman on a disabled boat, as well as being a fellow sailor who had rerigged his entire boat in Palmyra's lagoon, Luke had been pulling for me to get my furler as much as me. Having it there was a relief for us both.

Luke left the diesel barrel at the dock (before I left, I would have to bring *Honu* there to pump the fuel into her tank) but had loaded the food and furler into the bed of his pickup. Together we carried the three-foot-deep plastic bins and the eight-foot-long cardboard box into a far corner of our office shed where I kept my ant study supplies. The foot-wide furler box flexed like something that might contain curtain rods or plumbing pipes. With my Leatherman pocketknife, I slit the five layers of Mylar tape Craig had wrapped around the cardboard in eight places. (He took no chances packing the expensive replacement gear for an ocean-going barge trip.) I worked the flaps open, and there were my gleaming new furler parts, the pieces inside clear plastic bags, and a new forestay, about the diameter of my little finger, roped into a coil to fit the box.

Craig and Pierre had one end of the forestay professionally swaged (a forging process in which one metal item is forced onto another) to the fitting that would hold it to the top of the mast. That was the part that had broken, and they were taking no chances. Over the swage, they had assembled the furler's top aluminum pieces, called foil extensions, I learned from the Harken instruction manual, into an eight-foot section. I should use this, Craig wrote on the front of the booklet, as a model for assembling the rest of the forty-foot-long tube. Flipping through the pages, I saw that my helpers had also highlighted in yellow the sections crucial to the correct assembly of the system.

Here, finally, was my burden to view and touch. It was the first time I had seen a Harken furler, different from the one I lost, and in pieces no less. The booklet's cover issued the following caution: "WARNING! STRICTLY FOLLOW ALL INSTRUCTIONS TO AVOID AN ACCIDENT, DAMAGE TO YOUR VESSEL, PERSONAL INJURY OR DEATH."

I had thought only my brain was trying to kill me. My new furler was, too.

The manual's six chapter titles contained subheadings, which contained caveats. ("Will the drum fit on the bow? See page 6.") Page two listed the enclosed parts—toggle assembly, cross pins, shackles, drum assembly, foil clamp, two-foot bottom foil, seven-foot foil, foil feeder, connector bushing, connector screws, connector wedge, halyard swivel, trim cap, trim cap screws. And there were thirty-five more pages containing such terms as "long link adaptor w/toggle" and "rod adaptor stud," and a list of the thirteen tools I needed to proceed.

Taking a deep breath to calm myself, I closed the box and pushed it to the back of the long table that held my ant supplies, sending rat droppings plinking to the floor. How I wished I could also push the worry I had about fitting the furler on *Honu* to the back of that table and send it crashing to the floor with the rat turds.

I tried not to fret, but thoughts of failure chewed their way to my stomach like shipworms. The stakes were so high. Death on page one. But if I let my anxiety over installing the system run wild, it would spoil my experience in Palmyra.

Standing in that shed, I ordered myself to stop agonizing over a box of hardware and get on with life in this fantastic place. When the time came to install the forestay and furler, I would do the best I could and what happened, happened. How ridiculous to waste my precious time here on the negative. Worrying about a busted toggle, a broken marriage, or a bunch of achy joints would get me nothing except stomachaches. *Let it go.*

The mindful decision worked, mostly. I left the shed more confident than fearful, more buoyant than burdened.

Later, Alex helped me load the two food bins from the four-wheeled wagon into the dinghy and onto the boat, where I spent the rest of the day finding places for the contents. By the time I finished, every nook and cranny in *Honu* held bags of rice, packages of macaroni, cans of tuna, jars of spaghetti sauce, boxes of freeze-dried meals, and on and on. I revised my estimate of having enough food to sail to Antarctica. I had enough to circle the globe.

21

*N*ow that we knew how quickly and thoroughly the hermit crabs could scarf down the ant bait, another topic of concern in the study became coconut crabs. Would the giant crustaceans gobble up the peanut butter and corn syrup, too? Could we prevent that? How would we keep them from eating the ant poison that we were planning to scatter throughout our plots on Eastern Island? And my burning question: What the heck do these things look like?

Discussion of how to manage coconut crabs frustrated me, since I had yet to see one. It was possible to live on Cooper Island for days, weeks even, and not see any of these crabs, because in prerefuge days anglers, passing sailors, and private caretakers hunted the crabs for food, making the slow-growing species scarce. (They don't become sexually mature until they're eight years old.) In addition, the crabs are primarily nocturnal, and with only headlamps and flashlights for light in the camp, few visitors or workers went walking in the forest at night.

In a positive twist on humans messing with native habitat, for reasons unclear the highest population density of coconut crabs in Palmyra was not on Cooper Island but on Sand Island, one of several created by the Navy in the 1940s. For the crabs' protection, therefore, Sand Island was strictly off limits to everyone except those involved in official research.

Fortunately for me and several Nature Conservancy volunteers, our official resident researcher, Alex, had set up some of his study sites on Sand Island. He invited me and a few others to help with the inspections. I jumped at this rare opportunity to see the giant coconut crabs in daylight before dealing with them in the ant plots at night. Luke, happy to reward his hard-working volunteers, lent us the Nature Conservancy's ten-person motorized flatboat, so-called because it had a flat bottom and could enter shallow water. (This boat, purchased by the Nature Conservancy, was not ordinarily available for Fish and Wildlife business.) We clambered aboard for the quick, calm, one-mile excursion across West Lagoon.

Because Sand Island had no docks, Alex anchored the small motorboat a pier's length off the narrow beach. We jumped into the knee-deep water, the standard mode of arrival at Palmyra's remote islands, and waded ashore.

I had thought Cooper Island was hard to get around, but that had been easy walking compared with Sand. With no visitors, Sand Island contained no paths, causing everyone, even Alex, to step high and slow, making each footfall deliberate. We followed him in silence, concentrating on picking our way around bird's-nest ferns the size of inverted umbrellas, scooting over rotting trunks and jutting branches, and high-stepping through vines that grabbed our legs like tentacles. The only mercy Sand Island offered was a scarcity of coconut palms, so we didn't have to worry about getting beaned by falling coconuts or stumbling over those already on the ground.

The trickiest plants to get through were stands of palmlike *Pandanus* trees, natives of Palmyra and other islands throughout the tropics, including Hawai'i, where artisans weave the two- to six-foot-long strip leaves into mats, hats, and baskets. The common tree is known by several names: *Pandanus* (scientific), *hala* (Hawaiian), and screw pine (English). The thirty- to forty-foot-tall *Pandanus* trees were a sight to behold in Palmyra's groves, where their aboveground roots, which anchor the trees in sand and loose soil, crossed one another like a convention of tripods. But the support roots, half buried in fallen leaves, often extended from the trunk farther than I anticipated and sent me sprawling. So unexpected were some of my stumbles that it seemed as if a jokester tree had stuck out a leg as I passed, just to see me trip. But that wasn't the hardest part of walking through a *Pandanus* grove. The trees are packing. Sharp thorns cover their roots, branches, and trunks, and the leaves' edges are serrated like steak knives.

After about thirty minutes of thrashing, we entered a mature *Pisonia* grove (the *Pisonia* trees on the west end of Sand Island still stood tall and healthy), where the cool, green shade of the lofty trees kept the undergrowth down to short ferns and spongy moss and made the walking easier. Alex halted us with a hand gesture.

"There," he said.

We gathered in a semicircle and followed his gaze to the ground.

I had seen photos of coconut crabs, but like most spectacles of nature, pictures don't do them justice. The crab's body was the size of a small tea kettle, about eight inches across the back. If you included the creature's six walking legs, three on each side and splayed in all directions, the crab was two to three feet wide.

Those legs. Besides being exceptionally long (they resemble those of its close relative the king crab), the walking legs bent in odd angles at the joints like a crab contortionist. Startled by the sudden appearance of a pack of trolls (us), the crab, in an impressive display of weaponry, raised its front two appendages. The claws weren't as long as the agile walking legs but made up for it in mass, at least quadruple in diameter and ending in massive pincers, a crustacean mix of Popeye's forearms and Edward Scissorhands.

And what a body. The coconut crab belongs to the hermit crab family, and like its relatives, as a youngster it backs into an empty snail shell to protect its soft rear end, the abdomen. Coconut crabs upgrade shell sizes as long as they can, but eventually their bodies outgrow even the largest of snails. Thereafter, to protect the naked abdomen—in this crab, about the size, shape, and texture of a grapefruit—the crab tucks it under its hard-shelled thorax or chest.

It's this folding of the rear part of the body beneath its center that, among other things, makes coconut crabs look so weird. You get the feeling that the creature is clutching a plump throw pillow to its belly. The first sight of the coconut crab made me wonder, *What's it carrying?* A closer look revealed the answer: its own rear end.

The shell on this coconut crab's back hung over the creature's sides like a knight had laid his shield there. But no coat-of-arms ever looked so lovely. The crab's color scheme consisted of autumn oranges, sunset yellows, and rusty shades of brown. The hues covered the exoskeleton on the crab's head and back in splotches and polka dots, and its long legs bore the fall colors in bars, bands, and stripes. I had never seen an animal so beautiful and so grotesque at the same time. The coconut crab's legs, abdomen, and colors were eye-openers, but the creature's head made me wonder if someone had slipped a little LSD into my tea.

The crab's eyes looked like maroon beads on the ends of black stalks that moved as we moved: *I'm watching you*, those mobile eyes said. From below the matchstick eyes extended two whiplike antennae, about as long as the crab's body, and from inside the base of those rose another pair of antennae, shorter, jointed, and bent like a pair of Zs. The four sensory organs moved in slow motion, apparently smelling us. When that crab aimed its feelers at me, I felt like I was being mind-probed by a Vulcan house pet.

Even the crab's head was an alien shape, rounded in back but coming to a point in front, like a backward teardrop. A tear is what you might shed if you ran into one of these crabs in a dark place and didn't know that they aren't aggressive. Everything about the coconut crab—its legs, antennae, eyes, size, shape, and color—looked so outlandish that the creature seemed like a genetic experiment gone wrong. The most common comment I heard from people regarding coconut crabs was, "They look like giant insects." Like a mythical beast from Narnia, the coconut crab is so ugly, it's cute.

The coconut crab stood its ground rather than run, raising one of its long walking legs straight up in the air and angling it toward the closest human foot. *Halt*, the gesture seemed to say. Such pluck. A six-inch-tall teapot challenging a fleet of steam engines.

As we tiptoed around the lanky creature, it dashed into the woods, running forward in noncrab fashion. Coconut crabs aren't obligate side-walkers like some crabs. Rather, they're flexible, easily running forward, sideways, or backward. We followed the creature to its nearby den, a hollow in the base of a robust *Pisonia* trunk. Inside the crab cave lay a pile of brown coconut fibers, an inviting daybed that looked soft and comfortable.

The well-named coconut crabs use all parts of the coconut, eating the white meaty interior (the copra) and using the brown fibers (which the crab had to shred to get to the copra) as home furnishing. Coconut crabs rest in their hollows during the day, emerging at night to search for food. The crabs aren't strictly nocturnal, though. Any time of day, at the slightest whiff of anything that might be edible, the scavengers venture out.

We left the brave warrior in peace in its parlor and soon found another, this one in exquisite shades of blue—powder, royal, and navy. *Why blue?* I wondered, but when the crab ran to, and froze on, the top of a decomposing pile of downed trees, their trunks blue-gray in the dappled light, I saw the benefit. Before our eyes, the crustacean almost disappeared, its hard shell blending in with bark chips and crumbling branches, its claws and edges indistinct from the decay around it. The camouflage was so good that if I hadn't watched the crab go there, I would likely have missed it.

How lucky I felt to be working on an atoll with full-grown, unafraid coconut crabs. Here were land animals that lay eggs in the ocean, carry a switchblade and Vice-Grips for silverware, steal anything they can carry, recycle food like vultures, resemble bugs, live for a century, and come in dazzling colors. To know one was to love one, and I did love those junior Godzillas. Still, much as I admired the crabs' beauty in color and singleness of form, after seeing several, the idea of having to catch one with my bare hands (gloves heavy enough to offer protection diminish one's grip) gave me pause. Hugging fluffy seabird chicks was one thing; carrying around living bolt cutters another.

BACK on Eastern Island, coconut crabs did indeed become the third species of moochers to invade our pilot study sites. Looking down at the enormous creatures antenna-waving their way around the baited areas, I knew I would have to do something totally different or the study would never occur. With hermit crabs, rats, and now the occasional coconut crab helping themselves to the bait, none was left for the ants.

My solution to this problem worked better than I dreamed possible. Cooper Island residents had a year or two earlier given up using standard wire cage traps to catch rats. Besides being inhumane, the traps became ineffective because the intelligent rats learned to steer clear of anything that looked like a cage. Finding about a hundred of the old mesh traps piled inside a cobwebby bunker, I discovered the answer to my problem. I cleaned spider webs and rat feces from the eighty or so cages that I needed and paddled them in bundles of twenty to each of my four sites. (The muscles I grew!) The task took me days, but it was time well spent. With my index card bait papers inside the large-weave wire cages, ants could easily get in, but crabs and rats could not.

The rats, to my surprise, even those on distant Eastern Island where such traps had never been used, didn't even try. We wondered if those brilliant mammals picked up a death smell or a stress scent from the previously used traps, because during the entire three-month study, I never saw one rat approach one cage. And that was the end of the rat problem.

The cages also defeated most of the coconut crabs, but not the largest of them. One day, I found one of my cage traps utterly destroyed. A frustrated coconut crab had tried so hard to get the food inside that it crushed the stiff wire to a mishmash of metal, ate the peanut butter and corn syrup in the card inside, and ambled away.

22

$\mathscr{A}$FTER we chose and flagged the ant plots, Alex worked almost exclusively on his doctoral research and left the fieldwork to me. I had been right about Palmyra all those months ago in Honolulu. It was my kind of heaven. My solo trips to Eastern Island brought me as close as I had ever come to nirvana. Without another human being to be seen or heard, it was just me, the atoll, and the animals, my own private paradise.

Each day I enjoyed exercise elation from the strenuous workout required to paddle upwind and upcurrent to Eastern Island. While counting ants and maintaining the sites in the shady *Pisonia* forest, I listened to seabirds raising their families in the canopies above, their peeps, squeals, and squawks sounding like a symphony of life amid the booming surf striking the outside barrier reef. I talked to the fiddler crabs, strawberry and purple hermit crabs, and the occasional coconut crabs and rats that crossed my path during my work. They felt like old friends and likely thought the same of me.

Okay, I admit to "spilling" a little peanut butter and corn syrup here and there. (This is like giving a dog a steak and saying, "Hey, he likes me.") But I didn't worry about spoiling these animals for future encounters with humans, because if there were any visitors at all, it would be researchers who would not hunt or harm the wildlife. After the ant study, this remote section of the atoll would revert to tropical wilderness.

On the way back to Cooper, drifting in my kayak with the wind and current, I reviewed the number of peanut butter and corn syrup paper squares I handled (four plots at twenty papers each totaled eighty), the ants I counted (about one hundred per square, making about eight thousand per day), and the knee bends I did to put down the squares and pick them up (one hundred sixty).

The joints in my hands may have ached, but the rest of my body glowed with good health.

On my kayak, I rigged a tiny sail on a makeshift mast so I didn't have to grip the paddle, and then lay back, gliding along like Cleopatra in her barge. Those one- to two-hour drifts home allowed me to wallow in the wildlife of Palmyra's lagoons.

Besides the sharks and rays, I watched frigatebirds try to steal fish from brown and red-footed boobies in aerial extravaganzas that made the Blue Angels look like trainees. The two- to three-pound frigatebirds worked their seven-foot wings and scissoring tails to climb, plunge, swoop, and turn. The heavier, less maneuverable booby birds couldn't compete with such tactics and sometimes upchucked their fish in midair. This, of course, caused a free-for-all among the pirates, experts trying to outmaneuver other experts to catch airborne food.

Some boobies hung onto their catch, flying for all they were worth to get to their nearby nests, even while getting poked and pecked. Sometimes this worked, but not always, because the frigatebirds had other tricks up their feathered sleeves, such as working in pairs. I once saw two frigatebirds approach an airborne booby from opposite sides, seize a leg each, and flip the poor thing upside down. I imagined the frigatebirds high-fiving each other as the fish in the booby's crop went flying. *Score!* A second later, though, the two team members were fighting over the booty.

Other boobies employed what I thought was a brilliant solution to attempted robbery. Since frigatebirds can't land on the water (they need a downstroke of their wings to take off), some boobies being chased simply landed on the lagoon's surface. Hasty individuals would take off too soon and get assaulted again, but the more patient birds remained on the water, waiting for the pirates to give up and go away. This worked so well that I wondered why all the seabirds bothered by frigatebirds didn't do it. I guessed that the birds that sat down and waited it out were older and more experienced.

I also wondered if the booby birds felt frustrated or worried about losing a chick's meal to a frigatebird. *No*, I decided, *that was too human.* Animals don't fuss and fume about what life gives them. They accept the circumstances they find themselves in and move on. Like Craig with his "shit happens." Suddenly, I missed him fiercely. How he would love seeing these animals in all their wild glory. But that thought soon flew off with the frigatebirds and booby birds, because I was having the time of my life in Palmyra. Whatever he was doing, I hoped Craig was too.

THE non-ant wildlife work continued, proving (as if I needed proof) that Palmyra truly was a plant and animal paradise. Between the ant work, Alex and I made several expeditions to band ground-nesting seabird chicks, taking with us several eager Nature Conservancy volunteers. The trick was to find the chicks during the week or two after they had reached adult size, since we were placing permanent adult-sized aluminum bands on their legs, but before they learned to fly, since catching them after that is nearly impossible.

One whole day we searched under low-branched bushes in the jungle for red-tailed tropicbird chicks. Because these spunky, fat youngsters stayed in their nests, to catch one you had to crawl on your belly like an infantry soldier, dodge sticks aiming to poke your eyes out, and make a quick grab for the chick before it backed even farther under its bush. The tropicbird chicks squawked like fiends and drew blood from fingers with the smallest nips of their sharp-edged beaks. This time we knew the reasons we were bleeding—and we still called it a good time.

Another day we tackled masked boobies; on another, we searched for brown boobies—two more ground nesters. Chicks of both species were usually more out in the open than tropicbirds, but that didn't make them easier to catch. Once they realized we intended to grab them, they made a run for it, sending us on a merry chase. Often it took three or four of us closing in a circle to catch the chicks, and even then they occasionally ducked between our legs and escaped.

Banding seabirds is hard, scratchy, dirty work, but I love it for that rare privilege of holding a seabird to my chest, smelling the ocean in its feathers, and feeling its heart beat with my own. The birds linked me to the pulse of the planet, a connection often missing in the modern world. My bird hugs made me feel that, Craig or no Craig, I would never truly be alone in this world.

FINALLY, after getting the plots flagged, the bait-theft problem solved, and adequate pre-poison ant counts conducted, it was time to move on to the challenges of distributing poison in a wildlife refuge. The seabirds would not be harmed because they ate only fish, but no one knew what effect the ant poison would have on the crabs, soil, or surrounding water. The study, therefore, had to include a way of measuring these things. Also, if we killed ants on the ground, we didn't know what, if any, impact this had on ants in the trees. If hoards of ants were up there raising families and farming scale, and never coming down, poisoning the ground wouldn't help the trees.

So I also had to count ants crawling up and down selected trees. This was easy because big-headed ants cut highways along the green, moss-covered tree trunks as neat as any interstate, and the ants traveled them religiously. All I had to do was make an ink mark on the tree next to such an ant road and count the individuals that passed the mark. When my thumb pressed a button on top of a round metal counter, it advanced a number with an audible click, and in that way, I stood counting each ant that crossed the line. *Click, click, click.* The ants cooperated immensely by running one behind the other and each staying strictly in its own lane.

The next chore was to dig a small ground well, mercifully in only one plot, to collect water samples. I was to dip out a jar of water from the well every few days and save it for Honolulu researchers to test for ant poison. If the toxins got into the groundwater, they could potentially leach into the lagoon and poison the fish. Given the small amount of ant poison we would use, the possibility of causing such damage was remote, but water samples would provide certainty.

On the days I collected water from the well, I would also scoop surface dirt with a plastic spoon from twenty random spots, different every time, in each plot, and deposit the soil into plastic containers made for that purpose. Along with the water jars, the containers of dirt would also be sent to Oahu to be tested for ant poison.

Such layer upon layer of monitoring is crucial if a study is to be judged sound and its conclusions are to be trusted, and my admiration for the Fish and Wildlife scientists who designed the ant study rose another notch. That cash-poor, bureaucracy-saddled agency is often criticized and repeatedly sued, but in my experience the investigators who work there are steadfast in their efforts to do the research right.

Alex got out a hole-digging tool and a pickax, and off we went to dig our well.

"I've never used a post-hole digger before," I said as we scattered our gear around our chosen spot.

I had eliminated the phrase *I don't know how* from my vocabulary, replacing it with *I've not done this before.* The power of this tiny shift in thinking never ceased to amaze me. Even if I didn't succeed, the fact that I was attempting something new made me feel more capable, more accomplished.

He handed me the pole. Its shovel-like blades at the lower end descended with a twist when you punched the dirt.

I raised the handle above my head and brought the blades down with all my might. Nothing happened.

"You have to hit the ground hard," he said.

Okay. *Punch.* My second attempt made barely a dent in the hard-packed soil, laden with roots and coral rock. After a few more tries, during which my hands throbbed and sweat dripped off my face, the ground remained maddeningly unbroken.

"Would you like me to give it a try?" Alex said.

Gee, let me think.

He pulled off his T-shirt, raised the handle, and smashed the tool down with rippling muscles that I hadn't seen since our passage to Palmyra. I had once wondered if admiring that bare chest meant I was a perverted old lady. No more. Now watching those lean muscles at work in that young man's body, I appreciated it as a work of nature, like black-tipped reef sharks, coconut crabs, and ants. I was also thankful that I had an understanding friend to help me do work beyond my strength.

Digging that four-foot-deep well was backbreaking work, Alex's back being the one breaking. After he loosened the ground and made some progress, he rested and I gave it another go. I actually managed to loosen and scoop some dirt with the tool, but I would hit a root or rock and Alex had to step in and smash it with the pickax. For the hundredth time on this journey, I was struck with—and appreciated—the strength of the males of our species. Of course, I knew women could do these things, too, but when it comes to heavy lifting and deep digging, a large testosterone-loaded body sure helps speed up the chores.

My lighter-weight chore came to getting down in the hole and throwing out loose debris by hand so Alex could get the digging blades to the bottom. Our bodies dripped dirt and sweat from head to toe. When Alex's hands began slipping on the pole, he was unable to apply the force he needed to punch through. I crashed into the woods, found a low-leaning coconut palm, and peeled off some of its clothlike bark to wrap around the tool's handle.

Alex smiled. "Woman gather. Man dig."

After several hours, we hit groundwater. Another hour or so of scooping gave us the depth we needed to lower a jar into the water and retrieve samples. We placed a four-inch-diameter PVC pipe down the hole, packed dirt around it, and rigged a wire and jar down its center to reach the water. It took one exhausting day, and buckets of sweat, but we had our well.

We were so tired we could barely drag ourselves back to the flatboat Luke had loaned us to transport the digging gear, too heavy for the kayaks. But when we got there, the sight of that perfect blue lagoon looked so invigorating that the two of us ran like muddy children into the water, clothes and all. This so startled the black-tipped reef sharks that they practically leaped from the surface in their rush to swim away.

It was dark by the time we got back to camp. After a hot shower and a fine meal, I basked in the quiet peace that came from the hard work of digging a hole in the ground. It had been a long time since I felt that good.

Craig's words the day I told him I wanted to sail to Palmyra came back to me: "If you think it will make you happy, do it." Back then, I didn't think anything would make me happy. Now I considered it a possibility.

23

In another arm of the pilot study regarding the effect of ant poison in the refuge, we tested waterproof, one-inch-long radio transmitters that we were to attach to the backs of randomly selected strawberry hermit crabs, making sure the radios sent a clear signal. The purpose was to enable us to follow the signals after we spread the ant poison to see if the crabs were alive and well or sick and dying. Alex and I epoxied twenty-four of the transmitters, about the size and weight of a single peanut in its shell, to the tops of the crabs' turban shells and turned them loose. The glue didn't harm the snail shells (not part of the crabs' bodies), and the crabs, accustomed to hauling around all sizes of adopted mobile homes, didn't seem fazed by the lightweight transmitters.

When we released them, the crabs took off in all directions, looking like tiny rescue dogs wearing gray, numbered backpacks. A few minutes later Alex walked around with a bulky receiver that resembled those antennas people once attached to their roofs for TV reception. He pointed it this way and that, like a water diviner, and picked up the crabs' signals.

But the next morning while testing the transmission strength, we got no signals at all. Had our twenty-four subjects traveled out of radio range so soon? we wondered. Searching the forest floor in the area, we found the problem. We detected no signals because the little darlings had spent the night pulling the costly radios off each other's backs, demolishing them in the process. The evidence of this destruction could be found in several areas where tiny radio components and red, yellow, and green wires lay scattered on the ground. Later we located several crabs with spots of epoxy on their snail shells, minus all evidence of the transmitters. The crabs had picked each other clean.

Whether the crabs viewed the radios as potential food or were just curious as to what the heck their neighbors were toting on their backs, we did not know. But it didn't matter. The radio-tagging arm of the study was over. The bottom line came in an e-mail from Honolulu managers. It was too expensive to redesign and replace the transmitters.

We were learning a lot from the ant study in Palmyra, but as often happens in nature, the information was not what we expected. But then, that's why people do studies.

Palmyra hosted another kind of native land crab represented by two species (genus *Cardisoma* for those who know crabs). Called "tupas" by residents of some South Pacific island nations, these were shy creatures, the average adult about the size of my outstretched hand. Like their coconut crab neighbors, they came in all colors. Some tupa shells, in their mottled reds, yellows, and browns, looked like cheese enchiladas. Others reminded me of nineteenth-century impressionist art, their pastel fades and moss greens as exquisite as any Monet.

Tupas like to soak in shallow stands of freshwater, and one day, while avoiding a fallen branch, I stepped into a puddle, startling a lounging tupa into a gallop. The larger-than-average (about a half-pound) crab ran sideways in typical crab fashion while holding up one enlarged front pincer. I followed the gorgeous creature—purple and red—to take a picture. The tupa stopped at a tree trunk, whirled around, and pointed the claw at me. The posture was defensive only, but bold nevertheless. Like all the crabs of Palmyra, tupas just want to be left alone. I took the photo and left the gutsy little Gauguin in peace.

Because the tupa's main defense is freezing in place and standing behind its large raised claw, the half-pound crabs are relatively easy to pick up. You bend down and grasp them from the back, easy enough because they're light to lift and, like all crabs, are unable to reach backward with their pincers.

We had to pick up tupas because we needed some kind of marker to see if the ant poison affected them. Since radio transmissions were no longer an option, I came up with the idea of identifying each tupa by fastening small colored zip ties to one of the crab's walking legs. But that, too, turned out to be an idea that nature abhorred. The day after we zip-tied a tupa, we found the looped leg lying free, without its crab, still bearing the pink and yellow bands we had loosely applied. We hoped the crab lost only its leg—when in danger, tupas can release a limb to escape a predator and grow it back during the next molt—and not its life. But it was also possible that the plastic ties acted like bright flags broadcasting the crab's hiding place to a hungry rat that killed the crab and ate all but the tagged leg.

We e-mailed this second crab setback to the Honolulu managers for advice. The Fish and Wildlife biologists working on the ant study there decided that because neither the hermit crabs nor the tupas were threatened species (only the coconut crabs are considered in danger of extinction), Alex and I could simply, for the first two or three post-poison days, scout the area on foot to look for sick or dead hermit crabs and tupas. Not exactly precision science, given these crabs' proclivity to hide, but it was the best we could do.

The slow-growing coconut crabs were another story. There was no way we would fence the crabs out of our poison areas. Besides the problem of having no fencing material, the crabs are crackerjack climbers and would be up and over in a flash. Nor could we cage and house the crabs in the rat traps during the poison fling. The traps were far too small. It was time to face the senior biologist's forewarning that long-ago day in the Honolulu Fish and Wildlife office: "You'll have to remove the coconut crabs from your study sites before you spread the ant poison."

Our only option was to carry the crabs residing in the ant study areas to a spot far from the sites. Coconut crabs move so slowly that the Honolulu researchers thought the ants would eat all the poison long before the big crabs could amble back to their home territories.

In order to remove the nocturnal crabs, though, we first had to find them. Well, what better lure for coconut crabs than coconuts? If we put out fresh copra as bait, all the crabs in that area would flock to the feast, where we would gather them up for their short journey elsewhere.

To keep the crabs from carrying the coconut treats off to their dens, Alex and I drilled one-inch-round scent holes in the sides of white five-gallon buckets with the plan of depositing fresh coconut chunks inside. The afternoon before Poison Day, we would seal the lids with duct tape and distribute the buckets around the plots. Later that night (the crabs are most active at night), we would return with headlamps to the vicinities of the fragrant buckets, pick up the crabs lured there, and carry them well outside the fifty-yard poison plots. The big scavengers would eventually wander back to the plots, but after we removed the buckets and threw the coconut meat far outside the areas, it would take a day or two for the crabs to return. By then the ants would have eaten all the poison. I worried that the ants might miss some poison and leave it lingering on the ground, but the ant expert assured me by e-mail that the ants would quickly scarf up every morsel.

This plan was all well and good until Alex showed me how to open a green coconut on the metal spike that the camp managers had set up for that purpose, and left me to crack another seventeen on my own. He explained as he demonstrated. The idea with a fixed coconut spike is to place one hand on each side of the coconut and smash it down on the sharp point, taking care not to impale one's fingers, palms, or wrists on the tip. A couple of good smashes tears the green husk, making it easy (for some people) to rip the rest of the husk away by hand.

After he left, I raised the ten-pound coconut above my head and smashed it down. The upward-pointing spike looked so much like a knife blade, however, that at the last second, fearing I would skewer my hand, I hesitated, lost power, and made only a miniscule hole in the green husk. Smashing over and over, I finally had a shred of husk to pull on. Alex had made peeling the strips off look easy, but the fibrous husk was so stiff and dense that by the time I got to the brown nut containing the white copra, which still had to be broken with a hammer, my arthritic hands were screaming.

I was learning when to push myself and when to ask for help.

I walked to our Fish and Wildlife office where Alex toiled away on compiling his data and explained the situation. He shut down the computer and returned with me to the spike. It was hard work for him, too, but in less than an hour Alex spiked and peeled open all sixteen remaining coconuts. It had taken me an hour to do one.

The coconut incident made a big impression on me. Coconut opening was clearly not my strong suit, and it was silly of me to keep trying. *Play to your strengths* became another of my new life mottos.

The incident also made me appreciate the power of the claws of a coconut crab. It may take a mature crab a day to reach the so-called meat (the white part) of a coconut, but the creatures are tiny compared with Alex, and they don't have metal spikes to get them started.

We carted the fuzzy brown coconuts to our storage shed, noisy with the skittering of rat feet, and I stood back while Alex hacked open the inner shells with a machete. In no time we had eighteen side-holed and lid-sealed buckets containing yummy-smelling coconut meat, the equivalent of piña coladas for crabs. In the late afternoon, we carried the buckets to the borrowed flatboat, motored to Eastern Island, and deposited the bait buckets around the plots' edges. That evening after dinner, we would come back and relocate the crabs lured by the coconut buckets.

By then, I had seen dozens of these fantastic creatures and found coconut crabs as much fun to watch as seabirds. I don't know if coconut crabs are unafraid of people in other places, but when I crossed paths with them, if I didn't startle them with a sudden movement, they didn't usually run. Often, the crab simply went about its business, which was usually pulling fibrous husks off a green coconut or poking into a brown coconut shell for a sweet treat.

I loved everything about coconut crabs—their kaleidoscopic colors, their twiggy walking legs, their Godzilla aspirations, and even those disconcerting eyes—and felt a flush of protective anger later when people asked me how they taste, or why killing just one would matter.

The crabs are scarce in their island homes today because too many residents and visitors have killed too many crabs. With human populations increasing, and coconut crab populations decreasing, people are killing small crabs that haven't yet reached reproductive maturity. It doesn't take a study to know that can't last. The math is simple. Coconut crabs live only on tropical oceanic islands, take nearly a decade to reach sexual maturity, are easy to catch, and are good to eat. The odds of these creatures thriving outside of refuges anywhere in the world are minuscule. Palmyra is one of coconut crabs' few havens.

Even so, there's no official word on whether coconut crabs are in danger of extinction. Since these crustaceans are widespread throughout the Pacific and Indian Oceans, making a comprehensive assessment of their trend—declining or stable—is difficult. The International Union for Conservation of Nature, the global authority on species endangerment, lists them as "Data Deficient," meaning that they are a species of concern, but researchers don't have enough information to declare their status.

In preparing for the ant study, I was so busy each day, and so tired after dinner each evening, that I didn't think at all about marriage, menopause, or aging, nor did I think about my voyage back to Honolulu. Much as I missed Craig, I couldn't picture myself at home. I couldn't picture myself anywhere except exactly where I was.

BECAUSE coconut crabs are more active at night than during the day, our crab searching had to be done in the dark. And we did have to search. Some crabs might already have found the bait buckets, but when we arrived, others would still be walking toward them, trying to pinpoint the source of their favorite scent. We couldn't wait for long after dark, though, because those walking can openers would open the buckets, carry off their prize, and be gone.

Five Nature Conservancy workers volunteered to help Alex and me find the crabs. None were biologists, but all were professionals (with degrees in physics, dentistry, engineering, math, and computer science) interested in helping wildlife, the reason they volunteered to work in Palmyra in the first place. Like Alex and me, these conservationists took the crab relocation seriously and felt privileged to be invited to work with us in protecting this singular species.

The idea was to carry the crabs fifty to a hundred yards from the sites Alex and I would poison the next morning. This was a safe distance away, our Honolulu experts felt, because the speedy ants would eat all the poison long before the plodding crabs returned. We divided into two teams. Four people, including Alex, all young men with strong shoulders, biceps, and forearms, volunteered to be crab catchers. The rest of us—another woman my age, her husband, and me—would stay in the clearing to weigh and measure the captured crabs.

We were measuring the crabs because information about them is sparse. Handling stresses wild animals, but since we had to pick up the crabs in the study areas to move them to safety, our Honolulu bosses decided to use the relocation as an opportunity to collect data that could be shared with other coconut crab researchers.

The plan was for the catchers to bring their crabs to a small lighted location where we three data collectors would, as quickly and gently as possible, weigh and measure the captives. Afterward, the catcher would carry his crab outside the flagged area, turn it loose, come back to the bucket area, and scout for another.

The arrangement suited me better than anyone knew. One of my biggest thrills of wildlife work was getting to feel, smell, and breathe with animals I might otherwise never even see. The brief handling required while weighing and measuring didn't harm the creatures and had been a cherished experience for me while working at Tern Island. At Palmyra, I found that I longed to touch the crabs' showy shells, peer into their stalky eyes, and examine—at a safe distance—those club-like pincers. But I worried about my ability to catch and carry an eight-pound crab with my arthritis-weakened fingers. Being a data collector solved the problem. While gathering size information, I could touch the crabs' backs to my heart's content. *My aging body might have new limits*, I thought, *but that doesn't mean the end of the fun. I just have to rethink the way to experience it.*

"Feeling good that we're finally getting started?" Alex said, seeing me smiling.

"Yes. And happy I get to pet a coconut crab."

The seven of us bustled around the Cooper camp collecting flashlights and loading the flatboat with tubs, scales, and measuring tapes for the evening hunt. This was my kind of hunting party. Capture the quarry as humanely as possible, collect some statistics to help others of its kind, and turn it loose in a safe place.

At dusk, Alex drove the flatboat to Eastern Island, where we unloaded the equipment and formed our teams. Alex, the only experienced coconut crab handler among us, explained how to safely pick up the creature. You wave one hand in front of the crab, and when the creature turns its pincers that way, you grasp the shell from the back with the other hand. To hesitate is to lose. If you allow the crab to whirl around, it can pinch, or at worst, lop a finger off your grabbing hand.

To demonstrate, Alex took us with him to a nearby coconut bucket where a young red-and-orange crab about the size of a saucer (including legs) had been busy poking a claw into one of the bucket's scent holes. When the crab turned toward Alex, he wiggled his fingers in front of the crab to get its attention and, in one quick, smooth motion, grasped its shell from behind and above with the other hand. As soon as Alex lifted the crab off the ground it went limp, as if to say, *Okay, you got me.*

"Once you're holding it like this," Alex said, his thumb and fingers on the rear edges of the creature's shield-shaped back shell, "you're safe. The claws can't reach above or behind the body."

The young crab hung motionless in Alex's grip, its long, angular legs suspended in midair like a toy robot with dead batteries. Even the red eyes and four antennae, normally roaming like searchlights, remained still. This is the coconut crab's defense once captured or cornered: become invisible by freezing.

Alex lowered the crab into one of our three-foot-deep plastic bins. It roused slightly when its legs touched the floor, but after briefly tapping its new surroundings with the tips of its legs and claws and touching the walls lightly with its feelers, it apparently deemed the blue storage container inescapable and again froze. Reassuring the crab, as brightly colored as a Christmas ornament, that it was in loving hands, I got to work.

In the past when I helped weigh seabird chicks, I had to, as gently as possible, put the startled, struggling creature into a cloth bag without hurting its flapping wings, flailing feet, or snapping bill. Then I attached the heaving sack to a hanging scale and tried to read a bouncing number. (The small scales we used were metal cylinders with numbers down the front, a handle at the top, and a hook at the bottom. You held the scale up by the handle and hung whatever you were weighing on the hook.) The seabirds didn't hold a grudge. They didn't know how, having evolved with no land predators. The instant I placed the chick back in its nest, it snuggled down content, seeming to forget the whole incident.

Weighing coconut crabs was easier. Not only were there no wings, legs, or beaks to worry about, but there was no struggle, either. All I had to do was tie a rope to the hook end of the scale and dangle the other end over one of the crab's front claws. It was as if I said, "Would you hold this a minute, please?" because the creature instantly did so, locking onto the rope as only a coconut crab pincer can.

Raising the scale with the motionless crab dangling over the tub, I read the number and subtracted the weight of the rope: 1.4 kilograms (three pounds), a little guy. The largest ones weigh about ten pounds. The crabs stop growing after they're forty years old but live to at least seventy. People have not been studying them long enough to know if they live longer, but educated guesses are that they do. The fact that some of today's coconut crabs emerged on Palmyra's beaches at the same time the U.S. Navy was altering the atoll for World War II boggled the mind. Also mind-boggling was the fact that before the atoll was declared a wildlife refuge, people killed those regal residents for appetizers.

I wondered what the crab thought, hanging there in midair with goblins gawking all around. Impossible to guess. When you wear your skeleton on the outside, you don't exactly exude expression. The creature surely felt threatened but played it cool, waiting for its moment to strike or run. I gave the small crab big points for composure.

The problem with weighing the crab by letting it hold the scale rope was getting the rope back. After a little tug-of-war, in which a great ape (me) was clearly going to lose to an immature crustacean, I let the crab keep its prize. As if I had a choice. While the creature's claws were busy, I used a tape to measure the width of the crab's back, called the carapace. Four inches. I ran my fingertips over the flame-colored shell, smooth and cool as Italian marble. *If Michelangelo had known coconut crabs*, I thought, *we would see them today in the Sistine Chapel.*

By the time I finished measuring and recording numbers, the creature had lost interest in the inedible rope and dropped it.

I probably could have caught and carried the smaller crabs one-handed without much joint pain, but I wasn't sure of my fingers' strength. It didn't matter. I had the far better deal. Like a mother with a newborn baby, I cooed, stroked, and teared up over the sublime beauty of the crabs in my tub.

A volunteer brought me a blue coconut crab, this one larger, at five pounds. I weighed it using the rope trick, but when it came to measuring its shell, the crab began turning in the tub.

"The bigger ones squirm more," Alex said, handing the crab a stick. "If you give it something to play with, that keeps the pincers occupied while you work."

While the crab pinched and pushed the stick, I measured the shell's width. A moment later, Alex lifted the crab by the back of its shell and carried it to safety.

A young yellow-and-tan crab arrived for my tub, and soon after, one of the crab catchers carried in a burnt orange whopper weighing nearly eight pounds. Each crab went into a single tub, each data taker weighed and measured it, and one of the transporters, wearing a headlamp, carried it into the black forest. The crab assessment center was up and running.

The fresh coconut pieces inside the buckets worked well. As predicted, the crabs massed to the scent of their favorite food, all nicely peeled and cracked for them. If left for long, those shearing experts would have torn the buckets apart or worked the lids off, seized the copra inside, and walked off into the forest, but they didn't get the chance. The hunters snatched up the crabs as soon as they appeared.

Rumor has it that coconut crabs climb trees to get coconuts. They can, but they don't have to. It takes a lot less energy to eat the ones already fallen to the ground. Nor are coconut crabs compelled to eat coconuts. They eat anything they come across, such as fruit, veggies, or dead animals.

Another name for the coconut crab is robber crab, because if the scavengers are attracted to something, they sometimes try to carry it off. "I have seen sandals, sticks, cooking pots, and even knives and forks stolen from jungle camps," one biologist wrote in 1947 of coconut crab thievery. "I once found a pair of crabs fighting over a silver wristwatch, taken from a pile of clothes."

My favorite video clip from Alex showed a crab dragging a machete, about twice as long as the crab itself, down a path. The crab had picked up the scent of the blade, which Alex had used to hack open a coconut.

We soon had an efficient assembly line going, and for an hour or so the teams hunted, weighed, measured, and relocated coconut crabs at least fifty yards from the ant plots. Not all the crabs were cooperative with the weighing rope. They all grabbed hold and hung tight while I weighed them, but some of the larger crabs refused to let go of the rope while in the tub. I had to lift the rope from the bin with the crab dangling below, lower both to the ground, and wait until the crab was good and ready to open its pincer.

Once the crab was outside the bin, I had to watch it closely, but not because it tried to run away. Rather, it stole our stuff. One crab dropped the rope and snatched the nearby yellow notebook we used for recording our data, a special pad with heavy plastic covers and thick waterproof pages made specifically for outdoor fieldwork. The crab crumpled it like a piece of Kleenex. One of the men picked up the crab and tried pulling on the free end of the book, but that just made the crab clamp down harder, wrinkling the covers and tearing the pages.

The man put the crab on the ground and backed into the shadows, tricking the crab into thinking the threat was gone. It worked. The crab soon dropped the book, at which time the volunteer stepped into view, lifted the crab, and carried it off. I straightened the wrinkled notes, which we could still read, but the crab's creased signature remained on the cover forever.

When the catchers came back from their searches empty-handed, the job of moving the coconut crabs out of harm's way was done. We collected the coconut-filled buckets, tore off the tape, lifted the lids, and walking far from the ant plots, gave the relocated crabs a big reward: we threw them the copra they so craved.

Loading up the boat, we moved the entire operation to the next site, and eventually the third. Several hours later we had weighed, measured, and relocated most of the local crabs, thirty-six in all, from the three sites to be sprinkled with poison the next morning. The crabs at the fourth site, the control area on Cooper Island, we left alone. That area would not receive ant poison, and therefore, the coconut crabs there didn't need relocating.

As we left, I silently thanked the crabs for cooperating by congregating near the buckets. This had been the theory, but after all we had experienced in getting the study launched, I was leery of theory. I also thanked the crabs for giving me a wildlife encounter I would remember forever.

We were ready, finally, to spread the ant poison, but it felt wrong to fling toxins around a refuge, even in the name of science. I worried we had missed some unforeseen factor in protecting the wildlife, plus I admired and respected ants. The insects have roamed our planet for a hundred million years, turning and aerating soil that allows water and oxygen to reach plant roots. The tiny farmers weren't trying to topple *Pisonia* trees. Like so much damage we humans cause in our struggle to live, it just happened.

Once dressed for the job, though, I wanted to pitch that poison as fast as possible and get out of those miserable hot clothes. This was federal government work, and even though our granular poison, a commercial brand called Amdro, is available to the public and used commonly in American yards, the rules for working with any kind of toxic materials were strict. Like surgeons, we wore masks, gloves, long pants, long-sleeve shirts, closed shoes, and socks to make sure no poison touched our skin. Unlike surgeons, however, we looked like clowns. The only long pants I had were gray pajama bottoms printed with red ants. Alex's long sleeves came in the form of a yellow-and-red flowered surf shirt, and the black bulky gloves that Fish and Wildlife sent to Palmyra gave us Frankenstein hands.

These outfits would have been warm to wear anywhere, but since I had grown accustomed to wearing only lightweight running clothes, the full-length clothing, rubber gloves, and face mask smothered me just standing still. When we needed the cooling rain that drenched us so often, the clouds parted and let the equatorial sun steam us like dim sums. Sweat soaked my hair and stung my eyes, running down my nose, armpits, chest, and back. A simulated hot flash.

I had never had a real one. Back home, after stopping estrogen, I had warm flashes in the middle of the night, but they were dry, like a fever. Suddenly at two in the morning, my eyes flew open, I threw off the covers, and lay there feeling heat radiate from my skin like an all-over sunburn. I cooled off in a few minutes, but with the warmth came a pounding heart from what felt like a jolt of adrenalin—great, another whacked out hormone in the chain gang of menopause—and that was the end of sleep for the night.

My current sweat bath came from wearing too many clothes in an equatorial jungle, but if this was how full-blown hot flashes felt, well, they're awful. How can a woman sit in a restaurant, go to work, do anything in public, when she's suddenly soaking wet? I dripped in empathy with my sweaty sisters, grateful that although I had a hard time with menopause symptoms, at least I never walked around looking and feeling like a wet noodle.

Half blinded by sweat, Alex and I each filled our plastic grass seed applicators with ant poison. We walked as fast as the rain forest allowed while holding a bulky plastic case with one hand and turning its crank handle with the other. The plots weren't overwhelmingly large—each half the size of a football field— but years of toppled trees, dead branches, rotting leaves, and bush and fern growth made the going slow. Also, there were hermit crabs and tupas to watch for and step around. Mercifully, we had few coconuts to dodge since Eastern Island hosted far fewer coconut palms than Cooper.

We pushed through, stumbling up and down each measured grid, trying to walk a straight line as we spewed out yellow grains of sweet poison, occasionally pausing to wait for each other to make sure we covered every square foot of ground.

Since the plots were kayaking distances apart on Eastern Island, after finishing the first site we shed our sweaty clothes, packed up the gear, paddled to the next plot, climbed back into the sodden shirts and damp pajamas, donned the sopping masks, and did it all again. It took most of the day to poison the three plots. When done, we collapsed on a log to drink the last of our water.

"Look," Alex said. "The ground is moving."

It had taken the ants only minutes to broadcast the message that a wealth of sweets had rained from above, and the forest floor had come alive as worker ants rushed to the bounty. I watched in silence, knowing the poison would kill the queens, the adults, and all the larvae in this area. But ants don't waste time grieving over fallen comrades. A fertile queen would soon find the empty real estate, settle down, and repopulate it. Exactly how many days that would take was my job to find out.

A plane arrived on Cooper with food and building supplies, but not my jib. Next plane, Luke said. I would have liked to lay eyes on the sail, but I couldn't complain. Even with the plane full, Craig managed to get aboard a package containing the repaired autopilot arm, a new backup autopilot, a six-pack of Diet Coke, two gallons of motor oil for *Honu*'s oil-thirsty engine, and a handwritten note about the dog, my sister, and condo doings. When I read it, I got so homesick that the lump in my throat felt as if I had balled the page up and swallowed it whole.

Betty, an emergency medical technician contracted by the Nature Conservancy to take care of any injuries that might occur during construction of the new buildings, arrived on the plane.

"I met your husband at the hangar," she told me. "He was dropping off some things for you."

"How is he?" I asked.

"Still tall and handsome," she said, smiling.

This gave me such a rush of pride, I felt like a giggly ninth grader. *The cute one is mine.*

In his package, Craig had also sent acetaminophen and ibuprofen for my arthritic fingers, a good thing since the sharks had been eyeing them with great interest lately, or so I imagined. After a day of ant counting, soil collecting, and water sampling, as my kayak drifted downwind home, I had gotten in the habit of trailing my throbbing hands in the cool water. One day the paddle slipped from the deck into the water and a shark instantly struck the tip. The fish didn't damage the paddle—the shark was just checking—but when I sat up and looked around, five black-tipped reef sharks lingered around the kayak. I don't know if my wiggly white fingers attracted them, or if they had been following me out of natural curiosity, but I stopped dragging my hands in the water.

Before the poison dispersal, my squares of peanut butter and corn syrup attracted about a hundred big-headed ants on each card. I got good at eyeballing groups of ten, which made the counting easier.

After the poisoning, the count at the three plots on Eastern Island got ridiculously easy: zero. All the big-headed ants, the dominant species in the vicinity, were apparently dead. It didn't take rocket science to conclude that the poison worked at killing big-headed ants, but that wasn't the question. What researchers needed to know was how long it took for the big-headed ants to recover or for another scale-farming ant species to move into the vacant territory. That interval would be the time to introduce the scale-eating ladybugs.

Therefore, I still put out bait in all four plots, counted ants at the control plot, and recorded zero at the others. This would go on until more ants showed up.

The second most abundant ant species in Palmyra were crazy ants (their official common name), also farmers of scale. Crazy ants get their name from dashing like mad in all directions rather than walking or running one behind the other. The unpredictable pathways make crazy ants harder for soldier ants to catch, but they didn't have to, at least in our study sites. Crazy ants knew better than to intrude into big-headed territory.

It took the crazy ants a couple of weeks to realize that the storm troopers in the football helmets were gone. And there was the key to the question I had been sent to help answer: how long does an Amdro-poisoned area on a Palmyra

Atoll island remain free of scale-farming ants? Official answer: two weeks. If researchers were going to introduce scale-eating ladybugs to the atoll, they had fourteen days after poisoning to do it.

For a few days after we spread the ant poison, Alex and I scoured the areas for dead hermit, tupa, and coconut crabs but found none. We did, however, find a sick rat after opening the peanut butter jar to prepare for an ant baiting. The rat, with cloudy-looking eyes, staggered toward us, apparently blind. The ailing animal wandered around our feet, smelling the food but unable to see either it or us. Rats, a serious problem for Palmyra's native species, were one of the subjects of Alex's research, but rats were not part of the ant study, and the unintentionally poisoned mammal touched our hearts. We spooned peanut butter into the jar's lid and set it in the rat's path, giving it an all-you-can-eat feast.

"Don't tell anyone I fed a rat," Alex said as we watched the creature eat.

Silly boy. I'm a writer.

Following the ant study to its conclusion, banding seabirds, maintaining *Honu*, and writing about marine life for my newspaper columns made time fly by. In fact, when I examined my life on Palmyra, I realized that I was busier and working harder than I had at home. And yet, I felt far more relaxed, as though enjoying a much-needed tropical vacation. Of course, lush tropical islands foster that feeling in people, but my home in Hawai'i was also such a place, and I had not felt at peace on Oahu for a long time.

The difference, I realized, was that I had ditched the notion that the changes I was experiencing in my life were negatives.

Because like a lot of baby boomers I swore that I would never get old, my aging had struck me as a train wreck of loss—of youth, looks, sexuality, the Twinship. Even my hands had gone off the rails. But with my decision to fix up the boat and sail to Palmyra, "something agreeable happened." (This is my positive spin on that Japanese friend's "something alarming happened.") The agreeable something was that I had come to see midlife changes not as losses but as gains. Youth isn't all it's cracked up to be, given all its angst about appearances, sex, commitments, and careers. With aging came my ability to see the folly in all that striving. At anchor in my own boat in Palmyra, I didn't care how I looked, who liked me or not, or what the future held in store.

In taking a big risk, I had learned how to make my own choices independent of Craig. For the first time in my life, I was comfortable being alone, meaning not half of something, no longer a fraction of a whole. I felt in charge. The captain of my own ship.

I loved the new me. Like the older, more experienced booby birds, I was content to sit on the water and wait. Something would happen.

Of course I had my moments—that busted forestay awaited—but overall I felt happier than I had in years. I had fulfilling work to do, big-time adventure to be relished, and excellent companionship to be enjoyed. By telephone, but it worked.

As the months remaining in the atoll turned to weeks, I woke up most mornings feeling good. But increasingly, the thought occurred to me: *What if home doesn't feel like home when I get there? Where will I go? How will I get the New Me back?*

I remembered Alex at Tern Island tossing out a question that seemed ridiculous a year earlier when I was desperate to work in Palmyra, but no planes or ships were available to take me there.

"Well," he had said, "You have a sailboat, don't you?"

24

W<small>HEN</small> Pierre and I installed *Honu*'s wind generator, people warned me
about its annoying whirring noise, but I loved the little windmill churning
up there on the mizzenmast. Besides making electricity, each time I rowed
home at night in Palmyra's pitch-black lagoon, it came in handy as a homing
beacon.

One dark and rainy night, typical evening weather in Palmyra, I watched
an after-dinner movie in the yacht club and afterward set out for *Honu* in wind
gusting to twenty knots and with visibility so poor I could barely see the end of
my eight-foot dinghy. After rowing much longer than my usual ten-minute
commute, I knew the wind had pushed me off course, causing the dinghy to
pass *Honu* and head into the vast reaches of the lagoon. (It was only a mile or so
across, but while rowing around on a black windy night with rain threatening
a deluge, the far side felt like vast reaches.) I turned the dinghy around, re-
oriented myself with a bobbing point of light on the shore, likely someone's
headlamp, and rowed in earnest, hoping to spot if not the outline at least a suggestion of *Honu*'s white hull. Nothing. Again I turned around and rowed some
more. After about fifteen minutes, I heard the faint whir of windmill blades.
Honu was guiding me home.

Steering toward the sound, I finally saw a hint of white in the black noth-
ingness. But spotting the hull and getting aboard were two different things.
I rowed to the stern, and as I made a grab for the boarding ladder, the wind
caught the rubber dinghy side-on and sent it shooting downwind, back into the
void. Rowing fast to get back while I could still make out the boat, I approached
Honu from the side this time, thinking to stand up and grab the rail before the
dinghy bounced off the hull. Standing up, though, I lost my balance, and lurched
for the boat. A second before I would have gone overboard, my fingertips touched

the rail. Carefully, still standing, I inched my way hand over hand to the stern and, panting with exertion, finally grasped the ladder.

Out there, all alone in the dark, I laughed out loud while climbing aboard. In my precaptain life, I would have panicked over losing the boat, missing the ladder, and almost falling in the water. But my voyage to Palmyra reset the bar. After sailing in massive waves with no forestay across hundreds of miles of open ocean, and kayaking most days to Eastern Island against wind and current, rowing in circles in Palmyra's lagoon felt like paddling around a kiddy pool. Not only was locating my boat and figuring out how to get aboard not scary—it had been sort of fun.

Later, snug in my cabin, I exchanged the wet towel on my bed for a dry one (in spite of my attempts to seal the deck, it still leaked rainwater) and lay down, my mind whirling with strategies for boat repairs, topics for columns, and lists of possibilities for *Honu* and me. Now when I crawled into that bunk, Craig was far from my mind. A bath mat for a bed partner suited me just fine.

I felt even better later that week when a supply plane arrived carrying my new jib. Inside the bag was a note containing two words, "Love, Craig." For a guy who normally signed his notes with a slash that bore only a distant resemblance to a C, this was pure poetry. I treasured the simple note. It told me we were emerging from this chapter of our lives as a new kind of couple, no longer twins, but two members of a team. Since the day I announced to him that I would be sailing *Honu* to Palmyra, I had grown, learned, and changed so much that I was practically a different person. Craig changed as well. How often I considered the irony of losing each other bit by bit when we lived together at home but then finding each other sentence by sentence on a satellite phone when hundreds of miles apart. From Palmyra I felt that Craig was not only proud of me for managing *Honu* but also missed me.

"Love, Craig" may have meant almost nothing to some couples, but for us it was a salute to my skippering skills and a hug that didn't let go.

THE day I chose to assemble and install the forestay and furler dawned bright and clear, the storm clouds that so often rumbled across the atoll nowhere to be seen. I rowed ashore and found Alex in the office working on his study statistics. I wanted to assemble as much of the gear as I could alone, and Alex, always pressed for time, was happy to be on call.

Opening the glossy, thirty-five-page Harken instruction manual, I began with page one, paragraph one: "Assemble the furler in a clean, dry place."

I hosed off three of the camp's blue tarps to keep sand and dirt from the furler's joints. Anchoring the tarps at the corners with rocks, I let the plastic sheets dry in the sun while I sat next to them and read the instruction booklet cover to cover.

The illustrations showed me that, when assembled, the furler would look like a hollow pole with a heavy wire, the forestay, running inside its length. The top end would attach to the mast top and the bottom end to the so-called drum that looks like a giant spool of thread. The drum contains the line that runs along the edge of the deck back to the winches, allowing the sailor to furl her jib from the safety of the cockpit.

My struggles with those premed courses all those years earlier had taught me how to learn complicated new concepts, and I approached the furler assembly the same way I had once approached genetics or physics: one step—sometimes one word—at a time. Most of the terms weren't new, but they made little sense at first read. (For instance: "Screw main threaded stud portion onto bronze nosepiece until flats align with two cotter pin holes in terminal body.")

Read with pieces in hand, though, and well-labeled drawings to study, the instructions slowly began to make sense. Hovering over my head like a storm cloud was the thought: *I must not do even one tiny part of this wrong.* Each time I realized that I didn't have a clear picture in my mind of how, say, the drum mechanism attached to the end of the cylinder, I would start at the beginning and read the manual again.

The long pieces, called foils, slid together like Lego blocks, turning into place on threads and made secure by screws. As instructed, before I turned each foil and screw, I squirted it with a dash of Loctite, a bright red liquid you apply to threaded fittings to keep them from accidentally loosening. I did this slowly and methodically, checking the book often. As the day wore on, several men in the camp, Nature Conservancy workers taking breaks from cabin building, stopped by to check my progress. A few offered suggestions, some helpful but some maddening, such as one know-it-all who, apparently harboring a death wish, snatched a pair of pliers from my hand to tighten a fitting he deemed loose. I knew it was loose. I hadn't gotten there yet.

"Give me those pliers," I said, holding out my palm.

"What?" the man said.

"The *pliers.* You took them out of my hand while I was using them."

"I'm just trying to help you."

"I know. But that's not helping."

"Okay, okay," the man said, placing the tool in my hand.

"Thank you," I said. "You can go now."

He shot me an angry look and stomped off with an open-handed shrug that said, *Women. Go figure.*

I was glad to see the back of him.

As the furler grew longer, my confidence grew with it. By midafternoon, I had the forty-some-foot-long furler assembled in one piece that looked exactly like the pictures in the manual. I couldn't wait to string it up. My boat would be sailable again.

Luke had promised to move the flatboat from the Navy pier so I could bring *Honu* in from the anchorage and there hoist the unwieldy, fifty-pound furler and forestay from the pier to the mast top with a halyard. Luke, however, was nowhere to be found.

Okay, if I couldn't bring *Honu* to the furler, I would bring the furler to *Honu*. I discussed possibilities with Alex and phoned Craig for his suggestions on how to go about it. This was the kind of nautical task Craig loved working out with me now, and we came up with a plan that included Alex. We would tie several kayaks together, tie the fifty-foot-long pole along their length, and paddle the furler flotilla to the boat.

The wind came up, breezy enough that I worried about all the things that could go wrong in the towing. The worst would be to drop my precious piece of equipment into the lagoon, where it would sink like a stone. I wondered if we should wait for Luke to appear, which could be any minute or several hours, but Alex liked the towing idea and left to prepare the kayaks.

Luke saved me from my vacillation by showing up at that moment with some of the construction crew he had promised to take fishing outside the atoll. I could bring *Honu* to the Navy dock, the one and only place in the lagoon to tie a large boat to a pier, he said, as long as I had vacated the spot by the time he got back.

I thought this good news, but Alex surprised me. "I like the kayak plan better," he said. "We don't have to haul up the anchor, tie *Honu* to that rusty dock, and later find the anchoring spot again."

"Moving the boat to the furler is safer for the furler," I said. "And *Honu* needs to be driven. It's been three months."

"But also," he said, "moving the boat will displace Bruce."

This was not my Bruce anchor he was referring to but a juvenile batfish that had taken up residence among the rungs of *Honu*'s boarding ladder. The first time we saw the four-inch-long fish a month earlier, Alex and I were in the dinghy near the ladder.

"Look," he said. "A baby batfish."

"That's a leaf."

"Look closer," he said.

"Oh. It *is* a batfish," I said, peering at the fish. The young of these odd-shaped fish mimic golden leaves adrift, and this one was doing an outstanding job of it. We don't have batfish in Hawai'i, but they're colorful members of South Pacific reefs, and Alex and I considered this youngster an honored guest. A pet. We named it after Batman's alter ego, Bruce Wayne, and checked it each time we boarded the boat.

"You're worried about Bruce," I said, staring at this man who would work for hours roping kayaks together and risk dropping several thousand dollars' worth of gear to the lagoon floor to avoid evicting a baby fish from a boarding ladder. I loved Alex for his soft heart, but sometimes it bordered on the bizarre.

"We're driving *Honu* to the dock," I said. "It's faster, takes fewer people, and there's less chance of an accident."

Because I also loved Alex for his willingness to change his mind and let it go with no hard feelings, I was not surprised to hear his cheerful reply. "Okay, Captain," he said. "Let's do it."

I rowed us in the dinghy to the boat, and Alex took his place at the electric windlass to haul up the anchor. Back at the wheel, I pressed the starter button. Nothing. "You miserable goddamn fucking machine," I hissed at the starter button. "We *fixed* you." On my next try, the engine started right up. Apparently that's why sailors swear so much. It works.

Alex walked back to the cockpit with the announcement that the windlass was dead.

This time pocketknives worked better than curses. Together we scraped rust and corrosion off the windlass control, a part less than a year old already brought down by salt air. When Alex pressed the up button, the windlass motor began turning its saucer-sized gear called the wildcat, pulling up the heavy chain link by link and dumping it with a clatter into the chain locker below deck. I went back to the wheel and, when the anchor clunked into its resting position on the bow, shifted into forward gear. Once again, my *Honu* was on the move. A rush of pleasure swept over me. How I loved driving my own boat.

Luke, who had moved his powerboat to the small dinghy dock to load up for the fishing expedition, watched me pull up to the big pier, nodding his approval as he caught a mooring line. Like many of the men there, Luke thought he knew the best way for me to proceed with installing the forestay and furler. Unlike the other men there, however, Luke, having recently replaced the rig on his own boat, knew what he was talking about.

"It's easy," he said of hoisting the gear. "You attach a line like this." He tied a short rope to the top foil. "Clip the main halyard on it. One of you climbs the mast to slip the clevis pin into the toggle [how proud I felt to know exactly what he meant], and the other manages the halyard. It's all yours, Captain," he said, and off he walked for his fishing trip.

"I'll climb the mast," I said to Alex.

He smiled. "I figured."

Five or six people, mostly our volunteer coconut crab helpers, gathered to watch. I invited one obliging young man onto the deck to help Alex manage the halyards, tricky since two of the three supported the mast at the bow. But Luke was right. It was easy. I climbed the mast steps, and Alex hoisted the furler, with the forestay inside it, up to me. I inserted the top of the forestay into the toggle, pushed through its boltlike clevis pin, and untied the line and halyard. My new furler and forestay dangled from the mast top. "It's in," I called down. Cheers came from below. The procedure had taken ten minutes.

As I stood on the top mast steps, I once again marveled that one little stainless steel fastener was all that supported the mast at the bow, the forestay and heavy furler at the top, and a sail filled with wind in the middle. There's nothing like putting your own boat systems together to fully understand why it's so unwise—and unsafe—to push a boat beyond its recommended limits.

Clevis pins are beefy bolts with a small hole through the end into which you insert a narrow cotter pin, an elegant assembly that prevents the clevis pin from slipping out of its toggle. But bending the arms of that heavy cotter pin required more strength than I had in my hands. I didn't care. I was at the top of my mast and, more important, so was my forestay.

I descended to the deck. Alex and I shared a hug.

"Congratulations," he said.

"I couldn't bend the cotter pin properly," I said.

"No problem," he said. We harnessed him in the bosun's chair, and in a flash, while I controlled the halyard as a safety line, he climbed the mast, bent the pin's legs, and came back down. On deck we smiled up at our success. "For a pair of biologists who are usually reading 'how-to-sail' books as we go along," Alex said, "we're doing okay."

"So far, so good," I said. "Now we have to make the furler work."

Alex and I walked to the bow to install the drum, reading the instructions aloud as we did so. We assembled the furler drum (a separate piece at the base of the furler), inserting toggles and pins to match the manual's illustrations.

I e-mailed photos home for Craig and Pierre's viewing. My nightmare, of course, was missing some crucial step and losing the whole works again. Every few pages the Harken booklet issued another warning about how, if incorrectly installed, the toggle could fatigue, causing "damage to the vessel, personal injury or death." Dang. There was that death thing again.

My assembly looked okay to me and to my Honolulu-based helpers, Craig and Pierre, and I had to let it go.

Because the gear needed testing, I organized a trial sail for later in the week. The day arrived with black clouds, heavy rain, and thirty-knot winds, and I wondered if it was wise to go outside the atoll in such rough weather with unproved gear. On the other hand, for a real test, I needed real wind. Everyone had different opinions of what I should do. I called off the sea trial.

The next week on furler test day, the starter and windlass behaved perfectly, and out the channel Alex and I motored. Three months earlier I had driven into that channel exhausted and miserable over my broken boat, collapsing marriage, and aching, aging body. This time I couldn't have been more awake and alert—or more content. The boat was fixed, the marriage seemed, well, less wobbly, and although I was still aging, I had a new life ahead to explore the effects and meaning of growing old.

An hour later, after unfurling and furling the jib several times in twenty knots of wind, I declared victory. The new furler, forestay, and sail worked perfectly.

The test sail, however, left the deck and cockpit a muddy mess, because when we hoisted the mainsail, a dozen or more mud dauber nests built by the ever-present wasps crashed to the deck and into the cockpit. From the burst-open mud nests spilled their creepy contents: dozens of spiders, still alive but unable to walk due to the sting of the wasp mother. After building a nest, a mud dauber mom catches and paralyzes spiders, carrying them to the nest as food for her single growing baby. They must eat a lot. I never saw the larval wasp, but one nest contained seven nickel-sized spiders.

I poured seawater onto the decks and into the cockpit, the broken adobe wasp homes turning into sticky clods of mud that required bucket after bucket to wash off. Through the scuppers also went the paralyzed spiders. Drowning, I thought, seemed a preferable death to being eaten alive.

That wasn't the end of the wasp problem, because by the time *Honu* got back in the anchorage, the mud dauber traffic on the boat was worse than ever. In addition to the usual pioneer wasps scouting out possible homesteads, mother wasps flew around and around the mast and sail, frantically looking for their lost nests. For days I watched those elegant air dancers fly in, out, and around the areas of their former nests, thinking, I imagined, *I know I put the nursery right here.*

Eventually the female wasps halted their frantic flights. Like me, they stopped wasting time and energy searching for something they lost and moved on to build something new.

25

few days later I was eating dinner in the new shoreline dining room, recently completed by the builders, when the light easterly wind turned to a strong westerly wind. That meant that, in terms of keeping the boat safe and secure, *Honu*'s anchor was facing the wrong way.

Luke squinted at the lagoon through the sudden downpour. "Susan," he said, "I think your boat is moving."

I stared. All the warnings I heard and read about the poor holding ground of Palmyra's lagoon had been true. The boat had turned around and was slowly but surely dragging its anchor along the lagoon floor.

Before rowing out to reset it, I decided to finish my meal. This rash notion lasted only about two seconds but was memorable because a few months earlier I would have been running for the door in heart-pounding panic. Now with my boat drifting unattended, I sat there chewing a bite of Melissa's lasagna. I raised the fork to my mouth and stopped. *Wait. What was I thinking?* Neither the starter nor the windlass worked reliably. If the engine wouldn't start, and we couldn't raise the anchor, *Honu* could end up on a reef.

And so I did, after all, run for the door in heart-pounding panic, rowing the dinghy like mad, praying the starter would work. Alex arrived just before me in his kayak and was already scraping new corrosion off the electrical connections on the windlass. We got lucky. Both the windlass and the motor worked on the first try, and in a few seconds I was driving into the wind while Alex pushed the button on the control that hauled up the anchor. We thought resetting it would be a cinch—we had done it there three times already—but the depth finder decided at that moment to take a vacation. The digital readout on its round screen in the cockpit indicated in feet the depth of the water below the boat, but now it flashed impossible numbers: 3, 188, 12, 97.

The timing for such a failure was terrible, but I was neither surprised nor particularly irked at turning on a boat machine and having nothing happen. Nothing new there. Without the depth finder, however, locating the one and only thirty-five-foot-deep berm in the lagoon would be impossible.

It gets dark fast in the tropics, and with the storm worsening, we soon found ourselves in pitch-black night with thirty-knot winds blowing rain sideways. Donning our foul weather gear, we turned on the deck light and dropped the anchor—all two hundred feet of chain with it—on the spot. If we were lucky, the anchor would hit the berm and dig in right there. If not, we would be in seventy to eighty feet of water, too deep for the anchor to hold the boat, but it would at least slow her drift.

Honu stopped moving, or so I thought, and we took a moment to marvel at dozens of moray eels squirming snakelike near the water's surface. Neither of us had ever seen anything like this frenzied thrashing. We didn't know if it was normal for these nocturnal fish, if they were stirred up by the storm, or if they were agitated and confused by the deck lights.

The boat's lights definitely disoriented the storm-disturbed seabirds, because they began crashing into the boat. One red-footed booby flew straight into the mast and tumbled to the deck, where it sat stunned but uninjured. The wind was so strong that Alex had to crawl to the bird. He held it above his head and it disappeared into the shrieking black night. As we cheered this successful launch, another booby crashed into the cockpit. Amid the pandemonium of flapping wings, panicky squawks, and driving rain, we caught and released that bird, too. A moment later, a gull-sized seabird known as a black noddy hit a stay and fell in the cockpit.

Black noddies are as delicate and graceful as their close cousins the white terns, only a bit bigger and all black. Noddies get their name from nodding. This behavior between adults looks like chivalrous bowing. *Honored to meet you*, one seems to say, dipping like knight to queen. *The pleasure is mine*, the other politely nods back. These courtly birds can be bold when threatened. On Tern Island I once stepped too close to a noddy's chick and the parent burst up and pecked me a good one on the forehead. The next time I passed by, the same bird hit my chest. The attacks from such small birds didn't injure me, but I got the message: *Get away from my kid.* From then on, I gave the area a wide berth.

The noddy that crashed into the boat was only dazed, and we helped it fly away.

"We have to shut off the lights," Alex shouted over the gale.

I went below deck, dripping rainwater, turned off the switches, and fetched headlamps, which we wore centered on each of our foreheads like a Cyclops eye. We couldn't see past the rails in the lashing rain and had to rely on radar and GPS to check our position. This is easier said than done because the swirling wind changed directions, causing the boat to swing this way and that on its anchor chain. We heard the links clanking but didn't know what it meant. Were we drifting? I squinted at the GPS.

"I think we're moving," I called to Alex, who was watching the radar screen below deck in the navigation station. The boat seemed to be inching slowly toward the tear-your-hull-to-shreds Navy pier.

"We are," he said, appearing in the cockpit. "What should we do?"

It still rankled when he asked me that, because usually I didn't know the answer. But I was getting used to people looking to me for decisions, and so I made one.

"Let's pull up the anchor and use radar to drive to the middle of the lagoon and re-anchor. If we drag, we'll keep going back by radar until the storm stops."

The radar, a green screen with a line sweeping around in a circle, gave us an accurate location of the islands surrounding the lagoon. In about ten minutes we dropped the anchor at the lagoon's center, giving us breathing time.

"Let's talk about this," I said as we sat in the lashing cascade of the cockpit. Water poured off our faces, down our necks, and inside our yellow jackets.

Our main problem, we decided, was not being able to see the shore, a disconcerting situation what with the depth finder flashing nutsy numbers like 192, 8, 67. Even with the radar and GPS drag alarms on, we needed a light on the corner of the pier to show us the position of the boat from moment to moment. The light had to be big enough for us to see but small enough to go unnoticed by the storm-berserk birds. Why seabirds fly into lights in howling wind and driving rain is not known, but they do it everywhere.

Searching the boat, we found a glass jar with a lid and dropped one of the flashing LED headlamps in it. Alex volunteered to take it to shore in his kayak. This was no small feat in the dark with howling wind and torrents of rain, but Alex, a strong paddler, impressed me with his willingness to go. Seconds after he left the boat I lost sight of him and the red kayak, but the flashing headlamp in the jar cut through the darkness like an energetic firefly. Placing the jar on a corner piling on the pier, Alex set a rock on top to secure it and paddled back to the boat against a wall of rain pebbles, guided by the pulsing of my own headlamp. It was a fine job performed in record time.

It amazed us how well this worked. How comforting to see that little blue-white light on the pier blinking merrily through the rain to show us, sort of, where we were.

We decided on one-hour watches. One of us sat in the cockpit focused on the light and GPS, occasionally going below to glance at the radar screen, while the other dozed in the sea berth of the main cabin. Around three in the morning, the rain lightened and the wind eased until finally it was safe for us to go to bed. Alex and I toweled off and collapsed, exhausted, in our respective cabins.

The departing storm left the atoll dead calm. The next morning Alex fixed the depth finder by free diving below the hull and scraping a thin layer of algae off its sounder. It surprised me to see so much marine growth on the hull, since I'd spent considerable money on antifouling bottom paint. I wondered if the boatyard had screwed that up, too. (They had. I later learned that the painter, a guy as friendly and apparently as clueless as Ned, had done something wrong in the epoxy process, so the paint peeled off the bottom in sheets.)

With the depth finder working, we set the anchor where it had lain before the storm and were back where we started. Alex volunteered to help clean up the boat, but as a thank-you for his all-night help, I refused this generous offer and sent him ashore.

What a mess that storm made. The day was still and hot, and everything on the boat steamed with moisture and stank of animal waste. When threatened, seabirds defecate and vomit to lighten their bodies for a faster getaway, and true to form, the crashed birds had thrown up their half-digested fish and pooped copiously. In addition, the wind had dislodged several more mud dauber nests, and under the shelter of the dodger, dozens of wounded spiders wiggled amid the broken walls of their fallen cells.

After dropping the suffering spiders over the side, I scrubbed the mud and fetid fish remains from beneath the cockpit's slatted benches and floorboards. But the rotting fish smell lingered, and after sniffing around the cockpit I found a six-inch-long, partially digested flying fish wedged in the mainsail's traveler track. When I tried to pick up this little noddy gift, it burst open, spewing liquefied fish guts all over me and the mainsheet. Thirsty, reeking, and dripping with sweat, I slumped in the cockpit and sighed. Living on a sailboat in the lagoon of a tropical atoll was heavenly, but it sure had its putrid moments.

I felt proud of getting through the storm unscathed. *Honu* was beginning to feel to me like I imagined Buttermilk, the horse on the *Roy Rogers Show* that proved itself in one hair-raising incident after another, felt to Dale Evans. This boat was mine to command.

Yet what next? Both of us to pasture? It saddened me to think of *Honu*, all fitted out for offshore voyaging, getting barnacles on her bottom in Honolulu's Ala Wai Harbor. I didn't want barnacles on my bottom either.

26

As the ants began coming back to my bait stations, I had to start tallying again. Crazy ants were harder to count than big-headed ants because crazy ants race around in stop-and-go zigzags. Peter, the ant man in Honolulu, wondered via e-mail how far the crazy ant pioneers were traveling to get the bait, a question impossible to answer. As a joke, I suggested that we glue one of our few remaining radio transmitters, each the size of your average bonbon, to an ant's back to find out. He wrote back, without any irony that I could detect, that the transmitters were too heavy.

I replied, "Since ants work so well together, we could harness a thousand together and have them haul the transmitter in a little cart." No answer.

It surprised me how few biologists I met during my Palmyra work (and in the rest of my life) had a sense of humor about their subject, because animals can be so much fun. After dinner one evening, I brought my nontoxic acrylic paints (harmless to snail shells and their hermit crab inhabitants) and artist brushes from the boat and organized a party to decorate empty turban shells I had collected during a Christmas picnic months earlier. The luncheon had been held on a low, rocky island that occasionally flooded during storms and therefore had no resident strawberry or purple hermit crabs to take advantage of the large, perfect turban shells that sometimes washed up there. Cooper Island's hermit crabs were so short of shells that some had to resort to using trash for homes. I saw one crab toting a blue Noxzema jar, and others wore the end fittings for PVC pipe.

Six Nature Conservancy people joined in the art project, all displaying great imagination. We gave our creations names to match their designs, such as Darth Vader (all black), the Patriot (red, white, and blue), and Roy G. Biv (the colors of the rainbow: red, orange, yellow, green, blue, indigo, violet).

When the paint was dry, we placed the shells near the compost heap, an area densely populated with hermit crabs. The next morning, not a shell remained.

I watched for the crabs in the painted shells, found three, and carried them to the dining room to take pictures. How we loved those crabs as the adorable creatures scuttled around the table in their bright, custom-painted homes. But not everyone thought so.

"Inappropriate," sniffed a University of California biologist. He was one of a party of ten who had flown to Palmyra to tag sharks for a week. "I'll have no part of this," he said and huffed out of the dining room.

I understood the biologist's negative reaction to humans putting their mark on nature at every opportunity, but I had a reason behind what seemed to him disrespectful playing around. Preserving wildlife in this day and age requires cooperation among all sorts of people with all sorts of backgrounds, and that often means lightening up on the academic and scientific front. To make a commitment, people need a connection.

"Look," a Nature Conservancy maintenance worker said when he saw a crab in the shell he had painted ambling down a camp path. "That's my crab." For that man, who worked long hours servicing generators, outboard motors, and all the other machines that kept the camp running, Palmyra's wildlife suddenly got personal.

Most other workers in the California research group were pleasant and friendly. A few were so impressed with my voyaging that they sat with me at dinner and peppered me with questions. Men only. The women weren't interested.

This didn't surprise me. A year earlier, when Craig was *Honu*'s captain and I her crew, I had been one of those women at parties and in boatyards edging away from the men's talk about the chores and concerns of a skipper during offshore voyages. I knew the language of open-ocean sailing, but like most women, I didn't think I was capable of doing it myself and therefore never tried.

If circumstances had been different, I might not have tried either. I didn't take on a traditionally male job to make a statement. I just decided to remove myself from a situation that was not working for me, and to get to my chosen destination I needed a boat. Who knew that skippering a thirty-seven-foot ketch through the middle of the Pacific Ocean would open up a whole new world? Not me. I was too busy at the time trying to figure out the meaning of the word "refit."

But from the first day that I said to Craig, "I'll make it so," my life changed forever. Learning that I could indeed skipper a sailboat made me feel strong, independent, and responsible. Never before had I experienced such satisfaction. How powerful I felt living on my own sailboat beneath the Magellanic Clouds, with a new forestay and furler, installed by me. How proud I was of *Honu*, my veteran of the seas, all tuned up and ready for another adventure.

Going back to Honolulu would pretty much close the door that I had recently kicked wide open. Even if Craig was there to welcome me back to the Twinship, I didn't want it anymore. We weren't twins needing the other for survival. We were individuals exploring a new kind of partnership. For the first time in years, I looked forward to the future.

THE crazy ants' regular visits to the bait sites meant that the study was at its end. A question had been posed—how long does ant poison knock back Palmyra's scale-farming ants—and answered: two weeks. I felt proud of my role as a data collector in this amazing atoll, but my job there was done. The research results and subsequent decisions as to how, when, and if to proceed with introducing ladybugs to Palmyra were now up to U.S. Fish and Wildlife Service managers. That was not going to be easy. As employees of a federal agency, they were hampered by oodles of regulations, endless lawsuits, and pathetically little money. But in spite of knowing that the ladybug project might never be approved or funded, the people I worked with had put forth tremendous effort to design and launch the ant study, the first step toward saving the stately *Pisonia* trees.

Nearly every day that I lived in Palmyra, the sight of native plants and animals poking through and crawling around military ruins, plantation remains, and fishing rubble touched my heart. Such persistence, both in nature and in the Fullard-Leo family, owners of Palmyra since 1922 who refused to sell the atoll for use as a casino, resort, or nuclear waste dump, inspired me. I was also impressed with the determination of the Nature Conservancy in raising the money to buy the atoll and working with the U.S. Fish and Wildlife Service to make it a National Wildlife Refuge. The rules and regulations involved in that designation certainly had its frustrations, but everyone hung in there to give Palmyra's plants and animals the safe haven they so desperately needed.

With the ant project over, and *Honu* repaired, it was time to make an exit plan. It would be hard to say good-bye to Alex, but I was happy for him. His next career step was a giant one. He would return to the University of Hawai'i and defend his thesis regarding the effects of rats and crabs on Palmyra's plants. As a result of his research, Alex had become an expert on the flora and fauna of Palmyra Atoll. Being awarded his PhD would make it official.

The author planning the next leg of her travels—to Tahiti.

After all this work and learning, the idea of sailing *Honu* back to Honolulu became less and less appealing. Sure, I could sail around the Hawaiian Islands again, but Craig and I had sailed in Hawai'i for years, and I knew that, as before, I would gradually stop taking the boat out. Also, sailing home would mean that my grand adventure was over. Sometimes I would pause at the dinghy dock, admire the boat's sparkly reflection in the glassy water of Palmyra's lagoon, and remember the sailor's adage: *To stay functional, boats must be used.*

One day, I dug the buried and creased charts of Tahiti and the other Society Islands out of the boat's nav desk, laid them out on the Nature Conservancy's large dining room tables, and examined them with new eyes. Tahiti lay about fifteen hundred nautical miles southeast of Palmyra. The voyage there would be upwind, a harder point of sail than Alex and I had experienced on our trip from Honolulu to Palmyra. Thinking about sailing there gave me the old pangs of fear and self-doubt, but they blended with new feelings of confidence, know-how, and my ache for another adventure. *The South Pacific.* Such appeal those three words hold.

"How would you like to sail to Tahiti?" I said to Alex as we examined the charts. He had wrapped up his research and was making arrangements with Nature Conservancy to fly to Honolulu. "You could fly home from there."

He thought about this proposal for all of two seconds. "I would love it," he said simply.

I called Craig and asked what he thought about *Honu* going south to Tahiti rather than north to Hawai'i. I was past feeling abandoned, lonely, or lovesick and was not asking for permission. Rather, I was sharing voyaging ideas with my cocaptain, who had been with me in spirit all along.

Craig didn't hesitate either. "Go for it," he said. "You earned it. Have some fun with the boat."

And that was that. I was sailing to Tahiti.

Over the next days, Alex and I talked about Tahiti with all the fervor of Fletcher Christian and his mutineers. We inventoried our food (more than enough), studied trade wind patterns and equatorial currents (easy to see on the pilot charts), and e-mailed Tahiti's marinas and airlines for reservations (confirmed). Once we had the South Pacific bug, we could take no more waiting. We made a date to set sail in a week.

As before, the weather didn't agree. On launch day, leftover wind and rain arrived with a vengeance from distant Hurricane Olaf, rattling the anchor chain and giving me nightmares. One night I jumped up at three in the morning in a panic that the boat was dragging anchor. I woke Alex in the V-berth, urging him to get up and watch with me as the boat crept closer to shore. When it turned out that we were not moving at all, that it had just been a bad dream, Alex joked about locking me in irons and assuming command.

While waiting for the weather to settle—this time we were not going to shove off in a storm—I started an art project. Calling cards in the form of T-shirts, lettered signs, mobiles, poetry, and artwork hung from the walls and rafters of the Yacht Club, mementos of passing boats telling of countless visits throughout the years. It was time to leave a message from *Honu*.

As a favor, a Nature Conservancy worker cut out the shape of a sea turtle from a piece of plywood. I painted it green and in white lettering wrote:

December, 2004—March, 2005
Sailing vessel: Honu
Home port: Honolulu

Captain: Susan Scott
First Mate: Alex Wegmann

I found a flat piece of weathered driftwood on the beach and on it painted a quote e-mailed by a reader of my newspaper column, forwarded to me in Palmyra by Craig:

> Twenty years from now you will be more disappointed by the things that
> you didn't do than by the ones you did. So throw off the bowlines. Sail away
> from the safe harbor. Catch the trade winds in your sails. Explore. Dream.
> Discover.

The reader attributed the quote to Mark Twain but I would learn later that it came from a book of letters by the mother of writer H. Jackson Brown Jr. Attaching the driftwood to the turtle, I hung the mobile from the ceiling and walked across the room to gaze at it. Years earlier, I would have read that quote and thought of Craig. His love of adventure was one reason I loved him so. Now, though, that mother's advice spoke directly to me, a woman who had sailed away from her safe harbor and, in doing so, became the captain of her own ship.

The next day, Craig called with an all-clear weather report. The starter turned the engine over on the first try, and with Alex calling out channel directions from the bow, I waved good-bye to the manta rays and sharks in the lagoon and to the boobies and frigatebirds overhead. With wasps in their tutus dancing a final farewell, I set sail for Tahiti.

Epilogue

$\mathcal{I}$T took twenty-four days to reach Tahiti, more than three times the length of the voyage from Honolulu to Palmyra. That's a story in itself, but deciding to do it was the hardest part. With my new forestay and furler, assembled and installed by me, I sailed *Honu* twenty-five hundred miles (because it was up-wind, I could not sail a direct route) and made it safely to the Society Islands, consisting of Tahiti, Raiatea, Bora Bora, and others. In the middle of the voyage, the cantankerous starter finally gave up the ghost. Alex and I rebuilt it at sea using another "how-to" book, and it worked fine after that.

But successful repairs were minor compared with my feeling of achievement. Stepping onto land in Bora Bora was one of the most exhilarating moments of my life.

I put *Honu* in dry storage in a Raiatea marina and boarded a plane for Hawai'i. In Honolulu, Craig was waiting for me at the airport with a Micronesian ginger lei, its heady scent and creamy petals special even to those of us accustomed to wearing leis.

He looked fit, relaxed, and happy. We approached each other with goofy smiles and hugged for a long, heartfelt moment.

"You look great," I said.

"You too," he said.

Without the satellite phone, where the urgency of dropped calls, costly minutes, and whistling wind made me speak up and talk fast, I felt a little tongue-tied. But it wasn't the telephone making the difference. We really had changed. During our twenty-five years together, Craig and I had been soul mates, lovers, and members of an exclusive Twinship, but we had not been equals. Now we were.

Excited by the language that captains share, we talked about the boat and the voyage all the way home. There he asked me to shower and dress up a little (in Hawai'i this means a clean aloha shirt and shorts, or a version of such) because he had a surprise. He drove me to a lovely waterfront restaurant that featured a Sunday brunch, and when the hostess escorted us to the table, there sat a dozen friends and family members.

"Welcome home," they shouted, standing and applauding. They draped me in flower leis, covered me with kisses, and squashed me with hugs. How lucky I felt to live in Hawai'i and have such a loving *ohana*.

Unlike the time I returned home from Tern Island a year and a half earlier, Craig seemed genuinely glad to see me. Michele said later he had spoken of me often while I was at sea, mentioning that he hoped the boat would perform well, that the weather would cooperate, that I was safe.

"It was so unlike him to worry," she said, "but he worried."

Now that I was home, our new regard for each other continued. We walked beaches, went on movie dates, made love. The sex was warm and tender. Once in the midst of it, I had a glimpse of myself in tears staring at the "I love you" message on the Raggedy Ann doll, wondering if he still did. He still did.

Both of us steered conversations away from touchy subjects, which was fine with me and fine with Craig. Neither of us wanted to dredge up pain from the past. Besides, that period was over now. Craig had always kept parts of himself to himself, while I once shared every detail of my life with him. No more. I had no secrets, but some experiences, and my thoughts about them, felt like mine alone to cherish or regret. Having this new private side felt surprisingly liberating. I was comfortable alone with my thoughts.

Craig and I had to work out which parts of ourselves we would keep private, though, because sometimes silence was hurtful. Christine moved to the mainland after I returned home, but Craig still frequently jogged, swam, and rode his bicycle alone or with other friends. He did not share the athletic part of his life with me, even when it involved going to another country for weeks at a time.

"Where's Craig going?" his scheduler asked me one day at Craig's business office.

"I didn't think he was going anywhere. Why?"

"He asked for a month off in June."

I drove home in a haze of hurt feelings, and there on his desk lay Craig's passport. Apparently he was leaving the country, but for what and with whom, I did not know.

"Why don't you tell me about your trips?" I said as calmly as I could manage when he came home.

"Because you get upset when I want to go somewhere with my friends. I was happy for you when you sailed to Tahiti with Alex, but you're not happy for me when I'm doing something I want to do."

"How can I be supportive if I don't know what it is?"

He paused. "It's a bicycle race. In France."

I wished he wanted me to go with him, not to ride but to go to the start and finish lines, have a rendezvous, share some fun. On the other hand, he would not want to travel in France the way I wanted to, which included art museums, historical sites, and country walks. He wanted vigorous workout time with like-minded athletes.

"I'm happy you get to race in France if that's what you want," I said.

"Thank you," he said. "It is."

Often I pondered how this new fraternal, as opposed to the former Siamese, Twinship would work. But rather than utter the dreaded phrase, "Can we talk?" I pondered alone and did not try to sneak it into conversations. Since Craig would rather scrub the bilge with a toothbrush than talk about his feelings, I did not insist that he do so. My friend Paula was right, at least for me and Craig: women talk, men act.

And Craig acted just fine. Any woman in her right mind would kill for a husband like him, a man who shares his money unreservedly, supports all her endeavors, and is a good lover besides. *Do whatever makes you happy* rang in my ears. Craig meant that for both of us. His work and sports, activities that make him happy, are his own to share, or not, as he chooses. My writing, art, and wildlife encounters are mine to steer in whatever direction feels right for me. It works for us. Like all long-term relationships, it's a work in progress.

As far as our joint history coming to a halt, I was wrong about that. Daily life, as well as our volunteer medical work in Bangladesh and occasional vacations together, provide us with shared experiences. Also, traveling separately and having our own adventures has opened a new kind of sharing and given us fresh topics of discussion. Telling stories to Craig, who fully appreciates the humor, irony, and/or frustration of the incidents, gives me a thrill similar to our early years when we were still discovering each other. "You will not believe what happened" is now a frequent start to our conversations.

That settled, I had a boat in Tahiti to attend to.

I flew back to the Society Islands and with various crew members sailed *Honu* to the Cook Islands, Tonga, Fiji, New Caledonia, and Australia. I did not expect Craig to join me. The so-called Coconut Milk Run was my adventure. He could come or not.

Craig did join me, once in Tahiti and twice in Australia. Each visit was better than the one before as we gradually settled the questions of who does what when cocaptaining a boat. We made decisions on sail trim, direction, and destinations jointly. I know some of the equipment I installed, such as the GPS and water maker, better than Craig, so those are mine to deal with. (I'm still a water Nazi, though. What if the machine breaks?) He's great at tuning the rigging, plugging leaks, and troubleshooting mechanical problems. They're his to fix, but now I've got my head in there with his, and I pay attention to his detailed explanations.

Alex continues to crew for me, and we often shrug our shoulders over the ant study at Palmyra. While we tagged crabs, spread poison, and counted ants, it turned out that nature had been busy cooking up its own surprise. Before Fish and Wildlife biologists could mount an attack on the ants farming scale, Palmyra's *Pisonia* trees began to recover. As fewer and fewer of the giants crashed to the ground, researchers questioned whether scale was the main problem or if something else had damaged the *Pisonia* roots, causing them to weaken and let go. A few months after the ant study, whatever ailed the trees seemed to have stopped, or at least slowed to the extent that the trees could fight back and begin to recover. Today researchers are monitoring the great trees to see what happens, but it will take time. Watching trees grow is a slow process.

Thanks in large part to Alex, Palmyra's ecological rat crisis ended in 2011. Two years after being awarded his doctorate by the University of Hawai'i, Alex led a team of forty researchers, biologists, and volunteers in distributing rat poison to every nook and cranny of the atoll's islands, including treetops, using boats, helicopters, and human hands. The poison was an anticoagulant that does not harm crabs or other invertebrates, and because seabirds eat only fish, they too were safe. To protect the ground-pecking migratory shorebirds, the project was done in the summertime when most birds were in their Arctic breeding grounds. Of the few shorebirds that remained, a veterinarian supervised their capture and care during the poisoning. Shorebirds are now wintering on Palmyra's islands in record numbers.

Alex and his team estimated that up to thirty thousand rats died in the project, but disposing of their carcasses was unnecessary. In approximately twenty-four hours, Palmyra's crabs had eaten every part of the rats' bodies, bones and all, leaving only piles of tiny teeth. If the Olympics had a recycling competition, crabs would go home with the gold.

How proud I felt to be Alex's friend as I watched him shape Palmyra's multimillion-dollar rat eradication project, organize mountains of supplies, and lead a small army of workers to a successful end. This sweet man with the boyish enthusiasm rose above his personal beliefs that all creatures have a right to live, and saw that when humans make mistakes, such as introducing rats to Palmyra, we have an obligation to try to make things right. The rats had to go. As unpleasant as that was for him (and most biologists), Alex followed through with sound science and practical strategies, and he got the job done.

With no rats to eat seedlings, native plants of several species, including great numbers of *Pisonia* saplings, are thriving on Palmyra's islands for the first time in decades. In the absence of rats, the islands' ground-nesting seabirds are having a baby boom, and the beaches are crawling with crabs. Fiddler crabs in particular are popping up over all the sand flats, Alex reports, and the baby coconut crabs that come ashore are surviving in higher numbers.

Palmyra Atoll is now one of the few places in the Pacific that provides assisted living for senior crustaceans. There, coconut crabs, tupas, hermit crabs, and fiddler crabs can live out their natural life spans without alien predators.

AFTER sailing to Palmyra, I found that skippering the boat, fixing the boat, or arranging to have the boat repaired kept me so busy, I often forgot about menopause and aging. These bodily processes chugged along, though, gnawing my joints, etching my face, and wrecking my skin. I have come to peace with those things mostly but get discouraged when I can't open a jar, or my knees ache after a hike, or I'm so forgetful it scares me. When that happens, I recall what my friend Tim, a doctor about my age, tells patients and friends concerned about aging.

"Don't think of it as growing old," he says. "Think of yourself as being chronologically gifted."

He's not joking. Growing old is a gift. A lot of people don't get the chance.

I am always amazed when women tell me that menopause was a nonevent for them. "My periods just stopped," some say, "and that was it. I felt fine." Well, my menopause nearly killed me. My middle to late fifties were as confusing and angst loaded as my stormy adolescence. And it ended just as gradually. As time passed, I simply had less and less anguish about aging until, one day, I felt comfortable in my new skin. It's a looser fit now, but it's also thicker in that

I don't care what others think of me nearly as much as I did before all this hormone swinging. It's one of the pluses of getting old.

I still take estrogen and progesterone because I sleep well when I'm taking it and don't when I'm not. Craig, through his weekly medical journal alerts, helps me keep up with the latest studies. Current advice is to take hormones as long as you need them to control problematic symptoms. An eighty-one-year-old friend of mine has also resumed taking estrogen. As with me, it allows her uninterrupted sleep, and she feels alert and well rested the next day.

Besides easing menopause symptoms, estrogen replacement appears, according to some studies, to reduce the incidence of osteoporosis, a concern for me given my already-creaky joints, and possibly dementia, a worry for everyone of a certain age. When I read those studies, I'm a little afraid *not* to take estrogen. I know there's a slight increase in the incidence of breast cancer and heart disease in women who take hormones, but since I have no family history of either, I have chosen to live with those risks.

My main comfort in taking the drugs is that people are now living longer than ever before, and as such, we are all laboratory rats in the long-term study of growing old. I will stay tuned to the latest research, and adjust my medications accordingly. In the meantime, I focus on the quality of my life in the here and now.

On his second trip to Australia, Craig took a month off work to sail with me from Lizard Island to Brisbane, a long, upwind passage.

"How come I get all the upwind sailing?" he said one day when the wind was blowing twenty-five knots directly from Cooktown, our destination.

"Because you're so good at it," I said. A surprise wave slammed the side of the cockpit and broke on Craig's face, soaking his T-shirt and shorts. "And," I added, handing him his foul weather jacket, "you don't whine."

We started laughing again on that voyage. He was relaxed, fun to be around, and such an expert sailor that the thousand-mile beat seemed half that. And even though he will always be light years ahead of me in nautical skills (he had been sailing fifty-odd years to my five), he considered me a true cocaptain of our boat. One day as the wind increased in strength, he asked if I thought we should put a double reef in the mainsail, or a triple.

"What do I know?" I said, thinking he was joking.

He was not.

"Susan," he said. "You sailed to *Australia*."

I learned a lot from Craig that month. It was my best vacation in years. Craig enjoyed it too. I know this because he told me so, plus it seemed to be true. And if not, well, that's his business. I no longer contemplate his silences or second-guess his meanings. I accept Craig's generosity, affection, and support as fine gifts from a good man, and I encourage him to seek his own adventures, as he encourages me. I am alone a lot, but I'm no longer lonely.

I love my new status as long-distance sailboat captain. Craig apparently does, too.

"You sailed this boat here [Cairns] from Honolulu?" an Aussie sailor said to Craig after spotting *Honu*'s home port on the transom.

"No," Craig said, pointing at me with pride. "My wife did."

Author's Note

Going to Palmyra

Given the distance involved and the expense of getting supplies to Palmyra Atoll, it will always be a hard place to visit. But for the determined traveler, it's possible. For information about how to go to Palmyra, go to http://www.fws.gov/palmyraatoll/visit.html. Whatever the cost in time, energy, or money to travel there, it's worth it. Palmyra Atoll is one of the most spectacular and unique marine wilderness preserves in the world. As such, it is part of the Pacific Remote Islands National Marine Monument, is a jewel in the Nature Conservancy's land rescue efforts, and provides a matchless scientific platform for the universities and institutions that call themselves the Palmyra Atoll Research Consortium.

As for cruising sailors, boats are allowed to anchor in Palmyra's lagoon for one week. Captain and crew can go ashore on Cooper Island only. Potable water is available, but the Nature Conservancy camp, limited in resources, offers no repair help, tool lending, or provisions.

If you want to help the oceans

Throughout this book I've shared the wonder I feel about the marine world, and attempted to show how it saved me during some hard times. Here I get to give back to the ocean by offering ideas about what we can do to help save that precious world.

In the big picture, we have to rebuild our societies in ways that maintain ecological balance. This giant undertaking often feels impossible but humans are an ingenious species, and I believe that scientists and inventors can find practical solutions to worldwide pollution, climate change, over-fishing, and habitat destruction. Concerned citizens can help by supporting environmental legislation and contributing money or skills to research projects, conservation groups, and organizations dedicated to protecting marine wildlife. Here are four I like and trust:

- The Nature Conservancy   http://www.nature.org/
- Island Conservation   http://www.islandconservation.org/
- Hawaii Audubon Society   http://hawaiiaudubon.org/
- The Marine Mammal Center   http://www.marinemammalcenter.org/

In the day-to-day picture, adopting small lifestyle changes not only helps the planet but also makes life a little brighter. The following efforts have made me more aware of my consumption, improved my health through exercise, and helped me make new friends:

- Leave the car at home. Run errands by bicycle or on foot.
- Reuse, recycle, and rethink how you consume electricity.
- If you live far from the ocean, visit marine parks and aquariums. Think of the animals there as ambassadors for their species. Let them win your heart and inspire commitment. My lifelong love of sea lions began at a marine park.
- While walking beaches, carry a bag to pick up trash. This has made me much more aware of our throw-away culture, and also inspired me to make art from marine debris. You can see my art and read my "Ocean Watch" columns at www.susanscott.net

Production Notes for Scott / *Call Me Captain*
Cover design by Julie Matsuo-Chun
Interior designed by George T. Whipple
    with text in Janson and display in Snell Roundhand Script and Black Script (SR)
Composition by Westchester Publishing Services
Printing and binding by Sheridan Books, Inc.
Printed on 60 lb. House White, 444 ppi.